# *Democracy*
## IN PRINT

April 3, 2009

Dear Ken & Mag,

Thanks for all you've done for the peace movement.

And thanks, too, for your hospitality!

Best,

Matt

# Democracy
## IN PRINT

THE BEST OF
*The Progressive* Magazine, 1909–2009

*Edited by*
MATTHEW ROTHSCHILD

THE UNIVERSITY OF WISCONSIN PRESS

The University of Wisconsin Press
1930 Monroe Street, 3rd Floor
Madison, Wisconsin 53711–2059

www.wisc.edu/wisconsinpress/

3 Henrietta Street
London WC2E 8LU, England

5   4   3   2   1

Printed in the United States of America

Library of Congress Cataloging-in-Publication Data
Democracy in print : the best of the Progressive magazine, 1909–2009 / edited by
Matthew Rothschild.
p.   cm.
ISBN 978-0-299-23224-5 (pbk. : alk. paper) — ISBN 978-0-299-23223-8 (e-book)
1. Progressivism (United States politics) 2. United States—Politics and
government—20th century. 3. United States—Politics and government—2001–
I. Rothschild, Matthew. II. Progressive (Madison, Wis.)
III. La Follette's weekly magazine. IV. La Follette's magazine.
JK271.D435   2009
320.51′30973—dc22
2008046312

To the memories of
ROBERT M. LA FOLLETTE SR., BELLE CASE LA FOLLETTE,
ROBERT M. LA FOLLETTE JR., PHILIP LA FOLLETTE, WILLIAM T. EVJUE,
MORRIS H. RUBIN, MARY SHERIDAN RUBIN, and ERWIN KNOLL—
all who edited *The Progressive* over the past 100 years.
And to progressives everywhere!

*The real cure for the ills of democracy is more democracy.*

—ROBERT M. LA FOLLETTE

# CONTENTS

# ACKNOWLEDGMENTS

This was a group effort if ever there was one. Thanks to Elizabeth DiNovella for doing a lot of the heavy lifting, not only in reading decades of the magazine's output but also in narrowing the selections. To Ruth Conniff and Amitabh Pal for tackling a couple of decades each and for reading over the entire manuscript and making thoughtful comments, and thanks to Amit also for hunting down reprint rights. Thanks to Nick Jehlen for designing the cover. Thanks to Dennis Best, Ben Lembrich, Ina Lukas, and Phuong Luu for retrieving old texts and making them usable in the computer age. Thanks to Diana Cook for copyediting this book, and for proofreading *The Progressive* for more than thirty-five years. Thanks to Jodi Vander Molen for proofreading this book. Thanks to Furaha Norton and Sarah Fau for their fine editing suggestions early on. And enormous thanks to Sheila Leary at the University of Wisconsin Press, for riding to the rescue at a delicate moment, and to Gwen Walker and Sheila Moermond for their excellent editorial advice, and to Andrea Christofferson, for her marketing efforts. Thanks also to Gail Leondar-Wright for her professional assistance in getting the word out.

Dennis Best, Andrea Potter, and Jodi Vander Molen of *The Progressive* helped raise crucial revenue for this book project and for our centennial celebration. Research for this book was made possible, in part, by the Argosy Foundation, the Brico Fund, the Buck Foundation, the Compton Foundation, Betty and Corkey Custer, Daniel Erdman, the Evjue Foundation, John and Mary Frantz, the Fund for Investigative Journalism, David and Betsy Gifford, Evelyn Haas, Victor and Lorraine Honig, Matt Johnson, the Kelly Family Foundation of Madison, Wisconsin, Pam and Don Lichty, Art and Sue Lloyd, the John D. and Catherine T. MacArthur Foundation, Michael Mann, Jeffrey Mayersohn, Richard Mazess, the Menemsha Fund, the Mosaic Foundation of R. and P. Heydon, Jack and Lucia Murtaugh, Christopher Oeschsli, the Purple Moon Foundation, Robert Redford, Lucy Rosenberg, Margaret Rosenberry, the Samuel Rubin Foundation, Natalie Sue Schmitt, Carol Sundberg, Phillip Willkie, and thousands of steadfast supporters of *The Progressive*.

Final thanks to the permanent outside board members of The Progressive, Inc.—Gina Carter, Dayna Cunningham, James Friedman, and Barb Kneer—who give generously of their time and their wisdom in exchange for six free lunches a year.

We're grateful to all the authors and copyright owners who gave us permission to reproduce their work in this anthology. Some of them requested specific citations, which follow.

James Baldwin, "A Letter to My Nephew," copyright © 1962 by James Baldwin. First published in *The Progressive*, December 1962. Copyright renewed. Collected in *The Fire Next Time*, published by Vintage Books. Reprinted by arrangement with the James Baldwin Estate.

Noam Chomsky, "The Bounds of Thinkable Thought," copyright © 1985 by Noam Chomsky. Used by permission of the author.

Sandra Cisneros, "Prayer for the New Millennium," copyright © 2007 by Sandra Cisneros. First published in *The Progressive*, July 2007. Reprinted by permission of Susan Bergholz Literary Services, New York, NY, and Lamy, NM. All rights reserved.

Eduardo Galeano, "The Curse of Columbus," copyright © 2007. First published in *The Progressive*, October 2007. Reprinted by permission of Susan Bergholz Literary Services, New York, NY, and Lamy, NM. All rights reserved.

Marilyn Hacker, "Rue Beaurepaire, I and II," copyright © 2002 by Marilyn Hacker. Collected in *Desesperanto: Poems, 1999–2002* by Marilyn Hacker. Used by permission of the author and W. W. Norton & Company.

June Jordan's essays and poem are reprinted by permission of the June Jordan Literary Estate, www.junejordan.com.

Maxine Kumin, "Poem for an Election Year: The Politics of Bindweed," copyright © 2001 by Maxine Kumin. Collected in *The Long Marriage* by Maxine Kumin. Used by permission of the author and W. W. Norton & Company.

Martin Luther King Jr.'s essay, "The Burning Truth in the South," was reprinted by arrangement with The Heirs to the Estate of Martin Luther King Jr., c/o Writers House as agent for the proprietor, New York, NY.

Adrienne Rich, "Veterans Day," copyright © 2002, 2001 by Adrienne Rich. Collected in *The Fact of a Doorframe: Selected Poems, 1950–2001* by Adrienne Rich. Used by permission of the author and W. W. Norton & Company.

# Democracy
## IN PRINT

# Introduction

## A History of *The Progressive* Magazine

MATTHEW ROTHSCHILD

Magazines are fragile plants—magazines of dissent especially so. Only a few manage not to die from neglect or mishandling or poor transplanting. *The Progressive* is one of those exceptional, hardy orchids.

Founded on January 9, 1909, by Senator Robert M. La Follette of Wisconsin, it was originally called *La Follette's Weekly*, and then simply *La Follette's*. In 1929, four years after La Follette's death, it continued as a weekly magazine called *The Progressive*, and in 1948 it became a monthly publication.

This publication has always been more than a magazine. It's the articulation of a mission.

On the very first page of the very first issue, La Follette laid it out.

"In the course of every attempt to establish or develop free government, a struggle between Special Privilege and Equal Rights is inevitable," he wrote. "Our great industrial organizations [are] in control of politics, government, and natural resources. They manage conventions, make platforms, dictate legislation. They rule through the very men elected to represent them."

Yet he was hopeful. "The battle is just on," he wrote. "It is young yet. It will be the longest and hardest ever fought for Democracy. In other lands, the people have lost. Here we shall win. It is a glorious privilege to live in this time, and have a free hand in this fight for government by the people."

The words of La Follette find an almost perfect echo in those of Bill Moyers, which we published ninety-five years later. Similarly, La Follette's statements denouncing the crackdown on civil liberties in 1917 recall those of Senator Russ Feingold in December 2001.

As we've pored over every single issue published by this magazine over the past 100 years, we've been amazed at all the echoes—the continuity of concern that represents itself year after year, decade after decade.

The themes ring out:

Combating corporate power
Championing civil liberties
Rallying for women's rights and civil rights and human rights and labor rights
Opposing war and empire

Preserving our environment
Defending a truly independent media
Reforming criminal justice
Building a sturdy safety net for all Americans
Democratizing our democracy

As La Follette himself put it, "The real cure for the ills of democracy is more democracy."

And we've achieved some more democracy over the last 100 years. Women gained the right to vote and reproductive freedom. The labor movement won the right to strike, the eight-hour day, the minimum wage, and an end to child labor. The civil rights movement interred Jim Crow. The gay rights movement, against long odds, asserted itself and made extraordinary progress toward equality over the last four decades. Unemployment insurance and workers' compensation, along with Social Security, Medicare, and Medicaid, have provided at least some cushion for people tossed hither and yon by capitalism and bad luck. The regulatory apparatus, established early in the Progressive years and strengthened during the 1960s and 1970s, created at least a scaffolding for holding business accountable. And the environmental movement, which began with Teddy Roosevelt and rose again with Gaylord Nelson and a myriad of activists, marches on today.

Yet there are many things that remain to be achieved.

It is disconcerting to read about the need for universal health care—back in 1917.

It is eerie to stumble upon an article demanding an end to the corrupting influence of money in politics—dated 1909.

It is frustrating to read article after article against the death penalty, starting with Leo Tolstoy's in 1910.

And it is amazing to see, time and time again, how our presidents continue to wage war "without authority from Congress" and "based on a flimsy pretext"—as *The Progressive* editorialized back in 1927.

The magazine has always been woefully undercapitalized, and the demands of running the publication, on top of his senatorial duties, took a toll on La Follette.

"La Follette loved his magazine," writes Nancy C. Unger in her biography, *Fighting Bob La Follette*. "He refused to acknowledge it as a perpetual drain either politically or personally, and willingly made up its deficits out of the family's finances."

Over time, things did not get easier.

On October 6, 1947, the headline on the cover of *The Progressive* read: "The End of *The Progressive*." Written by then-editor Morris H. Rubin, the notice began: "This is the last issue of the present *Progressive*. . . . For years we have fought a losing rearguard action against the soaring costs of production. . . . We have sweated out the financial problems of *The Progressive*, nights, Saturdays, Sundays, and holidays."

But just as Morris Rubin and his diligent, smart, steady wife, Mary Sheridan Rubin, were exhausted from sweating it out and prepared to lay down their editors' pens, the readers of the magazine came to the rescue with thousands of donations, big and small, and the magazine resumed publication in 1948.

So it has been for the last six decades, as the readers of *The Progressive* have continually kept the magazine alive. And they've done so for a reason: They believe in its mission. When I interviewed for my first job at *The Progressive*, I asked the editor, Erwin Knoll, what that mission was. He had an immediate and immodest answer: "to save the world." Later, after worrying about the magazine's finances for years, I asked Erwin how we were going to make it. An atheist, he responded: "God will provide."

This book is not intended to be leaden or moth-eaten. It's meant to be savored. We've chosen only articles and items that stand up on their own. We hope they'll engage you and inspire you, and sometimes amuse you. Taken together, they'll give you a clear picture of the essence and vitality of progressivism, an indigenous political movement that shows signs of resurging again today. This book also presents a romp through the last century, and it offers some signposts for the road ahead. It should be appreciated not only by people who today identify as progressives but also by anyone with an interest in American politics or journalism. And we hope it will stand as a monument to progressive thought in America.

As you can imagine, it took a painful process of pruning to make our final selections. We omitted such luminaries as Lincoln Steffens, Helen Keller, and George Orwell. And, with a few exceptions, we decided against showcasing the elected officials who wrote for us, including Hubert Humphrey, JFK, George McGovern, and Adlai Stevenson. We even skipped the interview we did with Barack Obama.

Instead, our governing principle was to offer the best writing in the magazine and to draw the arc of each issue from the earliest years up to today.

In striving to make this book enjoyable to read, we've condensed and edited most of the pieces. We've presented a chapter of original political poetry published in our pages since 1995. And we've included interviews with fascinating people we've talked to over the past twenty years.

It's been humbling for all of us who've worked on this project. We are custodians of this great institution, which has housed the likes of Jane Addams and Louis Brandeis, James Baldwin and Martin Luther King, June Jordan and Philip Berrigan, Theodore Dreiser and Dolores Huerta, Norman Thomas and Ralph Nader, John Kenneth Galbraith and Molly Ivins, and so many other great writers and activists, poets and actors, political comics and engaged intellectuals, right up to the present, with Barbara Ehrenreich and Eduardo Galeano and Howard Zinn.

Yet we're more than curators. We sponsor this tour not just so you may marvel at the work gathered here but also so you may take it to heart, grapple with the ideas, and, if you end up agreeing with them, join the progressive movement, however you can, for there is much yet to be done.

As La Follette said, "The battle is on." And yes, with a little luck and a little more pluck, "here we shall win."

PART I

# Championing Civil Liberties

Teh right to free speech, the right to free assembly, the right to petition the government for a redress of grievances, the right to practice any religion or no religion, the right to privacy—all these are sacred.

Fighting Bob La Follette defended these rights throughout his career. And when the mobs (including senatorial ones) yelling "traitor" came after him for opposing U.S. entry into World War I, he stood his ground—for himself and for all of us. His case for wartime dissent came in one of the greatest speeches ever delivered in the U.S. Senate, and so we kick off this chapter with an excerpt from that address.

*The Progressive's* belief in the First Amendment led it to publish Theodore Dreiser's defense of the Communist Party's political rights in 1931, echoed by Justice Hugo Black thirty years later. *The Progressive* was also in the forefront of the effort to expose McCarthyism, which Robert Hutchins and Morris Rubin address in this chapter. By the way, the magazine's special issue on McCarthyism in April 1954, entitled "McCarthy: A Documented Record," was the most popular one we ever published, selling more than 300,000 copies—ten times the number of the magazine's subscribers at the time.

Defending the First Amendment has occasionally put *The Progressive* on the outs with some of its allies. Nat Hentoff, who once famously said that the sex drive is second only to the censorship drive, denounced intolerance on the left on our college campuses. And *The Progressive* upheld the right of Nazis to march in Skokie, and never sided with those who would ban pornography.

The biggest violator of our rights is the U.S. government, especially the Executive Branch, as Senator Russ Feingold twice reminds us in this chapter. In words that recall the poet Langston Hughes, Feingold notes that the government can turn this into a country without basic rights, but then "that country wouldn't be America."

# Free Speech and the Right of Congress to Declare the Objects of the War

ROBERT M. LA FOLLETTE
NOVEMBER 1917

*Speech delivered on the Senate floor, October 6, 1917*

Mr. President, I rise to a question of personal privilege.

I have no intention of taking the time of the Senate with a review of the events which led to our entrance into the war except in so far as they bear upon the question of personal privilege to which I am addressing myself.

Six Members of the Senate and fifty Members of the House voted against the declaration of war. Immediately there was let loose upon those Senators and Representatives a flood of invective and abuse from newspapers and individuals who had been clamoring for war, unequaled, I believe, in the history of civilized society.

Prior to the declaration of war every man who had ventured to oppose our entrance into it had been condemned as a coward or worse, and even the President had by no means been immune from these attacks.

Since the declaration of war the triumphant war press has pursued those Senators and Representatives who voted against war with malicious falsehood and recklessly libelous attacks, going to the extreme limit of charging them with treason against their country.

This campaign of libel and character assassination directed against the Members of Congress who opposed our entrance into the war has been continued down to the present hour, and I have upon my desk newspaper clippings, some of them libels upon me alone, some directed as well against other Senators who voted in opposition to the declaration of war.

One of these newspaper reports most widely circulated represents a Federal judge in the State of Texas as saying, in a charge to a grand jury—I read the article as it appeared in the newspaper and the headline with which it is introduced:

DISTRICT JUDGE WOULD LIKE TO TAKE SHOT AT TRAITORS IN CONGRESS
*Associated Press leased wire*
HOUSTON, TEXAS, OCTOBER 1, 1917

Judge Waller T. Burns, of the United States district court, in charging a Federal grand jury at the beginning of the October term to-day, after calling by name Senators STONE of Missouri, HARDWICK of Georgia, VARDAMAN of Mississippi, GRONNA of North Dakota, GORE of Oklahoma, and LA FOLLETTE of Wisconsin, said:

9

"If I had a wish, I would wish that you men had jurisdiction to return bills of indictment against these men. They ought to be tried promptly and fairly, and I believe this
court could administer the law fairly; but I have a conviction, as strong as life, that this
country should stand them up against an adobe wall tomorrow and give them what they
deserve. If any man deserves death, it is a traitor. I wish that I could pay for the ammunition. I would like to attend the execution, and if I were in the firing squad I would not
want to be the marksman who had the blank shell."

I find other Senators, as well as myself, accused of the highest crimes of which
any man can be guilty—treason and disloyalty—and, sir, accused not only with no
evidence to support the accusation, but without the suggestion that such evidence
anywhere exists. It is not claimed that Senators who opposed the declaration of war
have since that time acted with any concerted purpose either regarding war measure
or any others. They have voted according to their individual opinions, have often been
opposed to each other on bills which have come before the Senate since the declaration of war, and, according to my recollection, have never all voted together since that
time upon any single proposition upon which the Senate has been divided.

I am aware, Mr. President, that in pursuance of this general campaign of vilifica-
tion and attempted intimidation, requests from various individuals and certain organizations have been submitted to the Senate for my expulsion from this body, and that
such requests have been referred to and considered by one of the committees of the
Senate.

If I alone had been made the victim of these attacks, I should not take one moment
of the Senate's time for their consideration, and I believe that other Senators who
have been unjustly and unfairly assailed, as I have been, hold the same attitude upon
this that I do. Neither the clamor of the mob nor the voice of power will ever turn
me by the breadth of a hair from the course I mark out for myself, guided by such
knowledge as I can obtain and controlled and directed by a solemn conviction of right
and duty.

But, sir, it is not alone Members of Congress that the war party in this country has
sought to intimidate. The mandate seems to have gone forth to the sovereign people
of this country that they must be silent while those things are being done by their
Government which most vitally concern their well-being, their happiness, and their
lives. Today and for weeks past, honest and law-abiding citizens of this country are
being terrorized and outraged in their rights by those sworn to uphold the laws and
protect the rights of the people. Citizens are being unlawfully arrested, thrown into
jail, held incommunicado for days, only to be eventually discharged without ever having been taken into court, because they have committed no crime. Private residences
are being invaded, loyal citizens of undoubted integrity and probity arrested, cross-
examined, and the most sacred constitutional rights guaranteed to every American
citizen are being violated.

It appears to be the purpose of those conducting this campaign to throw the country into a state of terror, to coerce public opinion, to stifle criticism, and suppress discussion of the great issues involved in this war.

In time of war the citizen must be more alert to the preservation of his right to control his Government. He must be most watchful of the encroachment of the military upon the civil power. He must beware of those precedents in support of arbitrary action by administrative officials which, excused on the plea of necessity in wartime, become the fixed rule when the necessity has passed and normal conditions have been restored.

More than all, the citizen and his representative in Congress in time of war must maintain his right of free speech. More than in times of peace it is necessary that the channels for free public discussion of governmental policies shall be open and unclogged. I believe, Mr. President, that I am now touching upon the most important question in this country today—and that is the right of the citizens of this country and their representatives in Congress to discuss in an orderly way frankly and publicly and without fear, from the platform and through the press, every important phase of this war; its causes, the manner in which it should be conducted, and the terms upon which peace should be made. I am contending, Mr. President, for the great fundamental right of the sovereign people of this country to make their voice heard and have that voice heeded upon the great questions arising out of this war, including not only how the war shall be prosecuted but the conditions upon which it may be terminated with a due regard for the rights and the honor of this Nation and the interests of humanity.

I am contending for this right because the exercise of it is necessary to the welfare, to the existence, of this Government, to the successful conduct of this war, and to a peace which shall be enduring and for the best interest of this country.

Mr. President, our Government, above all others, is founded on the right of the people freely to discuss all matters pertaining to their Government, in war not less than in peace, for in this Government the people are the rulers in war no less than in peace. And before this great fundamental right every other must, if necessary, give way, for in no other manner can representative government be preserved.

I say without fear of contradiction that there has never been a time for more than a century and a half when the right of free speech and free press and the right of the people to peaceably assemble for public discussion have been so violated among English-speaking people as they are violated today throughout the United States. Today, in the land we have been wont to call the free United States, governors, mayors, and policemen are preventing or breaking up peaceable meetings called to discuss the questions growing out of this war, and judges and courts, with some notable and worthy exceptions, are failing to protect the citizens in their rights.

It is no answer to say that when the war is over the citizen may once more resume his rights and feel some security in his liberty and his person. Now is precisely the time when the country needs the counsel of all its citizens. In time of war even more than in time of peace, whether citizens happen to agree with the ruling administration or not, these precious fundamental personal rights—free speech, free press, and right of assemblage so explicitly and emphatically guaranteed by the Constitution—should be maintained inviolable.

But more than this, if every preparation for war can be made the excuse for destroying free speech and a free press and the right of the people to assemble together for peaceful discussion, then we may well despair of ever again finding ourselves for a long period in a state of peace. With the possessions we already have in remote parts of the world, with the obligations we seem almost certain to assume as a result of the present war, a war can be made any time overnight and the destruction of personal rights now occurring will be pointed to then as precedents for a still further invasion of the rights of the citizen. This is the road which all free governments have heretofore traveled to their destruction.

> —ROBERT M. LA FOLLETTE, a leader of the Progressive movement, was a governor and senator from Wisconsin. He founded *The Progressive* in 1909. He ran for president on the Progressive Party ticket in 1924.

## Theodore Dreiser Denounces Campaign Against Communists

THEODORE DREISER
SEPTEMBER 1931

Barring Communism in America is bringing about, and will continue so to do, an unprecedented suppression of political views. Even now Congress is receiving reports on a bill to exclude all alien Communists in the United States. The Fish Committee wants all alien Communists here to be exported. This means that every unnaturalized Communist to the man living in this country will be deported merely because of his political views. Is he a thrifty person? What are his reasons for following his economic beliefs here? These absolutely pertinent questions are to be utterly discarded as naught.

Not only that, but all Communists desiring to enter the United States will have the door shut in their faces. And though this restriction of immigration to this country is quite new, further barring of those who so keenly desire to reside here forebodes, to my mind, not only an unwise deprivation but a downright weakening of the mentality of America. For hitherto, most certainly it has been able to accept and assimilate immigration and to stand on its own two feet. In addition, knowing the general trend of the government in abolishing divergent though well-grounded politics, Hamilton

Fish, in his recommendations to Congress, demands the immediate suppression of all Communist newspapers and magazines. In other words, there is to be here only one form of political thought and that capitalistic.

By the proposed exclusion of the Communists, as I see it, the loss of constitutional rights will be highly involved. Privacy will be a joke in this country. The Fish Committee recommends that the Department of Justice be financed to equip itself with an elaborate secret service to take the names and activities of all radicals. This, in addition to being a black list of labor, would constitute a black list of thought. More, this program of the United States government to make Communism a crime means to the very heart, the end of free speech, assemblage, and other property rights

—THEODORE DREISER, novelist, was the author of *An American Tragedy* and *Sister Carrie*, among other works.

## What Are We Afraid Of?

ROBERT M. HUTCHINS
DECEMBER 1950

We hear on every side that the American Way of Life is in danger. I think it is. I also think that many of those who talk the loudest about the dangers to the American Way of Life have no idea what it is and consequently no idea what the dangers are that it is in.

You would suppose, to listen to these people, that the American Way of Life consisted in unanimous tribal self-adoration. Down with criticism; down with protests; down with unpopular opinions; down with independent thought. Yet the history and tradition of our country make it perfectly plain that the essence of the American Way of Life is its hospitality to criticism, protest, unpopular opinions, and independent thought. A few dates like 1630, 1776, and 1848 are enough to remind us of the motives and attitudes of our ancestors. The great American virtue was courage.

We ought to be afraid of some things. We ought to be afraid of being stupid and unjust. We are told that we must be afraid of Russia, yet we are busily engaged in adopting the most stupid and unjust of the ideas prevalent in Russia, and are doing so in the name of Americanism.

The worst Russian ideas are the police state, the abolition of freedom of speech, thought, and association, and the notion that the individual exists for the state. These ideas are the basis of the cleavage between East and West.

Yet every day in this country men and women are being deprived of their livelihood, or at least their reputation, by unsubstantiated charges. These charges are then treated as facts in further charges against their relatives or associates. We do not throw people into jail because they are alleged to differ with the official dogma. We throw them out of work and do our best to create the impression that they are sub-versive and hence dangerous, not only to the state, but also to everybody who comes near them.

The result is that every public servant must try to remember every tea party his wife has gone to in the past ten years and endeavor to recall what representatives of which foreign powers she may have met on these occasions.

The cloak-and-stiletto work that is now going on will not merely mean that many persons will suffer for acts that they did not commit, or for acts that were legal when committed, or for no acts at all. Far worse is the end result, which will be that critics, even of the mildest sort, will be frightened into silence. Stupidity and injustice will go unchallenged because no one will dare to speak against them.

To persecute people into conformity by the non-legal methods popular today is little better than doing it by purges and pogroms. The dreadful unanimity of tribal self-adoration was characteristic of the Nazi state. It is sedulously fostered in Russia. It is to the last degree un-American.

—ROBERT M. HUTCHINS was the president of the University of Chicago from 1929 to 1945.


# Freedom's Most Effective Weapon

MORRIS RUBIN
APRIL 1954

Joe McCarthy has struck repeatedly at the letter and the spirit of our Bill of Rights by using methods of intolerance and intimidation in an effort to create a national climate of hysteria, fear, and suppression.

The "ism" added to his name has become a generic symbol of guilt by accusation, character assassination, the big lie, and the repudiation of our country's traditional devotion to fair play and a fair trial.

He has impaired the functioning of some of our most important defense laborato-ries, and he has battered at the morale of those who administer our country's program of military defense.

He has exercised a decisive influence, for the worse, on our civil service and our for-eign service.

He has left his mark of intolerance on the government, the churches, the schools and colleges, the literature and the press of our country.

He has appointed himself a one-man purge squad committed to smearing and destroying those who disagree with him.

It is a dangerous error, we are convinced, for the forces of decency in America to fail to regard any man and his "ism" with deep seriousness. His power today comes in great measure from our failure to fight back earlier. The evidence is overwhelming that McCarthyism cannot long survive where the people are given the truth about the character of his "crusade."

—MORRIS RUBIN was the editor of *The Progressive* from 1940 to 1973.

# The Manifest Destiny of America

JUSTICE WILLIAM O. DOUGLAS
FEBRUARY 1955

We have staked our security, our ability to survive, on freedom of the mind and the conscience. So spoke Jefferson, Hamilton, and Madison. So say the great majority of us today.

That conception of freedom is the most novel principle the world has known. It leaves political and religious discourse unlimited and unrestrained. It leaves the mind free to pursue every problem to the horizon, even though the pursuit may rile a neighbor or stir his ugly prejudices.

History has recorded example after example of rulers who decreed what men must think, what cause they could espouse, what views they might embrace.

Man's experience with those laws and practices was a bitter one. The persecutions and oppressions of those early days make up some of the blackest chapters of intolerance.

History shows that the main architects of repressive laws were often men of good intentions. Their reasons sometimes had the ring of patriotism to them: protection of the safety of the state against subversive ideas. Their reasons often had overtones of religious fervor: the conviction that the soul of man needed but one faith and creed.

Jefferson, Madison, and Hamilton knew this history. So did the other Founding Fathers. And when it came to drafting our Bill of Rights they took bold action. They placed political and religious controversy beyond the reach of government; and by that act alone they launched on this continent a unique experiment in government.

Our Bill of Rights rejects the philosophy that political and religious controversies should be regulated in the public interest. It leaves no room for regulation.

The Founding Fathers believed, however, that the antidote to advocacy was counter-advocacy. They believed that if a subversive idea was presented from a platform or soapbox, the remedy was not to jail the speaker, but to expose the fallacy or evil in his cause, to submit his ideas to pitiless analysis, to explode his thesis in rebuttal.

Under our way of life a man should never go to jail for what he thinks or espouses. He can be punished only for his acts, never for his thoughts or beliefs or creed.

—WILLIAM O. DOUGLAS was a Supreme Court justice from 1939 to 1975.

# The Last Best Hope

JUSTICE HUGO L. BLACK
AUGUST 1961

[The continued whittling away of basic American liberties by the U.S. Supreme Court has no more articulate and courageous opponent than Justice Hugo L. Black. Typical of the magnificent if losing battles he has been waging was his dissenting opinion in the recent case *Communist Party of the United States of America v. Subversive Activities Control Board. The Progressive* is happy to present a condensed version of Justice Black's memorable decision, which received so little attention in the nation's press.—The Editors.]

I do not believe that it can be too often repeated that the freedoms of speech, press, petition, and assembly guaranteed by the First Amendment must be accorded to the ideas we hate, or sooner or later they will be denied to the ideas we cherish. The first banning of an association because it advocates hated ideas, whether that association be called a political party or not, marks a fateful moment in the history of a free country. That moment seems to have arrived for this country.

The Subversive Activities Control Act of 1950 here involved defines "Communist action" organizations and requires them to register with the Attorney General, giving much information of every kind with regard to their property, income, activities, and members. The Communist Party has been ordered to register under that Act by the Subversive Activities Control Board and has challenged the validity of that order on the ground, among others, that the Act is unconstitutional in that it amounts to a complete outlawry of the Communist Party. The contention is that this Act, considered as a whole and in its relation to existing laws which affect members of the Party, imposes such overhanging threats of disgrace, humiliation, fines, forfeitures, and lengthy imprisonments upon registered organizations and their members, most of which burdens become effective automatically upon registration, that it will be impossible for the Party to continue to function if the registration order is upheld.

The plan of the Act is to make it impossible for an organization to continue to function once a registration order is issued against it. To this end, the Act first provides crushing penalties to ensure complete compliance with the disclosure requirements of . . . registration. Thus, if the Party or its members fail to register within the time required by the Act, or if they fail to make annual reports as required, or to keep records as required, each individual guilty of such failure can be punished by a fine of $10,000, by imprisonment for five years, or both, for each offense, and each offense means "each day of failure to register" or "each listing of the name or address of any one individual" either by the organization or by an individual. Thus, for a delay of thirty days in filing required reports, a fine of $300,000 and imprisonment for 150 years could be imposed by a trial judge.

Having thus made it mandatory that Communist organizations and individual Communists make a full disclosure of their identities and activities, the Act then proceeds to heap burden after burden upon those so exposed. Certain tax deductions allowed to others are denied to a registered organization. Mail matter must be stamped before the organization sends it out to show that it was disseminated by a "Communist action" organization, with all the treasonable connotations given that term by the recitals of "fact" in the Act. Members of a registered organization cannot hold certain jobs with the government, or any jobs with private businesses engaged in doing certain work for the government. Members cannot use or attempt to use a passport and cannot even make application for a passport without being subject to a penalty of five years in the penitentiary. The Act thus makes it extremely difficult for a member of the Communist Party to live in this country and, at the same time, makes it a crime for him to try to get a passport to get out.

This whole Act, with its pains and penalties, embarks this country, for the first time, on the dangerous adventure of outlawing groups that preach doctrines nearly all Americans detest. When the practice of outlawing parties and various public groups begins, no one can say where it will end. In most countries such a practice once begun ends with a one-party government.

Talk about the desirability of revolution has a long and honorable history, not only in other parts of the world, but in our own country. This kind of talk, like any other, can be used at the wrong time and for the wrong purpose. But, under our system of government, the remedy for this danger must be the same remedy that is applied to the danger that comes from any, other erroneous talk—education and contrary argument. If that remedy is not sufficient, the only meaning of free speech must be that the revolutionary ideas will be allowed to prevail.

—HUGO L. BLACK *was a Supreme Court Justice from 1937 to 1971.*

# On Secrecy

DANIEL SCHORR
JULY 1976

It is now some four months since the *Village Voice* appeared, or exploded, with the House Intelligence Committee report. Since February 23, when I was suspended with full pay by CBS, the question put to me most often by concerned Americans has been: "Who are you to flout the decision of our elected Representatives and publish their report, which they have decided to keep secret?"

It is an important question, and a suitable question for our bicentennial year, because it touches on the meaning of the Constitution. Suspension, like hanging, is wonderful for concentrating the mind.

I have read the stirring statement of James Iredell, later a Justice of the Supreme Court, that if Congress tried to exercise any other power over the press than regulating copyright, "then they will do it without any warrant from this Constitution and must answer for it as for any other act of tyranny."

And I have read, a great many times, from the opinion of Justice Hugo Black in the Pentagon Papers case in 1971: "In the First Amendment, the Founding Fathers gave the free press the protection it must have to fulfill its essential role in our democracy. The press was to serve the governed, not the governors. The Government's power to censor the press was abolished so that the press would remain forever free to censure the Government. The press was protected so that it could bare the secrets of government and inform the people. Only a free and unrestrained press can effectively expose deception in government."

Justice Black's was an individual opinion, but it was good enough for this individual. He said nothing about avoiding publication in an anti-establishment paper; indeed, he issued a reminder that the press as a whole was meant to be anti-establishment. How can we bare secrets and expose deception in government if the Government—Executive or Legislative branch—can decide when we are allowed to do it?

It seems reasonable to say that the Government should be able to protect its secrets. But it would seem more reasonable if there existed complete confidence in those who wield the "secret" stamp. This nation has just passed through three years of revelations that the "secret" stamp and the national security label were used to conceal wrongdoing, conspiracy, and illegality. The delicate cord of trust that linked this nation, and its press, to its elected leaders has snapped. There is today no unquestioning trust that what a President or a Secretary of State calls "a national security matter" is indeed a national security matter and not a personal security matter or a personal embarrassment matter. It will be a long time before national security and secrecy will again be accepted without question by the American people, and especially by the journalistic community. Acceptance of secrecy requires a consensus of confidence in those who call things secret.

—DANIEL SCHORR has been a journalist for more than sixty years, working for CBS, CNN, and NPR. He is the recipient of a Peabody and a George Polk award.

## When Nice People Burn Books

NAT HENTOFF
FEBRUARY 1983

It happened one splendid Sunday morning in a church. Not Jerry Falwell's Baptist sanctuary in Lynchburg, Virginia, but rather the First Unitarian Church in Baltimore.

On October 4, 1981, midway through the 11 a.m. service, pernicious ideas were burned at the altar.

As reported by Frank P. L. Somerville, religion editor of the *Baltimore Sun*, "Centuries of Jewish, Christian, Islamic, and Hindu writings were 'expurgated' because of sections described as 'sexist.'

"Touched off by a candle and consumed in a pot on a table in front of the altar were slips of paper containing 'patriarchal' excerpts from Martin Luther, Thomas Aquinas, the Koran, St. Augustine, St. Ambrose, St. John Chrysostom, the Hindu Code of Manu V, an anonymous Chinese author, and the Old Testament." Also hurled into the purifying fire were works by Kierkegaard and Karl Barth.

The congregation was much exalted: "As the last flame died in the pot, and the organ pealed, there was applause," Somerville wrote.

I reported this news of the singed Holy Spirit to a group of American Civil Liberties Union members in California, and one woman was furious. At me.

"We did the same thing at our church two Sundays ago," she said. "And long past time, too. Don't you understand it's just symbolic?"

I told this ACLU member that when the school board in Drake, North Dakota, threw thirty-four copies of Kurt Vonnegut's *Slaughterhouse Five* into the furnace in 1973, it wasn't because the school was low on fuel. That burning was symbolic, too. Indeed, the two pyres—in North Dakota and in Baltimore—were witnessing to the same lack of faith in the free exchange of ideas.

What an inspiring homily for the children attending services at a liberated church: They now know that the way to handle ideas they don't like is to set them on fire.

The stirring ceremony in Baltimore is just one more illustration that the spirit of the First Amendment is not being savaged only by malign forces of the Right, whether private or governmental. Campaigns to purge school libraries, for example, have been conducted by feminists as well as by Phyllis Schlafly. Yet, most liberal watchdogs of our freedom remain fixed on the Right as the enemy of free expression.

For a salubrious change, therefore, let us look at what is happening to freedom of speech and press in certain enclaves—some colleges, for instance—where the New Right has no clout at all. Does the pulse of the First Amendment beat more vigorously in these places than where the yahoos are?

Well, consider what happened when Eldridge Cleaver came to Madison, Wisconsin, last October to savor the exhilarating openness of dialogue at the University of Wisconsin. Cleaver's soul is no longer on ice; it's throbbing instead with a religious conviction that is currently connected financially, and presumably theologically, to the Reverend Sun Myung Moon's Unification Church. In Madison, Cleaver never got to talk about his pilgrim's progress from the Black Panthers to the wondrously ecumenical Moonies. In the Humanities Building, several hundred students and others outraged by Cleaver's apostasy shouted, stamped their feet, chanted "Sieg Heil," and otherwise prevented him from being heard.

After ninety minutes of the din, Cleaver wrote on the blackboard, "I regret that the totalitarians have deprived us of our constitutional rights to free assembly and free speech. Down with communism. Long live democracy."

And, raising a clenched fist while blowing kisses with his free hand, Cleaver left. Cleaver says he'll try to speak again, but he doesn't know when.

The University of Wisconsin administration, through Dean of Students Paul Ginsberg, deplored the behavior of the campus totalitarians of the Left, and there was a fiercely denunciatory editorial in the *Madison Capital Times*: "These people lack even the most primitive appreciation of the Bill of Rights."

It did occur to me, however, that if Eldridge Cleaver had not abandoned his secularist rage at the American Leviathan and had come to Madison as the still burning spear of black radicalism, the result might have been quite different if he had been shouted down that night by young apostles of the New Right. That would have made news around the country, and there would have been collectively signed letters to the *New York Review of Books* and *The Nation* warning of the prowling dangers to free speech in the land. But since Cleaver has long since taken up with bad companions, there is not much concern among those who used to raise bail for him as to whether he gets to speak freely or not.

It is difficult to be a disciple of James Madison on campus these days.

—NAT HENTOFF, one of the preeminent journalists on civil liberties issues, writes for the *Village Voice*, among other publications.

## Lesbian Writer Fights Feminist Censors

HOLLY METZ
AUGUST 1989

Joan Nestle writes about lesbian life, and members of Women Against Pornography (WAP) picket her speeches and call for censorship of her work. Some lesbian opponents of pornography want to ban from women's bookstores magazines that feature Nestle's explicitly sexual writing, along with other "unacceptable" contributions.

"The anti-pornography movement is helping to create a new McCarthy period in the lesbian community," Nestle writes in *A Restricted Country*, her 1987 collection of theoretical essays, erotic poetry, and fiction. Lesbians who do not follow a prescribed mode of behavior "are distanced and told we are not feminists, even though many of us have spent years building the movement." She fears these women will be exiled from their own communities, then served up for state punishment like the labor organizers and social activists of the 1950s—convicted, Nestle says, "by innuendo, association, and labeling."

In her essay "My History with Censorship," the forty-nine-year-old writer recalls the state's tools of repression during those times. Motivated by "one prevailing view of how to make the country safe," the House Un-American Activities Committee routed out dissenters. Nestle and other students protested at its meetings, cheering those who refused to testify.

Joan Nestle also came out as a lesbian during the 1950s, a time when police vice squads routinely raided New York City's gay bars. There, too, she witnessed daring opposition. In the "deviant criminalized world of butch-femme lesbians in Village bars,'" Nestle writes, "I learned how to take brutal insults to personal dignity and keep wanting and loving. Here I learned first what a community of women could do even when we were called the scum of the Earth."

Knowing the vice squad might arrest them simply for dancing together, these working-class lesbians risked their jobs, daring to claim erotic independence. There was no "movement" to back them up. "They faced the forces of the state in the most vivid and concrete way," Nestle recalls.

A civil-rights activist since her teenage years, Nestle co-founded the Lesbian Herstory Archive in 1972, a depository for the diaries, newsletters, photographs, and paintings, of working-class lesbians—women the burgeoning women's movement had abandoned, she says.

Joan Nestle considers her writing revelatory—"the breaking open of the earth to see something that needs to be seen." As she sees it, when a way of loving is censored, its participants are put beyond the pale. They can live in shame, or resist: "If desire is a monument to what the reactionary forces in this world would like to destroy, then it can't be a secret any more."

What seems to anger Nestle most about feminist anti-pornographers is their unwillingness to recognize that women have varied experiences of both sexual danger and sexual celebration. Insisting that they were acting to "save women," WAP people even testified before former Attorney General Edwin Meese's commission against pornography—right alongside sheriffs upholding their raids on gay bookstores.

During one of the hearings, Nestle and eight other women sat in the front row wearing signs around their necks reading CENSORED.

"Politically," she says, "the setting is one that will *not* save women, and in fact will do terrible damage to sexual minorities. They take it upon themselves to say that those who want to explore another territory, one of sexual complexity and independence, should be silenced. I will never accept it."

—HOLLY METZ has been writing on social, cultural, and legal issues for over twenty-five years.

# Your Urine, Please

BARBARA EHRENREICH
MARCH 2000

The fascination with urine remains undimmed through the ages. Until the arrival of scientific medicine, physicians subjected it to careful visual scrutiny, expecting the color and clarity to reveal an exact diagnosis. Today, it's the corporate class that seems transfixed by the predictive powers of piss: 80 percent of large employers insist on testing job applicants' urine—or occasionally hair or blood—for damning traces of illegal substances. You can be the best qualified applicant in all other ways, but if your urine speaks against you, you're out. Experience, skill, enthusiasm, and energy—pee trumps them all.

A report released last September by the ACLU, "Drug Testing: A Bad Investment," summarizes studies showing that drug testing does not lower absenteeism, improve workplace safety, or achieve any of the other goals claimed for it by the anti-drug warriors. This should be no surprise: The tests mainly detect marijuana, which lingers in the body far longer than cocaine or heroin, and drug-testing labs are often alarmingly inaccurate, in both the false-negative and false-positive directions. In addition, smart drug users have all kinds of ways of foiling the test, from the herb goldenseal (available in health food stores) to vials of drug-free, battery-warmed urine (available on the Web). More to the point, most drug users confine their drug using to their off hours, when it can have little or no possible effect on their job performance. The residual mental effects of a weekend joint, for example, are about as powerful as those of a Saturday night beer—i.e., nil. Not to mention the fact that one of the most disabling and addicting drugs, alcohol, isn't usually tested for at all.

And what exactly would it mean for drug testing to "work," anyway? An argument could be made for testing airline pilots and school bus drivers, on the grounds that an off-hour user might, just possibly, be tempted to toke up while landing a 747 or driving on ice-coated streets. But retail and cleaning service workers? In my town, Winn-Dixie tests applicants for a $6-an-hour job stacking Cheerio boxes; Howard Johnson tests applicants for bed-making jobs. Hudson News, which can be found in New York area airports, greets customers with a sign boasting that it's a "drug-free workplace," but is the newspaper you buy there any more interesting if the cashier is an abstainer rather than a stoner? An alcoholic rather than a cokehead?

Speaking of newspapers, the *New York Times*, the *Los Angeles Times*, and the *Washington Post* all test their editors and writers—a practice that may actually make these papers less interesting, or at least help account for their unrelieved blandness. This is not because druggies make better reporters (though who knows?), but because any journalist sheep-like enough to submit to a urine test should, on this evidence alone, be barred from a profession that claims to value fearlessly independent thinking.

In other areas, drug testing may actually be counterproductive. First, there's the cost. The ACLU reports that in 1990 the federal government spent $11.7 million to test 29,000 employees, only 153 of whom tested positive—amounting to a cost of $77,000 to detect each putative drug user! Then there's the likely effect of testing on morale. A 1998 study found that testing "reduced rather than enhanced productivity" by as much as 29 percent, apparently because it leads to a certain surliness among the workers.

So why, in contempt of all the evidence, does American business remain so slavishly addicted to drug testing? Part of the answer has to be that drug testing is now a billion-dollar industry, meaning that an awful lot of people have a stake in its health and longevity. Capitalism is supposed to operate in a briskly rational fashion, but profits can perpetuate any kind of foolishness. Hence, for example, the Congressional fondness for obsolete weapons systems: It doesn't matter if they can't fly or even if the Pentagon has adamantly rejected them; they keep Lockheed Martin and Boeing content.

Sheer herd mentality—"peer pressure," as it's known in the anti-drug movement—also contributes to the drug-testing habit. I once asked a hotel owner why he tests his employees, and he said, in so many words: Everyone else is doing it, and I don't want to be the one who gets stuck with all the druggies and low-lifes who can't get a job anywhere else in town. This sounded vaguely reasonable until he added that he couldn't, ha ha, pass one of those tests himself, which made me wonder: If one pothead can make all the company's top decisions, why can't another one be trusted to push a broom?

Nor can we eliminate the kinkier charms of drug testing—to the employer, that is. In some testing protocols, the hapless worker has to pull down her pants in front of a lab technician or attendant and then pee in the presence of that forbidding audience. This is not a medical procedure; it's a rite of humiliation, designed to send the employee the message: We own you, all of you, and our ownership extends way beyond 5 p.m. Similarly for those intrusive pre-employment "personality tests," with true-or-false propositions like "I often feel overwhelmed by self-pity." It's not really our urine that they want—or our blood or our hair — but our souls.

There are a few small, hopeful signs. Faced with a severe labor shortage, some Internet and computer firms are abandoning testing rather than drive away qualified applicants. In safety-sensitive industries, a few companies have taken up the far more pertinent practice of "performance testing"—gauging an employee's motor skills just prior to work.

But the damage to democracy has already been done. In a decade of testing, millions of Americans have grown inured to this invasion of their bodies and private lives, readily trading their Fourth Amendment protection from "unreasonable search" in exchange for a job. And submission, no less than drugs, can be a hard habit to break.

—BARBARA EHRENREICH, social critic, is the author of *Nickel and Dimed, Bait and Switch*, and *The Land Is Their Land*, among other works.

# That Country Wouldn't Be America

SENATOR RUSS FEINGOLD
DECEMBER 2001

[*Editor's Note*: On October 11, the Senate voted ninety-six to one in favor of an anti-terrorism bill that severely infringes on our civil liberties. The only senator to vote against it was Russ Feingold, Democrat of Wisconsin. What follows is an excerpt from his floor statement that day. On October 25, the Senate voted on the final version of the bill. This time, it was ninety-eight to one, with Feingold again the odd man out.]

There is no doubt that if we lived in a police state, it would be easier to catch terrorists. If we lived in a country where the police were allowed to search your home at any time for any reason; if we lived in a country where the government is entitled to open your mail, eavesdrop on your phone conversations, or intercept your e-mail communications; if we lived in a country where people could be held in jail indefinitely based on what they write or think, or based on mere suspicion that they are up to no good, the government would probably discover and arrest more terrorists or would-be terrorists, just as it would find more lawbreakers generally.

But that wouldn't be a country in which we would want to live, and it wouldn't be a country for which we could, in good conscience, ask our young people to fight and die. In short, that country wouldn't be America.

I think it is important to remember that the Constitution was written in 1789 by men who had recently won the Revolutionary War. They did not live in comfortable and easy times of hypothetical enemies. They wrote the Constitution and the Bill of Rights to protect individual liberties in times of war as well as in times of peace.

There have been periods in our nation's history when civil liberties have taken a back seat to what appeared at the time to be legitimate exigencies of war. Our national consciousness still bears the stain and the scars of those events: The Alien and Sedition Acts, the suspension of habeas corpus during the Civil War, the internment of Japanese Americans during World War II and the injustices perpetrated against German Americans and Italian Americans, the blacklisting of supposed communist sympathizers during the McCarthy era, and the surveillance and harassment of anti-war protesters, including Dr. Martin Luther King Jr., during the Vietnam War. We must not allow this piece of our past to become prologue.

Preserving our freedom is the reason we are now engaged in this new war on terrorism. We will lose that war without a shot being fired if we sacrifice the liberties of the American people in the belief that by doing so we will stop the terrorists.

—RUSS FEINGOLD is the junior senator from Wisconsin.

# The New McCarthyism

MATTHEW ROTHSCHILD
JANUARY 2002

Donna Huanca works as a docent at the Art Car Museum, an avant-garde gallery in Houston. Around 10:30 on the morning of November 7, before she opened the museum, two men wearing suits and carrying leather portfolios came to her door.

"I told them to wait until we opened at 11:00," she recalls. "Then they pulled their badges out."

The two men were Terrence Donahue of the FBI and Steven Smith of the Secret Service.

"They said they had several reports of anti-American activity going on here and wanted to see the exhibit," she says. The museum was running a show called "Secret Wars," which contains many antiwar statements that were commissioned before September 11.

"They just walked in, so I went through with them and gave them a very detailed tour. I asked them if they were familiar with the artists and what the role of art was at a critical time like this," she says. "They were more interested in where the artists were from. They were taking some notes. They were pointing out things that they thought were negative, like a recent painting by Lynn Randolph of the Houston skyline burning, and a devil dancing around, and with George Bush Sr. in the belly of the devil."

There was a surreal moment when they inspected another element of the exhibit. "We had a piece in the middle of the room, a mock surveillance camera pointed to the door of the museum, and they wondered whether they were being recorded," she says.

All in all, they were there for about an hour. "As they were leaving, they asked me where I went to school, and if my parents knew if I worked at a place like this, and who funded us, and how many people came in to see the exhibit," she says. "I was definitely pale. It was scary because I was alone, and they were really big guys."

She is a freshman at Durham Tech in North Carolina. Her name is A. J. Brown. She's gotten a scholarship from the ACLU to help her attend college. But that didn't prepare her for the knock on the door that came on October 26. "It was 5:00 on Friday, and I was getting ready for a date," she says. When she heard the knock, she opened the door. Here's her account.

"Hi, we're from the Raleigh branch of the Secret Service," two agents said.

"And they flip out their little ID cards, and I was like, 'What?'

"And they say, 'We're here because we have a report that you have un-American material in your apartment.' And I was like, 'What? No, I don't have anything like that.'

"'Are you sure? Because we got a report that you've got a poster that's anti-American.'
"And I said no."

They asked if they could come into the apartment. "Do you have a warrant?" Brown asked. "And they said no, they didn't have a warrant, but they wanted to just come in and look around. And I said, 'Sorry, you're not coming in.'"

One of the agents told Brown, "We already know what it is. It's a poster of Bush hanging himself," she recalls. "And I said no, and she was like, 'Well, then, it's a poster with a target on Bush's head,' and I was like, nope."

The poster they seemed interested in was one that depicted Bush holding a rope, with the words: "We Hang on Your Every Word. George Bush, Wanted: 152 Dead." The poster has sketches of people being hanged, and it refers to the number who were put to death in Texas while Bush was governor, she explains.

Ultimately, Brown agreed to open her door so that the agents could see the poster on the wall of her apartment, though she did not let them enter. "They just kept looking at the wall," which contained political posters from the Bush counter-inaugural, a "Free Mumia" poster, a picture of Jesse Jackson, and a Pink Floyd poster with the quotation: "Mother, should I trust the government?"

At one point in the conversation, one of the agents mentioned Brown's mother, saying, "She's in the armed forces, isn't she?" (Her mother, in fact, is in the Army Reserve.)

After they were done inspecting the wall, one of the agents "pulled out his little slip of paper, and he asked me some really stupid questions, like, my name, my Social Security number, my phone number," she says. "Then they asked, 'Do you have any pro-Taliban stuff in your apartment, any posters, any maps?'

"I was like, 'No, I don't, and personally, I think the Taliban is just a bunch of assholes.'"

With that, they left. They had been at her apartment for forty minutes.

"They called me two days later to make sure my information was correct: where I lived, my phone number (hello!), and my nicknames," she says.

Brown says she's "really annoyed" about the Secret Service visit. "Obviously, I'm on some list somewhere."

Welcome to the New McCarthyism.

—MATTHEW ROTHSCHILD is the editor of *The Progressive* and the author of *You Have No Rights*.

# Treated Like a Criminal

## How the INS Stole Three Days of My Life

Behrooz Arshadi, as told to Mark Engler
March 2003

My name is Behrooz Arshadi. I am forty-eight years old, and I work in marketing for a minority publication in Los Angeles. My wife and I came to this country in 1987. We were running from the situation in Iran, looking for a better life. We have a seven-year-old daughter, who was born in the United States.

We've been applying for our green cards for years. We're at the end of the process, waiting for our interview. This fall, my lawyer told me the INS had ordered Iranian immigrants like me who were not U.S. citizens to report in. I decided to go on the last day, Monday, December 16.

I arrived at INS at about 10 a.m. There was a long line, and I had to wait and wait and wait. INS officers finally interviewed me about seven hours later for about twenty minutes. They asked me all the questions they already knew, basic questions that I had provided answers to long ago. They already had them in my file: "What is your mother's name? Your father's name? Where do they live?"

One agent asked me to wait. After about half an hour, an officer came and said, "You will have to be detained."

"Why?"

"Although you are married to an American citizen, you are out of status."

I was shocked. I'm not married to an American. Obviously, the guy didn't know what he was talking about. He didn't know anything about my case.

Though he didn't charge me with any crime, he handcuffed me and took me downstairs. They put me in what they called a "tank," and there were six such tanks. Inside, it was thirty-by-thirty, with eighty to ninety people inside. It was so crowded. The tank had two benches next to the wall and two open toilets. There wasn't space even to sit.

At one point, they took us out for fingerprinting and photos, and they made us put all our belongings in a bag—our ties, our watches, whatever we had. We kept only our clothes because they didn't provide any.

Other than that processing, they kept us in the tank until 5 a.m. They didn't talk to us. They didn't tell us what they were doing, why we were there, why they detained us. And they didn't give us blankets or warm clothing or anything. It was very cold. I was wearing my regular suit. This is Southern California, so it's a light suit. The air conditioning was going all the time. People were shivering. No one had a bed to sleep on. You couldn't even sit.

At about 5 a.m., they chained us all and took us by bus to the Pasadena jail about twenty minutes away. They put us in regular cells. We slept there, but only for a half hour. Then they woke us up for breakfast. I felt terrible. I hadn't slept the whole night.

Later, they took us back to the INS. To keep us busy, they moved us from tank to tank every few hours. Counting us and counting us and counting us. I imagine we were about 500, maybe 600, people. Some had come to the INS to register on Thursday or Friday of the previous week. And they were still waiting. Then there was collective punishment: If someone said something, the INS agents would make the whole group stand and wait for an extra hour.

The tanks had phones, so I called my wife and my lawyer. They were working to get me out on bond. I had to make collect calls. Later on, I found out it was $4 or even $6 for a call. The officers wouldn't say anything to us about our cases, about what we had to do, about what would happen next. Anything. It went on again until 5 a.m. the next day. It was very cold.

This time, they took us to San Pedro prison. When we arrived, they gave us clothes and blankets. It was also the first time I'd had coffee in all this time. They let us sleep for one hour, then walked us around the yard.

After that, we went back to the INS. It was 7 p.m. before they interviewed me again, this time for about five minutes. "What is your father's name? What is your mother's name? Where are you working?"

At 5 a.m. on Thursday morning, they sent us to Lancaster County jail. They stripped us buck-naked. They looked under our testicles. Under our tongues. Butts. Wherever. Then they gave us T-shirts and jumpsuits and put us in cells. There were showers. It was the first time I had a shower in three days.

They finally decided to release us without bail. But they told us we had to go back within one month to post bail. I don't think they wanted to keep us longer than seventy-two hours because then they would have had to charge us. They never charged me with anything. They said I would receive a letter from the INS. They call it a notice to appear in court, in front of a judge. They made me sign for it.

I received a letter in the middle of January saying that they had carefully reviewed my case. They canceled my bail and the notice to appear in court. I just had to appear for my regular green card interview. My case was back where it was before, and the INS had stolen three days of my life.

What was the purpose? The people who are coming for these registrations are trying to comply with the law. They're working people, good people, people with families. We were not criminals, but they treated us like that.

I wish what happened to me will never happen to anyone else. They didn't beat us up or anything like that. They didn't need to beat us. Whatever they did was enough to crush us. I slept only four hours during that time. I felt total frustration.

On Thursday, I was one of the last ones released. They finished processing me at about midnight. They released a group of us to the Metrolink station in Lancaster. We were waiting to go to the train and an officer said to us, "Are you citizens of the United States?"

We laughed and said no.

The officer said, "Then why don't you go back to your fucking country?"

I didn't tell my daughter where I had been. I didn't want her to worry about me being in jail—which she knows as a place for bad people, for criminals.

I told her that I went to see a friend in San Diego.

> —BEHROOZ ARSHADI is an Iranian-born businessman who lived in Los Angeles for many
> years. Mark Engler is a writer based in New York City and a senior analyst with Foreign
> Policy in Focus.

# Our Job Is Not to Stand Up and Cheer When the President Breaks the Law

SENATOR RUSS FEINGOLD
APRIL 2006

*Speech delivered on the Senate floor, February 7, 2006*

Mr. President, last week the President of the United States gave his State of the Union address, where he spoke of America's leadership in the world, and called on all of us to "lead this world toward freedom." Again and again, he invoked the principle of freedom, and how it can transform nations, and empower people around the world.

But, almost in the same breath, the President openly acknowledged that he has ordered the government to spy on Americans, on American soil, without the warrants required by law.

The President issued a call to spread freedom throughout the world, and then he admitted that he has deprived Americans of one of their most basic freedoms under the Fourth Amendment—to be free from unjustified government intrusion.

The President was blunt. He said that he had authorized the National Security Agency's domestic spying program, and he made a number of misleading arguments to defend himself. His words got rousing applause from Republicans, and even some Democrats.

The President was blunt, so I will be blunt: This program is breaking the law, and this President is breaking the law. Not only that, he is misleading the American people in his efforts to justify this program.

How is that worthy of applause? Since when do we celebrate our commander in chief for violating our most basic freedoms, and misleading the American people in the process? When did we start to stand up and cheer for breaking the law? In that moment at the State of the Union, I felt ashamed.

Congress has lost its way if we don't hold this President accountable for his actions.

This goes way beyond party, and way beyond politics. What the President has done here is to break faith with the American people. In the State of the Union, he also said that "we must always be clear in our principles" to get support from friends and allies that we need to fight terrorism. So let's be clear about a basic American principle: When someone breaks the law, when someone misleads the public in an attempt to justify his actions, he needs to be held accountable. The President of the United States has broken the law. The President of the United States is trying to mislead the American people. And he needs to be held accountable.

To find out that the President of the United States has violated the basic rights of the American people is chilling. And then to see him publicly embrace his actions—and to see so many Members of Congress cheer him on—is appalling.

The President is not a king. And the Congress is not a king's court. Our job is not to stand up and cheer when the President breaks the law.

That is one of the reasons that the framers put us here—to ensure balance between the branches of government, not to act as a professional cheering section.

We need answers. Because no one, not the President, not the Attorney General, and not any of their defenders in this body has been able to explain why it is necessary to break the law to defend against terrorism. And I think that's because they can't explain it.

Instead, this Administration reacts to anyone who questions this illegal program by saying that those of us who demand the truth and stand up for our rights and freedoms have a pre-9/11 view of the world.

In fact, the President has a pre-1776 view of the world.

Our Founders lived in dangerous times, and they risked everything for freedom. Patrick Henry said, "Give me liberty or give me death." The President's pre-1776 mentality is hurting America. It is fracturing the foundation on which our country has stood for 230 years. The President can't just bypass two branches of government, and obey only those laws he wants to obey. Deciding unilaterally which of our freedoms still apply in the fight against terrorism is unacceptable and needs to be stopped immediately.

In a nation built on freedom, the President is not a king, and no one is above the law.

I yield the floor.

PART 2

# Combating Corporate Power

Acentral tenet of progressivism is that corporations have way too much power over our economy and our political system. La Follette viewed this as the central issue of his day, and he railed against corporate power throughout his career.

To curb the power of the "industrial overlords," as he once called them, *The Progressive*, under the stewardship of his widow, Belle Case La Follette, and his sons, Bob Jr. and Phil, regularly published "the Progressive Platform." To look at that today is to marvel at its sweep: It calls for public ownership of oil and minerals, utilities, transportation, and banking. And it stresses the need for farmers' co-ops and consumers' co-ops, as well as a powerful trade union movement.

You can really feel the tension in the struggle against the economic overlords when you read the piece by Harold Ickes, who was FDR's secretary of the interior. Writing in 1938 when the largest corporations were threatening to engage in a capital strike, Ickes warned about "big business fascism."

Corporations are killers. Ralph Nader, Jane Slaughter, and Morton Mintz all write about this fact in their own ways. But none does so with as much emotional power as Ron Hayes, who lost his son in an industrial accident, an accident that could have been prevented if the company had operated up to code, and if the Occupational Safety and Health Administration had done its job.

In writing about corporate power, *The Progressive* has had the great fortune of publishing terrific stylists, like John Kenneth Galbraith, who graced our pages more than once, and especially Molly Ivins, who anchored *The Progressive* with her column for twenty years. Her contribution in this chapter gives you a taste of her salty indignation, which was a reader favorite for so many years.

# Punish the Real Offenders

ROBERT M. LA FOLLETTE
MAY 27, 1911

The Standard Oil Company is guilty. It is ordered by the United States Supreme Court to dissolve its present organization within six months. So flagrant has been its violation of the anti-trust law, that its eminent lawyers were not able to prove it even "reasonably" innocent.

But is it punishment merely to compel the Standard Oil Company to change its form of organization? We heard immediately after the decision was handed down that there was no panic in Standard Oil headquarters; on the contrary, this company's stock was stronger in Wall Street, and officials of the trust announced that business would be carried on as usual, with each constituent company operating under the direction of its own officers. Does this look as if the public is given even "reasonable" relief from this monopoly?

What about the men under whose direction these illegal practices were carried on? Are they not to be called to account?

Offenses such as these with which the Standard Oil Company stands convicted were not committed of themselves. They were the work of human hands and human brains, and the men responsible for them should be summoned to court.

We cannot have justice as long as the petty offender is jailed and the big lawbreaker allowed to go his way.

If the heads of trusts were sent to prison for willful lawbreaking, such as this, there would be fewer violations of the Sherman law. Fines they laugh at, "dissolution" weakens them not a bit, and the law is specific enough. We quote from the Sherman Act: "Every person who shall make any such contract or engage in any such combination or conspiracy shall be deemed guilty of misdemeanor, and, on conviction thereof, shall be punished by fine not exceeding five thousand dollars or by imprisonment not exceeding one year, or by both said punishments, in the discretion of the court."

Plain justice demands that the men in back of this Standard Oil villainy be punished.

## Borah Tells How Our Wealth Is Divided

SENATOR WILLIAM E. BORAH
MAY 2, 1931

Today, 3 percent of the American people own 75 percent of its wealth. Let us be a little more liberal. Let us say that 4 percent own 80 percent of its wealth. I would not take it from them, but I do think there ought to be a political party in this country—if not a political party, then political voices—which shall worry more about the 96 percent than they worry about the 4 percent.

—SENATOR WILLIAM E. BORAH represented the state of Idaho from 1906 to 1940.

## The Progressive Platform

JANUARY 5, 1935

1. Public ownership of natural resources and those activities with a public interest—light, heat, power, and transportation.
2. The elimination of war profits; government monopoly on the manufacture and sale of munitions; a plebiscite on wars which would send American soldiers to foreign soil.
3. High inheritance and income taxes to be levied on the beneficiaries of monopoly.
4. The development of a strong farmers' cooperative movement and also consumers' cooperatives.
5. The development of a strong trade union movement.
6. A government-owned central banking system to break the grip of the money trust by carrying out, among other things, the congressional power "to coin money and regulate the value thereof."
7. Adequate old age pensions and unemployment insurance.
8. Adequate poor and unemployment relief and the restoration of purchasing power in the hands of the great masses of the people.

# Lawless Big Business Must Be Controlled to Save Democracy

HAROLD ICKES, SECRETARY OF THE INTERIOR
JANUARY 8, 1938

Here in America it is the old struggle between the power of money and the power of the democratic instinct.

In the last few months this irreconcilable conflict, long growing in our history, has come into the open as never before, has taken on a form and an intensity which makes it clear that it must be fought through to a finish—until plutocracy or democracy—until America's sixty families or America's 120 million people win.

Economic power in this country does not rest in the mass of the people as it must if a democracy is to endure. Wealth is not equitably distributed nor do its owners in the main even manage and control it. On the contrary, wealth has become so great and so concentrated that as a matter of fact, it controls those who possess it.

About one-half of the wealth of this country is in corporate form, and over one-half of it is under the domination of 200 corporations, which in turn are controlled by what Ferdinand Lundberg in his recent book referred to as "America's Sixty Families."

Eight years ago America's sixty families had held in their hands, since the close of the World War, complete dominion over the economic and political life of the country. They had lulled the American people into the conviction that if the people would grant conditions in which these sixty families would have confidence that they would do as they pleased, the sixty families would put capital to work; enterprise would boom, wages would rise, stocks would soar, and there would be two cars in every garage.

The people gave the sixty families this confidence; gave the sixty families this trust in their benevolent despotism—in short, gave the sixty families then what they ask for today, and what happened? Out of their divinely claimed genius as managers of private enterprise the sixty families promptly led the American people into the worst peacetime catastrophe ever known.

Then the disillusioned people changed the government.

The new government bailed the sixty families out of the consequences of their own mesmeric miscalculations and their unintelligent leadership of the system of private enterprise of which they had pretended to be master managers. It preserved the corporate structures in which their capital was invested from going through the wringer of bankruptcy and reorganization and stock assessment. And it preserved the management structure from going through the wringer to squeeze out incompetence and big salaries. Then government sought to modify the way in which the business of the nation was done so that business confidence would be based upon the well-being and purchasing power of 120 million people at the bottom standing on their own feet rather than upon the license of the sixty families at the top and upon their premises, in return for that license, to permit the gravy of their benevolence to trickle down upon the exploited millions at the bottom.

Government did get the economic system back on its feet; did succeed in doing a job where the sixty families had failed.

Government had the system back on its feet so well at the time of the elections of 1936 that, as the president said in his Chicago speech, the patients—over their panic and raising their salaries—felt strong enough to throw their crutches at the doctor.

And last spring government had the business of the country turning over so well that it thought it could safely heed the pleas of private enterprise to government and abandon the economic initiative.

Pursuant to these pleas government cut down public expenditures to keep up purchasing power in order to meet the insistence of private enterprise that business confidence would be greater if government would take steps to balance the budget—assuaged the fears of the head of the biggest bank in the United States about runaway inflation—and turned over to the managers of private enterprise the responsibility they had said that they were eager and willing to assume.

And what happened?

Two things. First, the sixty families that were masterminding private enterprise proved to have learned nothing nor forgotten nothing since 1929 about the management of business under modern conditions. They made the same mistakes they had made before 1929. They ran the stock market up and helped it get started down. They did little or nothing to increase the purchasing power of labor to make up for the government withdrawals and then ran prices to the sky so that the consumer refused to spend what they graciously let him earn.

Second, the sixty families, unwilling to learn to do business upon the democratic terms of 1937, began to make demands and threats.

To Franklin D. Roosevelt and the overwhelming millions who have three times approved his policy they have made a threat like that which Nicholas Biddle of the Bank of the United States 100 years ago made to Andrew Jackson—a threat that they will refuse to do business at all unless the president and the Congress and the people will repeal all that we have gained in the last five years and regrant them the suicidal license they had enjoyed in 1929.

To the 120 million people of the United States they have made the threat that the professional operators of the American economic system and the professional managers of the capital funds of the United States—capital to which every American man and woman over four generations has contributed sweat and blood—will refuse to operate that economic system, will refuse to let that capital be employed unless they are once more given full power to wreck American democracy in their own sweet way.

To the 120 million people of the United States they have made the threat that, unless they are free to speculate free of regulations to protect the people's money; unless they are free to accumulate through legal tricks by means of corporations without paying their share of taxes; unless they are free to dominate the rest of us without restrictions on their financial or economic power; unless they are once more free to do all these things, then the United States is to have its first general sit-down strike—not of labor, not of the American people, but of the sixty families and of the capital created by the whole American people of which the sixty families have obtained control.

If the American people call this bluff, then the America that is to be free will be a democratic America, a free America.

If the American people yield to this bluff, then the America that is to be will be a big-business Fascist America—an enslaved America.

—Harold Ickes served as FDR's secretary of the interior.

# The Profit in Highway Slaughter

Ralph Nader
May 1966

[*Editor's Note*: In all the controversy over General Motors' private investigation of Ralph Nader—the young attorney who is one of the automobile industry's severest critics—little detail has been revealed in the mass media about his specific charges that the industry bears responsibility for an appreciable part of the slaughter on the nation's highways. The following is a condensation of Mr. Nader's testimony before the Senate subcommittee on automobile safety.]

Under present conditions there is little economic incentive for the automaker to concern himself seriously with automobile casualties and collisions—for the costs and penalties are not upon him. Actually, the more cars depreciate through collisions, the greater the demand for new and used cars. Only when there is a real threat of cost or other adverse feedback, as in the mass litigation over the 1960–'63 Chevrolet Corvairs, does a manufacturer take notice and correct, as General Motors did for the Corvair rear suspension system after those four tragic model years. But such feedbacks are very infrequent and, until the Corvair cases, never on a mass basis.

Neither do automobile collisions and injuries threaten the economy generally—at least there is no felt threat to the economy as there would be if, for example, a pest attack destroyed most of the cotton crop. For the costs of the highway epidemic are essentially economic demands feeding a vast highway accident service industry composed of medical, hospital, police, legal, insurance, repair, and administrative services.

To put it squarely, death on the highway produces incomes and profits for hundreds of thousands of people and companies. It is a multibillion-dollar industry whose dynamics are hardly about to be in the direction of self-liquidation. The energies of lawyers and physicians (to choose the skills ideally most subject to professional standards of conduct) are so taken up in the care and handling of post-accident problems that they have had little time, even if they had the inclination, to exert effective and sustained efforts toward prevention of collisions and injuries.

Thus, the economics of the highway accident industry and the operational health of the highway transport system do not breed self-correcting forces and the attention of government that obtains to a substantial degree in other forms of transportation. This condition has made the annual toll of 50,000 dead and millions injured the most expendable horror of our technological society. In America, life is cheapest on the highway.

How tragic are the results and how costly is the impact on purchasers of America's largest consumer durable. The car buyer pays more than $700 (according to a study by Massachusetts Institute of Technology, Harvard, and University of Chicago economists), when he buys a new car, for the cost of the annual model change which is mostly stylistic in content. Consider how much safer today's automobile would be if over the past two decades the car buyer received annually a substantial safety advance—both in the operational and crashworthy aspects of his automobile—for that $700 payment.

Instead, cars are being built which, standing still, can kill adult and child pedestrians who fall or are inadvertently pushed into their sharp points and edges. And passengers can die in collisions at speeds as low as five miles per hour. Is it any wonder that, at present rates, at least one out of every two living Americans will either be killed or injured (disabled beyond the day of injury) in an automobile collision?

A genuine democracy has to provide for the participation of the public in decisions relating to technology whose use is so fraught with tragedy to millions of people. There is an old Roman adage which says: "Whatever touches all should be decided by all." The automobile touches us all in the most ultimate ways. The safety the motorist gets when he buys his car should not be determined solely by manufacturers—especially a tightly knit few—whose interests are necessarily those of profit-parochialism.

—RALPH NADER, consumer advocate, wrote *Unsafe at Any Speed*, founded many public citizen groups, and has run several times for president as a third-party candidate or independent.

# Valley of the Shadow of Death

JANE SLAUGHTER
MARCH 1985

I used to believe everybody's daddy worked for Union Carbide. Mine did—he was a chemical engineer—and so did most of the daddies in our neighborhood.

It was a neighborhood of "Carbide housing." Carbide had paid to have some war workers' homes barged forty miles downriver and re-erected three miles from the company's factory in Institute, West Virginia, near Charleston. Carbide's young employees bought the transplanted houses and started their families there.

After we left that neighborhood, I met girls whose fathers didn't work for Union Carbide. I felt sorry for them; they couldn't go to Cliffside or Carlisle, Carbide's summer camps, where a two-week stay cost $20 in the late 1950s.

I thought about my Carbide childhood when I heard, early last December, that a cloud of poisonous MIC gas had killed 2,500 people who lived near a Carbide plant in Bhopal, India. The plant in Institute is the only other one that produces methyl isocyanate (MIC).

I remembered a Saturday night in April 1955, when my parents were getting ready to go to the monthly dance sponsored by Carbide. Suddenly, we heard a loud boom.

"That's the plant," said my father, and he rushed off to investigate. Later, we learned that a reactive chemical called acrolein had blown the top off a tank car. Eight workers were hurt in the explosion and fire, and the fire department evacuated the residents of Institute.

Chemicals in the air were a fact of life, like sunshine or rain. As one of my friends put it, "Certain towns just had their certain smells. South Charleston was sulfur. Nitro was rotten potatoes." Nobody who was employed by Carbide would admit to minding much.

My sister, who worked for Carbide for several years, making her way from typist to systems analyst, says some Carbide employees refer to their status as "sucking off the tit of Big Mama Carbide." The company is the largest private employer in West Virginia's Kanawha Valley, with about 7,000 workers on the payroll. Top scale for an operator at the Institute plant is $12.50 an hour.

So I wasn't really surprised to find, when I went back to the Valley a few weeks after the Bhopal tragedy, that most people were angry not at Carbide but at Carbide's critics. There were, to be sure, some residents who feared a gas leak and worried about the lack of a decent evacuation plan. But many more resented the questions being asked about Carbide's integrity and competence. Their concern was that the adverse publicity about Bhopal could cost them their jobs, which are doubly precious in the state that has the nation's highest unemployment rate.

More than 400 employees of Carbide's Technical Center rushed to sign a Sunday newspaper ad last December reaffirming their faith in the company. Letters to editors of area papers argued that Carbide's factories were safer than the highways, and that the insecticide Sevin, made from MIC, was not a hazardous substance but a lifesaver.

The Carbide plant in Institute, like the one in Bhopal, has thousands of close neighbors. Many live in private homes, but there are also some 4,500 students at West Virginia State College and 250 to 300 blind and disabled enrollees at the West Virginia Rehabilitation Center. There is no clear plan for evacuation in case of emergency.

At a community meeting held in Institute a few days after the Bhopal tragedy, residents asked officials what they should do if a gas leak occurred. State Health Director

Clark Hansbargar told them to put wet cloths over their mouths, check the wind direction, and walk crosswind. Residents pointed out that heading crosswind if the wind was blowing in its prevailing eastward direction would mean swimming the Kanawha River or climbing a mountain.

A *Charleston Gazette* telephone poll of Kanawha County residents, taken after Bhopal, found that 62 percent believed that a comparable disaster could occur in West Virginia. But only 15 percent of the respondents said they had no confidence in the safety of the Valley's chemical plants, while 40 percent professed to be "very confident" and the rest "somewhat confident."

Don Wilson, who lives one mile east of the Institute plant, says his lungs were burned in 1975 by a gas emission from Carbide. He placed a three-line newspaper ad to hear from others who had been injured by toxic air, and received more than twenty-five calls.

"Most of them had had similar experiences; some of them had cancer," Wilson recalls. "But they had relatives who worked for the chemical industry and they were reluctant to get involved. . . . You will not find people who work for the chemical industry saying anything bad about the chemical industry.

"We will have to have a Bhopal here," he told me. "We will have to have a hundred to a thousand people die here. The chemical industry will be allowed to monitor itself until there is a disaster."

—JANE SLAUGHTER works for *Labor Notes* in Detroit.


# Tobacco Roads
Delivering Death to the Third World

MORTON MINTZ
MAY 1991

In 1989, the World Health Organization asked a special group of consultants to make the first-ever calculation of how many people now living will be killed by tobacco-caused diseases if current smoking patterns persist. They reported in April 1989 that nearly one-tenth of the world's population is doomed—500 million babies, children, and adults.

Many of those will be in the less-developed nations where, thanks in good part to U.S. exports, cigarette consumption is increasing sharply.

For Asia and the Third World, there are enormous health implications in U.S. Government promotion of cigarette exports. The United States is the leading cigarette exporter. In 1989, despite a 3 percent decline in cigarette production, U.S. manufacturers sent 100 billion cigarettes abroad, more than twice as many as in 1983. And, to supply a growing export market in the first half of 1990, production rose about 2 percent.

While tobacco smoking has become less popular here, U.S. cigarette companies have tried to expand their sales to Japan, Taiwan, South Korea, and Thailand. These countries imposed trade restrictions that substantially barred cigarette imports, thus protecting their own domestic tobacco monopolies.

Except for Japan's, these monopolies were, for the most part, lethargic, tame enterprises. They did, or were permitted to do, very little advertising and promotion, particularly to women and children. As sowers of addiction and death, they were minor leaguers; to become major leaguers, they would require the prod of the aggressive, sophisticated transnational cigarette companies.

This, to be sure, is not how U.S. Trade Representative (USTR) Carla Hills views it. "I don't see how health concerns can enter the picture if the people are smoking their own cigarettes," she told a news conference in January of last year.

The U.S. transnationals' initial export efforts generally failed, leading them to seek help from tobacco-state legislators led by Republican Senator Jesse Helms of North Carolina, from such power brokers as Michael Deaver, Ronald Reagan's friend and former White House chief of staff, and, decisively, from the Reagan Administration itself.

The tobacco companies' clout came from Section 301 of the Trade Act of 1974. If a nation refuses to remove "discriminatory" or "unfair" trade barriers to U.S. products, Section 301 empowers the Government to retaliate, principally by raising tariffs against that nation's exports to painful, even unbearable levels.

The pivotal and most recent Section 301 action in behalf of the cigarette industry was initiated by the Bush Administration against Thailand, following Reagan Administration actions against Japan, Taiwan, and Korea.

Thailand has long banned the import and sale of foreign cigarettes, but by 1989 smuggled cigarettes—an estimated eighty-five million packs—accounted for 5 to 8 percent of domestic sales. By resolution in April 1988, the Royal Thai Government cabinet, as part of a comprehensive anti-smoking campaign, forbade all direct and indirect advertising and sports sponsorship of cigarettes, whether domestic or foreign. In February 1989, the Thais passed a law: "Advertising of tobacco is totally prohibited in all forms, direct and indirect, in all media." Even this failed to remove all ads for U.S. brands from billboards and print media. In February 1990, for example, a "Salem" billboard was erected at the Pro-Am Golf Championship.

Hills began threatening to retaliate harshly against Thai exports (which include furniture and canned tuna) unless Thailand lifted all of its restrictions. Protesting her "strong-arm tactics," Senator Edward Kennedy said, "Free trade is not a license to export lung cancer or ride roughshod over the anti-smoking laws of other nations."

In October, the Thai cabinet, bowing to relentless pressures and fears of drastic retaliation against exports to the United States, agreed to end the import ban. A few weeks later, the Bush Administration dropped its threat to impose sanctions on Thailand.

By 1986, 62.5 percent of all Japanese men smoked—the highest rate in the developed world. Lung cancer, once uncommon, increased thirty-four-fold among Japanese men in thirty-five years. In November 1987, the Sixth World Conference on Tobacco and Health in Tokyo recommended that the Japanese government prohibit cigarette advertising and promotion. The recommendation was ignored by the Japanese government, which gets 3 percent of its revenues—$12 billion a year—from tobacco taxes and the profits of its tobacco monopoly.

But Japan did hold down competition from foreign cigarettes with high tariffs and restrictions on manufacture and distribution. Voluntarily, it also restricted cigarette advertising that targeted women and children. In September 1985, President Reagan directed his trade representative, Clayton Yeutter, to begin a Section 301 action.

"American cigarettes still claim less than 2 percent of the Japanese market," Senator Helms complained in a letter to Prime Minister Nakasone in July 1986. "Your friends in Congress will have a better chance to stem the tide of anti-Japanese trade sentiment if and when they can cite tangible examples of your doors being opened to American products."

Three months later, in October 1986, the Japanese government caved in, signing an agreement that gave American companies what they wanted—or, as a Japanese newspaper put it, the government used tobacco as "a blood offering" to protect Japanese exports.

Three weeks after ending the Japanese Section 301 investigation in October 1986, President Reagan determined that Taiwan also unfairly restricted the sale of U.S. tobacco products. USTR asked Taiwan to repeal a government ban on TV ads although, of course, the United States has prohibited just such advertising since 1971. Taiwan refused, but agreed to permit print cigarette ads. Within six weeks, in December 1986, Taiwan agreed to give U.S. companies free access to its market and thus staved off retaliation against its exports.

The Korean government, working with the Korean Monopoly Corporation, had nearly closed its cigarette market to imports before 1988. Its restrictions included a law, modeled on World Health Organization standards, which prohibited all cigarette advertising and promotional activities except for certain point-of-sale ads.

At Reagan aide Michael Deaver's perjury trial, it came out that two years earlier, in 1985, Philip Morris had paid him $250,000 to try to secure concessions from South Korea. Deaver told then-President Chun Doo Hwan, Lori Heise wrote in *World Watch*, that "the tobacco issue was tied to South Korean textile exports, which were threatened by protectionist legislation pending in Congress."

A few months later, the situation played out much as Deaver had predicted it would; Reagan vetoed the protectionist textile bill, and South Korea unilaterally yielded non-discriminatory market access to U.S. cigarettes.

"I have never smoked, have no desire to do so, and believe this addiction to be a terrible human tragedy," Yeutter wrote to Dr. C. Everett Koop, the antismoking crusader who served as Surgeon General in the Reagan Administration. "However, what we are about in our trade relationship is something entirely different."

During President-elect Bush's inaugural festivities seven weeks later, Yeutter, nominated to be Secretary of Agriculture, was the guest of honor at a reception. The host was Philip Morris.

—Morton Mintz is an investigative reporter who worked for the *Washington Post* for thirty years.

# They Killed My Son

Ron Hayes

December 1995

Friday, October 22, 1993, began like a hundred Fridays before it. It was the last day of my workweek, I was in a job I loved, and I had a great family. I even had a special treat that day: lunch with my wife. But this Friday was the day that ruined my life. At 1:30 p.m., I got the call that every parent dreads: a cold, hard voice said, "Mr. Hayes, your son Pat has been killed."

It became a day of firsts: the first time I would identify my child's body; the first time I would search for the words to tell our other children what had happened; the first time I would pick out a casket. This task was so hard, but the hardest part of all came on Monday, when we had to close the casket forever. I held on as long as I could with five or six men pulling against me, but it was inevitable. I had to close the top and send my son's body away forever. No more touching; no more hugging; no more kissing. He was gone.

What makes it all even more unbearable is the needless nature of his death.

Pat was killed on the job because the company he worked for didn't bother to provide a safe workplace, and the Occupational Safety and Health Administration (OSHA) didn't have the will or the resources to insist that the company do so.

Pat was nineteen years old. He went to work that morning looking forward to a weekend of doing what he loved most, hunting, but this was not to be. He worked for the Showell Farms Chicken Processing Plant in De Funiak Springs, Florida, for $5 an hour. His supervisors told him to go into the corn silo and start scraping the kernels off the side of the bin, while an augur at the bottom sucked the corn down. This dangerous procedure, called "walking the corn," is against the law. Company officials knew it was life-threatening; still they sent their employees in on a daily basis without proper training or safety equipment. According to one company official, "Showell Farms operates under the roll-of-the-dice philosophy; we won't change our ways until something bad happens."

Well, something bad happened to my son Pat. He was smothered under sixty tons of corn kernels. He died at 10:05 a.m., but because the company didn't have an emergency-action plan, as required by law, it took rescue workers five and a half hours to recover his body. His face was so contorted in pain, you could see two tear streaks down his cheeks.

Showell Farms was no stranger to OSHA. Over the preceding eighteen years, OSHA had conducted twenty inspections at plants owned by this company, issuing a total of more than 100 citations, including willful and serious violations. But these citations did not make the company clean up its act.

After Pat died, OSHA investigated Showell Farms once again. The investigating officer determined that the company had willfully violated OSHA standards and determined that Pat's death could have been prevented. The officer issued a report, finding six willful violations and proposing a penalty of $530,000. But then higher-ups at OSHA caved in. The area director reduced the six willful violations to a lesser ranking of "serious," and lowered the total fine to only $30,000.

To say the least, my family and I were devastated by these changes. Showell Farms was delighted. "The company broke its neck to get down there and pay the fine," one OSHA official said.

I have since found out that OSHA had been helping the company for years; nearly all of the past penalties had also been reduced.

An internal OSHA audit revealed that Pat's death did, in fact, involve a willful violation of safety standards, and that the OSHA area director was wrong to reduce the violation and the fine. A high-ranking OSHA official later told us, "OSHA was afraid of the company. That's why they didn't pursue the case."

OSHA's handling of the investigation into Pat's death was hardly unique. The agency reduces 99 percent of fines over $50,000, and collects only thirty-three cents for every dollar it levies in fines. I can only conclude that OSHA is in the pocket of big business. It's high time the American worker woke up and started taking this agency back.

This is a matter of life and death not just for my family but for thousands of other families across this country. About 10,000 Americans die on the job every year; 70 percent of these work-related deaths could be prevented if companies would do the right thing by their employees, and if OSHA had the power and the will to enforce safe working conditions.

We need to make health and safety protections stronger, not weaker. We don't need to cut OSHA; we need to improve OSHA so that safety laws are properly enforced. That's the only way businesses will understand that they cannot get away with breaking the law and risking people's lives.

My son is gone forever, but members of Congress can still save lives. They can stop cutting inspections and enforcement. They can stop making health and safety standards weaker. And they can start protecting working people like Patrick Hayes.

In workplaces all over the country, Pat's death is being replayed day after day. And if Congress has its wish, many more parents will be getting the dreaded phone call that I got that Friday afternoon two years ago.

Patrick, this is a father's promise, beloved son: you will always be in our hearts and minds, and we will fight to make things better in your honor. You did not die in vain, son. In your death, others will live.

—RON HAYES has advocated tirelessly for workplace safety and established Families in Grief Hold Together after the death of his son.

# Free Market Fraud

JOHN KENNETH GALBRAITH
JANUARY 1999

Most economists commit what I, in a professionally cautious way, call innocent fraud. It is innocent because most who employ it are without conscious guilt. It is fraud because it is quietly in the service of special interest.

Let's begin with capitalism, a word that has gone largely out of fashion. The approved reference now is to the market system. This shift minimizes—indeed, deletes—the role of wealth in the economic and social system. And it sheds the adverse connotation going back to Marx. Instead of the owners of capital or their attendants in control, we have the admirably impersonal role of market forces. It would be hard to think of a change in terminology more in the interest of those to whom money accords power. They have now a functional anonymity.

But most of the people who use the new designation—economists, in particular—are innocent as to the effect. They see nothing wrong with their bland, descriptive terminology. They pay no attention to the important question: Whether money—wealth—accords a special power. (It does.) Thus the term innocent fraud.

The fraud also conceals a major change in the role of money in the modern economy. Money, we once agreed, gave the owner, the capitalist, the controlling power in the enterprise. So it still does in small businesses. But in all large firms the decisive power now lies with a bureaucracy that controls, but does not own, the requisite capital. This bureaucracy is what the business schools teach their students to navigate, and it is where their graduates go. But bureaucratic motivation and power are outside the central subject of economics. We have corporate management, but we do not study its internal dynamics or explain why certain behaviors are rewarded with money and power. These omissions are another manifestation of fraud. Perhaps it is not entirely innocent. It evades the often unpleasant facts of bureaucratic structure, internal competition, personal advancement, and much else.

This innocent or not-so-innocent fraud masks an important factor in the distribution of income: At the highest levels of the corporate bureaucracy, compensation is set by those who receive it. This inescapable fact fits badly into accepted economic theory, so it is put aside. In the textbooks, there is no bureaucratic aspiration, no reward for bureaucratic achievement, no bureaucratic enhancement by merger and acquisition, and no personally established compensation. Bypassing all of this is not a wholly innocent fraud.

A more comprehensive fraud dominates scholarly economic and political thought. That is the presumption of a market economy separate from the state. Most economists concede a stabilizing role to the state, even those who urgently seek an escape from reality by assigning a masterful and benign role to Alan Greenspan and the central bank. And all but the most doctrinaire accept the need for regulation and legal restraint by the state. But few economists take note of the cooptation by private enterprise of what are commonly deemed to be functions of the state. This is hidden by the everyday reference to the public and private sectors, one of our clearest examples of innocent fraud.

Take the common outcry about corporate welfare. Here the private firm, as it is called, receives a public subsidy for its product or service. But what is called corporate welfare is a minor detail. Far more important is the full-fledged takeover by private industry of public decision-making and government spending.

The clearest case is the weapons industry. Given the industry's command of the Congress and the Pentagon, the defense firms create the demand for weaponry, prescribe the technological development of our defense system, and supply the needed funds—the defense budget. There is no novelty here. This is the military-industrial complex, a characterization that goes safely back to Dwight D. Eisenhower.

Any notion of a separation between the public and a private sector—between industry and government—is here plainly ludicrous. Nonetheless, the absorption of public functions by the arms industry is ignored in all everyday and most scholarly economic and political expression. And what is so ignored is in some measure sanctioned. I hesitate here to speak of innocent fraud; it is far from being socially benign.

What we must seek in these matters is reasonably evident. It is the use of plain language to express the clear truth. We can then take pleasure from the discomfort the truth so often evokes.

—JOHN KENNETH GALBRAITH, economist, diplomat, and writer, was the author of *The Affluent Society*, among many other works.

# Wake Me When We're Equal

MOLLY IVINS
APRIL 2001

Excuse me, but this is special, unmerited favor for rich people. At first, Citizens for Tax Justice claimed 43 percent of the total tax cut would go to the richest 1 percent of people in America. This caused various Administration flunkies to have a hissy fit, so Citizens For redid their math, and it turned out that they were wrong—45 percent of the tax cut goes to the richest 1 percent.

Bush's whine on this figure was: "But, but, you're including repeal of the death tax." (The "death tax" is what Republicans call the estate tax because they're just so gosh-darn cute.) This is very complicated, so pay attention: The reason we include repeal of the estate tax while figuring the effects of the Bush tax cut is because it is included. This is a fiendishly clever liberal ploy, but there it is. Would you like to take out the effects of the estate tax? OK: The richest 1 percent get only 36 percent of the tax cut that way. Even guys from the Heritage Foundation admit this. If the richest 1 percent got only 2 percent of the tax cut, wouldn't that be 100 percent more than they are relatively entitled to? When George W. says "across-the-board tax cut," what does he mean?

If we were to totally abandon the principle of progressive taxation and pretend that Steve Forbes really won the election, we would give the richest 1 percent, despite their skyrocketing share of both income and accumulated wealth, a tax cut proportionate to the share they pay—which is about 20 percent of all federal taxes, including income, estate, etc. I can't imagine why we'd do that, but at least you could make a case for it, sort of, in a way.

My favorite moment in the debate (so far) was when Tucker Carlson of *Crossfire* claimed that those of us who point out the massive injustice of this tax cut are not only "populists" [!], guilty of fomenting "class warfare" [!], but we are also, to quote the impeccably bow-tied Carlson, "vulgar." I just about swooned on the spot. Oh, no! Not vul-gah! My late mama would have *died*, had she not already croaked, upon hearing me accused of such a thing. On the other hand, my late, beautifully bred mother did not raise any damn fools.

The Bush tax cut is inexcusable. Pointing that out is not "vulgar." Passing the damn thing is vulgar.

The subtext of the reporting on the perfectly disgusting Marc Rich pardon *should be* that all those who are disgusted are guilty of horribly vulgar populism. As a now-forgotten Sunday-morning chatter announced in horror: "This could cause people to think that the rich can buy their way out of the justice system."

No shit.

Been going to Texas prisons for a long time. Seen nobody rich on Death Row yet. You mean, MONEY has something to do with justice in this country?

I'm relishing those right-wingers who affect to be horrified by the impending possibility of "egalitarianism." Should we all be reduced to the same economic status by
nefarious populist methods of "income redistribution," William F. Buckley Jr. and the
clerk at your grocery store checkout counter will be as one in unbecoming pursuits
such as clipping the coupons that are not from investments but for 10 percent off on
the forty-seven-ounce bottle of Prell.

This would give me a nightmare about how to measure social merit, if I did not
have the elementary brain to notice that we're actually headed in the opposite direction: Wake me up when impending egalitarianism is a problem. In the meantime,
oligarchy is eating our ass, our dreams, our country, our heritage, our democracy, our
justice, and our tax code.

—MOLLY IVINS, the great progressive journalist out of Texas, was the author of *Molly Ivins Can't
Say That, Can She?* and *Bushwhacked*. She wrote for *The Progressive* for twenty years.

# PART 3

# Renouncing Empire

The difference between the progressivism of La Follette and that of Teddy Roosevelt can be boiled down to this: Roosevelt was an imperialist, and La Follette, like Mark Twain, an anti-imperialist. La Follette opposed U.S. intervention in Mexico, as well as in Europe. He decried the war profiteers and saw them dictating U.S. foreign policy.

Throughout the last 100 years, *The Progressive* has opposed almost all U.S. interventions, the lone exception being World War II, though La Follette's sons were isolationists until Pearl Harbor. During that war, *The Progressive* remained open to conscientious objectors, and it began to publish the writings of Milton Mayer, an acerbic pacifist. His contribution in this chapter, where he goes after Churchill, is a classic.

This chapter also includes two articles that discuss the Vietnam War, one by Tom Harkin, who wasn't yet a senator, and another by the great journalist David Halberstam. In addition, it offers a sample of some of the amazing investigative reporting *The Progressive* has done over the years. Allan Nairn's "Behind the Death Squads" and Thomas Nagy's "The Secret Behind the Sanctions" reveal how, with malice aforethought, the U.S. government created policies that would take a ghastly toll.

If isolationism is one response to empire, progressive internationalism is a far more preferable one. *The Progressive* has helped articulate this philosophy, with profound contributions from Arundhati Roy, Eduardo Galeano, and Howard Zinn. In "The Scourge of Nationalism," Zinn challenges us to put down our flags and "assert our allegiance to the human race, and not to any one nation."

# Why War?

ROBERT M. LA FOLLETTE
MARCH 18, 1911

Why is the President massing troops on the Mexican border? What reason has he for making a warlike demonstration which is sounding an alarm in every quarter of the world? What canon of international law can be invoked, to justify rushing a formidable army, equipped for battle, to the very boundary line of a country at peace with our government? What precedent of intervention can he offer as an excuse for meddling in the internal affairs of Mexico at this time? Can he forecast the complications with foreign powers which may result?

Congress should require the President to give a strict accounting of this extraordinary use of the army and navy.

The whole affair seems incredible. It is unprecedented. In a time of profound peace the President hurls the army and the navy to the borders of a friendly nation. A quarter of the standing army put in the field with equipment, ammunition, and supplies as for active war. The start was made under the thin pretense that it was a "Military Maneuver." This is quickly laid aside and correspondents traveling with the President on his southern jaunt announce that the purpose is "to stamp out the Mexican insurrection," and if necessary to this end, to "intervene."

That is to say, to invade this, our neighboring republic.

If this means anything it means war. To all intents and purposes it is the beginning of hostilities against the Mexican Republic.

The Constitution vests in the Congress the right to make war. And rightly so. The people pay the bill, and give their lives. It is right that they should be consulted. The time is past—at least we thought the time had passed—when wars were made by kings to serve their selfish purpose.

But we are told this is not war. It is "intervention."

Never in our history have we done this thing before.

Our troubles with Spain are fresh in mind. Taft had before him the example of a line of Presidents from Grant to McKinley who for a period of nearly thirty years exhausted every resource of statesmanship and diplomacy to avoid intervention. Their wisdom and foresight should have admonished him to pause and consider the consequence likely to result from his acts as he rushed his orders that Monday night to mobilize an army on the Mexican frontier and then hurried away to Augusta to play golf.

His illustrious predecessors knew that intervention spelled war. They knew that "war is hell." In the case of Cuba, more than two hundred thousand helpless natives were killed in the long struggle for liberty and still intervention was not invoked. Our commerce with the island valued at more than a hundred million annually was totally destroyed and intervention was not suggested. Millions upon millions of the property of American citizens was laid waste and yet no President advised intervention. American citizens in Cuba were imprisoned and cruelly maltreated in violation of treaty and international rights and still the then President did not call for intervention. Not until the United States battleship *Maine* was blown up, killing 266 men and officers—and even then, not until Congress authorized intervention did President McKinley order the American fleet to Havana.

We "intervened" in Cuba, but it was Congress—not the President—who took that action, and it meant war. And in Cuba we intervened to help a people struggling for their liberties. We did not intervene to throttle insurrection. We did not use our ships and army to uphold the tyranny of Spain.

Yet we are told by the President of the United States that "the Mexican insurrection will be stamped out" at any cost. Since when has the government taken sides against an oppressed people struggling for liberty?

Did President Taft's affable hobnobbing with President Diaz last autumn open a new chapter in American history? What is the reason for this unauthorized declaration of war against the struggling Mexican people and this unwarranted and unaccountable use of the military establishment of our republic against a peaceful neighbor?

Is it because Henry W. Taft, brother of the President, is a director in Pierson and Son, an English corporation—the largest single financial interest in Mexico?

Is it because J. P. Morgan & Co., or Kuhn, Loeb & Co., or Speyer & Co., are the fiscal agents for the bonds issued by the Diaz government, and heavy holders of securities and concessions obtained from the dictator Diaz?

Is it because Attorney General Wickersham was until lately a director in the American-Hawaiian company, the corporation holding contracts for the transportation of raw sugar from Hawaii via the Teheuntepec railway, one of the properties of the Pierson company?

Is it to be found in any former law associations between Henry W. Taft and Attorney General Wickersham, which did business under the name Strong, Cadwallader & Co., a firm now represented heavily in Mexican interests?

Is there any connection between the warlike demonstration against Mexico and the recent conferences in New York, participated in by such men as the American minister to Mexico, Henry Lane Wilson, the fiscal agent of Diaz, Jose Limantour, and Morgan?

Is it possible that the army and navy of the United States are being used as a sideshow of a gigantic Wall Street gamble?

Have we come to this point, that patriotism, valor, and life and death are openly made the pawns of Wall Street's politicians, to be moved about as suits the greater profits of Wall Street's master spirits?

# The Armed Ship Bill Meant War

ROBERT M. LA FOLLETTE
MARCH 1917

I am opposed to the United States making war upon England for her ruthless violations of our neutral rights just as I am opposed to making war upon Germany because of her relentless violation of our neutral rights.

The belligerents upon both sides are desperate to the verge of madness. Germany is bordering upon starvation. England, according to Lloyd George, is facing actual want. France is beginning to feel the pinch of hunger. Revolution, whose first warnings were food riots, has taken place in Russia. Shall we, to maintain the technical right of travel and the pursuit of commercial profits, hurl this country into the bottomless pit of the European horror? Shall we bind up our future with foreign powers and hazard the peace of this nation for all time by linking the destiny of the American democracy with the ever-menacing antagonisms of foreign monarchies?

Our intervention will confuse the issue, bring new alignments, force other neutral nations to take sides, giving to the horrible conflict now approaching a climax a fresh intensity, increased fierceness, and prolong it indefinitely.

Now, in the third year of the war, the stricken world finds that all these efficient instruments of woe to mankind cannot accomplish a big enough slaughter to force a victory. Starvation—race starvation—starvation of men, women, and children—has become the terrible, relentless, merciless issue of this war madness among civilized Christian nations.

How can we, with the history of the past three years mapped out so vividly before us, assume that the entrance of the United States upon the bloody field will stop the war?

In God's name, let us not deceive ourselves. We stand at the head of the neutral nations, outside the territory swept by this war mania. Shall we break the peace of the neutral half of the world? Shall we take on the awful responsibility of dragging in one side, and pushing in on the other, until every quarter and corner of the Earth is one battlefield?

Who shall then set limits of time or space upon its ravages?

And for what? For commercial advantage and fat profits, beneficial to a limited number of our dollar-scarred patriots.

If the silent masses who found opportunity for expression at the November election could today make themselves heard above this clamor for war, instigated and sustained by the money power and a subjugated press, they would with even a stronger voice, pray God that this country be kept out of war.

# Defense or Imperialism?

ROBERT M. LA FOLLETTE
FEBRUARY 1921

There will never be another time when it will be so easy to induce the nations of the earth to reduce armaments as the present.

Our navy today is vastly superior to any except Great Britain's. Our coast defenses are declared on the highest authority to be "the best in the world." Counting the men just released from service as a potential reserve, we have the largest army of trained soldiers on earth.

With a total estimated wealth equal to that of any two nations in the world, and larger than Great Britain and Japan's combined, this country must choose whether it will lead the movement to disarm or set the pace in a new competition which can only lead to war.

The people—who must pay the staggering price of a race in armaments—are opposed to such a program. They have no foreign investments to protect, and no dividends, derived from armor contracts, at stake.

Conceding the right of the owner of capital to invest his money where he pleases, the people must force Congress to declare against the policy of using the State Department and the military arm of the Government for collecting private claims for those seeking large profits in foreign lands.

When our capitalists withdraw their money from this country to stake it on the turn of fortune's wheel in some foreign land, let them take the gambler's chance.

If money is to be spent to make their foreign risks secure, let it be their own money.

If lives are to be risked to protect their Mexican mines—their Central and South American concessions—let it be their own lives that take the hazard.

It is time for the people to call a halt. Every man and woman in the country should make senators and congressmen understand that they will be held to account if under the dishonest plea of preparing for the national defense they rebuild the American navy to serve the wicked aims of conquest and imperialism.

# Armed Intervention in Nicaragua

ROBERT M. LA FOLLETTE JR.
JANUARY 1927

"We denounce the mercenary system of foreign policy under recent administrations in the interests of financial imperialists, oil monopolists and international bankers, which has at times degraded our State Department from its big service as a strong and kindly intermediary of defenseless governments to a trading outpost for those interests and concession-seekers engaged in the exploitation of weaker nations, as contrary to the will of the American people, destructive of domestic development and provocative of war." (La Follette–Wheeler Platform, 1924)

The armed intervention of the United States in Nicaragua under the Coolidge Administration is a startling example of the "mercenary system of foreign policy under recent administrations in the interests of financial imperialists, oil monopolists and international bankers," which was so vigorously denounced in the La Follette–Wheeler platform of 1924. Without authority from Congress, American marines have been landed in Nicaragua.

This armed invasion of a friendly republic and the support of the government of General Diaz are justified by the Coolidge administration under the flimsy pretext of protecting American lives and property in Nicaragua. In spite of repeated demands in the press and elsewhere, upon the State Department to furnish the names and places where American lives and property have been threatened or endangered, no answer has been forthcoming.

To understand why a great and powerful nation of 105 million people should be using its power and prestige, and its armed forces, in bending to its will a small weak republic of 638,000 people, helpless and practically defenseless, a few facts must be reviewed.

In 1910, the finances of Nicaragua having become involved, the State Department sent a Mr. Dawson to that country. He worked out what was known as the Dawson plan, which was subsequently embodied in a three-party loan treaty between the State Department, the Nicaraguan government, and certain New York bankers. The United States never ratified this treaty and it became a dead letter, but while it was under consideration by the Senate, Brown Brothers & Company, the U.S. Mortgage and Trust Co., and Seligman & Company "refinanced" Nicaragua. Under the terms of the loan the American investors were given 51 percent of the stock of the Nicaraguan railroad and the Nicaraguan National Bank. In all, approximately $6 million was loaned to this little country over a period of years by our benevolent Wall Street bankers. In spite of the tremendous interest charges and the excessively harsh terms upon which the money was loaned, Nicaragua was able by 1924 to buy back 51 percent of the stock in the bank and the railroads and to pay off the balance of the loan.

In 1911 American marines were landed in Nicaragua, and following fighting in which 150 Nicaraguans were killed, Diaz, now president, who was then a clerk employed by American interests, was made President of Nicaragua. Shortly after this "American-made" Nicaraguan President was installed he negotiated a treaty with the United States whereby this government was given a perpetual option on the canal route which lies across Nicaragua. Senator Borah, Chairman of the Senate Foreign Relations Committee, has stated "that was no treaty at all. It was nothing more than a treaty of the United States with itself." From 1912 to 1925, American marines were maintained in Nicaragua. During that period of time elections for President and Vice President have been held every four years but under the watchful eyes of our State Department, backed by the American marines, men have been selected for the two highest offices in that republic who were satisfactory to our State Department, and of course to the Wall Street bankers who "owned" the country through their loans.

The Coolidge Administration has blundered badly. It has undertaken intervention in Nicaragua pure and simple. It has undertaken that intervention in behalf of a government whose chief claim for support is its willingness to accept dictation from our State Department and the American business interests which seek to exploit Nicaragua. The inevitable result of this harsh, bullying and unjustifiable action is to set the nations of South and Central America against us.

The maintenance of the Coolidge Administration's position means the launching of this government upon a frank course of imperialism and exploitation. Carried to its logical conclusion this policy will require the maintenance of a tremendous navy and a huge standing army. In the end it will mean sacrificing the lives of thousands of American boys in winning for American international bankers the opportunity to exploit the rich natural resources of our sister republics in Central and South America.

—ROBERT M. LA FOLLETTE JR. served as U.S. senator from Wisconsin from 1925 to 1947.

# We Have Got to Lick Churchill Too

MILTON MAYER
NOVEMBER 23, 1942

The worst blow the United Nations has received in this war was dealt them on November 10. It was dealt them not by Adolf Hitler, but by Winston Churchill.

If the United Nations recover from the blow that Churchill dealt them on November 10, they will be able to withstand all the forces of all the Hitlers that will ever rise upon the earth. The Hitlers may strike at their body, which is only mortal; Churchill struck at their soul.

"He disclaimed anew"—I am quoting the Associated Press report of his speech—"any British designs for new territory, but added firmly: 'We mean to hold our own. I have not become the King's first minister in order to preside over the liquidation of the British Empire.'"

Can the cause which we advance as democracy withstand this blow?

Can men fight and die, yes, and kill, for liberty, equality, and fraternity when their leader is their enemy?

Can the last, best hope of earth survive the assault which Churchill has launched at its heart?

I hope so.

I hope so because I am one of those who argued, before Pearl Harbor, that the democracies were morally unprepared, and I have hoped, since Pearl Harbor, that I would prove to have been ignominiously wrong.

I have hoped that we would turn out to be fighting for the rights of men, all men, everywhere, and always. I have hoped that we would turn out to be idealistic enough not to expect to achieve these rights by next Thursday, or a week from Thursday. And I have hoped that we would be realistic enough to know that we would never achieve them at all if we did not set out at the very start, however great the distance and however slow the road, to achieve them in the end.

My hopes are dimmed by Churchill's assault, but my hopes are unimportant compared with the hopes of the people in Germany, France, Japan, and India who want to be free. Where can they turn now, the people in Norway, China, Malaya, and Russia who want to be free? And the people of America, who want to fight for freedom, and *only* for freedom, where can they turn now?

Churchill has told them all, and all of us, that as long as he has power the slaves shall not go free. He has told them, and all of us, that he is fighting, and that we are fighting alongside him, for human slavery and not against it. He has told them all, and all of us, that we who subsist fatly and shamefully on the homeless and the hungry must put away our shame and fight for our fat.

He has told us that our quarrel with Hitler is not a quarrel between freedom and tyranny, but a quarrel between tyrants. He has told us that we are fighting for the oldest of all orders, the order that enslaved us to lust and blood and gold, the order that Hitler alone among historians calls new. He has told us, this leader of ours, that Armageddon is after all only a cellar in which the thieves are disputing the loot on the basis of seniority.

My friends, Winston Churchill does not intend to free the 390 million people whom he described in 1935 as "the brightest star in the Emperor's crown." He does not intend to free the 100 million who comprise the lesser stars in the Emperor's crown. He does not intend to free the Indians, who contribute two shillings to every English pound of profit, nor the Malaysians, nor the Arabs, nor the Africans who contribute only two or three bob. He intends to "hold our own."

We cannot win this war by beating Hitler; we have got to beat Churchill, too. We cannot win this war by freeing our enemies' victims from our enemies abroad; we have got to free ourselves from our enemies at home. We cannot win this war by driving the fascists from the Wilhelmstrasse; we have got to drive them from Downing Street too.

—MILTON MAYER, journalist, teacher, and Quaker, was the author of *They Thought They Were Free: The Germans, 1933–1945*. He wrote for *The Progressive* from the 1940s to the 1980s.

# Vietnam Whitewash

## The Congressional Jury That Convicted Itself

THOMAS R. HARKIN
OCTOBER 1970

The trip I was about to embark on was one designed to uncover, first hand, the facts about the U.S. involvement in Vietnam—the cold facts, not propaganda. By the time I returned I had learned some of the rawest realities of Vietnam, but, even more important, I had also learned some shattering truths about one of the major committees of that high ruling body of our Government: the House of Representatives.

"The members of this Committee will be better prepared than anyone who has gone over to Vietnam on a fact-finding trip . . . we will not be led around by the nose . . . this will be a 'no briefings' trip."

This statement was made by Representative G. V. "Sonny" Montgomery, Mississippi Democrat and chairman of the House Select Committee on U.S. Involvement in Southeast Asia, during the week preceding the Committee's departure for South Vietnam.

I accompanied the Committee on its two-week trip to Southeast Asia as a member of the staff, appointed by Representative Neal Smith of Iowa.

Another staff aide, Ken Lester, and I met with Don Luce, an American who has been in Vietnam—with some return trips to the United States—since 1958. Author of *Vietnam: The Unheard Voices*, Luce has a wide range of Vietnamese friends from his long work among the Vietnamese people, and a comprehensive command of the language. He is now working for the World Council of Churches in Vietnam.

Naively, I told him that this Committee wanted to get away from the "canned briefings," and I asked Luce if he could introduce me to people in Saigon who would meet with the Committee and give their independent views on the war. He showed us a report he was translating into English. Five students had been released from Con Son prison just a month before, and had written a report, accompanied by drawings, of the conditions on Con Son, and of their confinement and torture in the tiger cages. The conditions they described were horrible. But the most shocking was the description of the use of the tiger cages. Luce said that he was acquainted with one of the students, and I asked him to see if the student would meet with us. The next day, Luce and Nguyen Loi came to our hotel.

Loi drew us a map from his memory of the location of the tiger cages. The entrance to the cages is well hidden, he said. It is a small, unmarked wooden door, around a corner and between a double wall. Sometimes, Loi said, wood is piled in front to hide it even more.

Frank Walton, chief of the Public Safety Directorate under AID for Vietnam, and his assistant, Randolph Berkely, accompanied us to Con Son. On the flight to the island, which lies about 140 miles southeast of Saigon, more than fifty miles from the nearest coastline, Walton and Berkely briefed us, and Walton gave us a "fact sheet" on Con Son. Dated July 2, 1970, the day before our visit, this "fact sheet" spoke in glowing terms of Con Son:

"Con Son," the "fact sheet" read, "has long held a reputation for being a 'Devil's Island.' This reputation still prevails, in spite of an enlightened and modern administration of the facility. Con Son is not a 'Devil's Island,' but on the contrary is a correctional institution worthy of higher ratings than some prisons in the United States."

As we approached the island, I asked Walton if Con Son was something like Alcatraz used to be.

"Oh, hell no," he replied, "Con Son is more like a Boy Scout recreation camp."

With the aid of the map, and a great stroke of luck, we were able to find the tiger cages. We found the little wooden door without much trouble, but Colonel Ve, the prison commandant, would not let us through, saying that the door was permanently locked. A guard on the other side, evidently hearing the Colonel's voice and thinking he wanted to go through with us, opened the door. Colonel Ve looked as though the sky had just fallen on him.

The conditions in the cages can only be described as inhuman. Each cell is about five feet wide, ten feet long, and ten feet deep. Into each cell are crowded as many as five people, with no fresh air, no sanitary facilities, no water, and no direct sunlight. Many of those in the cages have their ankles shackled to an iron bar about two feet off the floor. They are sometimes kept this way for months and years. None of the men could stand because their legs were paralyzed from being shackled and beaten. Colonel Ve admitted they couldn't walk, but he attributed it to infantile paralysis. When I asked him why they were shackled, he said it was to keep them from breaking out at night.

There were about 250 men in the tiger cages in one building, and about 250 to 300 women in another set of cages in another building. Above the cages were buckets of lime dust that the guards throw down on the prisoners when they make noise or beg for food or water. The lime dust causes severe burning of the tissues when it comes in contact with moist skin, eyes, and lungs.

We talked with many of the prisoners, and learned that none was there for criminal offenses unless such protest acts as failure to salute the flag are considered crimes. ("These are very bad people," Colonel Ve told us. "They won't salute the flag. They won't salute the United States flag.")

After the story of our findings became public, many people, Congressmen included, tried to say that Luce was not interpreting correctly, and that he was building up a story. However, I had a tape recorder hidden in a briefcase during our entire visit to Con Son, and captured all the conversations in the tiger cages on tape. I also took some pictures of the tiger cages, which were later published in *Life* magazine. Colonel Ve was the first to get upset about my taking pictures. He angrily demanded I turn over the film to him. When I refused, he went to Walton, who became very disturbed, and said I was guilty of a "breach of protocol."

Chairman Montgomery finally said that he felt that it was the consensus of the group that Tom Harkin would turn over the pictures to the Committee so it could take whatever action it felt necessary. I told Representative Smith what I wanted to do with the pictures. I told him that I thought about getting them before the public, so that they would see what is happening, and public pressure might be brought to bear on the government to change these conditions.

"Oh, no. That's all wrong. Public pressure never solved anything. Publicity never does any good," replied Smith.

I could not believe my ears. That was the most public-be-damned statement I had ever heard from an elected official in our Government. I always believed, and still do, in the force of public opinion, and that the surest safeguard against tyranny is a free and informed public.

At first I didn't know what to do. If I spoke out, I would have to resign my job with the Committee, which, in any event, would expire in another twenty days. However, speaking out would also cost me my job with Representative Smith—the job that had gotten me through my first year of law school, that I was counting on to get me through the next two years. An even more painful consideration was my long acquaintance and friendship with Neal Smith. We had mutual friends, some of whom worked for him in his office and back in his Iowa district. What would they think? Would they break their friendship with me, thinking I was a "traitor"?

While I pondered these factors, the words of those in the tiger cages came back to me.

The Buddhist monk: "I have been beaten. . . . I have been shackled. Still I speak for peace. . . . I only ask that when you leave, you guarantee our safety from retaliation by the guards."

The eighteen-year-old girl, a former high school student: "Please tell your people and ours what is happening to us."

A middle-aged man: "I have been here a long, long time. . . . My legs are now paralyzed."

The voices we heard as we were leaving the tiger cages: "Please give us food . . . water . . . make them stop throwing the lime on us . . . please, vegetables . . . please . . . our only crime is that we ask for peace."

I thought to myself: how many people find themselves in my position, knowing the truth and able to do something about it, yet do not speak out for fear of losing friends or causing themselves personal discomfort?

There was really no question about my decision. I called the press, disclosed the existence of the tiger cages, and released my pictures.

—THOMAS R. HARKIN has served as U.S. senator from Iowa since 1990. His photos of the tiger cages appeared in *Life* magazine.

# How It All Began

DAVID HALBERSTAM
APRIL 1973

Where, then, are the roots of it? How did it happen? How in fact could it happen? Did the roots invisibly grow while we still slept, watched the more visible crises mount at Berlin, in the Congo, in the Middle East? It did not, after all, just happen in February 1965, when Lyndon Johnson, with the consent of those around him, began the bombing, or in July 1965, when he first sent combat troops. Too much had been prepared long in advance. And why, if there was no great chorus of enthusiasm for what he was doing, was there such a mute acceptance of his course from the Congress, the press, the business community—indeed, the State Department itself?

Could we really have a country in the seventh enlightened decade of an enlightened and rational twentieth century, the United States, anti-colonial in its origins and traditions, pick up a colonial war where the French had left off without a single officer from the Department of State resigning? The answer is yes, we could. Why had the men who might have doubted been winnowed out, how had the course been set? Where had the damage been done? Why did intelligent, rational men go against the course of history, against, finally, common sense, so that the United States would end up in Vietnam, in the words of the late Bernard Fall, "walking in the same footsteps as the French, although, dreaming different dreams"?

The answers, it seems to me, lie in the damage done to the Government, the Democratic Party, and the press by the Joseph McCarthy period, and by the general tensions created in the domestic reaction to the Cold War. To blame it all on McCarthy is far too simple; he was merely a crude symptom of the time, an accident looking for a place to happen, a name grafted on an era. Indeed, the fears that his name evokes had existed even before his famous speech in Wheeling, West Virginia, in February 1950, and the foreign policy accommodations to those fears had already begun to take place.

In Vietnam one of the most crucial of these decisions took place in May 1950, before McCarthy was a household word, before the Korean war broke out: the decision to supply military aid to the French in Indochina. Secretary of State Dean Acheson's decision, not his successor, John Foster Dulles's. It was a fateful moment, for until then we had not supported the French cause. We had resisted the French claim that this was part of the great global struggle against world Communism, that the French were fighting for freedom in Vietnam, that their enemy was our enemy. From the very start, in 1945, we had refused French requests for troop ships to return the white colonial troops to Vietnam. Other requests for military aid had followed, and we had always rejected them. Acheson himself in the past had referred to the French cause as a colonial war, loath though he was to pressure the French to do anything about it.

May 1950 changed all that. Acheson threw the switch, deciding to give the French military support and therefore—even more important as far as American history was concerned—moral support. (One does not give military aid without legitimizing the cause as well.) His reasons were two-fold. The first was his abiding concern to stop the Communists in Europe: Acheson felt that a strong Europe required a strong West Germany, and increasing German steel production was the best means of reviving that economy. The French had been recalcitrant, uneasy about mounting German strength; yet they desperately needed economic aid for Indochina. A deal was made, what Acheson later would call a simple quid pro quo: West German steel production could go up, and the United States would give major military assistance to the French in Vietnam. On May 8, after making his deal with Robert Schuman, Acheson announced: "The United States Government, convinced that neither national independence nor democratic evolution exists in any area dominated by Soviet imperialism, considers the situation to be such as to warrant its according economic aid and military equipment to the Associated States of Indochina and France in order to assist them in restoring stability and permitting these states to pursue their peaceful and democratic development." What would follow was two billion dollars in American aid, and growing American support; by 1954 we who had once doubted the cause were more enthusiastic for the French to continue than they were. It was no longer a colonial war but a just war, a war for freedom: the West against the Communists.

The second reason behind Acheson's decision was dictated to a large extent by American political terms. The storm against the Administration's Asia policies was already brewing; the Republicans, hungry after eighteen years out of office, were willing to exploit the fall of China, and to accuse the Administration of betraying American interests there. The word they used was "treason." China had gone Communist, not because of the fickle quality of history, but because the Democrats had harbored Communists in the State Department. Acheson was already on the defensive; he was trying to protect as best he could his favorites among the Asia people from the headhunters. The smell of witch-hunt was in the air. Now Acheson was trimming; he had been charged with losing one country, and he did not want to endanger his President and his party by losing another.

This was an easy time to sell fear and demagoguery: The country had moved head first from isolationism into superpower status. The normal tensions between great powers were made more intense first by the addition of *ism* to the struggle—Communism versus capitalism—a factor which gave it a moral-religious distinction, and then by the added threat of the atomic bomb. It was a particularly dark chapter in American life: our foreign policy had become locked into an all-encompassing blind and total anti-Communism. Intelligence, enlightened self-interest, traditional anti-colonialism, and old-fashioned common sense—our guidelines in the past—had been supplanted by ideological purity and domestic fear. And if Acheson had accommodated to a certain degree, Dulles, who followed him, was far worse; he made peace quickly with the right, and his peace offering was the Asian experts and Asian office of the State Department. He did not want trouble with Congress, and Asia was the price: in a move of historic proportion and appalling consequences, he opened the doors of his department to the loyalty and security people. Thus would American policy-making on Vietnam be poisoned by the McCarthy period, and vital organs—the Democratic Party and the Department of State—damaged beyond easy repair.

Under Kennedy, the State Department was a badly damaged instrument, filled with fear and ignorance, devoted largely to the preservation of myths. Yet no one could admit this, could admit that the policy-making in this stylish and modern Administration was still mired down in a darker past. No wonder, then, that seemingly intelligent men made such unwise choices. It was all a Greek thing: as a nation we had stood by during the McCarthy period and allowed, with a kind of national consent, a group of witch hunters to destroy good men who had performed honorable public services. No one had challenged it then, nor challenged the legacy of what had happened. Now, a decade later, with the war in Vietnam, we got what we deserved.

—DAVID HALBERSTAM, journalist and war reporter, wrote *The Best and the Brightest*, among other works.

## Behind the Death Squads

ALLAN NAIRN
MAY 1984

Early in the 1960s, during the Kennedy Administration, agents of the U.S. Government in El Salvador set up two official security organizations that killed thousands of peasants and suspected leftists over the next fifteen years. These organizations, guided by American operatives, developed into the paramilitary apparatus that came to be known as the Salvadoran Death Squads.

Today, even as the Reagan Administration publicly condemns the Death Squads, the CIA—in violation of U.S. law—continues to provide training, support, and intelligence to security forces directly involved in Death Squad activity.

Interviews with dozens of current and former Salvadoran officers, civilians, and official American sources disclose a pattern of sustained U.S. participation in building and managing the Salvadoran security apparatus that relies on Death Squad assassinations as its principal means of enforcement.

Over the past twenty years, officials of the State Department, the Central Intelligence Agency, and the U.S. armed forces have:

conceived and organized ORDEN, the rural paramilitary and intelligence network described by Amnesty International as a movement designed "to use clandestine terror against government opponents." Out of ORDEN grew the notorious Mano Blanco, the White Hand, which a former U.S. ambassador to El Salvador, Raul H. Castro, has called "nothing less that the birth of the Death Squads";

conceived and organized ANSESAL, the elite presidential intelligence services that gathered files on Salvadoran dissidents and, in the words of one U.S. official, relied on Death Squads as "the operative arm of intelligence gathering";

enlisted General Jose Alberto "Chele" Medrano, the founder of ORDEN and ANSESAL, as a CIA agent;

trained leaders of ORDEN in surveillance techniques and use of automatic weapons, and carried some of these leaders on the CIA payroll;

provided American technical and intelligence advisers who often worked directly with ANSESAL at its headquarters in the Casa Presidencial;

supplied ANSESAL, the security forces, and the general staff with electronic, photographic, and personal surveillance of individuals who were later assassinated by Death Squads. According to Colonel Nicolas Carranza, director of the Salvadoran Treasury Police, such intelligence sharing by U.S. agencies continues to this day;

kept key security officials—including Carranza, Medrano, and others—on the CIA payroll. Though the evidence is less conclusive about Major Roberto D'Aubuisson, presidential candidate of the right wing ARENA party, some of his close associates describe him as a former recipient of CIA funding;

furnished intelligence files that D'Aubuisson used for a series of 1980 television broadcasts in which he denounced dozens of academics, trade unionists, peasant leaders, Christian Democrats, and members of the clergy as communists or guerrilla collaborators. Many of the individuals D'Aubuisson named in his television speeches were subsequently assassinated. The broadcasts launched D'Aubuisson's political career and marked the emergence of the paramilitary front which later became ARENA;

instructed Salvadoran intelligence operatives in the use of investigative techniques, combat weapons, explosives and interrogation methods that included, according to a former Treasury Police agent, "instructions in methods of physical and psychological torture";

and, in the last decade, violated the Foreign Assistance Act of 1974, which prohibits spending U.S. funds "to provide training or advice or provide any financial support for police, prisons, or other law enforcement forces for any foreign government or any program of internal intelligence or surveillance on behalf of any foreign government."

The use of the term "Death Squad" has, in some respects, fostered a profound misunderstanding of El Salvador's official terror apparatus. It conjures up images of discrete bands of gangsters randomly cruising the countryside in search of opportunities to kill. In fact, the term more meaningfully applies to a system that can dispatch a soldier at any time to kill a selected victim. Another misunderstanding about the Death Squads arises from the fact that they came to public notice in the United States in connection with the spectacular emergence of Roberto D'Aubuisson as a powerful political figure. U.S. officials who want to shield the Salvadoran government from culpability in the Death Squads, as well as some liberals who want to undermine D'Aubuisson's electoral prospects, have promoted the mistaken notion that the Death Squad phenomenon—this sprawling institution with a twenty-year history and tens of thousands of victims—is the personal instrument of one diabolical man.

U.S. complicity in the dark and brutal work of El Salvador's Death Squads is not an aberration. Rather, it represents a basic, bipartisan, institutional commitment on the part of six American Administrations—a commitment to guard the Salvadoran regime against the prospect that its people might organize in ways unfriendly to that regime or the United States.

—ALLAN NAIRN is a journalist and human rights activist currently living in Indonesia.

# *The Secret Behind the Sanctions*

THOMAS J. NAGY
SEPTEMBER 2001

Over the last two years, I've discovered documents of the Defense Intelligence Agency proving beyond a doubt that, contrary to the Geneva Convention, the U.S. government intentionally used sanctions against Iraq to degrade the country's water supply after the Gulf War. The United States knew the cost that civilian Iraqis, mostly children, would pay, and it went ahead anyway.

The primary document, "Iraq Water Treatment Vulnerabilities," is dated January 22, 1991. It spells out how sanctions will prevent Iraq from supplying clean water to its citizens.

"Iraq depends on importing specialized equipment and some chemicals to purify its water supply, most of which is heavily mineralized and frequently brackish to saline," the document states. "With no domestic sources of both water treatment replacement parts and some essential chemicals, Iraq will continue attempts to circumvent United Nations Sanctions to import these vital commodities. Failing to secure supplies will result in a shortage of pure drinking water for much of the population. This could lead to increased incidences, if not epidemics, of disease."

The document goes into great technical detail about the sources and quality of Iraq's water supply. The quality of untreated water "generally is poor," and drinking such water "could result in diarrhea," the document says. It notes that Iraq's rivers "contain biological materials, pollutants, and are laden with bacteria. Unless the water is purified with chlorine, epidemics of such diseases as cholera, hepatitis, and typhoid could occur."

In cold language, the document spells out what is in store: "Iraq will suffer increasing shortages of purified water because of the lack of required chemicals and desalination membranes. Incidences of disease, including possible epidemics, will become probable unless the population were careful to boil water."

Recently, I have come across other DIA documents that confirm the Pentagon's monitoring of the degradation of Iraq's water supply.

One document in this series, "Medical Problems in Iraq," is dated March 15, 1991. It says: "Communicable diseases in Baghdad are more widespread than usually observed during this time of the year and are linked to the poor sanitary conditions (contaminated water supplies and improper sewage disposal) resulting from the war. According to a United Nations Children's Fund (UNICEF)/World Health Organization report, the quantity of potable water is less than 5 percent of the original supply, there are no operational water and sewage treatment plants, and the reported incidence of diarrhea is four times above normal levels. Additionally, respiratory infections are on the rise. Children particularly have been affected by these diseases."

Another document, "Status of Disease at Refugee Camps," is dated May 1991. The summary says, "Cholera and measles have emerged at refugee camps. Further infectious diseases will spread due to inadequate water treatment and poor sanitation."

The reason for this outbreak is clearly stated again. "The main causes of infectious diseases, particularly diarrhea, dysentery, and upper respiratory problems, are poor sanitation and unclean water. These diseases primarily afflict the old and young children."

Yet another document, "Health Conditions in Iraq, June 1991," says that in one refugee camp, "at least 80 percent of the population" has diarrhea. At this same camp, named Cukurca, "cholera, hepatitis type B, and measles have broken out."

The protein deficiency disease kwashiorkor was observed in Iraq "for the first time," the document adds. "Gastroenteritis was killing children. . . . In the south, 80 percent of the deaths were children (with the exception of Al Amarah, where 60 percent of deaths were children)."

As these documents illustrate, the United States knew sanctions had the capacity to devastate the water treatment system of Iraq. It knew what the consequences would be: increased outbreaks of disease and high rates of child mortality.

The Geneva Convention is absolutely clear. In a 1979 protocol relating to the "protection of victims of international armed conflicts," Article 54, it states: "It is prohibited to attack, destroy, remove, or render useless objects indispensable to the survival of the civilian population, such as foodstuffs, crops, livestock, drinking water installations and supplies, and irrigation works, for the specific purpose of denying them for their sustenance value to the civilian population or to the adverse Party, whatever the motive, whether in order to starve out civilians, to cause them to move away, or for any other motive."

But that is precisely what the U.S. government did, with malice aforethought.

—THOMAS J. NAGY (tom500k@yahoo.com) was formerly a tenured professor. All documents cited in his original article can be accessed via Google or a comparable search engine.

# The Algebra of Infinite Justice

ARUNDHATI ROY
DECEMBER 2001

It must be hard for ordinary Americans, so recently bereaved, to look up at the world with their eyes full of tears and encounter what might appear to them to be indifference. It isn't indifference. It's just augury. An absence of surprise. The tired wisdom of knowing that what goes around eventually comes around. The American people ought to know that it is not them, but their government's policies, that are so hated.

Bush's almost god-like mission—called Operation Infinite Justice until it was pointed out that this could be seen as an insult to Muslims, who believe that only Allah can mete out infinite justice, and was renamed Operation Enduring Freedom—requires some small clarifications. For example, Infinite Justice/Enduring Freedom for whom?

In 1996, Madeleine Albright, then the U.S. Ambassador to the United Nations, was asked on national television what she felt about the fact that 500,000 Iraqi children had died as a result of economic sanctions the United States insisted upon. She replied that it was "a very hard choice," but that all things considered, "we think the price is worth it." Albright never lost her job for saying this. She continued to travel the world representing the views and aspirations of the U.S. government.

So here we have it. The equivocating distinction between civilization and savagery, between the "massacre of innocent people" or, if you like, the "clash of civilizations" and "collateral damage." The sophistry and fastidious algebra of Infinite Justice. How many dead Iraqis will it take to make the world a better place? How many dead Afghans for every dead American? How many dead children for every dead man? How many dead mujahedeen for each dead investment banker?

The American people may be a little fuzzy about where exactly Afghanistan is (we hear reports that there's a run on maps of the country), but the U.S. government and Afghanistan are old friends. In 1979, after the Soviet invasion of Afghanistan, the CIA and Pakistan's ISI (Inter-Services Intelligence) launched the CIA's largest covert operation since the Vietnam War. Their purpose was to harness the energy of Afghan resistance and expand it into a holy war, an Islamic jihad, which would turn Muslim countries within the Soviet Union against the communist regime and eventually destabilize it. When it began, it was meant to be the Soviet Union's Vietnam. It turned out to be much more than that. Over the years, through the ISI, the CIA funded and recruited tens of thousands of radical mujahedeen from forty Islamic countries as soldiers for America's proxy war. The rank and file of the mujahedeen were unaware that their jihad was actually being fought on behalf of Uncle Sam.

In 1989, after being bloodied by ten years of relentless conflict, the Russians withdrew, leaving behind a civilization reduced to rubble. Civil war in Afghanistan raged on. The jihad spread to Chechnya, Kosovo, and eventually to Kashmir. The CIA continued to pour in money and military equipment, but the overhead had become immense, and more money was needed.

The mujahedeen ordered farmers to plant opium as a "revolutionary tax." Under the protection of the ISI, hundreds of heroin processing laboratories were set up across Afghanistan. Within two years of the CIA's arrival, the Pakistan/Afghanistan borderland had become the biggest producer of heroin in the world, and the single biggest source on American streets. The annual profits, said to be between $100 and $200 billion, were ploughed back into training and arming militants.

In 1996, the Taliban—then a marginal sect of dangerous, hard-line fundamentalists—fought its way to power in Afghanistan. It was funded by the ISI, that old cohort of the CIA, and supported by many political parties in Pakistan. The Taliban unleashed a regime of terror. Its first victims were its own people, particularly women. It closed down girls' schools, dismissed women from government jobs, enforced Sharia law—under which women deemed to be "immoral" are stoned to death and widows guilty of being adulterous are buried alive.

Operation Enduring Freedom is being fought ostensibly to uphold the American Way of Life. It'll probably end up undermining it completely. It will spawn more anger and more terror across the world.

The U.S. government and governments all over the world are using the climate of war as an excuse to curtail civil liberties, deny free speech, lay off workers, harass ethnic and religious minorities, cut back on public spending, and divert huge amounts of money to the defense industry. To what purpose? President Bush can no more "rid the world of evildoers" than he can stock it with saints.

It's absurd for the U.S. government to even toy with the notion that it can stamp out terrorism with more violence and oppression. Terrorism is the symptom, not the disease.

Terrorism has no country. It's transnational, as global an enterprise as Coke or Pepsi or Nike. At the first sign of trouble, terrorists can pull up stakes and move their "factories" from country to country in search of a better deal. Just like the multinationals.

The September 11 attacks were a monstrous calling card from a world gone horribly wrong. The message may have been written by bin Laden (who knows?) and delivered by his couriers, but it could well have been signed by the ghosts of the victims of America's old wars. The millions killed in Korea, Vietnam, and Cambodia, the 17,500 killed when Israel—backed by the U.S.—invaded Lebanon in 1982, the 200,000 Iraqis killed in Operation Desert Storm, the thousands of Palestinians who have died fighting Israel's occupation of the West Bank. And the millions who died, in Yugoslavia, Somalia, Haiti, Chile, Nicaragua, El Salvador, the Dominican Republic, Panama, at the hands of all the terrorists, dictators, and genocidists whom the American government supported, trained, bankrolled and supplied with arms. And this is far from being a comprehensive list.

For a country involved in so much warfare and conflict, the American people have been extremely fortunate. The strikes on September 11 were only the second on American soil in over a century. The first was Pearl Harbor. The reprisal for this took a long route, but ended with Hiroshima and Nagasaki. This time the world waits with bated breath for the horrors to come.

Someone recently said that if Osama bin Laden didn't exist, America would have had to invent him. But, in a way, America did invent him. He was among the jihadis who moved to Afghanistan in 1979 when the CIA commenced its operations there. Bin Laden has the distinction of being created by the CIA and wanted by the FBI.

But who is Osama bin Laden really? Let me rephrase that. What is Osama bin Laden? He's America's family secret. He is the American president's dark doppelgänger. The savage twin of all that purports to be beautiful and civilized. He has been sculpted from the spare rib of a world laid to waste by America's foreign policy: its gunboat diplomacy, its nuclear arsenal, its vulgarly stated policy of "full-spectrum dominance," its chilling disregard for non-American lives, its barbarous military interventions, its support for despotic and dictatorial regimes, its merciless economic agenda that has munched through the economies of poor countries like a cloud of locusts, its marauding multinationals that are taking over the air we breathe, the ground we stand on, the water we drink, the thoughts we think. Now that the family secret has been spilled, the twins are blurring into one another and gradually becoming interchangeable.

Now Bush and Bin Laden have even begun to borrow each other's rhetoric. Each refers to the other as "the head of the snake." Both invoke God and use the loose millenarian currency of Good with a capital G good and Evil with a capital E evil as their terms of reference. Both are engaged in unequivocal political crimes. Both are dangerously armed—one with the nuclear arsenal of the obscenely powerful, the other with the incandescent, destructive power of the utterly hopeless. The fireball and the ice pick. The bludgeon and the axe. The important thing to keep in mind is that neither is an acceptable alternative to the other.

President Bush's ultimatum to the people of the world—"If you're not with us, you're against us"—is a piece of presumptuous arrogance. It's not a choice that people want to, need to, or should have to make.

> —ARUNDHATI ROY is a writer and activist. She won the Booker Prize for *The God of Small Things.*

## Heckled in Rockford

CHRIS HEDGES
JULY 2003

[*Editor's note*: This was a commencement speech delivered at Rockford College on May 17 before a hostile crowd. Audience reaction is in brackets.]

I want to speak to you today about war and empire. The killing, or at least the worst of it, is over in Iraq. Although blood will continue to spill—theirs and ours—be prepared for this. For we are embarking on an occupation that, if history is any guide, will be as damaging to our souls as it will be to our prestige, power, and security. But this will come later, as our empire expands. And in all this we become pariahs, tyrants to others weaker than ourselves. Isolation always impairs judgment, and we are very isolated now.

We have forfeited the goodwill, the empathy the world felt for us after 9/11. We have folded in on ourselves, we have severely weakened the delicate international coalitions and alliances that are vital in maintaining and promoting peace. And we are now part of a dubious troika in the war against terror with Vladimir Putin and Ariel Sharon, two leaders who do not shrink in Palestine or Chechnya from carrying out acts of gratuitous and senseless violence. We have become the company we keep.

The censure, and perhaps the rage, of much of the world—certainly the one-fifth of the world's population which is Muslim, most of whom I will remind you are not Arab—is upon us. Look today at the fourteen people killed last night in several explosions in Casablanca. And this rage, in a world where almost 50 percent of the planet struggles on less than two dollars a day, will see us targeted. Terrorism will become a way of life. [*"No!"*] And when we are attacked, we will, like our allies Putin and Sharon, lash out with greater fury.

The circle of violence is a death spiral; no one escapes. We are spinning at a speed that we may not be able to hold. As we revel in our military prowess—the sophistication of our military hardware and technology, for this is what most of the press coverage consisted of in Iraq—we lose sight of the fact that just because we have the capacity to wage war does not give us the right to wage war. This capacity has doomed empires in the past.

"Modern Western civilization may perish," the theologian Reinhold Niebuhr warned, "because it falsely worshiped technology as a final good."

The real injustices—the Israeli occupation of Palestinian land, the brutal and corrupt dictatorships we fund in the Middle East—will mean that we will not rid the extremists who hate us with bombs. Indeed, we will swell their ranks. [*Whistles.*] Once you master people by force, you depend on force for control. In your isolation, you begin to make mistakes. [*"Where were you on September 11?"*]

Fear engenders cruelty; cruelty . . . fear, insanity, and then paralysis. [*Hoots. "Who wants to listen to this jerk?"*] In the center of Dante's circle, the damned remained motionless. [*Horns.*] We have blundered into a nation we know little about and are caught between bitter rivalries and competing ethnic groups and leaders we do not understand.

Iraq was a cesspool for the British when they occupied it in 1917. It will be a cesspool for us, as well. [*"God bless America," a woman shrieks.*]

As someone who knows Iraq, speaks Arabic, and spent seven years in the Middle East, I know that if the Iraqis believe rightly or wrongly that we come only for oil and occupation, they will begin a long, bloody war of attrition.

As William Butler Yeats wrote in "Meditations in Times of Civil War," "We had fed the heart on fantasies / the heart's grown brutal from the fare." [*Horns. "I never would have come if I knew I had to listen to this," a woman yells.*]

This is a war of liberation in Iraq, but it is a war now of liberation by Iraqis from American occupation. And if you watch closely what is happening in Iraq, if you can see it through the abysmal coverage, you can see it in the lashing out of the terrorist death squads, and the murder of Shiite leaders in mosques, and the assassination of our young soldiers in the streets. It is one that will soon be joined by Islamic radicals, and we are far less secure today than we were before we bumbled into Iraq. [*"U.S.A., U.S.A.," some in the crowd chant.*]

We will pay for this, but what saddens me most is that those who will, by and large, pay the highest price are poor kids from Mississippi or Alabama or Texas who could not get a decent job or health insurance and joined the army because it was all we offered them. For war in the end is always about betrayal, betrayal of the young by the old, of soldiers by politicians, and of idealists by cynics.

—CHRIS HEDGES, journalist and author, wrote *War Is a Thing That Gives Us Meaning* and *American Fascists*, among other works.

# The Scourge of Nationalism

HOWARD ZINN

JUNE 2005

Is not nationalism—that devotion to a flag, an anthem, a boundary so fierce it engenders mass murder—one of the great evils of our time, along with racism, along with religious hatred? These ways of thinking—cultivated, nurtured, indoctrinated from childhood on—have been useful to those in power, and deadly for those out of power.

National spirit can be benign in a country that is small and lacking both in military power and a hunger for expansion (Switzerland, Norway, Costa Rica, and many more). But in a nation like ours—huge, possessing thousands of weapons of mass destruction—what might have been harmless pride becomes an arrogant nationalism dangerous to others and to ourselves.

Our citizenry has been brought up to see our nation as different from others, an exception in the world, uniquely moral, expanding into other lands in order to bring civilization, liberty, democracy.

That self-deception started early. When the first English settlers moved into Indian land in Massachusetts Bay and were resisted, the violence escalated into war with the Pequot Indians. The killing of Indians was seen as approved by God, the taking of land as commanded by the Bible. The Puritans cited one of the Psalms, which says: "Ask of me, and I shall give thee, the heathen for thine inheritance, and the uttermost parts of the Earth for thy possession."

When the English set fire to a Pequot village and massacred men, women, and children, the Puritan theologian Cotton Mather said: "It was supposed that no less than 600 Pequot souls were brought down to hell that day."

It was our "Manifest Destiny to overspread the continent allotted by Providence," an American journalist declared on the eve of the Mexican War. After the invasion of Mexico began, the *New York Herald* announced: "We believe it is a part of our destiny to civilize that beautiful country."

It was always supposedly for benign purposes that our country went to war. We invaded Cuba in 1898 to liberate the Cubans, and went to war in the Philippines shortly after, as President McKinley put it, "to civilize and Christianize" the Filipino people.

As our armies were committing massacres in the Philippines (at least 600,000 Filipinos died in a few years of conflict), Elihu Root, our Secretary of War, was saying: "The American soldier is different from all other soldiers of all other countries since the war began. He is the advance guard of liberty and justice, of law and order, and of peace and happiness."

Nationalism is given a special virulence when it is blessed by Providence. Today we have a President, invading two countries in four years, who believes he gets messages from God. Our culture is permeated by a Christian fundamentalism as poisonous as that of Cotton Mather.

How many times have we heard Bush and Rumsfeld talk to the troops in Iraq, victims themselves, but also perpetrators of the deaths of thousands of Iraqis, telling them that if they die, if they return without arms or legs, or blinded, it is for "liberty," for "democracy"?

Nationalist super-patriotism is not confined to Republicans. When Richard Hofstadter analyzed American presidents in his book *The American Political Tradition*, he found that Democratic leaders as well as Republicans, liberals as well as conservatives, invaded other countries, sought to expand U.S. power across the globe.

Liberal imperialists have been among the most fervent of expansionists, more effective in their claim to moral rectitude precisely because they are liberal on issues other than foreign policy. Theodore Roosevelt, a lover of war, and an enthusiastic supporter of the war in Spain and the conquest of the Philippines, is still seen as a Progressive because he supported certain domestic reforms and was concerned with the national environment. Indeed, he ran as President on the Progressive ticket in 1912.

Woodrow Wilson, a Democrat, was the epitome of the liberal apologist for violent actions abroad. In April of 1914, he ordered the bombardment of the Mexican coast, and the occupation of the city of Vera Cruz, in retaliation for the arrest of several U.S. sailors. He sent Marines into Haiti in 1915, killing thousands of Haitians who resisted, beginning a long military occupation of that tiny country. He sent Marines to occupy the Dominican Republic in 1916. And, after running in 1916 on a platform of peace, he brought the nation into the slaughter that was taking place in Europe in World War I, saying it was a war to "make the world safe for democracy."

One of the effects of nationalist thinking is a loss of a sense of proportion. The killing of 2,300 people at Pearl Harbor becomes the justification for killing 240,000 in Hiroshima and Nagasaki. The killing of 3,000 people on September 11 becomes he justification for killing tens of thousands of people in Afghanistan and Iraq.

What makes our nation immune from the normal standards of human decency?

Surely, we must renounce nationalism and all its symbols: its flags, its pledges of allegiance, its anthems, its insistence in song that God must single out America to be blessed.

We need to assert our allegiance to the human race, and not to any one nation. We need to refute the idea that our nation is different from, morally superior to, the other imperial powers of world history.

There have always been men and women in this country who have insisted that universal standards of decent human conduct apply to our nation as to others. That insistence continues today and reaches out to people all over the world. It lets them know, like the balloons sent over the countryside by the Paris Commune in 1871, that "our interests are the same."

—HOWARD ZINN, professor and author, wrote *A People's History of the United States*, among many other works.

# The Curse of Columbus

EDUARDO GALEANO
OCTOBER 2007

Did Christopher Columbus discover America in 1492? Or was it the Vikings before him? And before the Vikings, what about the people who lived there? Didn't they exist?

Official history relates that Vasco Núñez of Balboa was the first man who saw both oceans, standing on a peak in Panama. Were the inhabitants of that area blind?

Who gave maize and potatoes and tomatoes and chocolate and the rivers and mountains of America their names? Hernán Cortés? Francisco Pizarro? Were the people who were already living there mute?

We have been told, and still are, that it was the pilgrims of the *Mayflower* that populated America. Had it been empty before?

Because Columbus didn't understand what the Indians were saying, he concluded that they didn't know how to speak. Because they wore no clothes, were gentle, and gave away everything they had, he concluded they lacked the capacity for reason. And because he was certain of having discovered the Orient by the back door, he believed they were Indians from India.

Afterwards, during the second voyage, the admiral promulgated an act establishing that Cuba was part of Asia. The document of June 14, 1494, stated as evidence that the crew of the three ships recognized it as such. Whoever said otherwise was given thirty lashes, fined 10,000 maravedíes, and had his tongue cut out.

The notary, Hernán Pérez de Luna, attested, and the sailors who could write signed at the bottom.

The conquistadors demanded that America be something it wasn't. And they treated the Americans as if they were what they imagined the pagans of the Orient to be.

Christopher Columbus said he saw on the shores of Cuba sirens with men's faces and chicken feathers, and supposed that not far from there men and women had tails.

In Guyana, according to Sir Walter Raleigh, there were people with eyes in their shoulders and mouths in their chests.

In Venezuela, according to Pedro Simon, there were Indians with ears so long they dragged on the ground.

In the Amazon, according to Christopher of Acuña, the natives' feet were shaped backwards, heels forward and toes behind, and according to Pedro Martín de Anglería, women mutilated one breast to be able to fire their arrows better.

Anglería, who wrote the first history of America, though he never set foot there, also affirmed that in the New World there were people with tails, and these tails were so long the natives could sit only in chairs with holes.

The Black Code prohibited the torture of slaves in the French colonies. But it wasn't to torture them but to educate them that slaves' masters whipped their backs and cut their tendons when they fled.

The Laws of the Indians, which protected those in the Spanish colonies, were quite moving. But the gallows and pillory set up in the center of every Main Square were even more affecting.

The reading of the Request for Obedience was very convincing. This occurred on the eve of the assault on each village. It explained to the Indians that God had come to the world and left St. Peter in his place, and that the successor of St. Peter was the Holy Father, and that the Holy Father has shown favor on the Queen of Castilla, who rules all this land. For this reason, they should go from here or pay tribute in gold, and if they don't or if they stay, war would be declared on them, and they would be made slaves along with their wives and children. But the Request was read in the middle of the night from the mountain in Spanish and without an interpreter, in the presence of the notary but no Indians, as they were asleep, miles away, and hadn't the faintest idea what was awaiting them.

Perhaps the most revealing episode in the history of the Americas occurred in 1563 in Chile. Indians besieged the fortress of Arauco, depriving the Spanish of food and water, yet Captain Bernal refused to surrender.

From the stockade he screamed out, "There will be more and more of us!"

"With what women will you make them?" the Indian chief asked.

"With yours. We will make them bear children who will be your masters."

The invaders called the original Americans idolaters because they believed that nature is sacred and that we are the brothers and sisters of all those with feet, paws, wings, or roots.

And they called them savages. But they were not wrong about this. The Indians were such savages that they ignored the fact that they had to obtain a visa, a certificate of good behavior, and a work permit from Columbus, Cabral, Cortés, Alvarado, Pizarro, and the pilgrims of the *Mayflower*.

—EDUARDO GALEANO, journalist and essayist, is the author of *Open Veins of Latin America*, *Memory of Fire*, and *Mirrors: An Almost Universal History*.

# PART 4

# Campaigning for Women's Equality

There was nothing more exhilarating, in going through the early years of *The Progressive*, than reading about the women's suffrage movement. Belle Case La Follette, wife of Fighting Bob, was one of the leading suffragists in the Midwest. The first woman to graduate from the University of Wisconsin law school, she helped make *The Progressive*, then known as *La Follette's*, a suffragist paper.

A few gems fell out of the old volumes when we opened them up. One was from Carl Sandburg on the occasion of the birth of his daughter. Another was a tiny but devastating riposte from Jane Addams on the ridiculous arguments against suffrage.

With that battle won, *The Progressive* maintained its commitment to women's equality. A piece by Susan Brandeis in 1930 noted that there were only 1,600 female lawyers in the 1920 Census. Daughter of a Supreme Court justice, she herself was denied a position at a large New York law firm simply because she was a woman.

*The Progressive* also played a part in exposing the evils of sexual abuse, with Jill Gay's "The 'Patriotic' Prostitute" and Bonnie Urfer's haunting "Memoirs of a Normal Childhood."

But the magazine exulted in the gains women have made across the board, including such fields as athletics. Ruth Conniff's "Awesome Women in Sports" shows young women not as victims but as champions.

Since 1990, *The Progressive* has been running monthly interviews. The one with Katha Pollitt in this chapter gives you a sense of how revealing those interviews can be.

# My Baby Girl

Carl Sandburg
february 10, 1912

It was just a week ago she came. Only seven days ago I saw her writhe and take breath, heard her first plaintive cry to her first morning in the world.

And when I walked away from the hospital in early gray daylight with a fresh rain smell in the air, treading the blown-down and scattered catalpa blossoms under my heels, I had above all else a new sense of a sacredness of life. A grand, original something the full equal of death or first love or marriage as an experience, this I knew I had touched. The whole white army of girl childhood was a trembling soft wonder I now understood better.

All that day and the next, however, I was compelled to draw on my resources of patience and humor. The remark of a startlingly large number of my friends was:

"Too bad it's a girl."

I learned it for the first time to be positively true that fathers and mothers generally know what they prefer as a first child and they prefer boys to girls. Could they have their choice from the God of Things as They Are, they would say:

"Give us a boy."

And so, while a few understood my joy, some actually took it as a half-grief, a kind of sorrow, and commiserated me:

"Too bad it's a girl."

Thus at the very start of life, prejudices and dispreferences follow the footsteps of one sex as against another.

"It is better to be a boy than a girl, better to be a man than a woman." This was the undertone and the oversong of those who proffered me gratulations.

And I have wondered how far they are right.

Tonight however, as I hold in my arms for a few moments, this new-come beginner in the game of life, I think I would as lief be this baby girl as any man alive.

For this baby girl, as sure as luck and health stay by her, shall see wonder on wonder that will be denied to our eyes. If she lives out fifty years, she will be a mingler in and a witness upon changes, developments, and advances that baffle all prophecy and forecast by us today. In her years, many new shapings will be worked on the hard mechanisms of wealth production, the curious codes of law and justice, and the heart-strings of human mercy and brotherhood.

She shall see women go forward and cast ballots and speak and write and with passionate earnestness take part in political movements. She shall sit in a gallery in the

House of Representatives in Washington and listen to the words of a woman member of that body.

She shall know the final destiny of the war game. Perhaps, even, she or her lover may watch with their own eyes fleets of air battlers so deadly destructive with explosives hurled at helpless cities below that the war game is abandoned forever and the nations of the earth disarm their troops and dismantle their navies.

She—this little soft-breathing thing in my arms—will be alive when typhoid, tuberculosis and babies born blind have become forgotten, improbable things. We are moving that way today. We edge toward it every year. We imagine and picture it. But she, my baby girl, will walk the streets of cities from which all dangers of the now commonest and deadliest diseases have been driven out.

In this week, when her name is registered among the births, woman, the common woman—the wife of the workingman—is the slave of a slave, cooking, sewing, washing, cleaning, nursing in sickness, and rendering a hundred personal services daily for a man who is himself not in power to dictate a constant job and living wage for himself.

My baby girl shall see the slave achieve freedom for himself and his class, and "the slave of a slave" broken away from the harsh interests that hold him in the dark today.

So rapid and sweeping are some of the advancements today, that I think it possible that the wise sweet mother who bore her, and I, her father, may look on these things forecasted. But whether we see them or not, sure it is that the world is moving forward with strides so fast and vast that all the Tribe of Intelligence agree that these and more beyond our reckoning will be.

All of this is more than guess, conjecture, and surmise. The achieved rights of life for men, women, and children are reaching farther and farther every day. So, I know that when my baby girl, on some night of moonlight and roses, says "Yes" to a man who asks her the Momentous Question, it will not be for money that she replies. It will not be for bread-and-butter and a home that her answer will be given. It will be a case of heart answering unto heart.

Time was when it may have been right to pity the baby girl. That time has gone by. I am glad it was a girl.

—CARL SANDBURG was a poet, journalist, and Lincoln biographer.


## If Things Were Reversed

JANE ADDAMS, as recorded by Belle Case La Follette
APRIL 6, 1912


What would be the state of the masculine mind if the voting women should present to them only the following half-dozen objections, which are unhappily so familiar to many of us?

First—Men would find politics corrupting.

Second—They would vote as their wives and mothers did.

Third—Men's suffrage would only double the vote without changing the results.

Fourth—Men's suffrage would diminish the respect for men.

Fifth—Most men do not want to vote.

Sixth—The best men would not vote.

—JANE ADDAMS, the founder of Hull House, was also a suffragist and a founder of the Women's International League for Peace and Freedom. She won the Nobel Peace Prize in 1931.

# May the Women of the United States Vote in 1920?

BELLE CASE LA FOLLETTE

FEBRUARY 1920

On the first day of May 1919, the U.S. House of Representatives passed by a vote of 304 yeas to 89 nays the joint resolution declaring that the right of citizens of the United States to vote shall not be denied or abridged on account of sex. On June 4, the U.S. Senate by a vote of 56 yeas to 25 nays adopted this same resolution.

At last, after many long years of struggle and sacrifice, the necessary two-thirds vote of both branches of the U.S. Congress had been secured for the amendment!

The final action came so easily, so much as a matter of course, that a casual observer judging from outward manifestations might easily have believed it was a matter of no great importance. I sat next to Harriet Taylor Upton in the Senate gallery at the time. Her father, as I remember it, was dean of the House of Representatives, when Mr. La Follette was the youngest member, and had ably championed during his long service this same amendment. From childhood Harriet has been in the thick of the fight. We squeezed hands and shed a few tears and that was all. There was no attempt at a great demonstration. The vice president did not have any excuse to rise and solemnly remind the galleries that such things are forbidden by the rules of the Senate.

This outward calm was not due to the absence of a deep undercurrent of feeling or lack of appreciation of the magnitude of the event. The stage had not been set. There had been no speech making. We knew in advance that we had the necessary two-thirds vote. The expected had happened.

The throngs of women suffragists as they left the galleries doubtless took long breaths of relief and offered silent prayers of thankfulness. But the victory was not yet complete. There was more work ahead. There was a new responsibility to discharge. Before this resolution could become an accomplished fact—really an amendment to the constitution of the United States—it must be ratified by the legislatures of three-fourths of the several states.

Since we are so confident, so sure, why this impatience, why 1920?

For my part, it is not because I expect it will make any great difference in the practical result, that I would have women vote in 1920, but, believing as I do, that the greatest menace to democracy is the lack of interest on the part of the governed, and believing that the first greatest benefit to the state of votes for women is the increased interest in public affairs which the discussion of political problems in the home inevitably brings, for this reason, I think it would be of immense value to the nation if women are enfranchised at the beginning of a presidential campaign, when the greater political enthusiasm will naturally tend to stimulate the largest number of women to register and to exercise the privilege of voting.

The issues of the coming campaign—peace and war, government ownership, industrial questions, universal military training, the high cost of living—are all problems within the experience and understanding and close to the hearts of women. For women to assume a direct share of the responsibility in government, at this great crisis in the world's history, will give tremendous impetus to the patriotism and fervor of all the people in the solution of problems now confronting us.

—BELLE CASE LA FOLLETTE was a writer, editor, suffragist, and champion of civil rights for African Americans. The wife of Fighting Bob La Follette, she helped keep *The Progressive* going after his death in 1925.

## Women's Wages in Government

MARY ANDERSON, Women's Bureau of the Labor Department, as recorded by Belle Case La Follette
DECEMBER 1926

I am sorry to say that through the information we receive in our investigations we find that many women, far too many, are not even receiving a living wage. We also find that, in comparison to wages paid to men, women's wages are very far down the scale—so far, in fact, that there is little semblance of equality between the wages of men and women. One of the prevailing thoughts which has fostered this inequality of wages has been that men are providers for the family and that women have only themselves to support, with their incomes supplemented by other members of the family when living at home.

But in investigations made by the Women's Bureau we have found that women are often providers for the family, and that they supplement the man's wages, while young girls more often than young boys take unopened pay envelopes home to their mothers. We have found, too, that the women have family responsibilities in addition to the matter of pay—the work in the home being left almost entirely to the women to perform after a day's work in the factory.

There are over 8.5 million gainfully employed women in the United States, and of these there are over 4 million employed in the producing and distributing trades. From the facts we have gathered we know that the future of the girl today is closely linked up with the conditions which prevail in the places where she works.

We want to see the girl made an efficient part of industry's machinery, but we also want to see that industry offers a future for the woman and is an institution which the girl can enter, and in which she can stay and prosper and grow.

The beginning has been made, and we find many places in many industries which are offering to women a living wage, hours short enough to allow for education and recreation after the day in the factory is over, working conditions which eliminate fatigue as far as possible, and an opportunity to advance in industry through opening up new activities for women, and through paying wages based on the job and not on the sex of the workers.

We who have worked in the industrial field for many years see much to encourage us, but we know there is still much to be done. The thing of the first importance to know is that women are an important factor and that they are a permanent factor in the industrial world. We know that the girl who goes into the factories and workshops of the country does so to meet a real need. We know that she is indispensable to industry and we know what so few people seem to recognize: that the girls of today, these flappers who are getting so much criticism and publicity, are most of them helping in the support of their families.

For years we have been hearing of the girl who works for pin money, who can afford to work for less than a living wage because she lives at home, who spends her earnings on silk stockings and fur coats. There may be some such girls; in fact, I presume there are, but I have known thousands of working women personally and I have known very few to whom such statements apply.

Through our special investigations we have studied men as well as women, so that we might have a basis for comparison, and what we already knew to be true: that a large majority of single women who live at home contribute all their earnings to their families. Nearly seven out of every ten single women who live at home turn over every cent to their mothers or fathers, getting back for themselves only what can be spared after the family needs are met.

—Mary Anderson was chief of the Women's Bureau at the Department of Labor from 1919 to 1944.

# Women and the Law

## Unjust Discrimination

SUSAN BRANDEIS
FEBRUARY 9, 1930

When the 1920 census was taken there were 1,600 women engaged in the practice of law in the United States. This number undoubtedly has been largely increased since then. I became a member of the profession subsequent to 1920. In this field, frankness impels me to say that the picture is rather gloomy, for women lawyers throughout the land, and particularly in the larger cities, are still discriminated against. In my own city, New York, one of the representative bar associations refuses to admit us to membership. Some of the large law firms refuse us employment. Upon my arrival in New York I sought employment with one of the large law offices which was denied me, although by way of consolation I was assured by the prominent lawyer at the head of the firm to whom I made my application, that were I of the opposite sex I could have almost any position I desired with his law firm.

Other large firms which give employment to very few women lawyers do so almost invariably upon a quota basis. We are thus in large numbers denied contact with the weighty and intricate legal problems which naturally gravitate to those law offices. In addition, we are discriminated against by many men and, I regret to be compelled to say, women who have not enough confidence in us, solely on account of our sex, to entrust to us legal matters of importance and magnitude. This further limits our field of activity. Yet many women lawyers have in official and other capacities shown efficiency and ability to cope with the most intricate legal problems. Women have also shown aptitude in the handling of complicated and important legal matters as assistants in the Attorney General's office. Assistant Corporation Counsel, Assistant District Attorneys. In private practice many have shown unusual ability in both civil and criminal law.

If I have any plea to make, it is that this unjust discrimination should cease and a step to bring that condition about would be for women to show a larger measure of faith in the ability of women at the bar to represent them in all legal matters no matter how complicated.

Once these discriminations are removed and women lawyers estimated solely upon merit, I feel certain we will soon produce outstanding women lawyers engaged in private practice comparable to the leaders among the men of the bar.

Women can raise many additional champions for themselves if they but give to women lawyers the support they deserve.

—SUSAN BRANDEIS, daughter of Justice Louis Brandeis, was one of the first women to argue a case before the U.S. Supreme Court.

# The "Patriotic" Prostitute

JILL GAY
FEBRUARY 1985

Germany's Rosie Travel sells sex tours to Thailand. "Anything goes in this exotic country," says the company's brochure. "Especially when it comes to girls. Still, it appears to be a problem for visitors to Thailand to find the right places where they can indulge in unknown pleasures. . . . Rosie has done something about this. . . . You can book a trip to Thailand with erotic pleasures included in the price."

Japan Air Lines (JAL) is a little more subtle. "In order to embellish and relish better the nights of Korea," its brochure advises, "you must start above all else with a Kisaeng party." In South Korea, Kisaeng women were traditionally hired to sing and dance at parties; today, however, the word is synonymous with prostitute. "A night spent with a consummate Kisaeng girl dressed in a gorgeous Korean blouse and skirt is just perfect," continues the JAL pamphlet. Kisaeng parties, it adds, have "become one of the nation's most charming attractions."

"I felt I was picking out a slave girl at a slave market," says one Japanese tourist about his visit to Korea.

The international sex trade has reached shocking proportions. Between 70 and 80 percent of male tourists who travel from Japan, the United States, Australia, and Western Europe to Asia do so solely for the purpose of sexual entertainment, according to *World View 1984*, a French political almanac. The Thai police estimated in 1982 that there were 700,000 prostitutes in the country—about 10 percent of all Thai women between the ages of fifteen and thirty. A 1982 International Labor Organization (ILO) study found some 500,000 prostitutes in Bangkok alone. In the Philippines, an estimated 200,000 prostitutes operate; in South Korea, 260,000.

But far from being alarmed by these figures, leaders of the affected countries are spurring the trade along. "Within the next two years, we are going to need money," said Thailand's vice premier, talking to a meeting of provincial governors in 1980. "Therefore, I ask of all governors to consider the natural scenery in your provinces, together with some forms of entertainment that some of you might consider disgusting and shameful because they are forms of sexual entertainment that attract tourists.

"Such forms of entertainment should not be prohibited . . . because you are morally fastidious. . . . We must do this because we have to consider the jobs that will be created for the people."

In South Korea, the government sponsors an "orientation program"; prostitutes are issued identification cards that serve as hotel passes. The card is a "Certificate of Employment in Entertainment Service."

"You girls must take pride in your devotion to your country," the women are told at the orientation sessions. "Your carnal conversations with foreign tourists do not prostitute either yourself or the nation, but express your heroic patriotism."

Though prostitution is called the world's oldest profession, the boom in Southeast Asia started with the U.S. presence in Vietnam. There were 20,000 prostitutes in Thailand in 1957; by 1964, after the United States established seven bases in the country, that number had skyrocketed to 400,000. Throughout the war, Bangkok was a favorite "rest-and-recreation" (R&R) spot for GIs. Similarly, the number of R&R centers in the Philippines increased from 20 to 600. And in South Vietnam itself, there were about 400,000 prostitutes at the height of the war—almost one for every GI.

"Saigon has become an American brothel," Senator J. William Fulbright noted. And the South Vietnamese government didn't seem to mind. "The Americans need girls; we need dollars," one official said. "Why should we refrain from the exchange? It's an inexhaustible source of U.S. dollars for the State."

When the American soldiers left in the mid-1970s, "the post-Vietnam slack was picked up by tourism," says an activist with Friends of Women, an organization based in Bangkok. The area around the U.S. military base at Subic Bay and the R&R center in Olongapoboth in the Philippines are the largest bases for prostitution in Asia.

But something other than the mere presence of soldiers and tourists accounts for the flourishing business.

"Sex tourism in the Philippines really took off during the period after 1972 when martial law was declared, and the government gave priority to export promotion," says Irene Santiago, a Filipina community organizer. "We needed a lot of dollars in order to pay off the foreign debt, so tourism was a major thrust for dollar earning. And with that, came the sex tourists mainly from Japan."

The sex trade has also figured in Thailand's economic development strategy, which calls for reducing investment in agriculture and aggressively pushing the export of goods produced in the cities. In a typical village in the north, as many as one-third of the families have no land, and three-quarters have less than the two acres needed for subsistence. Many send their daughters to Bangkok to work as prostitutes.

And some women opt for the profession because they don't care to work in the hazardous export-oriented plants. "You get cancer working in factories, we get abortion and VD working as prostitutes," one woman says. Prostitution now vies with sugar as Thailand's second largest producer of foreign exchange.

Taew grew up as one of eight children in northern Thailand. Her two elder sisters worked as prostitutes to American GIs at the base at Udon. When the U.S. Air Force left in 1975, her sisters came back to farm the land. But the soil was too poor to support them, so they went back to work as prostitutes in the cities. Then they got married, and the family lost its major source of income.

So Taew was sent to Bangkok to find work. She made $1.50 a day mixing cement and steel, then $20 a month as a housemaid. Later she tried waitressing. Still struggling, she was finally persuaded to sell her virginity for $400, of which she received $100. "Taew did not like it a bit," the ILO study reported. "She cried for several days afterward." Taew sent her earnings home so her family could build a well for drinking water.

After her parents kept writing Taew letters asking for more money, Taew relented and went back to work as a prostitute.

Taew's story is not an aberration.

Women's groups around the world have begun to mobilize against the international big business of prostitution. Such demonstrations are essential if the sex trade is to come to a halt. But they are not likely to succeed unless there are more profound changes, both in the presence of the U.S. military and in the export-oriented development strategies of Asian countries that depend on foreign exchange—at the expense of their most impoverished women.

—JILL GAY has written and worked on issues of women's rights and global health for more than two decades.

# Memoirs of a Normal Childhood

BONNIE URFER
OCTOBER 1986

I had a normal childhood. It was filled with violence and abuse. Most of it I don't remember. Some things I will never forget.

The first time I was abused by a man I was six years old. His name was Elmer, and he managed the gas station next to our house. One summer day I walked over to visit him. He led me behind the counter, sat down on a chair, and lifted me onto his lap.

I was scared, I was always scared.

The first thing I heard as I sat on Elmer's lap was a zipper opening. He took my hand and led it behind me where I felt something soft, something very strange and wobbly and squishy. I remember trying to figure out what it was I was touching without looking. I didn't know. Then as my hand was guided over the soft thing it began to get hard and large. I wanted to cry. I still didn't know what it was. I didn't know until I grew up and had an adult relationship with a man. But I never forgot that day at Elmer's gas station and I never went back. Shortly after that episode Elmer took my brother on a trip with him.

When I was eight years old I visited my cousins with my family. My aunt needed to be picked up from work about twenty miles away through backcountry roads. My cousin Tim was going to get her and asked if I'd ride along. I said yes.

I was scared, I was always scared.

We were somewhere on our way when he stopped the car and started fondling my body and kissing me. I was so angry, I flew into the backseat where I kicked and kicked as hard as I could each time his hands came toward me. He finally stopped trying, told me I sure wasn't part of the family, and drove on to pick up his mother.

When I was eleven years old I went to the grocery store for my mother. When I got there I wandered up and down the aisles looking for the items ordered. On my way down one side aisle a man came toward me from the opposite direction. I didn't look at him.

I was scared, I was always scared.

As he went by I thought I saw his penis out of his pants. I hurried by, not wanting to disappoint my mother by leaving the store without the supplies I was sent for. I went down the next aisle; so did he. And his penis was out of his pants. I ran out of the store and went home with nothing but tears running down my face.

One warm day when I was thirteen my grandfather came to town to visit us. It was always a very special event and a big deal was made of his time in the city. We were preparing a picnic outside, so that's where most people were, except for my mother, my grandfather, and me. My mother walked down the stairs and went outside. That left me and my grandfather.

I was scared, I was always scared.

He was standing close behind me when the door closed behind my mother. As soon as it slammed, his hand went down the front of my pants. In the next second the door opened, and as fast as his hand went in, it came out. I never let myself be alone in the same room with my grandfather again.

I am only one person and these are only a few of the things I remember. There was the time I was ice skating, going from the pavilion onto the ice. As I walked out the door the hand of someone going in cupped my breast and squeezed.

Again and again and again I was scared. I felt so abused, so used, so low.

All of my life I remembered these things, and now I'm telling. For the first time in all of these years I can say it wasn't my fault and for the first time I'm recognizing and hearing from other women that they too had an uncle who managed to brush his hand across their breasts every time there was a hug to be given, or a family friend who always wanted the girls to sit on his lap so he could fondle their breasts or put his hand down their pants when no one was looking.

It's time we all started telling the truth about our normal childhoods.

—BONNIE URFER runs Nukewatch, a nonprofit in Luck, Wisconsin, that is dedicated to the abolition of nuclear weapons and nuclear power and to the preservation of the environment.


## Awesome Women in Sports

RUTH CONNIFF
MAY 1993

For the last few days I've been tearing pictures out of magazines—*Shape, Runner's World, Sports Illustrated*—collecting photographs of women athletes. I found a great shot of Gail Devers, Olympic gold medalist in the 100 meters, bounding out of the starting blocks, and I ripped out an ad for running shoes that shows two women striding side by side, silhouetted against an enormous blue sky.

I am pinning up these pictures on a bulletin board in the basement locker room of my old high school, Madison East, where I coach girls' track. I decided to make the bulletin board at the beginning of this year's season, ostensibly to provide information—weekly announcements, workout schedules, team records, etc.—but also for sneakier reasons. One is to do a little public relations for track (gym classes pass through this locker room every day, and I'm hoping to win a few new recruits). Another reason is to boost the girls' morale. The bulletin board I captured runs the length of one wall of the locker room. Covered with purple and gold paper and glossy photos, it stands out. My hope is that it will reflect a picture to the girls who walk by it of energy and optimism and strength. Hence my hunt through magazines for inspiring images of women in sports.

The ads do reflect a significant demographic change in attitude and self-image among American women. It's a change that has everything to do with more women playing sports.

Most of all, I see the change in women's images of themselves on a daily basis among the girls I coach.

The other day at practice, some girls on my team were talking about the hard-body heroine of the movie *Terminator 2*. One of the girls said she watched the movie with her boyfriend. "He said he wouldn't mind having a body like that, but he doesn't find her physically attractive," she said.

"Well, excuse me, but I find her physically awesome," one of the other girls remarked, to noises of assent from her teammates.

I like eavesdropping on these conversations.

Last year, at the beginning of the season, the girl who considers the Terminator woman awesome didn't want to lift weights, for fear she would get too "built."

That was before she became freshman city champion in the half mile. Now she's hooked. She worked hard to earn her varsity letter in cross-country and showed up for pre-season weight-training for track. She and the other runners on the women's team have developed a touching camaraderie over the past couple of years, as well as a kind of jock swagger that has subsumed some of the cloying cuteness a lot of high-school girls cultivate.

My own experience as an athlete has been so rewarding, and so central to who I am now, that it pains me to think of all the girls in school who might never discover the pride and confidence that come from challenging themselves and excelling in a sport.

Shortly after I moved back to my hometown, I went to see a neighbor of mine compete in a high school gymnastics meet. I remembered her as a little girl, doing cartwheels and splits on the sidewalk outside her house. While I was away at college, she had grown up into a state-ranked gymnast. Watching her at the meet, surrounded by other girls in ponytails and sweats, warming up, getting nervous, and focusing fiercely as they got ready to compete, brought back a flood of memories. That's when I decided to coach.

It was all there, the way I remembered it, when I first returned to a high-school cross-country meet. Tough girls with French braids from small Wisconsin towns (whose numbers used to include Susie Favor) warming up together, striding side by side in intimidating packs, their nylon pants and jackets rasping as they moved in unison. The smell of Icy-Hot and nervousness. One new girl on my team wept in terror before her race, begged me not to make her do it. She did it. She threw up. She couldn't believe she made it. At the end of the season I gave her the Team Spirit Award because she improved so dramatically, became a cross-country zealot—full of pride in herself and joy—and was her teammates' biggest booster. That feeling of elation, of victory, comes over and over again from testing yourself and surviving the test—kids sprinting their hearts out and throwing themselves across the finish line.

I knew a woman at Yale who posed as one of *Playboy*'s "Women of the Ivy League." She also happened to be the girlfriend of a runner on the cross-country and track teams. I remember seeing her at a cross-country meet. A group of us were standing at the finish line, covered with mud from running, cheering as the men's team came in. She came tripping across the grass, looking radically out of place in a fur coat and high heels, sinking into the soft ground, and waited on the sidelines for her boyfriend. I remember feeling sad when I saw her, outside the circle of happy track people, hugging and laughing, filled with shared, post-race euphoria. She could hardly walk, much less run, and she seemed infinitely far away from taking part in that event. I felt grateful for my muddy shoes and sweat clothes, grateful that I could be there fully and freely participating, not as a kind of crippled ornament standing on the sidelines.

So that's why I'm busy covering the wall with sports pictures and recruiting girls to run track. If I have anything to do with it, when I'm an old woman I'll be running road races with a crowd of other women, young and old, and every single one of us will be awesome.

—RUTH CONNIFF is the political editor of *The Progressive*, where she has worked since 1991.

# What Shall I Wear?

ELIZABETH KARLIN
OCTOBER 1994

A good friend sent me a baby-blue bulletproof vest after Michael Griffin killed Dr. David Gunn, so that I would have something to wear to work at the clinic where I do abortions. It came in a bag stamped FEMALE, and it fits quite well. I rarely wear it, though—not because it is hot and constricting, which it is, but because when I put it on, I am keenly aware of the parts of me that aren't covered. When friends ask how come I don't wear the vest, I answer, "What's the use? They'll just shoot me in the head."

And so it happened. Dr. John Britton, sixty-nine, wearing his bulletproof vest, and his bodyguard, James Barrett, seventy-four, vest status unknown, were shot in the head and killed. June Barrett, sixty-eight, a nurse, was shot in the arm. Paul Hill, a dedicated Christian terrorist who belonged to a group advocating murder of us abortion providers, shot them while they were sitting in their truck. Since then, I have been practicing crouching on the passenger-side floor of the car. My stiff hips get in the way of a quick disappearance, but after flicking the rearview mirror, I can drive backwards. They never taught me this in medical school.

At the office, things are much the same, but on the Monday after the killings the phone is busier than it has been in months. Women are trying to make appointments before I, the doctor, am oiled.

Some of our patients make an appointment without even being able to say the word "abortion." That is how I know we're losing. Here it is, 1994, twenty-one years after the *Roe v. Wade* decision, and every day I hear from at least one patient who believes that abortion is a secret, horrible crime—a torture practiced in some filthy subcellar, away from the prying eyes of even the doctor's own staff.

Nine out of ten women who come into my office have often repeated this sentence: "I would never have an abortion." When they face me and I ask them why they're crying, my patients who are minutes away from having an abortion say, "I don't believe in abortion."

Like me, these women read all around them that abortion is bad, and murder is bad, too, and has about the same moral severity. But abortion is a symptom, not the disease. It is itself a fundamental part of poverty, of despair, of a life gone wrong, of poor education in contraception. We will never reduce the number of abortions because we are not even interested in treating the disease. My patients are bruised women who have the worst abusive relationships, are alcoholics, are physicians and lawyers, are people who believe in the diaphragm, are pill failures, and are those whose doctors took them off the pill.

They are not bad. They are women. But their marginalization will allow the most horrendous behavior outside our offices and our homes.

Since the latest murders in Pensacola, I have had no protesters at my office. When I started doing abortions four years ago, they came daily. They put on some huge demonstrations outside both my home and my office. More recently, a few people pray outside the clinic. They carry a big sign, THEY KILL BABIES HERE! They call in sweet voices, "Liz, we love you. We love you. Come here and talk to us. You don't have to go in there." And when it is clear that I am going in there, they start to scream. "You will go to hell. Get over here and talk to me now. God will make you suffer." The transformation from saint to banshee is eerie. I would not be surprised if they showed up with weapons one day.

My daughter says she is checking out the medieval-armor room at the Metropolitan Museum of Art in New York. A Jewish friend who witnessed the Nazi occupation of Austria and knows a thing or two about violence suggests I wear a flak helmet as well. One provider already does.

I have learned to do a safe abortion. I have learned to counsel the most troubled women I have ever seen. I am learning not to judge. I am learning to teach what I know to medical students and residents. What I haven't learned yet is what the hell to wear to work.

—ELIZABETH KARLIN, a physician, ran the Women's Medical Center in Madison, Wisconsin, until her death from cancer in 1998.

# An Interview with Katha Pollitt, Columnist for The Nation

RUTH CONNIFF
DECEMBER 1994

Q: Do you think that you are one of a few people who believes women and men are the same kind of creature?

KATHA POLLITT: No. Lots of people think it. But the other strand of feminism is also quite strong. And it's much more fashionable. And the reason is that it explains the world we see without resorting to the concept of sexism. What it says is that women don't have power because they don't want power.

Q: What do you think about Emily's List—an organization that gives money specifically to women candidates?

POLLITT: Well, I'm glad you're asking me this question. I have a very complicated relationship to Emily's List, which is this: I belong to Emily's List. I send money to people on their list. But at the same time that I am writing out my little checks, I am wondering, why am I doing this? These politicians quite often are not particularly enlightened or feminist or liberal.

I think that people in American politics are always looking for shortcuts. For example, if we elect women, will they automatically on the whole, on average, defend the interests of women, and be less warlike, and be more honest and altruistic and all this kind of thing? I think that, yeah, if you elect a feminist she's going to do that. But just being a Democratic woman is not going to do that. There's an illusion that women have only women's interests at heart. Women have all the interests of their class, just like men do.

Nonetheless, given identical politics, I'd rather have a woman than a man in office, because I think there's a value in gender equity for its own sake. There are all kinds of issues where men and women do see things differently, not because women are lateral thinkers and men are hierarchical, but because women have a different life experience, and so they have different fears and different hopes as well.

But these kinds of small and marginal and subtle differences—you can't make a political movement out of them. It can't be made out of voting for a this-colored person or a this-gendered person as if they'd almost unconsciously carry out your goals.

Q: What do you think about the prospects for organized left-wing politics in this country?

POLLITT: I guess I would have to say at the risk of startling or bothering some of our readers, I don't think there is a Left in this country. There are liberals in this country. But I don't know of any movement, really, that mounts any kind of fundamental challenge to capitalism, and to the basic way this country is organized. The way things are set up I think there is very little space to enact even liberal politics. And so I feel that when we speak about the Left we're speaking about three people.

Q: Surely more than three.

POLLITT: Well, sure, You're one person, I'm another. I'm not saying there's nobody. What I'm saying is there isn't a social basis for this politics. There isn't an organization. What is the leftwing organization? The Nation Associates?

There are little things, there's this brush fire over here and these workers over there. But there isn't anything like an organized political movement. And the minute one develops, it collapses back into the Democratic Party again.

Q: What do you think of declarations of post-feminism, that many women say they are not feminists?

POLLITT: The idea that you need other people to make common cause with in order to achieve a goal feels to many people like failure. That's why you have a lot of working-class people who anathematize unions. I get letters from women like this who say, "I'm a Republican, I have an MBA, and everyone tells me I can't make it but I know I will. Because I'm determined and I'm the best, you see."

The American ideology is "If you're the best you don't need anybody." So that makes it very hard for joining a political movement based on solidarity not to seem like weakness and a confession of your own inability to succeed by your own efforts. Now what people in America have a hard time getting through their heads is that, first of all, nobody succeeds entirely by their own efforts, but also, not that many people succeed.

Q: What do you think of the debate about pornography?

POLLITT: I have a lot of sympathy for a very deep critique of heterosexuality. But what I don't have a lot of sympathy for is spending enormous amounts of political energy on the futile attempt to get rid of certain kinds of images.

People like to argue about pornography because it's about sex. And it relates to certain academic feminist interests having to do with representation. But as politics, it is a true waste of time.

And it's worse than a waste of time, because not only does it use up energy that could be better devoted to something else, it places feminism in the camp of those who think that women are less sexual than men, that women's sexuality is less diverse and perverse than men's.

It's very interesting that the women's movement in thirty years has not been able to get paid parental leave, something that many other countries have, something that's very modest, but actually would help people a lot. It has not been able to get a national system of day care—something else that exists in many countries. But it has been able to inject into the public discourse the views of Andrea Dworkin and Catharine MacKinnon on pornography.

I think it's been able to do this because it's hitching a ride on a feeling that is already very deep, which is Puritanism: Sex is bad, looking at it is bad, thinking about it is bad, and masturbation isn't very good either.

When is the last time someone made a case for pornography and said, you know, I like it? It's a pleasure. It's harmless. I don't beat and rape women. But I enjoy watching dirty movies. This is a case that is very, very rarely made, because people are ashamed of it. At the same time, they want to do it. And I think the shame and the wanting to do it are related. That's how Puritanism works.

You'll notice that feminist critics of pornography agree that sex is a kind of violence, that it's exploitative. But take your garden-variety act of sex; they all agree that what is going on here is essentially sadomasochism, really. And that's its central feature. None of them have much use for the idea that sex is amusing, that it can be light, that it can involve affection or friendship, that people can laugh while they have sex, that it can really be rather sweet. I think the kind of sex I have described is the kind of sex that lots and lots of people have. And it is one of the things that people like about having sex.

I come away from reading about this debate thinking, it's all so grim. Is sex really all that grim? You know, especially when you consider, if you believe these sexual surveys, women are having more pleasure in bed than they've had since they started trying to figure out women's sexual experience in some kind of a pseudoscientific way. And yet when you read all this you just think, it's all so grim and hateful, why would anybody bother?

They just have no sense of the subtlety of it all—that sex can be used to express a lot of different feelings. So you see, I'm still a romantic. I still believe in love.

# An Interview with Gloria Steinem

L. A. WINOKUR
JUNE 1995

Q: I know you're fond of the term "radical," preferring it, in many ways, to "feminist." Ever since Michael Dukakis refused to own up to the "L" word during the 1988 Presidential debates, terms like "liberal" have come under attack.

GLORIA STEINEM: I never liked "liberal." I always preferred "progressive," or some other term, to it. "Liberal" felt to me to be a little too top-down. It seemed too much like people making poverty policies in Washington. I think we have to name ourselves. I like the term "feminist." I feel very proud of it. I feel I'm a feminist before I'm an American. Before I'm a writer. The first feminist was somebody who believed women were equal to men. I also treasure the word "radical," which means going to the root. It needn't have the connotation of violence that has been given to it in its usage. To me it means that if you don't go to the root of a problem, you're not only putting a Band-Aid on a wound too deep, but you're not being effective.

Q: Do you see the socialization process of boys and girls as changing for the better?

STEINEM: It seems as if the imagination of change has to always precede the reality of change. And there are some areas in which our imagination is already there, and we're working on the structure and on the reality. And there are some areas in which our imagination isn't there yet. We imagined, and therefore convinced the country and are now working on the reality, that women can do what men can do. But too few of us have imagined, and therefore we haven't convinced the country, that men can do what women can.

As a result, a problem for many women now—the women who have jobs, at least—is that they have two jobs: They're taking care of the kids and taking care of the house, and they're working outside of the home besides. It was always the problem of poor women. Now it's the problem of middle-class women. So now we'll do something about it because there's a critical mass of women having this experience. We need to know in our hearts that men can raise children just as well as women can, and we need to be willing to raise our boys to raise children. We've done something toward raising our daughters more like our sons, but fewer of us have had the courage to raise our sons more like our daughters. And that's very, very important.

The source of gender roles—which in turn becomes the source of incomplete human beings, violence, and the cult of masculinity—is the experience you had as a little child, when you were totally nurtured and raised by women. So you think women have to be the nurturing ones. And you only see men in positions of authority and, thus, think men have to be authoritative. That's the source of the gender roles. It really is the root, or radical, view of gender.

—L. A. WINOKUR is a freelance writer in California.

## Dulcet Tones

MOLLY IVINS
OCTOBER 1995

The seventy-fifth anniversary of the suffrage of women provided a happy summer hiatus, a pleasant orgy of "you've come-a-long-way-baby" editorials. And so we have. What's depressingly familiar is the reaction to all our advances. Our opponents still haven't found any new adjectives to use against us. "Shrill," "strident," "hysterical," and "aggressive" remain the putdowns of choice. The favored argument is still the ad hominem (Latin teachers, please help: is "argumentum ad feminem" possible?) attacking the femininity of feminists.

Lucy Stone's daughter observed, "Crowds expected a woman's-rights advocate to be a tall, aggressive, disagreeable woman, with masculine manners and a strident voice. Instead they found a small, quiet woman with gentle, unaffected manners, and the sweetest voice ever possessed by a public speaker. That voice became famous."

Dulcet tones, girls, dulcet tones when discussing domestic violence, lest you, too, be called "shrill."


## An Interview with Ani DiFranco, Folksinger

MATTHEW ROTHSCHILD
MAY 2000

Q: One of your songs is called "Hello, Birmingham." It's about Dr. Barnett Slepian, the obstetrician and abortion doctor who was gunned down in Buffalo, New York, in 1998, right?

ANI DIFRANCO: I'm from Buffalo, and I live there now. I was not in the city when the shooting occurred, but I was there soon after. And the whole idea that, you know, a doctor who performs abortions is not safe in his own home, it just makes the atmosphere so claustrophobic. So I remember returning back to Buffalo and there was this feeling of dull fear just hanging over the city.

That's another terrifying circumstance in our country right now: the rightwing Christian terrorism that is occurring and not being addressed and dealt with as it should be. And Buffalo, New York, has long been a shit-magnet for these kinds of extremists. We had, I can't remember how many years ago, the first "Spring of Life," where all of these anti-abortion people besieged the city. They would camp outside women's clinics and just raise hell. They would make what is often one of the most difficult days in a young woman's life that much more difficult.

Q: You talk in the song about you yourself going to an abortion clinic.

DIFRANCO: Yes, I was eighteen, in Buffalo, and at that time there were only a few people screaming very angry things at me as I was walking into the clinic. And it was before a lot of these bombings and shootings started to occur with more frequency, so I wasn't fearing for my life at the time. But I think now I would.

The responsibility of birthing future generations rests on the shoulders of young women, and there are so many burdens that go along with that, and there's so much that a young woman faces and has to deal with that we're often on our own. And then to compound that with a fear for your life, with mortal fear, I think is just so terribly wrong. We can't see our way to actually trying to help young women in this journey, in this responsibility. Instead, we make it almost impossible.

Q: On *Up, Up, Up, Up, Up, Up* (1998), you say, "God's work isn't done by God. It's done by people." What are you driving at there?

DIFRANCO: How unfortunate it is to assign responsibility to the higher up for justice amongst people. My spirituality tends to be more in the vein of, if there is a God it exists within us, and the responsibility for justice is on our shoulders. What if we just looked to each other in this way? What if the steeples didn't all point up? What if they all pointed at us, and we had to care for each other in the way that we expect God to care for us? I'm much more interested in that.

Q: Do you consider yourself a descendant of Woody Guthrie?

DIFRANCO: Absolutely. You know, I just come from that whole community that grew out of Woody and Pete [Seeger] and the People's Songs Movement.

Q: Does being a popular performer ever get asphyxiating?

DIFRANCO: Oh, yeah. Oh, yeah. Don't get me complaining because I could go all day! One basic ridiculous assumption that I've encountered is that success equals compromise. When I first started being recognized in mainstream media, there were a lot of people crying "Sellout!" just by the automatic assumption that I must be doing something different now, that I must have sold my soul in order to be appearing in that magazine. The assumption being that political dedication equals obscurity. If there's anything I do, it's change and grow. I'm just a living being. Every year of my life I seem to learn that everything I know is wrong. I may not be the person you expect me to be, that I was two years ago, or five years ago, and I may not fit whatever image of me you have in your mind.

Q: Is that why you say on *Little Plastic Castle* (1998), "Someone call the girl police"?

DIFRANCO: Yeah, you know, I learn so much about societal, cultural dynamics through my constant growth. My whole early prehistory, you know, shaved-headed little girl in overalls and big old boots. There were very practical reasons why I looked like that. In my own life, I wanted to move away from the life I led as a teenager, playing in bars where I had long hair and looked very feminine and the attention I got was very male and very sexually oriented. There was just that vibe. You know, young chick.

I found that not conducive to my work, or to what I was trying to do. So, cut my hair off. Changed my shoes. And bang, boy, did that change the environment of my performances.

And then after many years of doing that, it's like, OK, I want hair to play with. Or, oooh, that's a pretty dress. And I remember the first time that I started walking out on stage in a dress and hearing young women screaming "Sellout!" They were just coming to know their own anger, and it hadn't deepened with an awareness that feminism is truly about women becoming themselves, and having choices, and I remember those angry, angry responses, and thinking, "Wow!"

Q: That didn't get to you?

DIFRANCO: It totally did. And there were so many things like that along the way, every little change.

Q: You never thought, screw this?

DIFRANCO: Oh, no. If anything, it makes me feel like I've got to fucking walk out there in gold lamé and pumps.

# PART 5

# Linking Arms with
# the Civil Rights Movement

In addition to being a suffragist, Belle Case La Follette was an antiracist agitator. She wrote about "the color line" several times in the magazine, and she led a campaign against segregation in the civil service in Washington, D.C. She and her husband demanded an end to lynching when the hideous practice was rampant. When she died in 1931, professor James Weldon Johnson hailed her in the following way: "Belle Case La Follette believed not only in justice for the Negro, she believed in the Negro."

The civil rights of all individuals, regardless of race, has been a central concern of the magazine, which decried the genocidal acts against Native Americans, the hostility to immigrants, the disdain toward people with disabilities.

When Japanese Americans were being rounded up into internment camps, one of the magazine's most prolific writers, Ernest L. Meyer, penned a first-person column reaching out to Sato, a Japanese American cook who had helped Meyer out in a time of need.

But it is the moral power of the black civil rights cause that rings loudest in these pages. A. Philip Randolph launches a campaign against Jim Crow in the military. Murray Kempton describes, with tremendous pathos, the trial of Emmitt Till's murderers. And Martin Luther King Jr., who wrote several times for *The Progressive* in the 1960s, lauds the students engaging in nonviolence.

Perhaps the finest piece of writing ever published in this magazine is the one by James Baldwin entitled "A Letter to My Nephew." He describes the crime of racism and how it crushes people into submission. Stripping it bare for his fifteen-year-old nephew, Baldwin writes: "You were born into a society which spelled out with brutal clarity and in as many ways as possible that you were a worthless human being."

# The Color Line

BELLE CASE LA FOLLETTE
AUGUST 23, 1913

Heretofore, in the streetcars, and, as I understand it, in the government service there has been no official discrimination against the colored people.

Since the advent of the new administration, however, there has been unquestionably a marked change, not perhaps so much in sentiment, as in the freer, stronger expression of the determination to impose upon the District of Columbia the usages of the Southern states in the matter of race segregation.

There has been talk before this of Jim Crow cars here, but it has been only talk. Very few have really believed that a movement for segregation of the races in the streetcars could be made to carry at the capital of the nation. But now the possibility is being regarded more seriously.

Segregation on the streetcars has no more foundation in right than segregation of pedestrians on the highway. It seems strange that the very ones who consider it the greatest hardship to sit next to a colored person in a streetcar entrust their children to colored nurses and eat food prepared by colored hands.

Men like Senator Vardaman and Representative Heflin are advocating with Southern vehemence the suppression of all opportunity for growth and advancement of the colored citizens of the United States. Such an announcement as follows is a proclamation of hate and strikes terror to the hearts of the colored race.

SHALL THE NEGRO RULE?

ALL OTHER QUESTIONS ARE MINIMIZED UNDER THE SHADOW OF
SOCIAL EQUALITY AND PREFERENCE FOR NEGROES
IN THE EMPLOY OF THE GOVERNMENT OF THE UNITED STATES
SENATOR JAMES K. VARDAMAN
AND OTHER PROMINENT SPEAKERS WILL ADDRESS THE PEOPLE AT A PUBLIC MEETING TO
BE HELD UNDER THE AUSPICES OF THE
NATIONAL DEMOCRATIC FAIR PLAY ASSOCIATION
WHICH STANDS FOR SEGREGATION OF THE RACES IN GOVERNMENT EMPLOYMENT, AND
"REORGANIZATION OF CIVIL SERVICE" AS DECLARED FOR IN THE NATIONAL DEMOCRATIC
PLATFORM OF 1912. AT THIS MEETING THE POLICY OF APPOINTING NEGROES TO
GOVERNMENT POSITIONS WILL BE FULLY AND FREELY DISCUSSED
AT OLD MASONIC TEMPLE, COR. 9TH AND F STS. N. W.
WASHINGTON, D.C.
WEDNESDAY NIGHT, AUGUST 6, 1913.

ADMIT BEARER                                                    AT 8 O'CLOCK

In our homes and on the streets we hear snatches of conversation that bespeak the fear and suffering caused by this new agitation. My cook asks me: "Is it true they can send us to Africa?

"What do I know of Africa?" she says, with choking voice. "I was born here. I have always lived here; and I wants to die here."

With all the traditions of a race but fifty years from slavery—indeed with no other tradition—with high officials, leaders of the party in power, talking of deportation, is it any wonder that even the younger generation are filled with apprehension and do not feel that security as to their rights which the newest immigrant enjoys?

There are over eleven thousand civil service employees working for the government. More than half of them are in the various departments here in Washington. These employees have competed with whites for their places, taking the same specified examination. I have the information direct from the secretary of the United States Civil Service Commission that except in positions where the physical qualifications are the important consideration, and in a few of the higher places drawing over eighteen hundred dollars a year, where personality is required, there is no means of knowing whether applicants are white or colored and, except for the handwriting, whether they are male or female.

The colored people are justly proud of success achieved on their own merit, like that gained in the Civil Service. This spirit, according to every ethical principle, should be encouraged by our government. It is the rock on which democracy rests. The colored people sense the meaning of any governmental discrimination against them with deep feeling, and the suggestion that the color line may be drawn in the government service has awakened a resentment I have never known before among the colored people here and, I understand, has aroused great indignation wherever the possibility of such a course has been discussed in centers of negro population elsewhere.

## Twin Evils of the Literacy Test
### Privilege and Race Discrimination
### Threaten the High Standard of This Country

LOUIS D. BRANDEIS
APRIL 1915

*Address before the New Century Club*

We, who are gathered here, know how strong are the arguments against the Literacy Bill. But let us not misconceive the situation. We are celebrating not a victory, but an escape. The danger remains. We have "scotched the snake, not killed it." It will recover from the blow; will rise again to renewed effort, and perhaps with greater strength. If we wish to protect our country from threatened danger, we too must be active, and we must be united. Effective defense demands above all things that we should perceive clearly the twin evils which are concealed under the cloak of the literacy test.

First: *The Evil of Privilege*. This immigration bill is not a literacy bill. It is an exclusion bill. It wishes to prevent others from sharing in the blessings which our country offers. If this measure had been one to insure the advance in the United States of literacy or education, then surely the people of Massachusetts would be united in its favor. From the time when the Pilgrim fathers, landing from Holland, brought with them our common school system, up to this day, when our forward-looking governor is working for university extension, the voice of Massachusetts has been emphatically and continuously for the spread and improvement of education. No state in the Union, no country in the world appropriates for education as much per capita as does Massachusetts. Massachusetts was the leader not only in the movement for free schools, but also in the movement to make attendance upon free schools compulsory.

The opposition of the great majority of the people of Massachusetts to the literacy test arises not from a failure to appreciate education, but from a recognition of its true value. Education is a means, not an end. Education is beneficent if used as an instrument of liberty, as a means to worthy ends; and as our President said, literacy is a test not of character, but of opportunity.

Second: *The Vice of the Exclusion Movement*, which is even more serious. It is not an accident that the test imposed by the restriction bill is literacy. The purpose of the bill was to restrict immigration from the Mediterranean and southwestern Europe. Literacy was adopted as a test because it was known that many of those people whom it was desired to exclude could not pass it. The movement thus springs from the conception or claim of race superiority. It involves necessarily race discrimination, and must lead to race antagonism. How dangerous such conception of race superiority becomes, the present war bears witness. The world is beginning to recognize that a lasting peace cannot come until this arrogant claim of race superiority shall have been abandoned; because the claim of race superiority is certain to be followed by the attempt of one race to dominate over the other.

Strange indeed is it that Americans should seek to foster this idea; for racial equality is the complement of democracy. Democracy rests upon two pillars: One, the principle that all men are equally entitled to life, liberty, development, and the pursuit of happiness; and the other, the conviction that such equal opportunity will most advance civilization. Aristocracy on the other hand denies these postulates. It rests upon the principle of the superman. It willingly subordinates the many to the few, and sacrifices the individual, insisting that civilization will be advanced by such sacrifices.

America, dedicated to liberty and the brotherhood of man rejected heretofore the arrogant claim that one European race is superior to another. America has believed that each race had something of peculiar value which it could contribute to the attainment

of those high ideals for which it is striving. America has believed that in differentiation, not in uniformity, lies the path of progress. Acting on this belief, it has advanced
human happiness, and it has prospered.

—LOUIS D. BRANDEIS served as a justice of the U.S. Supreme Court from 1916 to 1939.


# Murdering Negroes

ROBERT M. LA FOLLETTE
AUGUST 1919

The mobbing of harmless, helpless Negroes in the capital of this country is the nation's
everlasting shame.

The responsibility for starting the riots, which ruled Washington for days, rests
upon disorderly lawless whites.

Peaceable, unoffending colored men and boys were beaten up and murdered by
brutes who boast of our white civilization.

A reign of hysteria and terror prevailed throughout the sections of the city where
the colored population resides. They feared a "new East St. Louis." They armed themselves as best they could and barricaded their homes. There were colored soldiers
among them who had served with distinction in France, some of whom had been
wounded "fighting to make the world safe for democracy."

While the United States Senate is debating the League of Nations, which would
make us the custodians of peace and the instructors in democratic ideals to less enlightened peoples, we were murdering innocent, intelligent, God-fearing, law-abiding
colored citizens at the back door of the White House.


# Lynching Punishes the Community

ANNA HOWARD SHAW
NOVEMBER 1919

Whenever I hear the claim made that we are unfit for self-government in this country,
I feel that it is somewhat justified by our supine attitude toward lynching. A community controlled by a mob is not a civilized community, and should be placed under the
control of a more civilized part of the country. One great objection to lynching is its
effect upon the community itself, particularly upon the young, and the lawlessness
and disregard for order which underlies lynching, when nine times out of ten it is not
because of abhorrence of the crime committed, but a desire on the part of the mob to

vent barbarous natures in some form or another upon those who are weak and incapable of retaliation. I am decidedly opposed to lynching and have an utter contempt for those taking part in it.

—ANNA HOWARD SHAW was a suffragist, a civil rights leader, and the first woman ordained by
   the Methodist Protestant Church.

# The Plunder Harvest in Indian Affairs

SENATOR BURTON K. WHEELER
SEPTEMBER 1929

I am glad to say a word to you regarding the plight of the American Indian, the only 100 percent American in the United States. They were to be our wards, we their guardians. A relationship of trust was created not only as to their property but as to their persons.

Their reservations were set aside for their sole and exclusive benefit. We were to exclude undesirable persons from entering upon the same. We were to guard their property as faithfully as the father or guardian protects his son's or his ward's.

We, in some instances, gave him the exclusive right to hunt large areas of forest lands. The land on the reservation was his to be held in trust by the government for the exclusive benefit of the Indian nation. The treaty was as solemnly entered into as was the treaty between Belgium and Germany and just as unceremoniously broken, not once, not twice, but many times, and by the congresses of the United States and by the chief executives of the United States. Not by one president or by one congress, but by successive congresses, and when the Indian came to Congress and complained and asked that he be permitted to go into court and sue the government for violation of his treaties he was told, in some instances, at least, that it was against the "economy program" of the administration. And this in the face of the fact that he was not seeking to go into an Indian court, but into the white man's court, and seeking to recover only what the white man's court might adjudge was justly due and owing to him.

There are approximately 225,000 Indians in the United States under the domination of the Indian bureau, and the bureau has under its control over $1 billion of Indian property.

The health conditions among the Indians are extremely bad. Almost without exception we found that 25 percent of the Indians were affected with tuberculosis. On one reservation we were told that 50 percent of them were affected. We found no proper facilities for the treatment of this dread disease on the Indian reservations.

It is a disgrace to think that this, the wealthiest of all governments, should permit such a sordid condition as this to exist among our wards.

For seventy years or more the government has been handling the monies of the Indian tribes derived from the leases and the sales of land, from the sale of valuable timber, oils and other minerals, from the sale of tribal cattle, and yet this guardian has never given his wards an itemized statement showing how much he received or how much was paid out or what for. Not only that, but no itemized statement has ever been rendered any individual Indian showing how his account stood. If there are cases where it has been done, no superintendent knew of the same.

The bureau says they can come to the office and they will tell them if they want to know. The Indian says, "When we got to the office we can't get in or we are told to get out." This is bureaucracy run mad.

For over seventy years the Indians have been under the tutelage of the Indian bureau. When we took them over we said to them, you are uncivilized, we are civilized. There was little, if any, crime among the Indians, divorces were unheard of, they were happy and had plenty of food. Today they are hungry and sick and poor.

The school system is archaic. The schools are old firetraps, plumbing poor, ventilation poor, and until recently corporal punishment was inflicted.

The superintendent on one reservation admitted he took six girls, ages ranging around sixteen to eighteen years, made them bend over a chair while he held their dresses tightly around their bodies and beat them with a strap—the Indians said it was a piece of a harness tug. One boy, so his parents said, was beaten across his back until it bled.

The tales of brutality told by the Indians, and in some instances admitted by the agents, resembled the stories of the dark days of slavery. Many of these schoolteachers and agents asked the question, "What are you going to do with them when they won't mind, if we can't inflict corporal punishment?"

That's the same question some slave owners asked. That's the same question husbands ask when charged with assault upon their wives.

Our present enlightened civilization believes there is a better way than brute force. But many Indian agents don't belong to our present civilization. They are living in a civilization that is passed. They are politicians, most of them, who hold their jobs through the influence of some senator or representative. They are appointed to pay some political debts for, lo, these many years. He has paid them to his sorrow and to his moral, physical and economic ruin.

Secretary Wilbur was quoted in the newspapers as saying something to the effect that the Indians should be given a "pickle." The trouble is, Mr. Secretary, that the Indians have had too many pickles. It isn't pickles they need but an honest, efficient, business-like administration of their affairs. They have been exploited and plundered by Indian traders, lumber concerns, oil companies, et cetera, until they have little of their resources intact.

You have heard how the Indian bureau fed the old indigent Indians. Well, they have given them rations—$1.06 every two weeks. They have fed some of them horse meat and rancid pork until one old Indian said he had eaten horsemeat until he whinnied in his sleep.

—Senator Burton K. Wheeler represented Montana in the Senate from 1923 to 1947.

# Sato

## A Letter to a Japanese American

Ernest L. Meyer
January 17, 1942

Sato, if you are still alive, and wherever you may be, I address this to you. Perhaps I do wrong in writing, for you are a Japanese, and at the moment we must hate the Japanese, just as we must hate the Germans and the Italians and the Vichy French and the Finns and the Fascists of Norway and Rumania and many scattered precincts of the globe. Aye, there are millions upon millions of people we now must hate but especially must we hold in contempt the Japanese, for "remember Pearl Harbor!"

I do remember Pearl Harbor, and the memory hurts, for the act was evil. And it is precisely because your countrymen, Sato, at the behest of lunatic warlords who control them, committed this evil act that I feel an obligation to write, lest you and men like you—and I feel there are many—be lumped with the villains. I do remember Pearl Harbor, but I remember also Seattle and you, Sato.

Let me recall. The story is personal, perhaps unimportant, but true.

There was a season in Seattle when I was desperately down in my luck. Penniless, workless, and without a friend in a strange city. In the frantic quest for jobs, it was the habit of me and a hundred others like me to crowd into an alleyway behind the pressroom of the *Post-Intelligencer* long before daybreak. We waited for the first city edition of the morning newspaper to roll off the presses, and when the newsboys emerged with their bundles we scrambled for their wares. Under a corner arc light we flipped open the paper to the want-ad section and scanned the columns with practiced eyes. We sought some nugget of hope in the mass of fake ads and blind ads, and when we found that nugget we ran like demons in the dawn to be first in line when shop or office opened in the morning.

Many a race I lost, Sato, but in the end I won both a job and your friendship.

One dawn under the arc light, I read: "WANTED—Short-order cook; must have experience; apply night manager, Palace Restaurant." The address was a mile distant, but my legs were long, and I won the race, leading a dozen others of the hungry horde by a full block.

Breathless, disheveled, I burst into the Palace Restaurant. Fortunately the night manager was still there, behind the cashier's counter. I still held the crumpled newspaper in my hand, and I indicated the want ad.

"Experienced?" asked the manager.

I had never cooked in all my life, but I blurted desperately:

"Two years. Spokane, Walla-Walla, Portland."

"Well, I'll try you out. Eight dollars a week, plus meals, of course. Hours 6 p.m. to 6 a.m.; half day off Sunday. Go back in the kitchen, and Sato, the head cook, will tell you what to do."

I went into the kitchen, relieved, but scared. You were there, Sato, in clean cap and coat and apron, fussing over the pots on the huge range, and when you looked up at me I said simply:

"I'm the new short-order cook. I lied to the manager. I said I had experience, but I've never even boiled an egg. I lied because I'm hungry and I need a job."

I remember, Sato, that you stopped stirring something in a big copper kettle and you looked at me for what seemed a long, long time. Then you said in your excellent and precise English:

"I, too, have known hunger. Take off your coat, put on the white jacket and apron there in the closet. And then come, and I will show you."

Sato showed me. Sato corrected my awkward fumblings, taught me the shortcuts and tricks of the trade. Sato covered up for me. When the night manager looked in, later, Sato said in the pidgin he affected for some people:

"Plenty good cook, this young feller."

I knew he lied, for he had done more than half my work for me. And when the night manager, smiling, had left and I blurted out some poor words of gratitude, Sato said:

"Say no more on this matter. I could see at once when you came in that you do not hate Japanese. This gives me much happiness."

At that time, so green was I on the Coast, I did not catch the full meaning of his remark. I did not know that it was the part of all good race-conscious whites to despise the yellow men. And though I might never have shared the common contempt, my blessed ignorance eased the way toward a friendship between me and Sato which became real and enduring.

On our precious half-Sundays off, and on many early afternoons, Sato and I would meet at an agreed spot and set out on long walking trips. We explored the waterfront, remote inlets of the Sound, and the thickly wooded shores of Lake Washington. Sato always carried a camera. Ah, the spy! But if investigators had studied his negatives, as I did, they would have felt thwarted.

For on them there was naught but the silhouette of a pine branch against the sky, his favorite theme, or a pattern of tangled spars of some battered coastwise freighter, or the strange traceries that bilge and oil leave on still water, or the span of a gull's wings when it settles, stiff-legged, on the crest of a wave. Nothing suspicious there, unless groping toward fugitive beauty, too, comes under the ban.

—ERNEST L. MEYER, jailed as a conscientious objector during World War I, was a journalist who wrote for *The Progressive* in the 1930s and 1940s.

# Revolt Against Jim Crow

A. Philip Randolph
MAY 1948

It was on March 31, 1948, that Grant Reynolds and I startled the assorted members of the Senate Armed Services Committee by promising to lead a civil disobedience movement against any conscription legislation based on segregation of Negroes.

I speak of "assorted" Senators because the committee has a mixture of Southern reactionaries, Northern conservatives, and at least one Republican liberal. As the country well knows by now, it was Senator Wayne Morse of Oregon who raised persistently the legal doctrine of treason. We made it plain that legal technicalities and the prospect of dire consequences were not going to stop the movement against Jim Crow conscription which has become the last resort for self-respecting Negroes.

This new technique in race relations—this announced intention to withdraw support from discriminatory institutions and to quarantine Jim Crow, this prospect of acute humiliation in the eyes of the world—has jolted the government and the military clique into feverish efforts to convince themselves and the country that Reynolds and I did not represent Negro sentiment.

Their efforts are predestined to disappointment, fortunately. I pointed out to the committee that many Negro veterans said "never again" as they kissed Army life good-bye. Regardless of any organized movement, it is certain that there would be spontaneous resistance to a draft based on racial discrimination and segregation. But even the almost illiterate youth who have been writing me penciled notes of thanks show that they grasp the essence of our civil disobedience proposal—namely, that a Jim Crow America, and particularly a Jim Crow Army, is not the proper instrument to spread democracy and peace across the universe, and that our submission again to military segregation would be the height of folly and the acme of futility.

Regardless of one's position on peacetime conscription per se—and my union is on record against it—segregation is an unmitigated evil in itself, and if the country is going to be afflicted with the poison of militarism, the supreme irony of a Jim Crow Army must be brought to an abrupt end.

—A. Philip Randolph, a civil rights and labor rights leader, founded the Brotherhood of Sleeping Car Porters.

# Intruder in the Dust

MURRAY KEMPTON
NOVEMBER 1955

Moses Wright has been a field hand in the Mississippi Delta for as many of his sixty-four years as he has been able to walk. For the last nine of them, he has cropped shares for G. C. Frederick, a planter near Money, Mississippi.

Before his troubles came, he was as much of a success as a field Negro could hope to be in the Delta. He even owned a narrow corner of land outright; with cotton at $175 a bale, he could expect this year to make a little more than $2,000 from the land he farms for Frederick.

It is the essence of the Mississippi Delta that white people live off Negroes. This month, in Sumner, the Negro picked cotton and the white man loafed open-mouthed around the county courthouse. The prime economic law is that the Negro owns nothing. He cannot even be a bootlegger for Negroes; Leroy Collins, a Negro, appears to have made his living selling sneaky pete to other Negroes; but he acted only as agent for J. W. Milam, a white storekeeper.

By these standards, Moses Wright was almost a man of substance. Around Money, Negroes and whites alike called him "Preacher," an honorary title for good Negroes as "Judge" is for white lawyers who have escaped disbarment for twenty years.

Moses Wright was not a man with much impulse to escape Mississippi. Once every three or four years, he and his wife, Elizabeth, would travel North on the Illinois Central—W. C. Handy's "Yalla Dawg"—and spend a few days with their Chicago relatives.

Wright's relatives were an astronomical distance removed from him. The farthest away seems to have been Mamie Bradley, Elizabeth Wright's niece, a $600-a-year federal worker living in a lower-middle-class section of South Chicago. She had been born Mamie Carthan in Webb, Mississippi, and been taken north when she was two. She was the widow of Louis Till, who had been killed in the war; their son Emmett was now fourteen.

Emmett Till was an average schoolboy who seems to have had most of the ambitions of the new Negro: he planned to go to college and learn a skilled trade, both expectations far above the cotton fields which were Moses Wright's destiny. One day, early in August, Elizabeth Wright suggested that Mrs. Bradley give Emmett a vacation in Mississippi. She was very happy with the invitation. On August 18 she went home early to help Emmett pack. While he was getting his clothes ready, she says she explained to him that Mississippi was not like Chicago, and that he must be especially polite to any white man he met and, in any crisis, be ready to go down on his knees.

Emmett appears to have been quite gay about the approaching adventure. As he was leaving, he picked up his father's old beat-silver ring, with its initials "L.T."; it had always been too big for him; he showed his mother that his finger was now large enough to wear it.

"Gee," she said to him, "you're getting to be a big boy now."

There were six boys at the Wright house in Mississippi. Their life appears to have been narrow enough to make any relief exciting. On Wednesday night, August 25, Moses Wright took them to church according to custom; he had hardly bowed his head there when the boys had sneaked out and taken his old car.

They rode up to Money, which is a row of stores and filling stations along the railroad track in the dust and there Emmett Till went into a store to buy a few cents worth of bubble gum. The store he chose was not one frequented by the Wrights; it was owned by Roy Bryant, a smoky-eyed young paratrooper, and the son of a fecund clan with a reputation for brawling, whose chief was his huge, balding thirty-six-year-old half-brother J. W. Milam. Bryant was an ill-tempered, edgy man and a merchant with small appeal to quiet customers like Moses Wright.

The night Emmett Till went there for his bubble gum, Roy Bryant was out of town, and the store was tended by his wife, Caroline, a high school beauty already chipping and fading at twenty-one. She and Emmett were alone in the store for a few minutes, and she is the last surviving witness to his conduct. With the Bryants in crisis, Caroline testified that Emmett, whom she described as a man, made her an indecent proposal. The only undisputed fact seems to be that he left the store with a suggestive "goodbye" and that, when he was in the car and she came out, he emitted a woowoo whistle.

It was a very small gesture, but one which Emmett's country cousins failed to report to Moses Wright, if only because it was part of an escapade which would have brought his wrath upon all of them. Moses Wright got his official notice of Emmett's capital crime at two o'clock the next Saturday morning.

He had come home from an evening at Greenwood and had been asleep an hour when he was awakened by a voice outside his cabin shouting, "Preacher, Preacher!" He arose to answer the summons; as he was going to his door, the voice went on:

"It's Mr. Bryant. I've come for the boy that did the talking at Money."

When he opened the door, there was J. W. Milam standing with a flashlight and a pistol. "I'd know Mr. Milam if I seen him in Texas," said Moses Wright afterwards. "I want the boy from Chicago," Milam said. Moses Wright took the invaders back to the bedroom where Emmett Till was sleeping with Moses Wright's son Simeon. J. W. Milam shook him awake and asked if he was the boy from Chicago. Emmett Till answered "Yes," and J. W. Milam said, "Don't say 'yes' to me or I'll whup hell out of you."

At the door, Elizabeth Wright pleaded for Emmett; she promised to give Mr. Milam any money he wanted. Moses Wright stood on the porch; there was a third man out there in the column of blackness. Afterwards, out of six decades of training as a field Negro, Moses Wright said that it seemed to him that the two raiders treated the third companion as though he "were a colored man." They did not know Moses Wright; they did not even know Emmett Till's name; they were to learn it from the newspapers later; they had been led to their objective by a Negro. In the Delta, even the nightriders have their body-servants.

And then Moses Wright entered a plea for Emmett that was rooted in his sense of place and tradition. He asked Milam just to take Emmett out and whip him. "The boy don't look like he's got good sense," he said. But Milam pushed Emmett out on the porch; as he went off, he turned and asked Moses Wright how old he was. Moses Wright said sixty-four; and Milam asked him if he knew anybody present. "'No,' he said, "'I don't know nobody' and they said I'd better not or I wouldn't live to be sixty-five."

They took Emmett out in the dark; J. W. Milam flashed his light on the boy's face out by the car. Moses Wright, standing on the porch, heard a "light" voice from the rear of the car say, yes, that was the boy; and then the car, with lights out, was gone down the road to Money.

Moses Wright went back in his house, and the boys told him what had happened in Money on Wednesday night. By now, Elizabeth Wright was hysterical; Wright drove her to Sumner for the Chicago train. Every day, for the next two weeks, she would write and tell him to concede defeat and come north.

But Emmett was gone and Moses Wright had to stay to find him. Afterwards, alone in his house with his gun, waiting for his crop to come in, he would explain his revolt only by saying that, if he had kept quiet, "They'd think I done it."

And so, that same Sunday afternoon, Moses Wright drove to Greenwood and told the story of Emmett Till's abduction to Sheriff George Smith. Bryant was a friend of Smith's; and, as a friend, Smith drove out to Bryant to ask him about the old Negro's complaint.

Smith found Bryant asleep in the back of the store on the hot Sunday afternoon which had followed his long Saturday night. They talked as friends in the sheriff's car; Smith asked Bryant whether he had taken a colored boy out of one of the cabins the night before. Bryant answered that he had brought a boy back to his store, decided that he was the wrong boy, and then turned him loose to find his way home. Thereafter, said Roy Bryant, the outraged husband, he had played cards all night with his kin.

The sheriff could do nothing but arrest J. W. Milam and Roy Bryant for kidnapping. They sat in Greenwood jail for three days while the rain came driving down. Moses Wright clung to his cabin; around noon Wednesday, Deputy Sheriff John Ed Cothran came there to report that a body which could be Emmett Till's had been found in the Tallahatchie River.

Moses Wright went out to the muddy Tallahatchie and was shown a body lying face down in a boat with its head beaten in. A sheriff's deputy turned it over, and Moses Wright saw it was Emmett. The ring the boy brought down from Chicago was still on the body's finger; the Negro undertaker pulled if off and gave it to Moses Wright.

The body lay on a slab in Greenwood for a day. A policeman took its picture and the print was buried somewhere in the city files. Dr. L. D. Otken, a local pathologist, came to certify death; he testified with considerable vehemence later that he hadn't touched it and had no views as to the cause of death. That was the closest the county came to an inquest; then the body was turned over to Moses Wright with the understanding that it would be buried at once in the graveyard at Money.

But then Mrs. Bradley called to tell him to ship the body to Chicago. He sent it off and went back to his cotton, seemingly unaware that, by now, Emmett Till's name cried out in every newspaper and that, just because he had gone to the sheriff to clear himself with Mamie Bradley, his life could never be what it had been.

J. W. Milam and Roy Bryant came to trial on Monday, September 19, in Sumner's fetid second-floor courtroom, bulging to its dirty lime-green walls with its all-white jury panel and with Bryants. They came with their little boys, who babbled and tottered and tugged at their daddies and from time to time aimed their empty water pistols at deputy sheriffs and went "boomboom." It was so hot that J. W. Milam said once that it was hard not to feel mean on a day like this one; but he is an indulgent father, and, from time to time, he would tickle his son Billy and both would laugh.

The courtroom was so crowded that there was no room for Moses Wright to sit down; he stood in the back, a thin old man, in a tieless shirt and his glasses and old, cracked shoes. There was a concerted, metronomic ballet of waving fans between him and the judge's desk before which Smith and District Attorney Gerald Chatham struggled to pick a jury which might, by some thin chance, believe Moses Wright.

On Wednesday morning, Moses Wright was called to the stand. He sat in that squeaking old chair and told the prosecutor, who kept calling him "Uncle Mose," what had happened on that Saturday night hardly three weeks before.

The moment came when he was asked to point out J. W. Milam as the man who came to get Emmett Till. Moses Wright stood up; he raised himself on his tiptoes, thrust out a skinny finger, and looked full into the heavy, violent face before him and said, "There he is." And, for good measure, as if to compound his crime, he turned a little and threw out the finger again and said, "There's Mr. Bryant." He seemed almost jaunty about it, but he sat down and thrust his body against the chair back, as though his conditioned flesh was rebelling against his new brave spirit; and then it was possible to understand that he was defying not just Milam but his own oldest habits.

Then he was offered up to Sidney Carlton for bulldozing, and the voice of the defense attorney was the voice of every white overseer that Moses Wright has heard since boyhood. Carlton roared and Moses Wright's rebellious flesh shrank back from habit, but his tongue forced him to the wildest piece of defiance a Delta Negro can accomplish; he stopped saying "Sir," and began answering Carlton's every lash with a "That's right" which was naked at the end. He ran the hardest half hour of the hardest life possible for an American, and in the end he clung to his story. Carlton let him up, and he went back to the witness room where at least there was a seat for him.

In the courtyard Moses Wright was saying that he'd try to hang on in Mississippi: "I'm so scrounged down in this country that I hate to leave it." Upstairs the defense was putting on three white witnesses, including the sheriff who had turned the body over to Moses Wright, all loudly swearing that it couldn't have been Emmett Till's body.

The defense was restrained; it had, after all, very little to worry about. There was only the detail of the ring on the body, and this was explained, very sedately, to the jury by J. W. Whitten, of defense counsel, a thin young man of infinite delicacy, who under ordinary circumstances wouldn't spit on the peckerwoods before him.

Whitten said his theory was that Bryant and Milam had sent the Till boy home just as they said they had. Moses Wright had driven down the road and met Emmett coming back. He had picked him up and gone in search of one of those enemies of good race relations who abound in Mississippi as they do in Chicago. And these people had planted an old corpse in the river with Emmett's ring on its finger.

The Delta Negro must have a kind of chemical sense of danger; there could be no other reason why, while the genteel young Mr. Whitten was thus putting the finger on him, Moses Wright went into the sheriff's office, collected his witness fee, and walked down the road, across the bridge that leads out of town.

The jury was out an hour and eight minutes and came back with the appointed not guilty verdict. Bryant and Milam heard it with cigars in their mouths, and thereafter luxuriated twenty minutes in the courtroom for the news cameras. There was no demonstration, partly because Judge Swango forbade it and partly perhaps because everyone except J. W. Milam was a little ashamed of himself.

Moses Wright went back to his cabin; he still hoped to gather his crop. A few days after the trial, when all the reporters had gone and the television cameramen with them, five carloads of white men drove down the road from Money and stopped at his cabin and raised the old cry of "Preacher, Preacher." Moses Wright hid in the fields; the next day he went to Chicago for whatever the city holds for a man whose hands know nothing but cotton. His crop appears to be a dead loss.

—MURRAY KEMPTON, journalist and social critic, wrote for the *New York Post*, the *New Republic*, *Newsday*, and the *New York Review of Books*. He won the Pulitzer Prize in 1985.

# The Burning Truth in the South

MARTIN LUTHER KING JR.
MAY 1960

An electrifying movement of Negro students has shattered the placid surface of campuses and communities across the South. Though confronted in many places by hoodlums, police guns, tear gas, arrests, and jail sentences, the students tenaciously continue to sit down and demand equal service at variety store lunch counters, and extend their protest from city to city. In communities like Montgomery, Alabama, the whole student body rallied behind expelled students and staged a walkout while state government intimidation was unleashed with a display of military force appropriate to a wartime invasion. Nevertheless, the spirit of self-sacrifice and commitment remains firm, and the state governments find themselves dealing with students who have lost the fear of jail and physical injury.

It is no overstatement to characterize these events as historic. Never before in the United States had so large a body of students spread a struggle over so great an area in pursuit of a goal of human dignity and freedom.

One may wonder why the present movement started with the lunch counters. The answer lies in the fact that here the Negro has suffered indignities and injustices that cannot be justified or explained. Almost every Negro has experienced the tragic inconveniences of lunch counter segregation. He cannot understand why he is welcomed with open arms at most counters in the store, but is denied service at a certain counter because it happens to be selling food and drink. In a real sense the "sit ins" represent more than a demand for service; they represent a demand for respect.

It is absurd to think of this movement as being initiated by Communists or some other outside group. This movement is an expression of the longing of a new Negro for freedom and human dignity. These students were anchored to lunch counter seats by the accumulated indignities of days gone by and the boundless aspirations of generations yet unborn.

In this new method of protest a new philosophy provided a special undergirding—the philosophy of nonviolence. It was first modestly and quietly projected in one community, Montgomery, when the threat of violence became real in the bus protest. But it burst from this limited arena, and was embraced by masses of people across the nation with fervor and consistency.

The key significance of the student movement lies in the fact that from its inception, everywhere, it has combined direct action and nonviolence.

This quality has given it the extraordinary power and discipline which every thinking person observes. It has discredited the adversary, who knows how to deal with force but is bewildered and panicky in the face of the new techniques. Time will reveal that the students are learning lessons not contained in their textbooks. Hundreds have already been expelled, fined, imprisoned, and brutalized, and the numbers continue to grow. But with the punishments, something more is growing. A generation of young people has come out of decades of shadows to face naked state power; it has lost its fears, and experienced the majestic dignity of a direct struggle for its own liberation. These young people have connected up with their own history—the slave revolts, the incomplete revolution of the Civil War, the brotherhood of colonial colored men in Africa and Asia. They are an integral part of the history which is reshaping the world, replacing a dying order with modern democracy.

The outcome of the present struggle will be some time in unfolding, but the line of its direction is clear. It is a final refutation of the time-honored theory that the Negro prefers segregation. It would be futile to deplore, as many do, the tensions accompanying the social changes. Tension and conflict are not alien nor abnormal to growth but are the natural results of the process of changes. A revolution is occurring in both the social order and the human mind. One hundred eighty-four years ago a bold group of men signed the Declaration of Independence. If their struggle had been lost they had signed their own death warrant. Nevertheless, though explicitly regretting that King George had forced them to this extreme by a long "train of abuses," they resolutely acted and a great new society was born. The Negro students, their parents, and their allies are acting today in that imperishable tradition.

—MARTIN LUTHER KING JR., the legendary civil rights leader, won the Nobel Peace Prize in 1964.

## "I Will Keep My Soul"

JAMES FARMER
NOVEMBER 1961

On May 4 of this year, I left Washington, D.C., with twelve other persons on a risky journey into the South. Seven of us were Negro, and six were white. Riding in two regularly scheduled buses, one Greyhound, the other Trailways, traveling beneath overcast skies, our little band—the original Freedom Riders—was filled with expectations of storms almost certain to come before the journey was ended.

Now, six months later, as all the world knows, the fire-gutted shell of one bus lies in an Alabama junkyard, and some of the people who almost died with it are still suffering prolonged illnesses. A dozen Freedom Riders nearly gave up their lives under the fierce hammering of fists, clubs, and iron pipes in the hands of hysterical mobs. Many of the victims will carry permanent scars. One of them lies in a Detroit hospital critically ill from a cerebral hemorrhage, a direct result of the beating he took. Others have lost their jobs or have been expelled from school because of their participation in the rides. More than 350 men and women have been jailed in a half dozen states for doing what the Supreme Court of the United States had already said they had a right to do.

Who were the Freedom Riders?

By what right did we seek to "meddle in the South's business"? Ever since the election of Rutherford B. Hayes to the Presidency in 1876, and the bargain with the South which it entailed, the Southern states have maintained that what they do with the Negro is their own business, and "outsiders" have no right to interfere. The Freedom Riders rejected this essentially states-right doctrine of race relations. None of us, in the North or in the South, can afford the moral luxury of unconcern about injustice.

So we came from all over the country, from both races and of all ages, to test compliance with the law, to exercise the right of all Americans to use all transportation facilities with the dignity of equality, to shake Americans out of their apathy on this issue and expose the real character of segregation to the pitiless scrutiny of a nation's conscience.

Outsiders? As Americans, from whatever state, all of us are Mississippians and Minnesotans, Carolinians and Californians, Alabamans and Arizonans. No American can afford to ignore the burning bus and the bloody heads of the mob's victims. Who can fail to be stirred by the new convicts for conscience, black and white, who walked with pride into Southern jails, especially in Mississippi, surrendering their own personal freedom in the struggle for a greater freedom for everyone?

Jail at best is neither a romantic nor a pleasant place, and Mississippi jails are no exception. The first twenty-seven Freedom Riders to arrive in Jackson saw the inside of two different jails and two different prisons—the Jackson City Jail, the Hinds County Jail, the Hinds County Prison Farm, and the State Penitentiary at Parchman. Jails are not a new experience for many of the Riders but the Freedom Riders were definitely a new experience for Mississippi jails. For the first time, penal authorities in the citadel of segregation had a glimpse of the new Negro and the emancipated white. I do not think these jailers will ever be quite the same again after their experience. Nor will the other prisoners, black and white, be the same again, after having seen in the flesh men and women who do not believe segregation to be in the very nature of things, and who are willing to defy it.

Prison authorities frequently said, and really seemed to believe, that other Negro prisoners like things the way they are and have no sympathy with us, and that it was for our own protection that we were isolated from them. However, whenever the guards were not present, the Negro trustees went out of their way to show their sympathy by word and deed. "Keep up the good work," one said. "I admire you guys and what you are doing," said another. "I wish I could do the same thing, but I have to do what these people tell me to do." They smuggled newspapers in to us, delivered notes and messages between our cellblock and that of the girl Freedom Riders, and passed on rumors which they had heard in the jail or in the community.

One night at the county jail, a voice called up from the cellblock beneath us, where other Negro prisoners were housed. "Upstairs!" the anonymous prisoner shouted. We replied, "Downstairs!" "Upstairs!" replied the voice. "Sing your freedom song." And the Freedom Riders sang. We sang old folk songs and gospel songs to which new words had been written, telling of the Freedom Ride and its purpose. We sang new words to old labor songs, too. One stanza rang out: "They say in Hinds County no neutrals have they met. You're either for the Freedom Ride or you 'torn' for Ross Barnett?" Then the downstairs prisoners, whom the jailers had said were our enemies, sang for us. The girl Freedom Riders, in another wing of the jail, joined in the Freedom Ride songs, and for the first time in history, the Hinds County jail rocked with singing of songs of freedom and brotherhood.

After a rumor of our imminent transfer to the state penitentiary had reached us, the jailer came quietly to our Freedom Riders cellblock. He called me, and we stood there with the bars between us, chatting. He did most of the talking. He told me about his family, his wife, and four or five children—the good records they had made in schools, including Ole Miss. He told me of his son's prowess in sports and of the children's marriages and his grandchildren. He told me, too, of his dislike of violence, and of his children's upbringing in that regard. The jailer stood there talking for more than an hour, in the first conversation we had had with him. This, I am sure, was his way of saying goodbye, and of telling us that he respects the Freedom Riders, and that whatever unpleasantness we might meet at the state penitentiary would be something of which he did not approve.

Mississippians, born into segregation, are human too. The Freedom Riders' aim is not only to stop the practice of segregation, but somehow to reach the common humanity of our fellowmen and bring it to the surface where they can act on it themselves. This is a basic motive behind the Freedom Rides, and nonviolence is the key to its realization.

America saw also the Freedom Riders' challenge to the traditions and fears which have immobilized so many Negroes in Dixie. In terminals in the South, and on the buses, many Negro passengers took the Freedom Riders' cue and dared to sit and ride "first class." This was another purpose of the Rides themselves: to break down the voluntary submission of Negroes to racial injustice, a submission created by generations of suppression with the rope and with fire and with economic reprisal. As I entered the white waiting room in one terminal in the South, a Negro woman passenger from the same bus caught my eye and anxiously beckoned me to follow her into the dingy but safe colored section. Moments later, when she saw me served at the lunch counter in the white section, she joined me for a cup of coffee.

In Jackson, Mississippi, forty-one Negro citizens of that community joined the Freedom Riders, ending up in their hometown jails. Now out on appeal bond, they report many threats of reprisals. But there is a new spirit among Negroes in Jackson. People are learning that in a nonviolent war like ours, as in any other war, there must be suffering. Jobs will be lost, mortgages will be foreclosed, loans will be denied, persons will be hurt, and some may die. This new spirit was expressed well by one Freedom Rider in the Mississippi state penitentiary at Parchman. The guards threatened repeatedly, as a reprisal for our insistence upon dignity, to take away our mattresses. "Come and get my mattress," he shouted. "I will keep my soul."

—JAMES FARMER, civil rights leader, founded the Congress of Racial Equality.

# A Letter to My Nephew

JAMES BALDWIN
DECEMBER 1962

Dear James:

I have begun this letter five times and torn it up five times. I keep seeing your face, which is also the face of your father and my brother. I have known both of you all your lives and have carried your daddy in my arms and on my shoulders, kissed him and spanked him and watched him learn to walk. I don't know if you have known anybody from that far back, if you have loved anybody that long, first as an infant, then as a child, then as a man. You gain a strange perspective on time and human pain and effort.

Other people cannot see what I see whenever I look into your father's face, for behind your father's face as it is today are all those other faces which were his. Let him laugh and I see a cellar your father does not remember and a house he does not remember and I hear in his present laughter his laughter as a child. Let him curse and I remember his falling down the cellar steps and howling and I remember with pain his tears which my hand or your grandmother's hand so easily wiped away, but no one's hand can wipe away those tears he sheds invisibly today which one hears in his laughter and in his speech and in his songs.

I know what the world has done to my brother and how narrowly he has survived it and I know, which is much worse, and this is the crime of which I accuse my country and my countrymen and for which neither I nor time nor history will ever forgive them, that they have destroyed and are destroying hundreds of thousands of lives and do not know it and do not want to know it. One can be—indeed, one must strive to become—tough and philosophical concerning destruction and death, for this is what most of mankind has been best at since we have heard of war; remember, I said most of mankind, but it is not permissible that the authors of devastation should also be innocent. It is the innocence which constitutes the crime.

Now, my dear namesake, these innocent and well-meaning people, your countrymen, have caused you to be born under conditions not far removed from those described for us by Charles Dickens in the London of more than a hundred years ago. I hear the chorus of the innocents screaming, "No, this is not true. How bitter you are," but I am writing this letter to you to try to tell you something about how to handle them, for most of them do not yet really know that you exist. I know the conditions under which you were born for I was there. Your countrymen were not there and haven't made it yet. Your grandmother was also there and no one has ever accused her of being bitter. I suggest that the innocent check with her. She isn't hard to find. Your countrymen don't know that she exists either, though she has been working for them all their lives.

Well, you were born; here you came, something like fifteen years ago, and though your father and mother and grandmother, looking about the streets through which they were carrying you, staring at the walls into which they brought you, had every reason to be heavy-hearted, yet they were not, for here you were, big James, named for me. You were a big baby. I was not. Here you were to be loved. To be loved, baby, hard at once and forever to strengthen you against the loveless world. Remember that. I know how black it looks today for you. It looked black that day too. Yes, we were trembling. We have not stopped trembling yet, but if we had not loved each other, none of us would have survived, and now you must survive because we love you and for the sake of your children and your children's children.

This innocent country set you down in a ghetto in which, in fact, it intended that you should perish. Let me spell out precisely what I mean by that for the heart of the matter is here and the crux of my dispute with my country. You were born where you were born and faced the future that you faced because you were black and for no other reason. The limits to your ambition were thus expected to be settled. You were born into a society which spelled out with brutal clarity and in as many ways as possible that you were a worthless human being. You were not expected to aspire to excellence. You were expected to make peace with mediocrity. Wherever you have turned, James, in your short time on this earth, you have been told where you could go and what you could do and how you could do it, where you could live and whom you could marry.

I know your countrymen do not agree with me here and I hear them saying, "You exaggerate." They do not know Harlem and I do. So do you. Take no one's word for anything, including mine, but trust your experience. Know whence you came. If you know whence you came, there is really no limit to where you can go. The details and symbols of your life have been deliberately constructed to make you believe what white people say about you. Please try to remember that what they believe, as well as what they do and cause you to endure, does not testify to your inferiority, but to their inhumanity and fear.

Please try to be clear, dear James, through the storm which rages about your youthful head today, about the reality which lies behind the words "acceptance" and "integration." There is no reason for you to try to become like white men, and there is no basis whatever for their impertinent assumption that they must accept you. The really terrible thing, old buddy, is that you must accept them, and I mean that very seriously. You must accept them and accept them with love, for these innocent people have no other hope. They are in effect still trapped in a history which they do not understand and until they understand it, they cannot be released from it. They have had to believe for many years, and for innumerable reasons, that black men are inferior to white men.

Many of them indeed know better, but as you will discover, people find it very difficult to act on what they know. To act is to be committed and to be committed is to be in danger. In this case the danger in the minds and hearts of most white Americans is the loss of their identity. Try to imagine how you would feel if you woke up one morning to find the sun shivering and all the stars aflame. You would be frightened because it is out of the order of nature. Any upheaval in the universe is terrifying because it so profoundly attacks one's sense of one's own reality. Well, the black man has functioned in the white man's world as a fixed star, as an immovable pillar, and as he moves out of his place, heaven and earth are shaken to their foundations.

You don't be afraid. I said it was intended that you should perish in the ghetto, perish by never being allowed to go beyond and behind the white man's definition, by never being allowed to spell your proper name. You have, and many of us have, defeated this intention and by a terrible law, a terrible paradox, those innocents who believed that your imprisonment made them safe are losing their grasp of reality. But these men are your brothers, your lost younger brothers, and if the word "integration" means anything, this is what it means, that we with love shall force our brothers to see themselves as they are, to cease fleeing from reality and begin to change it, for this is your home, my friend. Do not be driven from it. Great men have done great things here and will again and we can make America what America must become.

It will be hard, James, but you come from sturdy peasant stock, men who picked cotton, dammed rivers, built railroads, and in the teeth of the most terrifying odds, achieved an unassailable and monumental dignity. You come from a long line of great poets, some of the greatest poets since Homer. One of them said, "The very time I thought I was lost, my dungeon shook and my chains fell off."

You know and I know that the country is celebrating one hundred years of freedom one hundred years too early. We cannot be free until they are free. God bless you, James, and Godspeed.

Your uncle,

James

—JAMES BALDWIN, essayist, novelist, playwright, poet, and civil rights advocate, wrote *Go Tell It on the Mountain, Notes of a Native Son, Another Country,* and the essay "The Fire Next Time."


# *"Arab"*

## Did You Flinch?

PAT AUFDERHEIDE

AUGUST 1984

I thought I was taking a part-time job, but it turned out I was joining a crusade. What's more, everyone knew it but me.

You, too, might have known enough to warn me about what I was getting into. To find out, just take this quick test: "Arab." Did you flinch?

Last summer, I was hired to edit a newsletter for one of the welter of small "cause" groups in Washington, the American-Arab Anti-Discrimination Committee (ADC). It was a freelance writer's dream: well-defined work for a few hours a week, interesting subject matter, access to a great copying machine.

The first hint that this was no ordinary job was the packet of clippings I waded through to assemble the first newsletter. They were gross caricatures of Arab sheiks and harem girls—all from staid mainstream press outlets.

These cartoons were enough to persuade me of the need for an ADC. The organization had been founded in 1981, after former Senator James Abourezk of South Dakota was shocked by the casual defamation of the Arabs in the FBI's Abscam sting. As he kept asking, "What if they'd called it Jewscam?"

So ADC had been established to defend the rights of Arab Americans. There are more than a million people—some say more than two million—of Arab descent in the United States. Most of them have been here for two and three generations, although some—like the Yemenis who constitute the second largest ethnic group among California's migrant workers—have arrived in the last decade. Few Arab Americans even own oil stock. Most are tired of hiding their ancestry, or of being treated as political scapegoats if they admit it. They would like to be seen as themselves, not as "the other side" of Jewish or Israeli interests in the United States.

The political implications sank in when I covered a story for the newsletter. Philadelphia's front-running mayoral candidate, J. Wilson Goode, had attended a fundraiser at the home of an Arab American. The next day, he found himself under attack as "pro-Arab." It didn't matter that his host and fellow guests were citizens; to Goode's opponent, they might as well have been PLO fighters—and Philadelphia might as well have been Tel Aviv.

Being Arab American is ipso facto a political statement, and this peculiar circumstance extends to anyone who works with Arabs. My contract assignment for the ADC turned into an embarrassment for many casual acquaintances.

"What are you up to these days?"

"I've got a job working for the American-Arab—"

"You what?"

It wasn't that they had anything against Arabs; they just couldn't believe what I had said. It made them nervous. I was committing an indiscretion. In Washington, you can work for the CIA and no one will blink an eye, but you can't say "Arab" without causing a stir. People always wait for me to excuse or explain my connection.

"Call me Monday to check that copy," I said to the editor of a film magazine. "I'll be at the office of the American-Arab Anti-Disc—"

"You're working where?" Pause. "Pat, we're on different sides of this. I couldn't work for those people."

"Oh, sure you could," I said, brimming with naiveté. "It's an anti-defamation group. You know, ethnics. Think 'Italian.' Equality of opportunity."

"I just have very strong feelings about the Middle East. I think we ought to just get out and stay out of there, let them all blow themselves up."

"But these are Americans," I said. "They eat Wheaties for breakfast. They read about Lebanon in the newspapers. Scratch them they bleed, and so on." But I had made him nervous. We disconnected, mutually disgruntled, having slammed ourselves up against the limits of liberalism a little too early in the day.

Working for "Arabs" is bad for a journalist's business. With that one word, you lose credibility. Suddenly, everything you do comes under close scrutiny. For instance, while writing a short children's book on the life of Anwar Sadat for a series on political leaders, I weathered several anxious telephone calls cautioning me "not to go overboard on the other side." No matter how I tried, I never could find out just what the other side's tack on Sadat would be—or even who was on the other side. But I did find out that after my manuscript had passed through several layers of approval, one editor asked, "Do you think we ought to check this with the Israelis?" Let's not even ask which Israelis he would check with. Let's ask, would this editor check a biography of Menachem Begin with "the Egyptians"?

I haven't had so much trouble telling people what I'm up to since I took a job at *In These Times*, which proudly calls itself "the independent socialist newspaper." Then, too, people looked at me pleadingly—"Don't try to convert me, please!"—when I told them what I did for a living. That, too, was a job for which I was expected to apologize.

I figured *In These Times* had given me great training for my work with the ADC, but a talk with Palestinian literary critic Edward Said, whom I had first met through *In These Times*, showed me the difference. He wasn't at all surprised to hear about the usual reaction to my bombshell announcement.

"Well, I'm used to it," I said confidently. "All those years at a socialist paper, you know."

"Yeah," he said, with a little laugh. "But now you're a socialist with leprosy."

—PAT AUFDERHEIDE, a senior editor at *In These Times*, is the director of social media at American University.

# The New Bigotry

MIKE ERVIN
DECEMBER 1984

Bigotry isn't dead, though it has taken on a more subtle identity. The old shrines of passionate ignorance, the "Colored Only" fountains and washrooms of the South, have been replaced by new monuments to intolerance.

The new bigotry isn't easily spotted because it isn't based on hatred for a particular race or sex. Few trip the blind or make fun of the "less fortunate." But cruelty is just one kind of conditioned ignorance that breeds bigotry. Even after living for twenty-eight years with a disability, I continue to run across new variations of the old theme.

Sometimes it's absurdly amusing. While buying yogurt in the grocery store, I'll notice someone observing me with a star-struck smile that says, "He's buying yogurt! How remarkable!" My purchase is seen as a superhuman feat; surely my disability must be so unspeakably dreadful that only superhuman strength could enable me to pick up a container of Dannon.

Others view me as subhuman, and my disability becomes synonymous with absolute physical and emotional dependency. The disabled are seen as orphaned infants who must be fed, hosed down, and protected.

Rarely am I viewed as just plain human. Bigotry works that way, sanctimonious indifference and inaction: It's OK to deny basic dignity to people who aren't exactly human.

When the Reagan Administration purged the Social Security disability rolls of what it regarded as lazy freeloaders, more than twenty of the hundreds of thousands who were miraculously cured of their disabilities by Presidential decree chose suicide. One man set himself on fire in front of a Social Security office.

These sacrifices on the altar of the new bigotry don't spark widespread indignation. The disabled can't even get on the bus, and there is little outcry.

The disability rights movement seems radical only because the bigotry it fights is so entrenched.

In a society based on hate, love is radical.

In a society based on oppression, freedom is radical.

In a society based on paternalism, independence is radical.

—MIKE ERVIN, a freelance writer and producer, is a disability rights activist with ADAPT.

## The Underclass Myth

ADOLPH L. REED JR.
AUGUST 1991

In recent years the image of an urban "underclass" has become the central representation of poverty in American society. In less than a decade the underclass has taken hold of the public imagination, and has come to shape policymakers' agendas concerning issues of race, urban decay, and social welfare. But what is the underclass? What is so compelling about that image? What is its significance in American political life?

The underclass idea rests on fuzzy and disturbing assumptions about poor people, poverty, and the world in which both are reproduced. Those assumptions amount to tacit—and sometimes explicit—claims regarding the defective nature of poor people's motivations, moral character, and behavior. They appeal to hoary prejudices of race, gender, and class.

If a thirty-five-year-old lawyer decides to have a baby without seal of approval from church or state or enduring male affiliation, we do not consider her to be acting pathologically; we may even laud her independence and refusal to knuckle under to patriarchal conventions. Why does such a birth become pathological when it occurs in the maternity ward in Lincoln Hospital in the South Bronx, say, rather than within the pastel walls of an alternative birthing center?

If a woman's decision expresses pathology because she makes it in poverty, then we have fallen into a tautology: she is poor because she is pathological because she is poor.

Female household-heading, for example, can result from a number of circumstances entirely beyond the control of women whose lives are compressed into that label. The same applies to unemployment or underemployment, and even long-term status as a welfare recipient can stem completely from impersonal forces. Characterizing those phenomena as behavior reveals a zeal for validating the underclass concept, and a fundamental inclination to seek the sources of poverty in deficiencies of individuals.

The underclass notion resonates with the ahistorical individualism rampant in the Reagan-Bush era. As a corollary, it is attractive to many petit bourgeois blacks because it flatters their success by comparison and, through the insipid role-model rhetoric, allows fawning over the allegedly special, tutelary role of the black middle class.

The idea of a behaviorally defined underclass also affirms an ensemble of racial and class prejudices that lurk beneath an apparently innocuous, certainly stupid tendency to reduce the social world to aggregates of good people and bad people. Simply, good people are people like "us," bad people are not, and the same behavior is assessed differently depending on the category into which the perpetrator falls.

An eighteen-year-old drug courier with a monogrammed BMW is pathological; an arbitrageur who strays too far onto the wrong side of legality is too clever for his own good—the stuff of tragedy. Dependency on AFDC breeds sloth and pathology; dependency on military contracts, tax abatements, or FHA loans does a patriotic service for the country, incubates family values, and so forth.

Finally, the underclass notion may receive the greatest ideological boost from pure sexism. For drug-crazed, lawless black and Hispanic men, the companion image is the so-called cycle of poverty, which focuses on women's living and reproductive practices as the transmission belt that drives the cycle.

The rhetoric of "family values," and of "disorganization," "deterioration," and "disintegration" stigmatizes female-headed households, which now are home to a majority of American children, and applies a hierarchy of propriety to the conjugal arrangements within which women might give birth. Of the master list of empirical indicators of pathology, most are observable only in women.

We are already seeing the policy fruit that this imagery bears. A judge in Kansas City has ordered children to use their absent fathers' names, presumably to strengthen obligation by establishing ownership. A Kansas state legislator has argued that impoverished women should be induced to accept Norplant birth-control implants as a way to hold down welfare costs and cut the size of the recipient population.

State welfare departments have taken up marriage brokering, as in a Wisconsin plan to offer cash inducements for women who marry their way off AFDC and to cut benefits for "unwed teenage mothers." These moves demonstrate unambiguously the repressive, antifeminist outlook lurking beneath the focus on family.

It is imperative to reject all assumptions that poor people are behaviorally or attitudinally different from the rest of American society. Some percentage of all Americans take drugs, fight in families, and abuse or neglect children. If the behavior exists across lines of class, race, and opportunity, then it cannot reasonably be held to produce poverty. If it does not cause poverty, therefore, we do not need to focus on it at all in the context of policy-oriented discussion about poverty.

We should fight for policy changes that will open opportunity structures: support for improving access to jobs, housing, schooling, real drug rehabilitation of the sort available to the relatively well off. A focus on behavior, after all, leads into a blind alley in policy terms. If we say that poor people are poor because they have bad values, we let government off the hook, even though conscious government policy—for example, in the relations between support for metropolitan real estate speculation and increasing homelessness, malnutrition, and infant mortality—is directly implicated in causing poverty.

I do not want to hear another word about drugs or crime without hearing in the same breath about decent jobs, adequate housing, and egalitarian education.

—ADOLPH L. REED JR. is a professor of political science at the University of Pennsylvania.

## My Father's Party

LUIS J. RODRÍGUEZ
APRIL 2008

My father was a Republican. Anybody who knows me may find this hard to believe. You could not find an apple as far away from the tree as the distance between my father and me. We didn't agree on many things, but mostly we disagreed on politics.

A little background: My father in 1956 made his final trip to Los Angeles from Mexico in his early forties when I was two years old. He had bought whole hog into "the American Dream." He worked hard—in dog food factories, construction, paint factories. He sold pots and pans, Bibles, and *chicharrones* (Mexican-style pork rinds). Finally, he landed a custodial position at a community college laboratory in the Los Angeles area, and that's what he did for fifteen years until he retired.

After several years of false starts—including getting evicted a few times, going bankrupt, losing one home—we finally bought a house in San Gabriel, California, in the late 1960s for $12,500 (his salary was around $14,000 at the time). It was a modest, wood-frame, two-bedroom for a family of six. Yet this made us one of the first Mexican families to own a home in the area.

I was thirteen years old and already in gangs and using drugs—hardly a model son for my parents. Their dreams failed to connect to anything I felt was important at the time. Something seemed hollow about my family pretending to "make it" when I knew otherwise: We may have bought a house, but we had money for barely anything else.

My dad fell for the materialistic lure of American capitalism. In the process, he often forgot he was a janitor—a highly qualified one, yes, but a janitor nonetheless. He dealt with growing debt by getting into more debt. He also had very little emotional connection with his children or with my mother. He was a hard guy to figure out, to influence, even to love.

Over the years, I saw his spirit get crushed.

When I got into revolutionary politics in my late teens and early twenties—a vital process in removing myself from crime and drugs—my father and I often argued. About unions (he hated them), civil rights (he felt people should stop complaining), and who should run the country (he loved Richard Nixon).

One time, my dad asked me to attend a meeting of a conservative political group. West San Gabriel Valley at the time had many middle-class, upwardly mobile white communities next to very poor Mexican barrios (which also included poor whites). A high school principal once told me the local school boards were overrun with John Birch Society members.

My father looked odd at this meeting. He was relatively short and brown-skinned, and was wearing an open shirt and slacks. The other men were tall, many gray-haired, in business suits and ties. I saw how awestruck my father looked among them. I was angry. To me, these men didn't deserve the respect of most people, let alone my father. I could see they cared little about his presence. They tolerated him. But he was invisible, as were the many working-class Mexicans surrounding their whitewashed suburbs. Their words at the meeting, I recall, were declarations of war against radicals (read "black and brown" radicals), hippies, peace activists, and more. They were declarations of war against people like me.

My dad and I never united around politics—or love, for that matter—until his death in 1992. He failed to recognize his class interests. He bought the wrong dream, the capitalist dream. It wasn't wrong for him to be for "the American Dream." But my point all along was (I guess I'm still arguing with my dad), which American Dream? The one that says everyone can get rich, or the one that promises freedom, equality, and justice?

—Luis J. Rodríguez is a poet, novelist, and activist. His books include *Always Running: La Vida Loca, Gang Days in L.A., Music of the Mill,* and *My Nature Is Hunger: New and Selected Poems, 1989–2004.*

# PART 6

# Joining the Cause of
# Gay Liberation

The gay liberation movement has been one of the most exciting of the last four decades—and one of the most successful. *The Progressive* weighed in early with a lovely piece by Richard Gollance, who worked in Hollywood before becoming a psychotherapist.

The interview with Harry Hay, one of the founders of the gay rights movement, offers a fascinating glimpse into how he organized the Mattachine Society during the McCarthy period.

The interviews with Randy Shilts and Larry Kramer spotlight the tireless work these two men did to press the government, as well as people in the movement, to take the AIDS pandemic seriously.

From Minnie Bruce Pratt, we get a first-hand account of what it feels like to be a mother discriminated against in the cruelest way because she is a lesbian. Ten years later, though, we can mark the distance the country has traveled, as Kate Clinton presides over gay marriages with joy and solemnity—and characteristic humor.

# I'm Proud to Be a Sissie

RICHARD GOLLANCE
MAY 1973

I've stopped worrying about whether or not I'm a Real Man. I like to dance, and sometimes when I'm walking along the beach, I'll dance right there. Sometimes I visit my friend Donna, who is "straight," and we play with fingernail polish, painting designs on each other's nails. I have a bright red scarf I like to wear around my head, like a gypsy. Maybe I'll sew this evening, or go for a motorcycle ride in the mountains this afternoon, or write a few scenes for a play I'm working on.

I don't consider whether my voice is deep enough or my presence authoritative enough. I don't have to do a mini-size version of the He-Man Strut or feel apologetic for being mini-size. And I won't surrender my life to an office. I work part time, just enough to support myself and that's all. Any other work I do will have to be meaningful to me.

This is a new freedom for me. Gentleness, introversion, slightness, or emotionality are dangerous in a boy, a sure sign that he may not be capable of meeting his male duty in the grownup world.

When I was very young, sometimes I played with dolls, or cried, or painted. I don't remember when the first pressures to change all that started, but gradually the agony of being made fun of and being called a "fairy" became the most horrible part of my life. Any situation could suddenly turn on me and leave me shattered. And my secret guilt about being homosexual intensified the need to hide and reconstruct the incorrect parts of my personality. As much as I tried, I never fully escaped the threat of imminent humiliation.

What hurts most now is realizing that my quest for masculinity and normality always involved restricting myself, never exploring or expanding myself. I wasted so much time and energy doing things I didn't enjoy. I remember my adolescence as a time of being constantly on guard.

There is no legitimate way for a boy in the suburbs to avoid baseball in the spring. Without raising a fuss, I would try out for the Little League, and every year wind up in the outfield of a third-string team where I couldn't do much harm. For encouragement, my parents would come to all the games, and at any family gathering, an uncle or a cousin was sure to ask my batting average, how my team was doing, what position I played: Was I a hero? Meals were rescheduled to accommodate practices, and buying a mitt was an event.

There was an annual ritual I became familiar with. It would start with my coach looking at me strangely after I threw a ball a few times. The routine: he would take me aside and ask me to have a catch with him, and I knew what was coming. He would try to be tactful (but make me realize, at the same time, that it was a serious problem) and say something like, "You're not following through when you throw the ball. You're doing it all wrong, like a girl."

The coach would then try to teach me the right way but, realizing me hopeless, would finally give up. I knew I was stuck in the outfield forever. Eventually I found an illegitimate way to avoid baseball in the spring. For several years I got sick for a few weeks every April or May. I dreaded the end of winter.

I finally discovered a spring sport. Distance running doesn't really require talent as much as it requires drive and a monumental need to prove something. Why else would you go around and around a track several miles a day and subject yourself to a grueling regimen whose only pleasure is the possibility of winning a race perhaps once a week? Why else go to bed early when all the next day promises is more timed laps and more calisthenics? I had that monumental need. Even after I established that I could be athletic and after I grew to hate the meaningless, repetitive exertion, I still continued. At last I had something to prove my precarious identity.

Every circumstance, every action demanded second-guessing. When I heard a sarcastic wolf-whistle as I walked in the school halls, I fashioned a grotesque walk that had virtually no wiggle in it. When I dated, the strong certainty and the impenetrable protectiveness I worked so hard to convey precluded any human communication and made the evening a torture. When I dressed, when I sat down and crossed my legs, when I carried a package, when I was angry at someone, when I chose books or magazines, or which classes to take, I always had to figure out if I was doing it the right way for a boy.

The details of my high school years may be singular, but few "gay" men escape similar traumas. Until about a year ago (I "came out" at seventeen; I'm twenty-three now), I wasn't able to accept being anything less than the strong one, the aggressor. I was afraid of being put down again for acting like a girl. While gay liberation helped me learn to like myself, the influence of feminists finally helped me transcend the contradictions between my needs and my fears. I was only convinced, step by step, as I felt the exhilaration of recovering those carefully lost parts of myself and seeing the shared delight of my friends, feminists and gay men, as I kept exploring. It was the first time I was given some reassurance about myself; perhaps my natural instincts weren't impossible after all. I didn't feel I had to stand outside and guard myself. It was a relief to lose that terrible self-consciousness.

When I go to bed with another man, we are each physically capable of being passive or active. For a long time, sex produced a subtle competition: who would give in? I could not ease up enough to enjoy being sexually passive; it was a defeat with a reward—closeness—that made it worth continuing nonetheless. Since I have relaxed and stopped thinking of sex as something akin to rape and plunder, the sensual pleasure has become dominant, and my bed adventures have lost that edgy strain of competition. One man is not the victor and the other the victim.

Some confused males are still stuck with their boyhood models: the spartan athlete, the fast-drawing gunslinger, the omnipotent billy-clubbed policeman, the blood-and-guts soldier, the computerized fast-talking executive, the remote intellectual, the awesome scientist, the unapproachable President of the United States. Life is still the great challenge for men to beat. All pleasures are to be withheld for future security. Men are enemies and women booty. If they ever shed their hard, masculine mechanisms, society and its life-denying institutions would cave in, from government to private enterprise, from the military to public education. But imagine for a moment what could replace it. Men and women wouldn't have to fit into slots. They could slide and explore and grow.

—RICHARD GOLLANCE is a psychotherapist in private practice in Los Angeles and Studio City, California.

# An Interview with Randy Shilts, Author of And the Band Played On

LAURIE UDESKY
MAY 1991

Q: You were one of the first openly gay reporters on a mainstream publication. In *And the Band Played On*, you talk about how gay and lesbian reporters are stigmatized; what has been your experience?

RANDY SHILTS: I have always been out, all my adult life. What was unique about me is that I was hired and everybody knew I was gay. So when I went to work at the *Chronicle*, everybody tried to outdo each other to be nice.

I think that's the strength one has when one is open. You tend to get the slights and the stigma when you're in the closet. And for good reason: When you're in the closet, when you're hiding it, you're acquiescing in a morality that says there's something to be ashamed of about being gay. Whenever you acquiesce in that way, you give the bigots the upper hand. Once you say, "Well, I'm gay and I'm not going to hide it," it forces bigots to assert their prejudice, and they rarely have the courage to do that. Most bigots are just bullies. Once you make them assert their prejudice, they won't do it.

Q: When you began writing about the AIDS epidemic, there was opposition in the media. How was that for you?

SHILTS: The biggest problems for me arose when my reporting put me in conflict with the gay community itself. That was the most psychologically trying. At the beginning, when I started writing about the epidemic, there were people who said, "Don't write about this, it's bad public relations." And, to me, it was so obviously a story. I had to write about it. I was accused of all kinds of horrible things—of being a self-hating gay person who had internalized homophobia. I was accused of trying to sensationalize this "rather minor" health story in order to sell papers for the *San Francisco Chronicle*. And that increased over the years, particularly as we got toward the bathhouse controversy. In my mind, it was always a business issue. Here were greedy businessmen who would kill anybody to make twenty-five cents. But the gay community did not interpret it as a business issue. It interpreted it as a civil rights issue. My reporting was aggressive, sometimes overly so. So there was this perception that I was out to subvert gay rights and that I didn't care about civil liberties and civil rights.

To me, the overriding issue was that civil rights wouldn't do us any good if we were all dead from this disease. At that point, there was a lot of denial.

It was a national story, but San Francisco is a very small town. I had been on television; people knew what I looked like. So I would walk down the street and people would scream at me. I had friends who refused to go to restaurants with me anymore, because waiters would come and insult me. There are people today who still despise me; if I go to a gay bar, there are still people who will insult me. That's the hardest thing.

Q: At the *Chronicle*, did you have to fight to get a certain viewpoint across in your reporting?

SHILTS: It was a matter, always, of breaking barriers, what was permissible to say. If you had told me ten years ago that we were going to have something about anal intercourse in the paper every day, the way we do today, I never would have believed it.

Q: *And the Band Played On* focuses primarily on white gay men. Recently, the AIDS Coalition to Unleash Power, ACT UP, split over issues relating to the fact that white gay men were primarily the leadership. What do you think happened that caused the split?

SHILTS: Everything to do with AIDS has to be measured against a deadline. Between 1 million and 1.4 million Americans are HIV-infected, according to the government, and we don't have forever to get the treatments. We know that everyone is working against this deadline—for most people it's about eleven years—and their immune systems will break down to the point that they will get one of the deadly AIDS diseases. All of our work, our scientific research, has to be judged by whether it's fast enough to save most of these people who are HIV-positive.

By shifting priorities away from treatments to take on a panoply of other social issues, ACT UP is deserting the one arena in which it has had profound effectiveness in order to work in another arena in which it will have minimal effectiveness. What really bothers me about this is that the clock is ticking away. And every day that you don't put pressure on the Government for treatments means thousands of people dying every day a few years down the road.

With treatments you can make a difference. National health care is going to cost $65 billion. We have a U.S. Congress that is incapable of passing even a routine budget. It either has to cut spending on other programs by $65 billion, which it won't do, or create new taxes to get $65 billion, which it won't do. So that's a long-term problem.

But we have a short-term problem with HIV: A lot of people are going to die. To say we shouldn't work for treatments because only wealthy people will get them—well, we don't have treatments in the first place.

Q: When did you start coming out as a gay man?

SHILTS: I was at Portland Community College in Portland, Oregon. For me, coming out was very political. I had gay sexual experiences, as we all did, from Boy Scouts on. For me there came a moment when I had to understand on a political basis. And it just hit one day. There's one sentence that explains it all in my mind: "I am right and society is wrong."

Every lesbian or gay man has to come to that conclusion in order to be well adjusted. When you're in the closet, what you're saying is, "Society is right and I'm wrong. Therefore, I will pretend that I am what society wants me to be."

I started by being involved in antiwar marches—the very early gay-liberation movements were involved in the antiwar movement, so I was around the gay-liberation people more. And once it hit me, a week later I told everybody. It was on May 19, 1972. I told every friend, everybody in my family, that I was gay. And I swore that I'd never live another day of my life in which people didn't know that I was gay.

—LAURIE UDESKY is a writer and editor on health care issues.

# One Good Mother to Another

MINNIE BRUCE PRATT
NOVEMBER 1993

In the *New York Times* photo, a young blonde woman sits staring, stunned. She holds up a large picture of her cherubic smiling little boy. At first this looks like a moment with which everyone sympathizes: a mother publicly grieving her child killed in a tragic accident or lost in a nightmare kidnapping. But in this photo, something jars slightly. There is no father next to the mother; her companion is a woman. The caption reads:

"A Virginia court's decision to remove a child from his mother because of her les-bianism is stirring controversy. Sharon Bottoms, left, lost custody of her two-year-old son, Tyler Donstou, to her mother." At that moment, perhaps the reader's sympathy wanes or turns to animosity.

But I know her look. I've sat in that desolate place. I've had my children taken from my arms, and I've felt that my children were almost dead to me because I could not hold them or touch them.

I had two boys whom I saw emerge, bloody and beautiful, from my body. I nursed them at my breast. I bathed their perfect tiny bodies and changed their diapers. I spoon-fed them baby-food spinach. I taught them how to tie their shoes. I rocked them through earaches and bad dreams. I drove them to their first day in kindergarten.

Then, suddenly, when they were five and six, when I fell in love with another woman and left my marriage to live as a lesbian, the world looked at me and saw an unfit mother. Suddenly, my husband had legal grounds to take my children away from me and never let me see them again.

Like Bottoms, I was also a "somewhat immature and undisciplined, though loving, mother"—after all, we were both mothers at twenty-one, barely out of girlhood. Like Bottoms, I was an "irregular job holder"—finishing a PhD in English literature. When I applied for teaching positions, the male interviewers would inquire, "How will you arrange child care? Are you planning to have more children? What will your husband do if we hire you?" And they never did.

But the standard for my being a "good mother" was not my parenting ability or financial stability. After all, my husband, a father at twenty-three and an unemployed graduate student, was no more mature in his role than I was in mine. No, I was con-sidered a fit mother as long as I was married and loyal to the man who was my hus-band. As soon as I asserted my independence, as soon as I began a life in which I claimed the human right to form intimate social and sexual relations with whomever I chose, specifically with other women, I was seen to be a perverted, unnatural woman by my husband, my mother, the people of the town I lived in, and the legal system.

The letter from my husband's lawyer said he was seeking custody because of my "unorthodox ideas about the place of the father in the home"—my heresy consisted of disagreeing with the idea that men were superior to, and should govern, women.

Though more than fifteen years passed between my agony at losing my children and that of Sharon Bottoms, the issues remain the same. This is true despite the fact that I lost custody of my boys to my ex-husband, their biological father, while Sharon has, at least for now, lost her boy to her mother, the child's biological grandmother, who sued for custody. The reason for denying us our children was the same: simply because we were in lesbian relationships.

In the words of Judge Parsons, who ruled in Henrico County Circuit Court against Sharon: "The mother's conduct is illegal and immoral and renders her unfit to par-ent." Illegal because in Virginia (and more than twenty other states and the District of

Columbia), sodomy—the "crime against nature" of lesbians and gay men—is still prohibited. And the 1987 U.S. Supreme Court, in *Bowers v. Hardwick*, actually stated in its majority opinion that it was maintaining the illegality of sodomy because that particular set of justices considered this kind of sex immoral, based on "traditional values."

Sharon Bottoms, as a lesbian in a committed relationship with another woman, is perceived as less fit to parent than her mother, whose live-in boyfriend for seventeen years was a man who, according to Sharon, sexually abused her twice a week during her teen years. Under the law and in the eyes of many people, Sharon's mother is more fit because she endorses heterosexuality as an institution and female subservience as a tradition, and presumably will pass these values along to her grandson. This arrangement is seen as being in the child's "best interests."

But should we not ask what kind of damage will be done to a boy if his sense of self depends on dominating another person? Should we not inquire about the immorality of teaching a child that love can only occur with state-sanctioned approval?

To see my boys, sometimes I drove roundtrip on three-day weekends, fourteen hours nonstop there, fourteen hours nonstop back. The youngest boy wrote in his school journal how he wished he could be with me more; the oldest boy talked to me late at night, on long-distance phone calls, about his depression, about how sometimes he just wanted to die.

I loved them, I called them, I saw them as much as I had time and money to do. We got through their baby years, pre-adolescence, and teens. When I finally asked the oldest, "What effect do you think my being a lesbian had on you?" he answered: "None. I think my personality was most shaped by not having you with me as a mother all those years, by having you taken away from me."

Now, with cases like that of Sharon Bottoms, the gay and lesbian community is fighting to end other inhumane limits on how all of us can live and love.

In 1976, when I went to a lawyer for help in my struggle for my children, he said to me, "This country is not ready for someone like you." Can we say now, in 1993, that we are ready for someone like Sharon Bottoms, just an ordinary woman, a part-time grocery clerk trying to raise a child on not enough money, but with the love and support of another woman who cares about both of them?

Let us declare, finally, that we are ready for this ordinary extraordinary woman who is saying to us, with her life, that to guarantee her right to be a lesbian and a mother is to take one more step toward liberation for all of us.

—MINNIE BRUCE PRATT is a poet, essayist, and activist who came out as a lesbian in North Carolina in 1975 and now lives in Jersey City, New Jersey. Her book of poems about her relationship to her sons as a lesbian mother, *Crime Against Nature*, was chosen as the Lamont Poetry Selection of the Academy of American Poets. She is doing antiracist and anti-imperialist organizing with the International Action Center and can be reached at www.mbpratt.org.

## An Interview with Larry Kramer,
## Playwright and Founder of ACT UP

L. A. WINOKUR
JUNE 1994

Q: In your play *The Destiny of Me*, several lines spoken by Ned or, if you will, the Larry Kramer character, really stand out in my mind. The scene takes place in the hospital. Ned, who is there seeking treatment for AIDS, is asked by his nurse about what happened between him and the crowd of gay activists protesting outside. He responds, "They look to me for leadership and I don't know how to guide them. . . . I wanted to be Moses, but I only could be Cassandra." Is this one of the fundamental dilemmas that haunts Larry Kramer? And, like the prophetic Cassandra, is it your destiny to go through life as a person possessed and tragically misunderstood?

LARRY KRAMER: It's a complicated question. There was a period when I really wanted to be a gay leader, the gay leader. And part of that is embedded in that answer. But it was preceded by and followed by what I'm going through now, which is not so much caring whether I was a leader or not, but just that what I said be listened to and acted upon. I was naive enough to believe—or to hope—that when *The Normal Heart* opened, the following day the world would be changed; Ed Koch would start doing something for AIDS; the *New York Times* would start writing about AIDS, and Ronald Reagan would fall into line. That's basically how strong I thought my argument was and that the world would respond to it. *The Normal Heart* was written for that purpose alone: to advise the world how awful everything was and how little was being done. There was that passion and urgency to it.

Of course, what I hoped would happen didn't happen, and the lesson I have learned since then is that I basically don't think one voice can make a difference in this country anymore. I don't particularly want to be that leader anymore, that Moses. But that doesn't mean I've stopped trying, or that I'm able to stop trying.

So I think the Moses/Cassandra stuff, in terms of where I am in my life now, is probably a little melodramatic. When I started ACT UP, I hoped that we had started a worldwide movement. I was conscious of the fact that I had these troops there. I can't say "at my disposal," because the problem with ACT UP was that it wasn't at anybody's disposal. It was democratic to a flaw.

But I sensed that with a certain kind of energy and effort I could probably take that movement and turn it into an army. For various reasons though—one having to do with the fact that they didn't want to be taken anywhere by me or anybody else, and another having to do with this conflict in my life between my political yearnings and my artistic ones, a conflict that makes it difficult for me to go all out for one or the other—I sort of let that moment slip. I don't know that I could have turned it into anything more than what it was turned into. But I do feel in some way that I have failed. . . . You say one person is dying every minute, or 100,000 are going to die next year, or 100 million are going to die by the turn of the century. It doesn't seem to scare anybody. After a while, you have to say, I really think this is being allowed to happen. You really have to say this is genocide.

Q: You have expressed strong feelings that people be open about being gay. For real progress on the AIDS front, is it necessary for people with the disease to also be public about that?

KRAMER: I think it would make it a lot easier, especially if people in power who are HIV-positive or who have AIDS were to do so. But I don't know that it's ever going to happen. We just have to keep fighting.

Politicians only respect one thing, and that's numbers and pressure. The gay community and the AIDS communities—and they're not necessarily the same communities—haven't been able to capitalize on that. So I tend to be very harsh on those of us who aren't in this fight in a confrontational way. I've been very critical of the gay community—especially the metropolitan gay communities—where it's not so difficult to be, if not out of the closet, certainly an active person politically. So one wonders whether there's a death wish. People participate in their own genocide.

# An Interview with Urvashi Vaid, Author, Executive Director, and Foundation Leader in the Lesbian and Gay Rights Movement

ANNE-MARIE CUSAC
MARCH 1996

Q: You talk about the gay and lesbian movement as transformative and redemptive. What do you mean by that?

URVASHI VAID: The redemptive potential of gay and lesbian sexuality is that it broadens and opens up gender rigidity. I don't think everybody should be straight or gay. And I don't think everybody should be gay at all, or will be. Some people are heterosexual. Some people are bisexual. And if sexuality were freed, truly freed, people would find their own comfort level with what they want to be.

I think gay relationships are really egalitarian, and they're refreshing in the context of the sexism of the world. We shouldn't give that up. And I also don't think we should give up the sexual wildness in our relationships. I'm in a monogamous relationship, so I'm not talking about monogamy/non-monogamy. But there's a way that we, by being conscious of sexuality and ourselves as sexual beings because we're gay, keep it really fresh.

Q: Is that what you're talking about in your book when you talk about joy?

VAID: Yes, I mean pleasure. I think gayness is about pleasure and pursuing pleasure. And that can be hedonistic, in the sense of pleasure for pleasure's sake. Or it can be moral, in the sense that it's eros, which has a moral dimension, which is about affirming life. Our relationships extend the definition of family. They don't undermine it or threaten it; they actually broaden it and bolster it beyond bloodlines. Family has always been tied to blood because of the whole inheritance thing, the need to protect private property. And so, gayness comes along and redefines family beyond this economic realm of inheritance and blood into this other emotional commitment and responsibility realm. I have a gay and lesbian family of friends—straight friends, gay friends, their kids—that to me is as important and strong and part of me as my sisters and their kids and brothers-in-law.

Q: And it has the potential to define family beyond national boundaries and racial boundaries, too?

VAID: Exactly, totally. The friendship circles that two people bring into each other's lives are probably more important than their so-called family. Gayness defines friends as family. And it also has a very community-minded definition of family. Gay people have a strong sense of responsibility to community that comes out of having to create institutions to take care of our own, but which is exactly the sense of civic community and civic responsibility that many straight people are bemoaning as being lost.

We have to change values, change cultural institutions, change economic forces to have a society in which gay people are viewed as equal, normal, healthy, natural human beings. I'm not part of a civil rights movement. I'm part of a liberation movement.

—ANNE-MARIE CUSAC is a poet, a journalist, and a professor at Roosevelt University. She worked for *The Progressive* for ten years as an editor and investigative reporter. She is the author of *Cruel and Unusual: Punishment in America*.

# An Interview with Harry Hay, Founder of the Mattachine Society, the First Modern Gay-Rights Group

ANNE-MARIE CUSAC
SEPTEMBER 1998

Q: What was it like coming out in the twenties and thirties?

HARRY HAY: You're talking about coming out to yourself and coming out to one or two other people. But it's not coming out to the people on the street you live on. In that time, you aren't a gay person, you aren't a homosexual person, you're a degenerate. And what you were suffering from was what was known as ostracism. Ostracism means *you don't exist at all.* And that's a very difficult situation to live with. As gay people, we had been chasing ostracism by that point for probably 300 years. You just knew that you should have dropped into your black hole.

Q: Did you feel those things?

HAY: I knew I was there, but I didn't believe what they said. I *never* believed what they said. I've always felt I carried a golden secret, a wonderful secret. Every time I thought about it, it made me feel warm. Up until I was eleven years old, I thought I was the only one of my kind in the world. I couldn't find anybody else who felt as I did.

There was a book by somebody called Edward Carpenter, *The Intermediate Sex.* I'm reading about Michelangelo and Alexander the Great, who were "homosexual"—a very long word. I don't know what that word means. So I go to look it up in the dictionary, and it isn't there.

Q: "Homosexual" was not in the dictionary?

HAY: No, it was not in the dictionary. I've always said, "If I had the sense I was born with and looked it up in the legal code, I would have found it." And it was in the penal code, of course. It wouldn't be in any American dictionary until 1938. And in most American dictionaries not until the Second World War. We had no words for ourselves. That's the important point—we didn't have words.

I read about this thing, and I know that word is me. It's about these people, and I and they have the same feelings. I know there are others. From there on out, my dream has *him* in it—whoever *him* is going to be—but there is another *him* somewhere.

At one point, I'm talking to Will Geer, the guy who was *The Waltons'* grandpa. He was also my lover, and he introduced me to the Communist Party. And I say, "All of us guys"—we didn't call ourselves "gay" yet, we didn't call ourselves "homosexual" yet, we called ourselves "temperamental"—"all of us temperamental guys, we should organize."

Will said, "For Christ's sake, you're out of your mind! What would we talk about? We're cocksuckers or nothing. What else?"

Maude Allen, a character actress from New York who was part of our company, was everybody's mother. And one day Maude says, "It would be a good idea if you underground guys got together." But she said, "You know what I think, if you're going to do it, *you're* going to have to do it." I said, "Me?" She said, "Who else?"

I was accustomed to walking alone. I'd find other people who agreed with me, but they also said, "I wouldn't dare mention it." I was the only one who would say, "We've got to stand." And they said, "Well, yes. And after you make it safe, then I'll stand, too. But you have to make it safe."

OK, so if I have to make it safe, I have to make it safe.

Q: How did you get the Mattachine Society going?

HAY: We set up these discussion groups. And we got the gay guys to come. They would all bring a girlfriend—a mother-in-law or an aunt, a cousin—but they would always bring a cover girl. We would salt ourselves in and around the group that was there. If a guy's eyes would shine a little bit more than usual, we would ask him to have coffee with us. Then we would show him a call to an underground society.

It worked. And the discussion groups were very cute. We might have a group of fifty people, and we would always talk about an issue out of chapter 5 of the Kinsey report. Somebody would raise his hand and say, "You know, I've got a cousin in Duluth." It was always a cousin in Duluth or Horners Corners. It wasn't L.A. And once in a while, he would slip and say, "I, I mean, my cousin." So we would hear about these various horrendous things that would happen to the cousin in Horners Corners. Then we would take this particular person and talk to him. And we began to get members for the Mattachine Society. We would then come out to each other. It was wonderful.

I remember hardened old queens who would show up, and they would be cynical, and they would be disparaging, and all of a sudden, this one particular hardened old guy, he started to cry. He said, "Look what I've had to put up with all my life, and nobody ever asked about these things before." And when he started to cry, he just broke open. Because all the things he'd been suffering were things that all the rest were suffering, too.

It caught on. We had a sphere of influence of about 5,000 people in the state of California under McCarthy, under the loyalty oath.

Q: What was your experience as a Communist, and how did McCarthyism affect you?

HAY: In 1934, when I first joined the party, I registered underground. Then, during the war years, we were able to come out because we had put the more difficult things for people to swallow temporarily on shelves. And we were all part of the war effort. So we had open Communist Party meetings all during the war.

After the war, it all clamped down again. During the Korean War, here on the West Coast, we had police inspectors on every block. Any house that had more than three cars in front was suspect. All the license plates were taken. They had discovered what house they were meeting in. They discovered who the people were. And then all you had to do was prove that you weren't what you weren't. You can't do that, as you know. It's the double negative thing.

In the Mattachine Society, underground as we were, we were infiltrated within six months. I have an FBI record. You'd be surprised. Every single member, every single Mattachine chapter—and there were chapters all over the country—were all infiltrated. We never knew who the mole was.

So you had a whole sense of terror. People were very, very careful in this period—1948, '49, '50. The McCarthy witch hunts, the loyalty oaths of people who had to be involved in the school systems, the Hollywood Ten.

"Pinko-commie-queer"—that was the thing you heard all over the place. Saw it in the movies.

Q: How did those two things—Communist and queer—get combined?

HAY: There were those who hated Communists, and there were those who hated queers. If you were both a Communist and a queer, then you were beyond the pale, by all means. That cut you off from everything. It broke people's spirit, and once your spirit breaks and you crawl, they keep pushing you and pushing you and pushing you.

Q: What can lesbians and gays do today?

HAY: Any time along the line where we can find a way so that we change something, that guy whom you have changed and the other people around him whom you have changed are going to, in turn, change others.

But that's being a thwart. That's not being confrontational. It's kissing them with a butterfly kiss as you go by. We have to be people who set each other free.

Give yourself permission to enjoy being gay. You do have to give yourself permission. You have been told you may not. Give yourself permission to be free.

# I Do Weddings

KATE CLINTON
JULY 2004

You've all heard my Peggy Lee lip-syncing "Is that all there is?" gay marriage whine. The next sound you'll hear is me jumping on the Same Sex Marriage Express. I am joining the Gay Marriage Industrial Complex!

Quite frankly, I am not going to let another gay wave pass me by.

I missed the rainbow tchotchke cash cow. Who knew?

I missed the gays on TV bonanza, but so did a lot of other actual gay people.

I missed the Gay Cruise treasure chest.

This time around, I will not be left at the altar.

If you can't beat 'em, join 'em, and that's just what I intend to do.

Judy Dlugasz, the founder of Olivia Cruises who does shipboard ceremonies (a twofer, she's brilliant!), told me how to get a minister's license from the Universal Life Church.

The ULC people will e-confer your ministership at no cost, but I splurged, and for $109, plus shipping and handling, I got the deluxe reverend package. In addition to my minister's license with my name in a very convincing liturgical font, it includes a wedding business training video for ministers and a revised and very helpful "Ultimate Wedding & Ceremony Workbook" for the planning-impaired.

I am most proud of my wallet-sized hologram license and the six-by-nine-inch orange laminated "Parking—Minister's Business" placard to display on my dashboard. The fine print says that parking privileges are not recognized in New York City, and that I am not authorized to do circumcisions. Otherwise I am good to go-d.

Like those itinerant clerics who traveled during the summer months and took over for vacationing priests, I hope to help out this summer in Provincetown, but without the pedophilia.

My wedding package, The Rite Stuff, includes one hour of pre-marriage counseling (because I don't want to hear much more about it than that); the ceremony itself (I'm very good with parents); and the reception after. My motto: "Every reception needs a wedding zinger."

My friend from Provincetown called me and my bluff and asked me to celebrate their union of thirty-two years. "We'll get the justice of the peace thing, but then we'd be honored to have you officiate in our living room, with a few friends. Then we'll go out to dinner."

And suddenly I am poring over my books, watching my video, worrying about my outfit, and writing a special ceremony for my good friends. I plan on mentioning the ups and downs and dish they've gone through together, that they lived through the AIDS plague, that they are the center of their often dysfunctional straight families, that they have to whack back their codependencies with large sticks, that they've both survived quadruple bypass surgeries and recoveries, that they care for their aging surviving parents, that they've raised thousands of dollars for the Provincetown AIDS support group, that they are hysterical to watch the Women's NCAA basketball finals with, and that they are spectacular loyal friends and boon companions to each other.

Part celebration, part roast, I am as nervous about this occasion as when I first began to perform. And honored beyond measure and surprised to be asked to celebrate my friends' love.

Get your licenses. Celebrate your friends. We'll make this marriage thing ours yet. As that old dyke Susan B. said, "Failure is impossible."

—KATE CLINTON, humorist and essayist, is the author of *Don't Get Me Started* and *What the L?* She also has recorded many comedy collections, including *Read These Lips* and *The Marrying Kind.*

PART 7

# Defending the Environment

Teddy Roosevelt was the first to make environmentalism government policy—and a hallmark of progressivism. Given La Follette's bitter differences with Roosevelt, it's quaint to hear Fighting Bob sing his praises here.

We couldn't help but be moved by the plaintive question in the 1911 article "Have You Ever Seen This Bird?" It was about the passenger pigeon, and alas, the deafening answer across the country was no.

Senator Gaylord Nelson of Wisconsin wrote several times for *The Progressive*, and his 1967 exposé of pollution helped plant the seeds for Earth Day. Denis Hayes's reflection on that day sounds the trumpet of the modern environmental movement. And his renunciation of the philosophy of growth for growth's sake is shared, as well, by Dave Foreman and Wendell Berry.

Jim Hightower anticipated the "slow food movement" by three decades with his 1975 article, "Fake Food Is the Future," while Winona LaDuke stresses the importance of sustainability. On a similar wavelength, Terry Tempest Williams talks about "respecting the land, the wildlife, the plants, the rivers, mountains, and deserts, the absolute essential bedrock of our lives."

Meanwhile, the threat of global warming lurks. *The Progressive* sent Bruce E. Johansen, a scholar on the subject, up to the Arctic Circle in 2001. Even back then he saw the disaster unfolding.

For hope, turn to the interview with Nobel Peace Prize–winner Wangari Maathai. It shows how the simple act of planting trees could turn back the forces of environmental destruction—and empower women at the same time.

## Teddy Roosevelt's Greatest Work

ROBERT M. LA FOLLETTE
MARCH 13, 1909

This globe is the capital stock of the race. It has just so much coal and oil and gas. These may be economized or wasted. The same thing is true of phosphates and many other minerals. Our water resources are immense, and we are only just beginning to use them. Our forests have been destroyed; they must be restored. Our soils are being depleted; they must be built up and conserved.

These questions are not of this day only, or of this generation. They belong to all the future. Their consideration requires that high moral tone which regards the Earth as the home of a posterity to whom we owe a sacred duty. The idea will ennoble any people upon which its real significance once more fully dawns.

This immense idea, Roosevelt, with high statesmanship, dinned into the indifferent ears of the nation until the nation heeded. He held it so high that it attracted the attention of the neighboring nations of the continent, and will so spread and intensify that we shall soon see world conferences devoted to it.

Nothing could be greater or finer than this. It is so great and so fine that when the historian of the future shall speak of Theodore Roosevelt, he is likely to say that he did many notable things, among them that of inaugurating the movement which finally resulted in the "square deal," but that his greatest work was inspiring and actually beginning a world movement for staying terrestrial waste and saving for the human race the things upon which, and upon which alone, a great and peaceful and progressive and happy race life can be founded. What statesman in all history has done anything calling for so wide a view and for a purpose more lofty?

## Have You Ever Seen This Bird?

C. F. HODGE
APRIL 8, 1911

Wisconsin was one of the last halting places of this fine pigeon—Passenger Pigeon— and it is now one of the most likely states in which to look for nestings, if any of the birds still exist.

With a flock of nesting birds to start with, we may be able to organize protection for the entire continent in such ways as to save this valuable and beautiful species and also save the good name of the American people.

We cannot organize a movement to "restore" or "save" a species that does not exist; but the moment a colony, or even a single pair, of nesting pigeons is found the Passenger Pigeon Restoration Club of America will be organized.

The State Game Commissions and State Warden service, sportsman's associations everywhere, and all the Audubon Societies will join in the work; the birds will be adequately protected by law, and be accorded the absolute freedom of the continent to feed and breed in safety anywhere in North America. As long as there is life there is hope.

If any nesting pigeons can be found and if they can then be effectively protected, in a few years we may have them back again filling our skies and transforming the most of our woods into beautiful and valuable life. This is an object well worthy of the best enthusiasm of every citizen of the United States and Canada. Theodore Roosevelt has expressed his desire to join the confirming party, when the first colony has been located.

One record indicates that a bird was killed in southern Virginia at Christmas. It is just this danger that the last stragglers will be ignorantly potted off that makes general publicity necessary. Everyone, everywhere, must be awakened to the danger and realize that there is a passenger pigeon problem in America.

This is only a part of a larger problem. Destructive forces have gone all too far in exterminating interesting and valuable American species. We are now turning toward "conservation," and strong movements are afoot in different states to bring back our splendid game birds, especially, to their ancient, native ranges. We may then hope to have our wild turkey back in our forest reservations, our wild swans and our wild geese and ducks nesting again along lakes and rivers, the prairie chickens booming in our fields and ruffed grouse drumming in every clump of woods and our bobwhite whistling along every roadside and from the top of every garden fence. In this glad procession we may still hope that the passenger pigeon will take the lead. Then, as its wanton destruction is the saddest, its restoration will be the gladdest story in the entire record of American natural history.

—C. F. HODGE, a Clark University professor, searched for the passenger pigeon for years to no avail.

# The National Pollution Scandal

SENATOR GAYLORD A. NELSON
FEBRUARY 1967

The natural environment of America—the woods and waters and wildlife, the clear air and blue sky, the fertile soil and the scenic landscape—is threatened with destruction.

Our growing population and expanding industries, the explosion of scientific knowledge, the vast increase in income levels, leisure time, and mobility—all of these powerful trends are exerting such pressure on our natural resources that many of them could be effectively ruined over the next ten or fifteen years.

Our overcrowded parks are becoming slums. Our birds and wildlife are being driven away or killed outright. Scenic rural areas are blighted by junkyards and billboards, and neon blight soils the outskirts of most cities. In our orgy of expansion, we are bulldozing away the natural landscape and building a cold new world of concrete and aluminum. Strip miners' shovels are tearing away whole mountains and spreading ugly wastes for miles around. America the affluent is well on the way to destroying America the beautiful.

Of all these developments, the most tragic and the most costly is the rapidly mounting pollution of our lakes and streams.

Every major river system in America is seriously polluted, from the Androscoggin in Maine to the Columbia in the far Northwest. The rivers once celebrated in poetry and song—the Monongahela, the Cumberland, the Ohio, the Hudson, the Delaware, the Rio Grande—have been blackened with sewage, chemicals, oil, and trash. They are sewers of filth and disease.

The Monongahela, which drains the mining and industrial areas of West Virginia and Pennsylvania, empties the equivalent of 200,000 tons of sulfuric acid each year into the Ohio River, which in turn is the water supply for millions of people who use and reuse Ohio River water many times over.

It is a definite possibility that the Great Lakes—the greatest single source of fresh water in the world—could be effectively destroyed by pollution in the years ahead. If this were to happen, it would be the greatest natural resource disaster in modern history.

That is the outline of this new American tragedy. It must be attacked for what it is—a sinister byproduct of the prosperous, urbanized, industrialized world in which we live.

—GAYLORD NELSON, the founder of Earth Day, was a senator from Wisconsin from 1962 to 1980.

# Earth Day
## A Beginning

DENIS HAYES
APRIL 1970

Other social movements have tramped across the dusty American stage. Many began in search of fundamental change; all failed. Our movement must be different.

Until recently, American movements tended to have a vulnerability. Relying heavily upon an economic analysis, they tended to focus at least in part upon material goals. And this made them vulnerable. The American economy can manufacture wondrous quantities of goods. So if a militant group wanted a piece of the pie, and was willing to fight for it, the economy would simply produce a little more pie and give it some. And with its material goals addressed, the movement invariably lost its teeth.

The contemporary revolution, however, does not rely upon an exclusively economic analysis, and its goals are not acquisitive. It will be impossible to "buy off" the peace people, to "buy off" the hippies, to "buy off" the young Black militants, to "buy off" the ecology freaks.

We can't be bought, because we demand something the existing order can't produce. We demand a lower productivity and a wider distribution. We demand things which last, which can be used and reused. We demand less arbitrary authority, and more decentralization of power. We demand a fundamental respect for nature, including man—even though this may sometimes result in "inefficiency."

Dissident groups accentuate different concerns, but our fundamental goals tend to be shared: ending exploitation, imperialism, and the war-based economy; guaranteeing justice, dignity, education, and health to all men. A focus on one concern does not mean a neglect of the others: We are able to seek more than one goal at a time. Those of us who have fought against the war will continue to do so until it is ended; those who have sought racial justice will not be satisfied until it is realized.

All these goals fall under a single unified value structure. This value is difficult to articulate, but posited most simply it might read: "the affirmation of life." This is a clear contradiction of most things for which America stands.

America is the New Rome, and is making Vietnam the new Carthage—razing her villages to the ground and salting what remains of her fields with long-lasting defoliants. America is the new Robber Baron—stealing from the poor countries of the world to satiate a gluttonous need for consumption. We waste our riches in planned obsolescence, and invest the overwhelming bulk of our national budget in ABMs and MIRVs and other means of death. Each of our biggest bombs today is the explosive equivalent of a cube of TNT as tall as the Empire State Building. And the only reason we don't have bigger bombs is that we don't have a means of delivering bigger bombs. Yet.

At the same time we are systematically destroying our land, our streams, and our seas. We foul our air, deaden our senses, and pollute our bodies.

America has become indifferent to life, reducing that vibrant miracle to a dead statistic. This callousness has allowed us to overlook the modest, intermediate consequences of our crimes. If 50,000 people are killed, if 10 million people starve, if an entire country is laid waste—we have learned to tuck the information into the proper file and write the affair off as a mistake.

We have to "unlearn" that. These aren't mistakes at all; they are the natural offshoots of the "growth generation"—of the neo-Keynesian mentality that still expects to find salvation in the continued growth of population and production. Nurtured in our frontier heritage as the shortsighted inhabitants of a bountiful, underpopulated country, this mental set (found in every economic text in our schools) has yet to grapple with the elementary fact that infinite expansion is impossible on a finite planet.

The implications of these old myths in the current setting are enormous. We now have the potential to destroy life on the planet, and in our rapacious plundering we are flirting with some frightening probabilities that we will do just that.

In a society in which death has lost its horror, with the slaughter of three wars under our belts and our streets full of mugging and indifference, a group of people—mostly young—is beginning to stand up and say, "No." We are beginning to say, simply, "We affirm life—a life in harmony with Nature."

Thousands of campuses and communities all across America will be taking part in Earth Day. Each will focus its attention upon the degradation of its local environment. Each will try to develop a holistic strategy for improvement. Some local groups are going to be reasonably moderate; others will be much more militant. None has any illusions about turning America around in one day, or one week, or one year. But it's a beginning.

April 22 is a tool—something that can be used to focus the attention of a society on where we are heading. It's a chance to start getting a handle on it all; a rejection of the silly idea that somehow bigger is better, and faster is better, world without limit, amen. This has never been true. It presumes infinite resources, and it presumes a mastery by Man over Nature, and over Nature's laws. Instead of seeking harmony, man has sought to subdue the whole world. The consequences of that are beginning to come home. And time is running out.

That is what April 22 is all about.

—DENIS HAYES, a leading environmental activist, helped coordinate Earth Day. He is the
   president of the Bullitt Foundation.


## Fake Food Is the Future

JIM HIGHTOWER
SEPTEMBER 1975

Most people think of food as something that farmers grow for people to eat. Not quite. The final step in manufactured food is being taken, and it is both eaters and farmers who are being stepped on. Synthetic food is here.

Having both the technological and economic power to redesign food, oligopolists are not hesitating to exercise it. "We might all be able to exist and flourish on a diet of three adequately compounded pills a day," wrote the head of Central Soya Company's chemurgy division in an article urging a shift to synthetic foods: "This is not an intriguing prospect for most people. And so it is practical to have the soy protein foods look like foods with which we are familiar." Ah, at least he would allow us the "appearance" of the real thing, though one detects a real inclination to sell us the pills.

The new farm is the laboratory, and the American provider is a multinational, multiproduct food oligopoly.

Milo Minderbinder, the amoral conglomerate builder of *Catch-22*, got stuck with bales of Egyptian cotton in one of his deals that went bad. To cut his losses, Minderbinder came up with the idea of coating bits of the cotton with chocolate and selling them as candy. We all laughed at this scene in Joseph Heller's novel, but it forced us to the discomforting admission that big business certainly would sell chocolate-covered cotton if it could.

They have, though with a little different twist. Instead of candy-coated cotton, such favorites as Baby Ruth and Butterfinger are cotton-coated candies. Standard Brands, the food conglomerate that now makes Baby Ruth and Butterfinger, does not use chocolate to coat its bars, but ladles on a synthetic substitute derived from cotton. At least Standard Brands is using a plant derivative. Peter Paul Mounds and Almond Joys now are coated with what is termed "an undisclosed brown substance," and even the president of the company has confessed, "I'm not sure exactly what it is."

Counterfeit chocolate is being offered by the candy makers because it is more profitable to them, not because it is better tasting or more nutritious. "It's a more lasting coating," explained a candy official to a *Newsday* reporter. "Nice gloss, nice shine, nice snap to the product." Monsanto has announced that its chemists have developed a total candy "system" that combines an artificial flavor with a bulking agent and gives the manufacturer the means to replace not only the chocolate coating but also the chocolate filling. A Monsanto executive noted that the system will offer candy makers a 17 to 20 percent saving. Does that mean that you can expect counterfeit chocolate candies to be 17 to 20 percent cheaper? No. Let that melt in your mouth.

Already, synthetics and substitutes hold 21 percent of the citrus-beverage market and high percentages of such markets as whipped toppings and coffee creamers. Imitation milk is now being marketed by two companies and is expected to take up to 10 percent of the fluid milk market by 1980. Pet, Carnation, and Borden are brand names that once were synonymous with real milk and milk products, but today these firms are among the largest marketers of such artificial milk products as nondairy coffee "whiteners."

In the new food economy, taste does not come naturally, but from a vial. Whether it is a tomato extender, a strip of fake bacon, or an imitation filling for doughnuts, the synthetic is tasteless. Fortunately, consumers are still picky enough to insist that at least some approximation of flavor exist. They get less than they bargained for. "Give us your flavor problem," says General Aromatic Products, a division of the Stepan Chemical Co. "Our staff of highly trained specialists continually search for flavors and flavor systems to meet the ever-increasing demands of the food industries." They offer a full line of standardized flavors, from bacon to strawberry, all of which come either as a liquid or in spray-dried form. For manufacturers of tomato soups, spaghetti sauces, ketchups, and other such items, this outfit provides a Cooked Tomato Flavor with a "taste like it came off grandma's stove." For processors of tomato juice and the like, the company sells Fresh Tomato Flavor that gives "the full vine-ripened, fresh, tomato effect."

The William M. Bell Co. has come up with Beef Flavor Imitation No. 11,001, advertising that "this is a most pleasing full bodied beef flavor and aroma, characteristic of prime roast of beef," adding that "it extrudes well in high protein foods, and is ideal in soups, gravies and other processed food where meat replacement is desired." Givaudan Corp. announced that it has responded to consumer demand for "naturally flavored" foods, by developing a series of "scientifically, reconstituted artificial oils."

The mind reels, to say nothing of the stomach.

—Jim Hightower, the writer, speaker, and agitator, was the Texas Agriculture Commissioner from 1982 to 1991. He produces *The Hightower Lowdown*, and he is the author, most recently, of *Swim Against the Current*, with his partner, Susan DeMarco.

# The Clamshell Alliance

## Getting It Together

Harvey Wasserman
September 1977

On July 9, 1976, the Public Service Company (PSC) of New Hampshire began leveling the town dump of Seabrook to prepare the site for construction of a nuclear power plant. It wasn't the company's first mistake, but it was definitely the biggest.

The people of Seabrook had already voted against the nuclear project, and the foundations had been laid for a locally based anti-nuclear campaign. The PSC bulldozers were a declaration of war against thousands of New England seacoast residents who had strong apprehensions about the plant, the thermal pollution it would spew into the Atlantic, and the hazards of radiation leakage, catastrophic accident, and disposal of nuclear wastes.

Within days, an umbrella coalition—the Clamshell Alliance—began planning a series of actions at the Seabrook site that would usher in a new age of political activism in the 1970s and pose a formidable threat to the electric industry's program of nuclear construction.

On Washington's Birthday in 1974, Sam Lovejoy struck a blow against the Montague plant by toppling a 500-foot nuclear-related weather tower at the proposed site. That action—and the documentary film that came out of it—became our call to arms.

Our assumption was that the nuclear industry could be beaten door-to-door, and our path led straight to Seabrook.

Through several weeks of meetings in the summer of 1976, representatives of New England grassroots organizations hammered out a new strategy. The Clamshell Alliance would employ mass civil disobedience. The actions, however, would be occupations, not demonstrations. The tactic of mass occupation, although untried in the United States, seemed to be our last resort. Nobody was winning any legal interventions, and there was no prospect of governmental action. We were not merely protesting nuclear construction—we were trying to stop it.

As an umbrella coalition, the Clamshell Alliance would help coordinate and focus the energies of the grassroots groups without imposing a rigid structure. All Clamshell meetings would operate on consensus rather than majority vote. There would be task-oriented committees, but no officers. The Alliance office would be a switchboard, resource, and convening center, but the decision making of the struggle would remain firmly in the hands of the local residents.

At the same time, all Clamshell actions would be organized along nonviolent precepts. In "affinity groups" of eight to twenty people, the occupiers were fully instructed in the legal ramifications of what they were about to do.

In the first occupation on August 1, 1976, eighteen occupiers—all from New Hampshire—walked along a mile of railroad track to become the first Americans to take part in mass civil disobedience at a nuclear reactor construction site. All had participated in a training session, though many of them knew each other well enough to act as an affinity group long before an occupation was ever contemplated.

On August 22, 1976, more than 1,500 Clamshell members rallied near the site and 180, representing all six New England states, occupied the PSC property. August 22 became our peaceful "shot heard 'round the world," and it made New England aware of nuclear power as nothing else short of a meltdown or a still larger occupation could have.

For many Alliance members, nonviolence is sine qua non, a deeply held religious commitment inseparable from their specific opposition to nuclear power. Nukes are, after all, engines of violence to both people and the planet, and that is the basic reason we oppose them. The nonviolent technique helped us draw the line between nuclear power as a technology of destruction and solar energy as one of peace.

Most important of all, however, the commitment to nonviolence has allowed us to attract a broad spectrum of people to both the nuclear issue and the prospect of personal participation in civil disobedience. Our unequivocal commitment to peace has opened neighborhood doors that might otherwise have been slammed shut.

With the help of nonviolence, we have witnessed the rise of a strong grassroots opposition in one of America's most conservative areas. In this growing struggle to stop nuclear reactors, we have found a coherence and a solidarity that have been missing from this country for too many years.

The atomic energy issue may, in fact, be the one to bring us all together. Nothing else short of war threatens the survival of the human race with such awesome finality. No other question cuts so deeply to the core of how we live, work, breathe, and make political decisions.

> —HARVEY WASSERMAN, writer, activist, solar power advocate, is the author of *Solartopia!* And with Bob Fitrakis, he exposed voting irregularities in Ohio in the presidential election of 2004.

## Earth First!

DAVE FOREMAN
OCTOBER 1981

The early conservation movement in the United States was a child—and no bastard child—of the Establishment. The founders of the Sierra Club, the Audubon Society, the Wilderness Society, and the wildlife conservation groups were, as a rule, wealthy pillars of American society. They were an elite band—sportsmen of the Teddy Roosevelt variety, naturalists like John Burroughs, outdoorsmen in the mold of John Muir, pioneer foresters and ecologists on the order of Aldo Leopold, and wealthy social visionaries like Robert Marshall. No anarchistic Luddites these.

When such groups as the Sierra Club grew into the politically effective force that blocked Echo Park Dam in 1956 and got the Wilderness Act passed in 1964, their members were likely to be physicians, mathematicians, and nuclear physicists. To be sure, in the 1950s and 1960s a few oddball refugees from the American mainstream joined the conservation outfits. But it was not until Earth Day in 1970 that the environmental movement received its first influx of real antiestablishment radicals as antiwar protesters found a new cause—the environment. Suddenly, in environmental meetings beards appeared alongside crew cuts—and the rhetoric quickened.

The militancy was short-lived. Along with dozens of other activists of the 1960s who went to work for conservation groups in the early 1970s, I discovered that a suit and tie gained access to regional foresters and members of Congress. We learned to moderate our opinions along with our dress. We heard that extremists were ignored in the councils of government, that the way to get a Senator to put his arm around your shoulders and drop a wilderness bill in the hopper was to consider the conflicts—mining, timber, grazing—and pare back the offending acreage. Of course we were good patriotic Americans. Of course we were concerned with the production of red meat, timber, and minerals. We tried to demonstrate that preserving wilderness did not conflict all that much with the gross national product and that clean air actually helped the economy.

Our moderate stance appeared to pay off when the first avowed conservationist since Teddy Roosevelt took the helm at the White House in 1977. Suddenly our colleagues—

self-professed conservationists—occupied important and decisive positions in the Carter Administration. Editorials proclaimed that environmentalism had been enshrined in the Establishment, that conservation was here to stay. A new environmental ethic was at hand: Environmental Quality and Continued Economic Progress.

But although we had access—indeed, influence—in high places, something seemed amiss. When the chips were down, conservation still lost out to industry. But these were our friends turning us down. We tried to understand the problems they faced in the real political world. We gave them the benefit of the doubt. We failed to sue when we should have.

But the moderate, subdued approach advanced by the major conservation groups contrasted with the howling, impassioned, extreme stand set forth by off-road-vehicle zealots, many ranchers, local boosters, loggers, and miners. They looked like fools. We looked like statesmen. Who won? They did.

"What have we really accomplished?" I thought. "Are we any better off as far as saving the Earth now than we were ten years ago?" I ticked off the real problems: world population growth, destruction of tropical forests, expanding slaughter of African wildlife, oil pollution of the ocean, acid rain, carbon dioxide buildup in the atmosphere, spreading deserts on every continent, destruction of native peoples and the imposition of one world culture (European), plans to carve up Antarctica, deep seabed mining, nuclear proliferation, recombinant DNA research, toxic wastes.

It was staggering. And I feared we had done nothing to reverse the tide. Indeed, it had accelerated.

And then: Ronald Reagan. James "Rape-'n'-Ruin" Watt is Secretary of the Interior. The Forest Service is Louisiana-Pacific's. Interior is Exxon's. The Environmental Protection Agency is Dow's. The cowboys have the grazing lands, and God help the hiker, coyote, or a blade of grass that gets in their way.

Maybe—some of us began to feel, even before Reagan's election—it was time for a new joker in the deck: a militant, uncompromising group unafraid to say what needed to be said or to back it up with stronger actions than the established organizations were willing to take.

We formed a new national group, Earth First! We set out to be radical in style, positions, philosophy, and organization in order to be effective and to avoid the pitfalls of co-option and moderation which we had already experienced.

We set out to demonstrate that the Sierra Club and its allies were raging moderates, believers in the system, and to refute the Reagan/Watt contention that they were "extremist environmentalists."

We set out to return some vigor, joy, and enthusiasm to the allegedly tired environmental movement.

We set out to provide a productive fringe, since it seems that ideas, creativity, and energy spring up on the fringe and later spread into the middle.

We set out to inspire others to carry out activities straight from the pages of *The Monkey Wrench Gang* even though Earth First! we agreed, would itself be ostensibly law-abiding.

And we set out to question the system; to help develop a new worldview, a bio-centric paradigm, an Earth philosophy. To fight, with uncompromising passion, for Mother Earth.

The name—Earth First!—was chosen deliberately because it succinctly summed up the one thing on which we could all agree: That in any decision, consideration for the health of the Earth must come first, or, as Aldo Leopold said, "A thing is right when it tends to preserve the integrity, stability, and beauty of the biotic community. It is wrong when it tends otherwise."

In a true Earth-radical group, concern for wilderness preservation must be the key-stone. The idea of wilderness, after all, is the most radical in human thought—more radical than Paine, than Marx, than Mao. Wilderness says: Human beings are not dominant, Earth is not for Homo sapiens alone, human life is but one life form on the planet and has no right to take exclusive possession. Yes, wilderness for its own sake, without any need to justify it for human benefit. Wilderness for wilderness. For grizzlies and whales and titmice and rattlesnakes and stink bugs. And . . . wilderness for human beings. Because it is the laboratory of 3 million years of human evolution—and because it is home.

Obviously, for a group more committed to Gila monsters and mountain lions than to people, there will not be a total alliance with the other social movements. But there are issues where Earth radicals can cooperate with feminist, Indian rights, anti-nuke, peace, civil rights, and civil liberties groups.

Action is the key. Action is more important than philosophical hair-splitting or end-less refining of dogma (for which radicals are so well known). Let our actions set the finer points of our philosophy. Earth First! would be big enough to contain street poets and cowboy bar bouncers, agnostics and pagans, vegetarians and raw steak eaters, pacifists and those who think that turning the other cheek is a good way to get a sore face.

For Earth First! it is all or nothing. Win or lose. No truce or cease fire. No surren-der. No partitioning of the territory.

Perhaps it is a hopeless quest. But is that relevant? Is that important? No, what is important is that one who loves Earth can do no less. Maybe a species will be saved or a forest will go uncut or a dam will be torn down. Maybe not. A monkey wrench thrown into the gears of the machine may not stop it. But it might delay it. Make it cost more. And it feels good to put it there.

—DAVE FOREMAN cofounded Earth First! After that, he helped found the Wildlands Project and the New Mexico Wilderness Alliance and the Rewilding Institute. He's the author of *Confessions of an Eco-Warrior.*

# An Interview with Wendell Berry, Writer, Farmer, Environmentalist

CAROL POLSGROVE and SCOTT SANDERS
MAY 1990

Q: We've had so much media hype on the environment recently. Should we take this seriously as an indication that people are coming to some point of awareness of environmental concerns?

WENDELL BERRY: I don't think we can take it seriously until people begin to talk seriously about lowering the standard of living. When people begin to see affluence, economic growth, unrestrained economic behavior, as the enemies of the environment, then we can take it seriously. But people are saying, "Give us everything we want and a clean environment," and that isn't a possibility.

Q: What are some things they want that they can't have?

BERRY: Unlimited amounts of plastic, for one. But almost all manufactured goods are causing pollution. We're in a situation in which we have problems but no environmentally sound solutions.

Q: For instance?

BERRY: I went to town yesterday to buy some chalk for a chalk-line, a carpenter's chalk-line. I came home with a bunch of chalk dust in a big plastic bottle. Almost everything you buy now comes in a plastic container. The roadsides are littered with trash—well, you see, you start pulling the thread and you find that everything's connected to everything else. Food from the fast food places is packaged in plastic trash. People are eating more junk food now—more fast food—because everybody's working. Why, all of a sudden, does it take two people working to support a household when not so long ago, one person working could support a household? Who's getting the money? Why is so much money needed? You can start with an issue of livelihood and wind up with an issue of the environment. And that's the connection that has to be made.

Q: What about the chances of some kind of grassroots leadership organized from below?

BERRY: That's where the hope is now. I don't see very much chance of the cities producing a grassroots movement that can directly cause change. The cities may finally exert a grassroots demand that can cause change, but the cities are helpless. The capacity of people in the cities to do things for themselves directly is extremely limited. They can't produce food; they can't produce building materials; they can't produce the materials needed for clothing; they're so cut off from the natural sources of their livelihood and so cut off from fundamental skills, most of them, that they can't directly do much of anything.

One of the hopes in agriculture, though, is that city people will demand a food supply that's safer and of better quality than the one they have now.

Q: And there are some signs of that?

BERRY: There are some signs of that happening. I hope it goes ahead and happens. What I'm looking toward is the possibility that the country people, who do still have some capacity to help themselves directly, will start doing so. I think what this means is simply the rebuilding of communities.

Q: Does that mean people moving to the country?

BERRY: Eventually it might mean that. What it means immediately, to me, is that the people who are left in the country are going to have to start helping each other again in practical and economic ways.

Q: Are you talking about co-ops?

BERRY: Well, no. I'm not necessarily talking about organizations at all. I'm talking about the unorganized institutions of families and neighborhoods. It's still an ordinary thing here for farmers to trade work. When there are neighborhood exchanges of labor, that works to the advantage of the neighborhood and not to the advantage of the larger economy.

The situation we have now, it seems to me, is that the larger economy—the national economy—is really being run for the benefit of very few people. It is preying upon and slowly destroying the local communities, everywhere. It's very clear that this is happening all over the rural United States. Rural America is a bona fide part of the Third World. It's a colony. Some parts are recognizably Third World— the Appalachian coal fields and the destroyed farm towns of the Middle West. But all of it is at one stage or another of moving toward Third World status. That is, everything we produce in rural America makes more money for other people than it does for the people who produce it.

They want our products as cheaply as they can be bought. They want to sell us their products as expensively as we can bear. They want our young people. We're destroying rural America and we're destroying the rural American communities.

But these communities still have access to land they can use in their own interest. They have access to materials they can use in their own interest. And they still have, to varying degrees, the fundamental skills necessary to work in their own interest. So the rural communities, it seems to me, are places you could look to for some kind of new start.

Q: Do you see any signs of that?

BERRY: Yes, there are some signs of it. One thing that reassures you, if you travel the country, is that scattered all over are people who are doing good work, who are trying to find the better ways. And they are finding some of them.

So the better possibility exists. The problem is getting the country as a whole to pay attention to it. Or getting any leader to pay attention to it. These leaders are a terribly cowardly bunch, by and large. They are terribly embarrassed and ashamed to propose anything different. They think it's unmanly to come up with something different; the manly thing is to stand on the prow and sail over the edge.

If you're going to sustain anything, you've got to have populations that are locally committed. The idea that you can destroy this place and go to another place is exhausted. We can't do that anymore.

—CAROL POLSGROVE taught journalism at Indiana University for many years. Her books include: *It Wasn't Pretty Folks, But Didn't We Have Fun?* and *Divided Minds: Intellectuals and the Civil Rights Movement.* SCOTT SANDERS teaches English at Indiana University and is the author of nineteen books, including *The Paradise of Bombs, Writing from the Center,* and *A Private History of Awe.*

## An Interview with Winona LaDuke, Native American Environmentalist, Green Party Vice Presidential Candidate with Ralph Nader

SONYA PAUL and ROBERT PERKINSON
OCTOBER 1995

Q: In the environmental movement, the word "sustainability" has become almost a cliché. How does your concept of sustainable economics and development differ from mainline understandings?

WINONA LADUKE: Native communities have an inherent advantage in understanding and creating sustainability. They have cultural cohesion and a land base, and both of these foundations are essential for any sustainable community. These days, there are a lot of New Agers creating "intentional communities," collective farms, housing, and so on, and I think it's great. But those who build community from scratch have much less going for them than we do. They have to make a community; we already have one. Indigenous peoples collectively remember who they are, and that memory creates a cultural fabric that holds us together. That's why rural, Native organizing is so vital. It can be the watershed of sustainability.

Q: How does this traditional understanding of sustainability shape your political work?

LADUKE: Take the White Earth Reservation. Here we have a sustainable-communities project. Its purpose is to sort out what is useful from our culture and from Euro-American cultures in order to move forward. On our organic raspberry farm, for example, we use tractors and other technologies. We also are investigating solar and wind power in the area. Innovations don't have to be indigenous, but they should at least make sense within our cultural practice and context. The question we ask ourselves is, "Does this technology fit?" As it turns out, it's a question of fundamental importance. It's natural to ask from the perspective of indigenous values, and it speaks to the entire framework of sustainability.

But the question of whether a product should be invented at all almost never comes up in the United States. If it did, we would live in a very different world. Products that don't biodegrade might never be produced, and our economy would have an inherent base of common sense. I believe that in order to build a sustainable society overall, indigenous peoples need to reinsert this criterion into the mainstream, "If the Creator didn't make it like that, should it be here?"

Q: What doesn't fit?

LADUKE: Sometimes you know something doesn't fit right away. For example, some people are using air boats to harvest wild rice now. But there is widespread opposition on the reservation because wild rice is a cultural wellspring. According to our traditions, the Creator gave us wild rice as a food, and the instructions on how to harvest it didn't include an air boat.

Q: What has your work with Greenpeace been like?

LADUKE: I've been on the board of Greenpeace since 1991 and have seen it undergo major changes. Greenpeace has grown from its "guys-on-boats" reputation to being capable of working closely with communities. When I first started, Greenpeace was suing some Indians to stop their subsistence harvest. Today, we have a sovereignty policy that prevents that type of interference. Now there is a lot more collaboration and discussion with Native peoples.

My work has been to support Native campaigns, leverage resources, and challenge Greenpeace's basic political agenda. We need to revisit who gets to decide what is an important and urgent issue. This is a fundamental question that needs to be asked of these white organizations, "Who has that right?"

Q: What would a model of traditional governance and decentralization mean for the United States as a whole?

LADUKE: It would undermine the entire structure of empire. If leadership and political power truly rested with local communities, then multinationals would find it impossible to poison their locales in the name of a "greater good." Absentee landowners would cease to exist, and small communities could preserve their distinct integrity. Cooperating on a smaller level could help everyone—Indian communities, Amish communities, urban enclaves, and so on. These can all be healthy, but they need to be nourished. As it is today, they are being technologically and culturally homogenized.

The last 400 years have been about building empires. This is not sustainable. Empires are about taking what doesn't belong to you and consuming more than you need. In order to move forward, we need to acknowledge this ongoing history. This is the fundamental paradigm of appropriation that remains unquestioned in America. We need to ask, "What right does the United States really have to this place?"

—SONYA PAUL (now Sonya Paul Gavin) works as the Office and Special Events Manager in the Vice Chancellor and Dean's Office of UCLA's Graduate Division. ROBERT PERKINSON teaches at the University of Hawaii–Manoa, specializing in criminal justice and empire.

## Arctic Heat Wave

BRUCE E. JOHANSEN
OCTOBER 2001

It's another warm day in Iqaluit, capital of the new semi-sovereign Inuit nation of Nunavut in the Canadian Arctic. The bizarre weather is the talk of the town. The urgency of global warming is on everyone's lips.

The temperature hit 82 degrees Fahrenheit on July 28 in this Baffin Island community that nudges the Arctic Circle. That's thirty-five degrees above the July average of 47, making it comparable to a 115- to 120-degree day in New York City or Chicago.

It is the warmest summer anyone in the area can remember. Swallows, sand flies, and robins are making their debuts, and pine pollen is affecting people as never before. Travelers joke about forgetting their shorts, sunscreen, and mosquito repellent—all now necessary equipment for a globally warmed Arctic summer.

In Iqaluit (pronounced "Eehalooeet"), a warm, desiccating westerly wind raises whitecaps on nearby Frobisher Bay and rustles carpets of purple saxifrage flowers as people emerge from their overheated houses (which have been built to absorb every scrap of passive solar energy) with ice cubes wrapped in hand towels. The wind raises eddies of dust on Iqaluit's gravel roads as residents swat at the slow, corpulent mosquitoes.

Welcome to the thawing ice-world of the third millennium. Around the Arctic, in Inuit villages connected by the oral history of traveling hunters as well as by e-mail now, weather watchers are reporting striking evidence that global warming is an unmistakable reality. Sachs Harbour, on Banks Island, above the Arctic Circle, is sinking into the permafrost. Shishmaref, an Inuit village on the far-western lip of Alaska sixty miles north of Nome, is being washed into the newly liquid (and often stormy) Arctic Ocean as its permafrost base dissolves.

A world based on ice and snow is melting away.

"We have never seen anything like this. It's scary, very scary," says Ben Kovic, Nunavut's chief wildlife manager. "It's not every summer that we run around in our T-shirts for weeks at a time."

"The glaciers are turning brown," he says, speculating that melting ice may be exposing debris and that air pollution may be a factor. Rivers have dried up that used to be spawning grounds for Arctic char.

Other changes are more menacing. During Iqaluit's weeks of record heat in July, two tourists were hospitalized after they were mauled by a polar bear in a park south of town. The bears are "often becoming shore dwellers rather than ice dwellers," says Kovic. The harbor ice at Iqaluit did not form last year until late December, five or six weeks later than usual. The ice also breaks up earlier in the spring, sometimes in May in places that once were icebound into early July. Polar bears usually obtain their food (seals, for example) from the ice. Without it, they can become hungry, miserable creatures, especially in unaccustomed warmth.

"The bears are looking for a cooler place," says Kovic.

On Hudson Bay in Manitoba, polar bears waking from their winter's slumber have found the ice melted earlier than usual. Instead of making their way onto the ice in search of seals, the bears walk along the coast until they get to towns like Churchill, where they block motor traffic and pillage the dump. Churchill now has a holding tank for wayward polar bears that is larger than its human jail.

Canadian Wildlife Service scientists reported in 1998 that polar bears around Hudson Bay were 90 to 220 pounds lighter than thirty years ago, apparently because earlier ice-melting has given them less time to feed on seal pups. When sea ice fails to reach a particular area, the entire ecological cycle is disrupted. When the ice melts prematurely, the polar bears can no longer use it to hunt for ring seals, many of which also have died, having had no ice to haul out on.

The offshore, ice-based ecosystem is sustained by upwelling nutrients, which feed the plankton, shrimp, and other small organisms, which feed the fish, which feed the seals, which feed the bears. Many Native people, who fish and hunt for their sustenance, are also deprived of a way of life. When the ice is not present, the entire cycle collapses.

Ice in many areas now melts earlier, sometimes as early as March, when the seals are having their pups. Because the ice breaks up too early, the pups often have not been fully weaned. Many of them starve or grow up in a weakened state. Warmer average temperatures may mean that the Arctic Ocean will become ice-free much of the year, imperiling populations of walrus and seal that feed on creatures living on the ice.

The Arctic's rapid thaw has made hunting, never a safe or easy way of life, even more difficult and dangerous. Last winter, Simon Nattaq, an Inuit hunter, fell through unusually thin ice and became mired in icy water long enough to lose both his legs to hypothermia, one of several injuries and deaths reported around the Arctic recently due to thinning ice.

Climate change has been rapid, and easily detectable within a single human lifetime. "When I was a child," said Sheila Watt-Cloutier, Canadian president of the Inuit Circumpolar Conference, "we never swam in the river where I was born, and now kids swim in there all of the time." Cloutier does not remember even having worn short pants as a child.

Gunter Weller, director of the Center for Global Change and Arctic System Research at the University of Alaska in Fairbanks, says mean temperatures in the state have increased by five degrees Fahrenheit in the summer and ten degrees in the winter over the last thirty years. Moreover, the Arctic ice field has shrunk by 40 percent to 50 percent over the last few decades and has lost 10 percent of its thickness, studies show.

Some Alaskan forests have been drowning and turning gray as thawing ground sinks under them. Trees and roadside utility poles, destabilized by thawing, lean at crazy angles. The warming has contributed a new phrase to the English language in Alaska: "the drunken forest."

"The people in my community are completely dependent on hunting, trapping, and fishing," says Rosmary Kuptana, who grew up in Sachs Harbour. "We don't know when to travel on the ice, and our food sources are getting farther and farther away. Our way of life is being permanently altered."

> —BRUCE E. JOHANSEN teaches at the University of Nebraska–Omaha and has written two dozen books, including several on Native American issues and on global warming. He is the author of the three-volume series *Global Warming in the 21st Century*.

# An Interview with Terry Tempest Williams, Writer, Environmentalist

DAVID KUPFER

FEBRUARY 2005

Q: How has your sense of place affected your outlook?

TERRY TEMPEST WILLIAMS: I come from an old Mormon family, six generations. Our ancestors came across the plains with Brigham Young in 1847, when he settled the Salt Lake Valley. I was raised in the interior American West. The space seemed infinite. It was a wonderful place to grow up. Our family spent most of our time together outside, so there was never a separation between the land, our family, and our spiritual life. For four generations, the Tempest family has made a living by putting in natural gas lines, water lines, sewage lines, optic fiber cables. Our family has made its livelihood from the land, digging trenches for hundreds of miles cross-country. You could say this is a real paradox, to destroy the land, yet love it at the same time. This is a typical story of Westerners, how we build community through change.

For me, it always comes back to the land, respecting the land, the wildlife, the plants, the rivers, mountains, and deserts, the absolute essential bedrock of our lives. This is the source of where my power lies, the source of where all our power lies. We are animal. We are earth. We are water. We are a community of human beings living on this planet together. And we forget that. We become disconnected, we lose our center point of gravity, that stillness that allows us to listen to life on a deeper level and to meet each other in a fully authentic and present way.

As children, we had access to all the open space imaginable. We would set up camps in rural Utah where the Tempest Company was at work laying pipe. We spent time in Wyoming, Idaho, Nevada, and Colorado—wild beautiful places. Now, many of these natural places have disappeared under the press of development.

Q: Do you look to your writing as a tool for your activism?

WILLIAMS: I do. I never will forget when I crossed the line at the Nevada Test Site in the Mojave Desert just outside Las Vegas. Before arresting me, the officer searched my body and found a pen and a notepad tucked inside my boots. "And these?" she asked. "Weapons," I replied. She quietly slipped my pant leg over my boots and let me keep them. Writing can be a powerful tool toward justice. Story bypasses rhetoric and pierces the heart. We feel it. Stories have the power to create social change and inspire community. But good writing must stay open to the questions and not fall prey to the pull of a polemic, otherwise, words simply become predictable, sentimental, and stale.

Q: What role should direct action play in the conservation and environmental movement?

WILLIAMS: It's a personal decision not to be taken lightly. I know when I chose to commit civil disobedience at the Nevada Test Site for the first time in 1988, it was not only a political decision but a spiritual one. I thought about this gesture, long and hard. I felt the gravity of its tradition, the seriousness of its action. I remember reading Gandhi's words and Martin Luther King's "Letter from a Birmingham Jail," along with Thoreau's essay. I went through nonviolent training led by seasoned activists at the Test Site sponsored by the Nevada Desert Experience. And I was not alone; there was a great solidarity among the men and women who were far more experienced about social actions than I was, including the Shoshone elders whose land the Test Site is on. So I think direct political action, civil disobedience, in particular, is something to be taken very seriously. I belong to "a clan of one-breasted women," where nine women in my family have all had mastectomies; seven have died, as a result of nuclear testing and radioactive fallout. We are downwinders. As we speak, my brother is in the last stages of lymphoma. There are times we have to put our body on the line for what we believe, for the injustices we see even within our own families.

Q: Could you speak to environmentalism in the Mormon Church?

WILLIAMS: At the heart of Mormonism is a high regard for community. That is its strength. I have great respect for that, and I think that for those of us living in Utah—for those of us who are Mormon, even if we are not orthodox—the way into an environmental conversation with the Mormon Church is through the door of community. And if we respect the Creator, then it logically follows that we respect Creation. I think of my great-grandmother Vilate Lee Romney, who came from good pioneer Mormon stock. She always said to us that faith without works is dead, so maybe that is the most important thing of all, to have our faith rooted in action. Our community in Castle Valley, Utah, gives me hope. It is a group of people who have committed to caring for a place, both human and wild. If I walked forever, I would never be able to cover this native ground of wonder and awe. I really do believe if there is hope in the world, then it is to be found within our own communities with our own neighbors, and within our own homes and families. Hope radiates outward from the center of our concerns. Hope dares us to stare the miraculous in the eye and have the courage not to look away.

—DAVID KUPFER is a freelance writer, environmental consultant, and organic grower.

# An Interview with Wangari Maathai, Winner of the Nobel Peace Prize

AMITABH PAL
MAY 2005

Q: What is the significance of the Nobel Committee expanding the definition of peace?

WANGARI MAATHAI: The metaphor that I have adopted is the metaphor of the African stool. The usual African stool has three legs, and the three legs represent for me peace, democracy, and sustainable, equitable management of resources.

Q: How did the Green Belt Movement get started and how did you forge the links between environmentalism and women's rights?

MAATHAI: Many women in rural areas said they were concerned about firewood, which was the main source of energy. They were concerned about water; there wasn't adequate clean drinking water. They were concerned about nutritious food, and they were concerned about poverty, especially among women. I immediately suggested that perhaps what we should do with these women is to plant trees. I saw the connection between land degradation and lack of water, so I continued with the program of tree planting. I started with a small group. Then it became two groups. Eventually, it was thousands of groups planting trees to restore the land and improve the quality of life.

Q: Why were you attacked for planting trees?

MAATHAI: Planting trees, per se, would not have been a problem. Nobody would have bothered me if all I did was to encourage women to plant trees. But I started seeing the linkages between the problems that we were dealing with and the root causes. And one of those root causes was misgovernance. The government had approved the clear-cutting of forests that were catchment areas for water and encouraged the cultivating of exotic plantations. It was the government that had allowed the people to go into the forests and to start cultivating food crops. All this had caused the massive destruction of forests, which could absorb water, which could give us normal rain patterns, and which could sustain the rivers. So I knew that even if I planted all the trees downstream, the stream itself was being destroyed by the government. It was important for us to address the government and to ask the government to stop destroying the catchment areas upstream.

The other problem we were facing was that a lot of our leaders in the government, especially in the 1980s, privatized a lot of these common goods. So I started raising my voice and educating the public on how the environment was being destroyed and who was destroying it. And how it was important for us to hold our leaders accountable for the better management of resources.

This is what the government did not like because the ruling elite was the beneficiary of these malpractices. And so their reaction was to intimidate, arrest, harass, in the hope that I would give up, or the people with whom I was working would give up, and the movement would die. We knew they were greedy and corrupt. So it was a matter of fighting corruption and fighting greed among the ruling elite.

The women were the major force in the movement. We were the ones who were being harassed. We were the ones who were being prevented from meeting. We were the ones who were the victims of the destruction that was going on. We, therefore, eventually adopted a campaign for our rights. So the tree planting campaign has always been in the forefront. It is the most visible campaign. But we branched into many other activities in an effort to deal with the root causes of environmental degradation.

Q: How do you respond to people who say fighting poverty takes precedence over protecting the environment?

MAATHAI: Poverty is both a cause and a symptom of environmental degradation. You can't say you'll start to deal with just one. You're trapped. When you're in poverty, you're trapped because the poorer you become, the more you degrade the environment, and the more you degrade the environment, the poorer you become.

So it's a matter of breaking the cycle. From the very beginning, that's what I was telling the women, that we cannot solve all the problems that we face: We are poor, we don't have water, we don't have energy, we don't have food, we don't have income, we're not able to send our children to school. There are too many problems we face. We have to break the cycle, and the way to break the cycle for us is to do something that is doable, is to do something that is cheap, do something that is within our power, our capacity, our resources.

Planting a tree was the best idea that I had because it is easy, it is doable, and you could go and tell ordinary women with no education: OK, this is the tree. It is now flowering. We're going to observe the tree until it produces seeds. When they're ready, we'll harvest them. We'll dry them, we'll put them in the soil. If they're good, we'll germinate them. We'll nurture them. We'll plant them in our gardens. If they're fruit trees, within five years we will have fruits. If they're for fodder, our animals will have fodder.

The tree for me became a wonderful way of breaking that cycle.

—AMITABH PAL is the managing editor of *The Progressive* and coeditor of the Progressive Media Project.

# PART 8

# Reforming Criminal Justice

Dostoevsky once said, "The degree of civilization in a society can be judged by entering its prisons."

By that yardstick, the United States is not very civilized.

Almost alone among advanced industrial countries, it still carries out the death penalty, a hideous practice that *The Progressive* has consistently opposed. Leo Tolstoy himself set the tone with the short essay La Follette published in 1910. The interview with Sister Helen Prejean details not only the inhumanity of capital punishment but also the class and race biases that so define it.

But it's not just capital punishment that besmirches the reputation of the United States. Anne-Marie Cusac, who for ten years covered the criminal justice beat for *The Progressive* and won the George Polk award for doing so, draws a disturbing comparison between the treatment of prisoners in the United States and the treatment of detainees at Abu Ghraib prison in Iraq.

A lot of criminal behavior stems from growing up in poverty or having a brutal childhood. And while each individual is responsible for the crime that he or she commits, we are wise as a society to investigate these circumstances. The great poet and essayist June Jordan does so better than almost anyone else in her surprising and extraordinary piece on Mike Tyson, "Requiem for the Champ."

# To the Hangmen's Managers and Sympathizers

LEO TOLSTOY
DECEMBER 3, 1910

I am naturally anxious to do all I can against evil, which tortures the best spirits of our time.

I think the present effective war against capital punishment does not need forcing; there is no need for an expression of indignation against its immorality, cruelty, and absurdity—every sincere thinking person, everybody knowing from youth the sixth commandment, needs no explanation of its absurdity and immorality; there is no need for descriptions of the horrors of executions as they only affect hangmen, so men will more unwillingly become executioners and governments will be obliged to compensate them more dearly for their services.

Neither the expression of indignation against the murder of our fellow men nor the suggestion of its horror is mainly needed, but something totally different.

As Kant well says, there are delusions which cannot be disproved and we must communicate to the deluded mind knowledge which will enlighten, and then the delusions will vanish by themselves.

What knowledge need we communicate to the deluded human mind regarding the indispensableness, usefulness, or justice of capital punishment in order that said delusion may destroy itself?

Such knowledge, in my opinion, is this: The knowledge of what is man, what his surrounding world, what his destiny—hence, what man can and must do and principally what he cannot and must not do.

We should oppose capital punishment by inculcating this knowledge to all men, especially to hangmen's managers and sympathizers who wrongfully think they are maintaining their position thanks only to capital punishment.

I know this is not an easy task. The employers and approvers of hangmen with the instinct of self-preservation feel that this knowledge will make impossible the maintenance of the position which they occupy, hence not only will they themselves not adopt it, but by all means in their power—by violence, deceit, lies, and cruelty—they will try to hide from the people this knowledge, distorting it and exposing its disseminators to all kinds of privations and suffering.

Therefore, if we really wish to destroy the delusion of capital punishment and if we possess the knowledge which destroys this delusion, let us, in spite of all menaces, deprivations, and sufferings, teach the people this knowledge because it is solely the effective means in the fight.

—LEO TOLSTOY, Russian novelist and pacifist, wrote *Anna Karenina* and *War and Peace.*

# Capital Punishment

BELLE CASE LA FOLLETTE
AUGUST 31, 1912

"Do you believe in capital punishment?" asked a United Press reporter over the telephone a few days ago. The occasion for the "interview" was that seven men were to meet death in the electric chair at Sing Sing and that two prisoners were condemned to be hanged here in the District of Columbia.

I cannot get accustomed to the fact that the laws and practice that prevail in the District of Columbia are so apt to be an example of unenlightenment. They are subject to the revision of Congress, and if there is a place where capital punishment should not exist, it is here in sight of the Capitol dome.

I do not object to the death penalty because I think it such a terrible thing for the individuals to whom it is administered, provided they are guilty of deliberate murder. Thousands of innocent people die daily from wrecks, drowning, and catastrophes of all kinds, who suffer more. History gives many examples of men and women who have met the headsman with a jest. And observers say that the average man, when he goes to his execution, usually keeps his nerve, even to eating a good breakfast. Nature prepares us all for the inevitable end.

But capital punishment is a survival of barbarism, and its existence is contrary to the best thought and practice of modern civilization. Some wardens say that life prisoners, particularly those who have committed murder under extenuating circumstances, who perhaps might never again violate the law, are much less a menace than those habituated to lesser crimes—professional, so to speak.

Broader understanding of the cause of crime and responsibility for it is tending slowly to revolutionize the plan of dealing with it. The highest authorities recognize that the struggle is social, not individual; that retaliation and retributive justice is impossible and the attempt to administer it does not lessen the evil-doing.

Investigation and experience have proved what common sense ought always to have told us: that solitary confinement, or worse, promiscuous herding of criminals in idleness and under harsh conditions, makes the savage more savage, and destroys the hope of improving those not wholly degraded.

Humane and scientific conditions in places of detention—sunlight, air, cleanliness, and methods of reformation—regular employment in healthful and varied and useful occupations, with a degree of compensation as an incentive together with indeterminate sentences, boards for pardon, probation—are all indications of the changed attitude of society toward those convicted of violations of the law.

Society is beginning to recognize its responsibility for crime and its obligation to at least administer the law so that its operation will not further degrade the offenders. It is wise economy—even though the first cost be somewhat greater—to direct the effort formerly expended in "punishment" of those imprisoned to fitting them to live and to earn a living, so they may return to the world better prepared to cope with temptation and with less likelihood of being a further menace to society.

# Death Punishment Does Not Deter Crime

Senator John J. Blaine
AUGUST 1927

I am convinced that the old doctrine of an eye for an eye and a tooth for a tooth cannot be sustained as the basis of punishment. Our present social organization, with the advance of science and the study of crime and its causes, will lead any thoughtful person to a conclusion quite contrary to the doctrine of vengeance or retribution.

Setting aside for the time the religious, moral, and ethical objections to taking human life by law, our attention is called to the practicability or the expediency of doing away with death sentences.

The states having no capital punishment for a ten-year period have a low homicide rate in comparison with death-penalty states.

If these facts prove anything, they prove that the death penalty has little or no effect as a deterrent.

There is no single fact in history that supports death sentences or corporal punishment involving the whipping post, the pillory, the stock, the putting out of eyes, scalping, cutting off ears, lips, nose, hands and feet, or other physical mutilation. Wherever those forms of punishment have prevailed crime has gone on unabated. In every jurisdiction where the purposes of punishment have been reformation and segregation, crime has been less flourishing.

Blindly employing the methods of the barbarous past will not cure the crime of murder, or other offenses.

Punishment by death is not a deterrent; the evidence on every hand proves that it is not a cure. The taking of human life as a mode of punishment is not justified in historical facts or human experience. It is cruel and barbarous; it cheapens life; it is morally and ethically wrong, unchristian, impractical, and inexpedient.

—Senator John J. Blaine represented the state of Wisconsin in the U.S. Senate from 1927 to 1933.

# Requiem for the Champ

JUNE JORDAN
APRIL 1992

Mike Tyson comes from Brooklyn. And so do I. He grew up about a twenty-minute bus ride from my house. I always thought his neighborhood looked like a war zone. It reminded me of Berlin immediately after World War II. I had never seen Berlin except for black-and-white photos in *Life* magazine, but that was bad enough: rubble, barren, blasted. Everywhere you turned, your eyes recoiled from the jagged edges of an office building or a cathedral, shattered, or the tops of apartment houses torn off, and nothing alive even intimated, anywhere. I used to think, "This is what it means to fight and really win or really lose. War means you hurt somebody, or something, until there's nothing soft or sensible left."

For sure I never had a boyfriend who came out of Mike Tyson's territory. Yes, I enjoyed my share of tough guys and gang members who walked and talked and fought and loved in quintessential Brooklyn ways: cool, tough, and deadly serious. But there was a code as rigid and as romantic as anything that ever made the pages of traditional English literature.

A guy would beat up another guy or, if appropriate, he'd kill him. But a guy talked different to a girl. A guy made other guys clean up their language around "his girl." A guy brought ribbons and candies and earrings and tulips to a girl. He took care of her. He walked her home. And if he got serious about that girl, and even if she was only twelve years old, then she became his "lady." And woe betide any other guy stupid enough to disrespect that particular young black female.

But none of the boys—none of the young men, none of the young black male inhabitants of my universe and my heart—ever came from Mike Tyson's streets or avenues. We didn't live someplace fancy or middle-class, but at least there were ten-cent gardens, front and back, and coin laundromats, and grocery stores, and soda parlors, and barber shops, and holy-roller church fronts, and chicken shacks, and dry cleaners, and bars and grills, and a takeout Chinese restaurant, and all of that kind of usable detail that does not survive a war. That kind of seasonal green turf and daily life-supporting pattern of establishments to meet your needs did not exist inside the gelid urban cemetery where Mike Tyson learned what he thought he needed to know.

I remember when the City of New York decided to construct a senior housing project there, in the childhood world of former heavyweight boxing champion Mike Tyson. I remember wondering, "Where in the hell will those old people have to go in order to find food? And how will they get there?"

I'm talking godforsaken. And much of living in Brooklyn was like that. But then it might rain or it might snow and, for example, I could look at the rain forcing forsythia into bloom or watch how snowflakes can tease bare tree limbs into temporary blossoms of snow dissolving into diadems of sunlight.

And what did Mike Tyson ever see besides brick walls and garbage in the gutter and disintegrating concrete steps and boarded-up windows and broken car parts blocking the sidewalk and men, bitter, with their hands in their pockets, and women, bitter, with their heads down and their eyes almost closed?

In his neighborhood, where could you buy ribbons for a girl, or tulips?

Mike Tyson comes from Brooklyn. And so do I.

In the big picture of America, I never had much going for me. And he had less.

I only learned, last year, that I can stop whatever violence starts with me. I only learned, last year, that love is infinitely more interesting, and more exciting, and more powerful, than really winning or really losing a fight. I only learned, last year, that all war leads to death and that all love leads you away from death.

I am more than twice Mike Tyson's age. And I'm not stupid. Or slow. But I'm black. And I come from Brooklyn. And I grew up fighting. And I grew up and I got out of Brooklyn because I got pretty good at fighting. And winning. Or else, intimidating my would-be adversaries with my fists, my feet, and my mouth.

I never wanted to fight. I never wanted anybody to hit me. And I never wanted to hit anybody. But the bell would ring at the end of another dumb day in school and I'd head out with dread and a nervous sweat because I knew some jackass more or less my age and more or less my height would be waiting for me because she or he had nothing better to do than to wait for me and hope to kick my butt or tear up my books or break my pencils or pull hair out of my head.

This is the meaning of poverty: When you have nothing better to do than to hate somebody who, just exactly like yourself, has nothing better to do than to pick on you instead of trying to figure out how come there's nothing better to do. How come there's no gym, no swimming pool, no dirt track, no soccer field, no ice-skating rink, no bike, no bike path, no tennis courts, no language arts workshop, no computer-science center, no band practice, no choir rehearsal, no music lessons, no basketball or baseball team? How come neither one of you has his or her own room in a house where you can hang out and dance and make out or get on the telephone or eat and drink up everything in the kitchen that can move? How come nobody on your block and nobody in your class has any of these things?

I'm black. Mike Tyson is black. And neither one of us was ever supposed to win anything more than a fight between the two of us.

And if you check out the mass media material on "us," and if you check out the emergency-room reports on "us," you might well believe we're losing the fight to be more than our enemies have decreed. Our enemies would deprive us of everything except each other: Hungry and furious and drug-addicted and rejected and ever convinced we can never be beautiful or right or true or different from the beggarly monsters our enemies envision and insist upon. How should we then stand, black man and black woman, face to face?

Way back when I was born, Richard Wright had just published *Native Son* and, thereby, introduced white America to the monstrous product of its racist hatred. Richard Wright's Bigger Thomas did what he thought he had to do: He hideously murdered a white woman and he viciously murdered his black girlfriend in what he conceived as self-defense. He did not perceive any options to these psychopathic, horrifying deeds. I do not believe he, Bigger Thomas, had any other choices open to him. He was meant to die like the rat he was, Bigger Thomas, cornered, and smashed to death, in his mother's beggarly clean space.

I never thought Bigger Thomas was okay. I never thought he should skate back into my, or anyone's, community. But I did and I do think he is my brother. The choices available to us dehumanize. And any single one of us, black in this white country, we may be defeated, we may become dehumanized, by the monstrous hatred arrayed against us and our needy dreams.

Poverty does not beatify. Poverty does not teach generosity or allow for sucker attributes of tenderness and restraint. In white America, hatred of black folks has imposed 360 degrees of poverty upon us.

And so I write this requiem for Mike Tyson: international celebrity, millionaire, former heavyweight boxing champion of the world, a big-time winner, a big-time loser, an African American male in his twenties, and, now, a convicted rapist.

Do I believe he is guilty of rape?

Yes I do.

And what would I propose as appropriate punishment?

Whatever will force him to fear the justice of exact retribution, and whatever will force him, for the rest of his damned life, to regret and to detest the fact that he defiled, he subjugated, and he wounded, somebody helpless to his power.

And do I therefore rejoice in the jury's finding?

I do not.

Well, would I like to see Mike Tyson a free man again?

He was never free.

And I do not excuse or condone or forget or forgive the crime of his violation of the young black woman he raped!

But did anybody ever tell Mike Tyson that you talk different to a girl? Where would he learn that?

Would he learn that from U.S. Senator Ted Kennedy?

Or from hotshot/scot-free movie director Roman Polanski?

Or from rap recording star Ice Cube?

Or from Ronald Reagan and the Grenada escapade?

Or from George Bush in Panama?

Or from George Bush and Colin Powell in the Persian Gulf?

Or from the military hero flyboys who returned from bombing the shit out of civilian cities in Iraq and then said, laughing and proud, on international TV: "All I need, now, is a woman"?

Or from the hundreds of thousands of American football fans?

Or from the millions of Americans who would, if they could, pay surrealistic amounts of money just to witness, up close, somebody like Mike Tyson beat the brains out of somebody else?

And which university could teach Mike Tyson about the difference between violence and love? Is there any citadel of higher education in the country that does not pay its football coach at least three times as much as its chancellor and six times as much as its professors and ten times as much as its social and psychological counselors?

In this America where Mike Tyson and I live together and bitterly, bitterly, apart, I say he became what he felt. He felt the stigmata of a prior hatred and intentional poverty. He was given the choice of violence or violence: The violence of defeat or the violence of victory.

Who would pay him what to rehabilitate inner-city housing or to refurbish a bridge?

Who would pay him what to study the facts of our collective history?

Who would pay him what to plant and nurture the trees of a forest?

And who will write and who will play the songs that tell a guy like Mike Tyson how to talk to a girl?

What was America willing to love about Mike Tyson? Or any black man? Or any man's man?

Tyson's neighborhood and my own have become the same no-win battleground. And he has fallen there. And I do not rejoice. I do not.

—JUNE JORDAN, poet, essayist, professor, activist, was the author of many books, including *Technical Difficulties* (essays), and *Directed by Desire: The Complete Poems of June Jordan.*

# An Interview with Sister Helen Prejean, Criminal Justice Activist and Author of Dead Man Walking

JUDY PENNINGTON
JANUARY 1996

Q: Do you think Americans have rejected the eye-for-an-eye image of God?

HELEN PREJEAN: I think there's a spiritual search going on in this country, but I'm concerned about the rightwing, fundamentalist stuff which offers such easy solutions. And you have this simplistic thing, too, of patriotism and religion: "God is with government. If government's doing it, God blesses it because government is authority and God is the ultimate authority." We have to get past that kind of thinking. Spirituality is rooted in personal integrity, community, and love.

Q: Are you saying that religion plays a part in upholding death and violence?

PREJEAN: It plays a very big part. Some polls show that the more often people go to church, the more they believe in the death penalty. I want to say that Christianity is domesticized, so acculturated—a comfortable religion of people, rather than a religion dealing with the real challenge of what Jesus was all about. I mean, Jesus had people of all classes and types eating together when the whole culture was about keeping people apart. Jesus moved across the whole spectrum of society and said, "This is what it means to have the kingdom of God, when people are sisters and brothers." In this country today, the most segregated day of the week is Sunday, when people go to church.

Churches are segregated, class-oriented. They preach about this personal God that will love and comfort me, and there's very little about standing in solidarity with the people who are suffering the most. Very little about building one body, one community—which means crossing over into the inner cities and building community together so that if one of us is hurt, all of us are hurt.

Q: How can you, as a radical thinker, be a nun in a Church that appears to be so ideologically conservative?

PREJEAN: It's not monolithically conservative, though; that's the key thing. On the death penalty, it's been hospitable to me, because the U.S. Catholic Bishops have been very strong against the death penalty, and so have a growing number of bishops around the world.

Q: What about other issues, though—how can you be part of a church with so many problems with its politics?

PREJEAN: Because all organizations I know of are weeding weeds. Some things are coming up right; some are coming up wrong. That's what it means to belong to any democracy, a religious community, the city of New Orleans. You can't expect that some people have all the light, and some have all the darkness. It's just human, the way things are. It's an evolving struggle. I feel like I'm following the gospel mandate, and part of that is being on the side of the poor and seeking social justice and social transformation. I don't have to wait for a bishop's permission to act, or to act only as they tell me to do.

Q: Your religious order has fully supported your work. Why is that?

PREJEAN: When you look at the biblical tradition of the prophets—Micah, Jeremiah, and Amos—you see prophets speaking out against injustice and linking it to God. That's very deep in the religious tradition, which, of course, Martin Luther King and the whole civil rights movement tapped into. You've got close to 3,000 people on death row in this country, and virtually all of them are poor. You begin to see how the thing pans out, how it really works.

Q: What are the inequities?

PREJEAN: One of them is that it depends on who gets killed. When a poor person or a person of color is killed, you won't see a DA pursue the maximum punishment. Politicians can use their rhetoric until the cows come home—that the death penalty is for "anybody that does these heinous, terrible crimes"—but it's really about who got killed. The status of the victim is the first thing to propel it.

The second thing is what kind of money is available for defense. If there's anything we've learned from the O. J. Simpson trial, it's that when you have a battery of defense lawyers, you are probably not going to be convicted. They've done their job all too well, and that's to raise questions about the evidence.

You compare that with poor people and the kind of defense they get. The most shocking thing to me, when I got into this, was that I presumed that poor people might not have the best defense but that it would be adequate. Then I found out one defendant whose attorney had visited with him for two half-hour periods to prepare his defense. One was on the morning of the trial. The jury was picked in a couple of days, guilt or innocence was decided in a few days, and he was sentenced to death by Friday afternoon. That's what happens to poor people.

Some of it is a pure lottery. A prosecutor in one county will go for the death penalty; another won't. Since the reinstatement of the death penalty in 1976, over 70 percent of all U.S. executions have taken place in five Southern states: Louisiana, Texas, Florida, Georgia, and Virginia.

Q: Why is that?

PREJEAN: Poverty. Race. The punishment for people who do things to white people in the southern states. You look at the Black Codes that were drawn up after Reconstruction. You see that legislatures actually wrote up codes for a white crime and a black crime. If a black man stole or raped: "Death penalty, death penalty." If a white person kills: "Well, we're gonna look at this." The punishment is far less.

Q: Did you ever feel, anytime in your life, that you were moving toward a certain destiny?

PREJEAN: Khalil Gibran has a line that says, "You will laugh all your laughter and cry all your tears." I think we all put our boats out on a current, set our little sails, and when we hit something that impassions us, and our little boat begins to go there, the wind whistles through our hair, and we know we're onto something. You become alive as you're doing it, and you begin to develop gifts you just didn't know you had. Jeremiah the prophet said, "I've got this fire burning in my bones. I've got to speak."

—JUDY PENNINGTON, a journalist and teacher of meditation, founded Eagle Life
Communications.

# Abu Ghraib, USA

ANNE-MARIE CUSAC
JULY 2004

When I first saw the photo, taken at the Abu Ghraib prison, of a hooded and robed figure strung with electrical wiring, I thought of the Sacramento, California, city jail.

When I heard that dogs had been used to intimidate and bite at least one detainee at Abu Ghraib, I thought of the training video shown at the Brazoria County Detention Center in Texas.

When I learned that the male inmates at Abu Ghraib were forced to wear women's underwear, I thought of the Maricopa County jails in Phoenix, Arizona.

And when I saw the photos of the naked bodies restrained in grotesque and clearly uncomfortable positions, I thought of the Utah prison system.

Donald Rumsfeld said of the abuse when he visited Abu Ghraib on May 13, "It doesn't represent American values."

But the images from Iraq looked all too American to me.

In February 1999, the Sacramento Sheriff's Department settled a class-action lawsuit alleging numerous acts of torture, including mock executions, where guards strapped inmates into a restraint chair, covered their faces with masks, and told the inmates they were about to be electrocuted.

When I read a report in *The Guardian* of London of May 14 that it had "learned of ordinary soldiers who . . . were taught to perform mock executions," I couldn't help but remember the jail.

Then there's the training video used at the Brazoria County Detention Center in Texas. In addition to footage of beatings and stun-gun use, the videotape included scenes of guards encouraging dogs to bite inmates.

The jail system in Maricopa County is well known for its practice of requiring inmates to wear pink underwear, and it is notorious for using stun guns and restraint chairs. In 1996, jail staff placed Scott Norberg in a restraint chair, shocked him twenty-one times with stun guns, and gagged him until he turned blue, according to news reports. Norberg died. His family filed a wrongful death lawsuit against the jails and subsequently received an $8 million settlement, one of the largest in Arizona history. However, the settlement included no admission of wrongdoing on the part of the jail.

The Red Cross also says that inmates at the Abu Ghraib jail suffer "prolonged exposure while hooded to the sun over several hours, including during the hottest time of the day when temperatures could reach 50 degrees Celsius (122 degrees Fahrenheit) or higher." Many of the Maricopa County Jail system inmates live outdoors in tent cities, even on days that reach 120 degrees in the shade. During last year's heat wave, the Associated Press reported that temperatures inside the jail tents reached 138 degrees.

In a Utah prison, Michael Valent, a mentally ill prisoner, died after spending six-teen hours nude in a restraint chair in March 1997. As it turns out, Valent's death has a connection to Abu Ghraib. Lane McCotter was serving as the director of the Utah State Prison system on the day that Valent was put in a restraint chair. After Valent died, McCotter resigned. Six years later, McCotter was in charge of reconstructing Abu Ghraib, though he has denied involvement in the abuses.

The point is not whether McCotter is personally responsible for Abu Ghraib. He is part of a well-established system.

In another incident reported by Amnesty International that happened during McCotter's watch, an inmate at the Utah State Prison "was shackled to a steel board on a cell floor in four-point metal restraints for twelve weeks in 1995. He was removed from the board on average four times a week to shower. At other times he was left to defecate while on the board. He was released from the board only following a court order."

A preliminary injunction banning the restraint chair in Ventura County, California, found that jail policy "allows deputies to require restrained arrestees to either urinate or defecate on themselves and be forced to sit in their own feces or 'hold it.'"

The practice of forcing prisoners to soil themselves allegedly occurred in Iraq, as well. On May 6, the *Washington Post* published a description of the abuses Hasham Mohsen Lazim said he had endured at Abu Ghraib. After guards beat, hooded, and stripped him, Lazim said, "Graner handcuffed him to the corner of his bed," where he remained for days. "We couldn't sleep or stand," Lazim told the paper. "Even to urinate, we had to do so where we sat."

A few days later, the *Post* reported similar allegations from Umm Qasr, where Satae Qusay, a chef, said he was forced to "urinate on himself when he was prohibited from using bathrooms."

Amnesty International has reports of "prolonged forced standing and kneeling" in Iraqi military prisons, as well as allegations of "the excessive and cruel use of shackles and handcuffs" at Guantánamo. Again, the Iraqi allegations seem almost to be ex-tracted from earlier Amnesty International writings on human rights in the United States.

Amnesty observed, "In Alabama, prisoners have sometimes been tied to a restraint pole (known as the 'hitching rail') as punishment, sometimes for hours in the swel-tering heat or freezing conditions. At Julie Tutweiler Prison for Women in Alabama, inmates have been handcuffed to the rail for up to a day."

In Iraq, the Red Cross evaluated people who had been subjected to solitary con-finement, and the organization discovered indications of psychological damage. The group's medical delegate said Iraqi prisoners were "presenting signs of concentra-tion difficulties, memory problems, verbal expression difficulties, incoherent speech, acute anxiety reactions, abnormal behavior, and suicidal tendencies. These symptoms appeared to have been caused by the methods and duration of interrogation."

Long-term use of solitary confinement happens in U.S. prisons all too often. Super-maxes are the most avid users of the technique. Prisoners at these ultra-high-security facilities often remain in isolation cells for nearly twenty-four hours a day. American prisoners also find long-term isolation psychologically traumatizing.

The *San Francisco Chronicle* reported in 2000 on a woman who had spent nearly four years in the hole at the secure housing unit of California's Valley State Prison for Women. She claimed to have had no human contact except for food trays that came through a door slot and threats from the guards outside her cell. She also said that the guards often denied her sanitary pads and toilet paper.

In 2001, a class action lawsuit filed by inmates of the supermax prison of Boscobel, Wisconsin, called the facility an "incubator of psychosis" and alleged that mental ill-ness was "endemic" at the prison. A judge ordered the removal of all mentally ill in-mates, which Ed Garvey, a court-appointed attorney in the case, says amounted to "about one-third of the prisoners." Some of the inmates at the Boscobel prison, includ-ing those who had the most severe reactions to their isolation, were juveniles.

"It was interesting that the International Red Cross was upset that prisoners were held more than thirty days in isolation and for twenty-three out of twenty-four hours," says Garvey. "In Boscobel, that's the case every day."

The Red Cross mentioned deaths in prison in Iraq, and the Pentagon is now look-ing at the deaths of at least thirty-three detainees in Iraq and Afghanistan. Two of these deaths have already been ruled homicides.

Inmates have died in U.S. prisons and jails under suspicious circumstances, as well. U.S. deaths that occurred in connection with the use of restraint chairs alone num-bered at least fifteen by 2002, according to Amnesty International. In U.S. prisons, in 2001 through 2002, there were eight homicides against inmates in custody that were not committed by other inmates. In U.S. jails, from 2000 through 2002, the number was thirty.

In conversations over the past few weeks, I have heard outrage and anger over the abuse at Abu Ghraib. I have rarely heard such reactions in connection with abuse of prisoners in the United States.

When we tolerate abuse in U.S. prisons and jails, it should not surprise us to find U.S. soldiers using similar methods in Iraq.

# PART 9

## Freeing the Media

The media reform movement took off in the early years of the twenty-first century. But La Follette saw the need for it his whole adult life. He founded *The Progressive* partly as a response to the inadequacies of the media all around him. And he discusses those inadequacies in his 1920 essay "People Demand a Free Press," which is as relevant today as the day he wrote it.

*The Progressive* has been lucky to be able to publish some of the leading media critics of the last century, including George Seldes, Ben Bagdikian, Noam Chomsky, and Robert McChesney, which we offer here.

It also has been able to showcase some of the journalists who are doing pioneering work. The interviews with White House correspondent Helen Thomas and *Democracy Now*'s Amy Goodman reveal what members of the media can do if they really care about what they are reporting and if they don't gag themselves with the bandanna of objectivity.

La Follette's word's still cry out:

"Do you want to be free, economically and politically free? Then begin at once. Organize! Organize in every state for a free and independent press."

# People Demand a Free Press

Robert M. La Follette
November 1920

It is vital to democracy that the voter should be able to form an intelligent opinion upon the issues of the day.

The press assumes to enlighten the people upon all public questions. It pretends to publish the facts on current events day by day, upon which the voter may rely in forming this voting judgment.

If the press were honest, if it printed the uncolored news, the real essential facts without bias, democracy would be safe.

The American public will think straight if given a fair chance. The great heart of the mass of mankind is right. It always beats in sympathy with human welfare.

But sound judgment may only be formed upon a sound basis of truth. When truth is distorted, when lies pass current for facts, when white is made to look black, and black white by a press that poisons its readers day by day, then the public is drugged into apathy or befooled into a wholly false opinion.

The people know the press is owned or controlled. They know that it is the servant of the combined groups which control Big Business, and through Big Business is rapidly acquiring the control of little business, line after line.

But foreknowledge that the press habitually misrepresents the facts, that it suppresses news, that it is unreliable on all issues involving public interest as against private monopoly—foreknowledge of all these facts cannot protect the public against its sinister influence.

So potent is the psychological effect of the printed lie, when artfully and persistently repeated, so destructive of all soundness of judgment are the deadly half-truths, the "doctored" news, the sly insinuations, the sensational falsehoods, retracted after they have served their purpose—and all the varied and multiplied forms of spurious, deceptive fabrication, willfully and wickedly printed from day to day by the Kept Press—that however thoroughly it be discredited, it is still the most powerful influence for evil, which menaces American democracy today.

The very life of democracy is committed to the voter. If he be ignorant or misinformed upon vital issues his ballot is a source of peril to the righteous decision of any issue.

The American pioneers sought to safeguard democracy by an effective system of universal education. Hence they established the public school as the foundation stone of the American commonwealth.

We have made education free, from the kindergarten to the primary, from the primary to the secondary schools, and on through the state universities.

This system of education—the most wonderful in all the world, with its hundreds of thousands of devoted teachers—has for its primary purpose the training of men and women for the grave responsibilities of citizenship.

All the way from the kindergarten to the university, the founders determined that the public school must be jealously protected against error and bias in textbook and teaching.

It was believed that the youth of the land would come from the public schools with open, unprejudiced minds trained to decide the issues of self-government as presented by an intelligent press.

But of what avail is our splendid system of education in preparing the voters to meet their responsibilities when the sources of current news are poisoned, and editorial comment controlled by sordid and mercenary influences. That control need not be through open ownership of the newspaper or magazine, though in many instances it is. But it is more frequently achieved through that community of interests, that interdependence of investments and credits which ties the publisher up to the banks, the advertisers, and the Special Interests.

The power that controls the press controls the American market.

It is doubtful if the American people can ever emancipate themselves from the merciless exploitation of the colossal monopoly which controls markets and prices, until they shall establish a free and independent press.

Men and women of America, do you want to break the stranglehold of monopoly, that takes toll, to the limit of its greed, out of your daily life?

Do you want to be free, economically and politically free?

Then begin at once. Organize! Organize in every state for a free and independent press.

## "Freedom of the Press" Bares Suppressed Facts Concerning Journalism

GEORGE SELDES
MARCH 21, 1936

There is a growing suspicion that the press is no longer what it claims to be, the "Tribune of the People," the "Voice of the Public," the "Upholder of Truth," the "Defender of Public Liberty," as thousands of newspaper mastheads daily proclaim it.

In the 1920s millions undergoing disillusion vaguely realized that they had been deceived by newspaper war propaganda. In the 1930s the myths of cyclical depressions and prosperity-around-the-corner again shook the confidence of the public.

"You can't believe a thing you read in the papers nowadays" has become a commonplace.

In the early days of 1935 mass meetings and conventions attended by thousands of persons have applauded general attacks on the press and specific charges against certain newspaper owners as agents of Fascism and breeders of war. There has been popular resentment against certain editors in the past but never to my knowledge as general an indictment against the press of the nation as we have today.

There are powerful forces which do not want the facts, from a millionaire's divorce to a war scare, presented truthfully. There are corrupting influences. Many newspapermen are subject to them without even realizing it.

As a reporter, I turned in the story of Andrew Mellon's divorce, stories of strikes, interviews with politicians and statesmen and news items concerning large corporations; eighteen months in the American army and ten years among the dictators of Europe made the newspaper game for me something like the thrilling thing it is in fiction. But from the first day to the last there was censorship, there was suppression of news, there was distortion and there was coloring of news, there was always an attempt by someone to mislead the public.

I do not say that the integrity of the world press has broken down completely: I do insist that attacks upon it are stronger than ever in the history of newspaper printing, and although this statement becomes self-evident when it is known that ten large nations, the dictatorships of continental Europe, no longer have a free press, I want to go further and show the attack upon its integrity in the free nations, France, Britain, and the United States especially, where, Deo volente, dictatorship may be avoided but where, unfortunately, another oligarchy, dictatorial big money and big business of the public utilities and the Teapot Dome kind, is always trying to destroy the foundations upon which free government is built.

> —GEORGE SELDES, journalist and media critic, was red-baited by Senator Joe McCarthy. Seldes wrote for mainstream outfits and then for *In Fact*, where he helped expose the health risks posed by cigarettes. He was the author of several books, including *Even the Gods Can't Change History* and *Witness to a Century*.

# The Media Monopolies

BEN H. BAGDIKIAN
JUNE 1978

All media with routine access to mass markets are already controlled by too few people. If we are serious about preserving maximum practical access to the marketplace of ideas and information, we ought to be deeply concerned.

The fifty largest broadcast chains already have three quarters of the audience. The fifty largest cable television companies have two-thirds of all subscribers. The fifty largest newspaper chains have more than two-thirds of all daily newspaper sales—and this is particularly troubling because concentration of control of daily newspapers has unique effects on all information media.

We would all benefit if we had a number of truly independent and comprehensive sources of daily news. But we do not.

When we talk about concentration of ownership of daily newspapers, we are talking about control of the only comprehensive and self-sufficient news system we have. There are more than fifteen hundred cities in the United States with daily papers, but only forty with competing newspaper managements. Of all cities with newspapers, 97.5 percent have newspaper monopolies.

This consolidation of monopolies is not something over the horizon; it is an accomplished fact. There are 1,760 daily papers in the country—a number that has remained stable since World War II. Of these, 73 percent are owned by 170 corporations. And now these 170 corporations are consuming each other, with large chains buying small chains, so that control is gathering with disproportionate speed among the few at the top.

In 1950, 20 percent of all individual daily papers were owned by chains; by 1960, it was 31 percent; by 1970, 47 percent. Today it is 62 percent.

Like beachfront property, independent daily papers are a disappearing commodity. So now big chains are buying small chains, multiplying the rate of concentration. Since 1960, the twenty-five largest newspaper corporations have increased their control of daily national circulation from 38 percent to 53 percent. Ten corporations now publish 37 percent of all newspapers sold daily in the United States.

Newspapers have followed other industries in another form of concentration—the conglomerate. But as with chains, there is a qualitative difference in the social impact of media conglomerates as against companies that make plastics or musical instruments. If an ordinary conglomerate uses one of its companies to further the interests of another of its companies, it may be unfair competition but it is largely an economic matter. If a conglomerate uses its newspaper company to further the interests of another of its subsidiaries, that is dishonest news.

At the present rate of concentration, we can expect that in less than twenty years almost every daily paper in the country will be owned by about ten corporations.

One reason concentration in the media is dangerous is that media power is political power. There is no reason why newspaper publishers and broadcast operators should not promote their corporate welfare the way other industries do. But it would be naive not to recognize that for politicians there is a difference between being asked to support a corporate bill for the computer industry and being asked to support something wanted by the newspaper publishers and broadcast managers in the politician's home district.

I doubt that even the most energetic chain-builder in the business would insist that it is socially healthy to have one corporation control every daily paper in the country. We now have twenty-five chains that control a majority of all papers sold daily. If one corporation in control is bad and twenty-five is good, what is the proper number? At what point should someone—presumably the Department of Justice or Congress—step in and say no?

But I don't believe that the Department of Justice or Congress will step in. They have not so far, and the pace of concentration has increased in the last decade. And I believe the Department of Justice and Congress do not step in precisely because concentrated control of the media also represents concentrated political and economic power.

If we believe in the indispensability of a pluralistic, marketplace of ideas and information, we cannot be complacent about a narrowly controlled management of that marketplace, whether it is governmental or corporate, benign or malicious. The greatest danger in control of the mass media is not, I think, the likelihood that Government will take control, but that the public, seeing little difference between narrow corporate control and narrow governmental control, will be indifferent to which dominates the media.

—Ben H. Bagdikian, journalist and media critic, worked as an editor of the *Washington Post*, was the dean of Berkeley's Graduate School of Journalism, and wrote *The Media Monopoly*.


# The Bounds of Thinkable Thought

Noam Chomsky
october 1985


In May 1983, a remarkable incident occurred in Moscow. A courageous newscaster, Vladimir Danchev, denounced the Soviet invasion of Afghanistan in five successive radio broadcasts. This aroused great admiration in the West. The *New York Times* commented accurately that this was a departure from the "official Soviet propaganda line," that Danchev had "revolted against the standards of doublethink and newspeak."

Danchev was taken off the air and sent to a psychiatric hospital. He was returned to his position last December. A Soviet official was quoted as saying that "he was not punished, because a sick man cannot be punished." In the West, all of this was understood as a glimpse into the world of Orwell's *1984*. Danchev was admired for his courage, for a triumph of the human will, for his refusal to be cowed by totalitarian violence.

Implicit in the coverage of the Danchev affair by Western media was a note of self-congratulation: It couldn't happen here. No American newscaster has been sent to a psychiatric hospital for calling an American invasion "an invasion" or for calling on the victims to resist.

We might, however, inquire further into just why this has never happened. One possibility is that the question has never arisen because no American journalist would ever mimic Danchev's courage, or could even perceive that an American invasion of the Afghan type is in fact an invasion or that a sane person might call on the victims to resist. If this were the case, it would signify a stage of indoctrination well beyond any achieved under Soviet terror, well beyond anything Orwell imagined.

Consider the following facts: In 1962, President Kennedy sent the U.S. Air Force to attack rural South Vietnam, where more than 80 percent of the population lived, as part of a program intended to drive several million people to concentration camps (called "strategic hamlets") where they would be surrounded by barbed wire and armed guards and "protected" from the guerrillas whom, we conceded, they were willingly supporting.

For the past twenty-two years, I have been searching for some reference in mainstream journalism or scholarship to an American invasion of South Vietnam in 1962 (or ever), or an American attack against South Vietnam, or American aggression in Indochina—without success. There is no such event in history. Rather, there is an American defense of South Vietnam against terrorists supported from outside (namely, from Vietnam), a defense that was unwise, the doves maintain.

In short, there are no Danchevs here. Within the mainstream, there is no one who can call an invasion by its proper name, or even perceive the fact that one has taken place. It is unimaginable that any American journalist would have publicly called upon the South Vietnamese to resist the American invasion. Such a person would not have been sent to a psychiatric hospital, but he would surely not have retained his professional position and standing. Note that here it takes no courage to tell the truth, merely honesty. We cannot plead fear of state violence, as followers of the party line can in a totalitarian state.

It is common now to deride any analogy between the Soviet invasion of Afghanistan and the U.S. invasion of Grenada, and indeed they differ radically in scale and character. A comparison with the U.S. invasion of South Vietnam would be more appropriate, but is inconceivable within the mainstream.

A kind of opposition to the Vietnam War did develop in the mainstream, of course, but it was overwhelmingly "pragmatic," as the critics characterized it, distinguishing themselves from the "emotional" or "irresponsible" opponents who objected to the war on principled grounds. The "pragmatic" opponents argued that the war could not be won at an acceptable cost, or that the goals were not clear, or that errors were made in execution. On similar grounds, the German general staff was no doubt critical of Hitler after Stalingrad.

How has this remarkable subservience to the doctrinal system been achieved? It is not that the facts were unknown. The devastating bombing of northern Laos and other attacks were suppressed by the media—these are called "secret wars," meaning that the government keeps them secret with the complicity of the press—but in the case of the American assault on South Vietnam, sufficient information was always available. The realities were observed, but not seen.

A closer look at the debate that did develop over the Vietnam War provides some lessons about the mechanisms of indoctrination. The debate pitted the hawks against the doves. The hawks were those, like journalist Joseph Alsop, who felt that with a sufficient exercise of violence we could succeed in our aims. The doves felt that this was unlikely, although, as Arthur Schlesinger explained, "We all pray that Mr. Alsop will be right," and "we may all be saluting the wisdom and statesmanship of the American government" if the U.S. succeeds (contrary to his expectations) in a war policy that was turning Vietnam into "a land of ruin and wreck." It was this book that established Schlesinger as a "leading war opponent," in the words of Leslie Gelb.

There is, of course, a possible position omitted from the fierce debate between the hawks and the doves which allegedly tore the country apart during these trying years— the position of the peace movement, which saw the war not merely as a "mistake," but as fundamentally wrong and immoral. To put it plainly, war crimes, including the crime of launching aggressive war, are wrong, even if they succeed in their "noble" aims. This position does not enter the debate, even to be refuted.

All agree that it was a "failed crusade," "noble" but "illusory" and undertaken with the "loftiest intentions," as Stanley Karnow puts it in his best-selling companion volume to the PBS television series on Vietnam, highly regarded for its critical candor. Those who do not appreciate these self-evident truths, or who maintain the curious view that they should be supported by some evidence, simply demonstrate thereby that they are emotional and irresponsible ideologues, or perhaps outright communists. They are outside the spectrum of thinkable thought.

All of this illustrates the genius of democratic systems of thought control, which differ markedly from totalitarian practice. Those who rule by violence tend to be "behaviorist" in their outlook. What people may think is not terribly important; what counts is what they do. They must obey and this obedience is secured by force.

Democratic systems are different. It is necessary to control not only what people do, but also what they think. Since the State lacks the capacity to ensure obedience by force, the threat to order must be excised at the source. It is necessary to establish a framework for possible thought that is constrained by the principles of the state religion. These need not be asserted; it is better that they be presupposed.

The critics reinforce this system by tacitly accepting these doctrines and confining their critique to tactical questions. To be admitted to the debate, they must accept without question the fundamental doctrine that the State is benevolent, governed by the loftiest intentions, adopting a defensive stance, not an actor in world affairs but only reacting—though sometimes unwisely—to the crimes of others.

If even the harshest critics tacitly adopt these premises, then, the ordinary person may ask, who am I to disagree?

Propaganda is to democracy what violence is to totalitarianism. The techniques have been honed to a high art, far beyond anything that Orwell dreamt of. The device of feigned dissent, incorporating the doctrines of the state religion and eliminating rational, critical discussion, is one of the more subtle means, though more crude techniques are also widely used and are highly effective in protecting us from seeing what we observe, from knowledge and understanding of the world.

There are no Danchevs here, except at the remote margins of political debate.

For those who stubbornly seek freedom, there can be no more urgent task than to come to understand the mechanisms and practices of indoctrination. These are easy to perceive in the totalitarian societies, much less so in the system of "brainwashing under freedom" to which we are subjected and which all too often we serve as willing or unwitting instruments.

> —NOAM CHOMSKY is an emeritus linguist at MIT and a leading critic of U.S. foreign policy and the media. His many books include *Manufacturing Consent* (with Edward Herman) and *Deterring Democracy*.

## Body-Bag Journalism

SUSAN DOUGLAS
APRIL 1997

"Here's a story that just could save your life," warns the baritone voice on the TV. "Experts will show you how you can protect yourself from being abducted. Details at 11:00." The next night, another story that could save your life: how to stand in an elevator so that if anyone attacks you, you can protect yourself.

The following night, a story designed to make us obsessive hand-washers à la Howard Hughes: a lurid account of all the lethal germs waiting to pounce on us from public doorknobs and escalator handrails, with tips on how to fend off these invisible predators. This is the new journalistic standard: If a story can't prevent your departure to the great beyond, it's not worth putting on the air.

Of course, these handy how-to stories don't come on right away—first you have to get through the murders, fires, automobile accidents, and robberies. Then there's the investigative reporting: an exposé on manicure shops that make all their clients soak their nails in the same water and, for Valentine's Day, a probe into which florist has the best roses. Then comes cotton candy: coverage of Elvis look-alikes or a beauty contest for cows.

Welcome to the local news. The "market" I live closest to, Detroit, is typical. The motto "If it bleeds, it leads" is in full force here, with as much as 54 percent of nightly news stories devoted to crime and disasters. Rocky Mountain Media Watch, in a 1995 study of 100 local newscasters around the country, found that 42 percent of their coverage reveled in mayhem. If there are no good disasters in the vicinity, the local news uses the wonders of satellite technology to import them: One night, a Detroit station led with footage of a bus that had crashed into the Charles River in Boston.

A study of the 11:00 news done by the *Detroit News* (just for the record, a scab newspaper) found that only 2 percent of the local news focused on the government and politics—that translates into eighteen seconds! There was zero coverage of poverty, education, race relations, environmental problems, science, or international affairs during the two months of the study.

Watching the local news in Detroit, you would never know there was a state legislature, a state court system, or a governor. Just when citizens need increased journalistic oversight of state government, they are getting almost none at all. Clinton and his Republican allies are devolving responsibility for public programs to the states, welfare being the most deplorable example, and the local media show no capacity for monitoring the states' actions.

Instead, the onslaught of body-bag journalism bludgeons the viewer into a state of cynicism, resignation, and fear—sentiments that serve a conservative agenda. George Gerbner, the former dean of the Annenberg School of Communication, called it the "mean-world syndrome." Simply put, the more TV you watch, the more inclined you are to exaggerate the level of crime in society, and to exaggerate your own vulnerability to crime. People who watch a lot of TV are much more likely to favor punitive approaches to crime—such as building more prisons and extending the death penalty—than are light viewers.

The orgy of mayhem on the local news isn't just revolting. It is dangerous. So, tonight, when they're zooming in on the bloodstains on the pavement, call them up. Tell them you hate it. More important, call their sponsors. Tell them you'd be inclined to buy their products, but you just feel too queasy to shop.

—SUSAN DOUGLAS is a professor of communications at the University of Michigan and the author of *The Mommy Myth*. She also is a senior editor at *In These Times*.

# Oligopoly
## The Big Media Game Has Fewer and Fewer Players

ROBERT W. MCCHESNEY
NOVEMBER 1999

When Viacom announced its offer to gobble up CBS for $37 billion in September, it capped off a decade of unprecedented deal-making and concentration in the media industries. The new Viacom would be one of only nine massive conglomerates—all of which took their present shape in the last fifteen years—that dominate the U.S. media landscape.

These giants—Time Warner, Disney, Rupert Murdoch's News Corp., Viacom, Sony, Seagram, AT&T/Liberty Media, Bertelsmann, and GE—to a large extent furnish your TV programs, movies, videos, radio shows, music, books, and other recreational activities.

They do a superb job of maximizing profit for their shareholders but a dreadful job of providing the basis for a healthy democracy. Their entertainment fare is tailored to the needs of Madison Avenue; their journalism to the needs of the wealthy and powerful.

By any known standard of liberal democracy, such a concentration of media power in a few self-interested firms run by some of the wealthiest people in the world poses an immediate and growing threat to our republic. As James Madison put it in 1822, "A popular government without popular information, or the means of acquiring it, is but a prologue to a farce or a tragedy, or perhaps both."

Far from regulating the media giants, the government has served as the handmaiden to these electronic robber barons.

This oligopoly would never have passed legal muster if the regulators at the Federal Communications Commission and in the antitrust division of the Justice Department were doing their jobs, or if the Telecommunications Act of 1996 were not railroaded through Congress.

The regulators have let these mergers slide, under tremendous pressure from the telecommunications and entertainment industry. Virtually no one in government is looking out for the public's interest in the media field.

Media concentration is not a new phenomenon, but it has accelerated dramatically in the last decade, and it is taking a new and dangerous form.

Classically, media concentration was in the form of "horizontal integration," where a handful of firms tried to control as much production in their particular fields as possible. The U.S. film production industry, for instance, has been a tight-knit club effectively controlled by six or seven studios since the 1930s. That remains the case today: The six largest U.S. firms accounted for more than 90 percent of U.S. theater revenues in 1997. All but 16 of Hollywood's 148 widely distributed films in 1997 were produced by these six firms, and many of those 16 were produced by companies that had distribution deals with one of the six majors.

The newspaper industry underwent a spectacular consolidation from the 1960s to the 1980s, leaving half a dozen major chains ruling the roost. U.S. book publishing is now dominated by seven firms, the music industry by five, cable TV by six. Nearly all of these are now parts of vast media conglomerates.

That's why looking at specific media sectors fails to convey the extent or the nature of the system today, for no longer are media firms intent on horizontal integration. Today, they seek "vertical integration," not only producing content but also owning distribution. Moreover, they are major players in media sectors not traditionally thought to be related. These conglomerates own some combination of television networks, TV show production, TV stations, movie studios, cable channels, cable systems, music companies, magazines, newspapers, and book publishing firms.

This has all come about seemingly overnight. In 1983, Ben Bagdikian published *The Media Monopoly*, which chronicled how some fifty media conglomerates dominated the entirety of U.S. mass media. By today's standards, that era was downright competitive.

The mega-media firms have enjoyed a staggering rate of growth in the last decade. In 1988, Disney was a $2.9 billion a year amusement park and cartoon company; in 1998, Disney had $22 billion in sales. In 1988, Time was a $4.2 billion publishing company and Warner Communications was a $3.4 billion media conglomerate; in 1998, Time Warner did $26 billion of business. In 1988, Viacom was a measly $600 million syndication and cable outfit; the new Viacom is expected to do $22 billion worth of business in the coming year.

Moreover, each of these firms averages at least one equity joint venture—sharing actual ownership of a company—with six of the eight other media giants. Rupert Murdoch's News Corp. has at least one joint venture with each of them. AT&T Liberty owns nearly 10 percent of both News Corp. and Time Warner. This looks more like a cartel than it does the fabled competitive marketplace.

Vertical integration enables a company to increase market power by cross-promoting or cross-selling a show.

If a media conglomerate has a successful motion picture, for instance, it can promote the film on its broadcast properties and then use the film to spin off television programs, CDs, books, merchandise, and much else.

Perhaps nowhere is the effect of concentrated corporate control on media more insidious than in journalism, democracy's lifeblood. I do not wish to romanticize the nature of U.S. journalism in the old days. It was highly flawed in key respects, and many of the current problems are only exaggerated forms of those that existed yesterday. But in today's corporate media system, journalism—and by that I mean the rigorous accounting of the powers-that-be and the powers-that-want-to-be, as well as wide-ranging coverage of our most urgent social and political issues—has nearly ceased to exist on the air and has been greatly diminished elsewhere. The reason is simple: Good journalism is bad business, and bad journalism can be very, very good for business.

—Robert W. McChesney is a professor of communications at the University of Illinois, Urbana-Champaign, and the cofounder of the media reform group Free Press. He is the author of many books, including *Rich Media, Poor Democracy* and *The Communication Revolution*.

# An Interview with Helen Thomas, White House Correspondent

ELIZABETH DINOVELLA
AUGUST 2004

Q: The White House press corps was pretty tame after 9/11, but now they are starting to challenge the President. What happened?

HELEN THOMAS: I think they are coming out of their coma. They finally are realizing they've been had. They finally realized that we went into a war based on false pretenses. And we were very much a part of that. We were the transmission belt for all of the spin and the alleged threats.

But there was the aura of 9/11. At these televised briefings there was an atmosphere among the reporters that you would be considered unpatriotic or un-American if you were asking any tough questions. Then it segued into a war where the public thought you were jeopardizing the troops if you asked certain questions. So I think we walked the line too much. The press corps is finally waking up to the fact that its job is to ask the questions that are so obvious. The American people were asking the questions. And they were wondering why the reporters rolled over and played dead. The President of the United States should be able to answer any question, or at least dance around one. At some time—early and often—he should submit to questioning and be held accountable, because if you don't have that then you only have one side of the story. The Presidential news conference is the only forum in our society, the only institution, where a President can be questioned. If a leader is not questioned, he can rule by edict or executive order. He can be a king or a dictator. Who's to challenge him? We're there to pull his chain and to ask the questions that should be asked every day, for every move.

Q: How did you see your role when you were a wire service reporter?

THOMAS: Straight reporting. Just the facts, ma'am. I wrote dull copy because I was afraid even a verb would sound pejorative or judgmental. I can honestly say I was never accused of slant in my copy. But I never bowed out of the human race since the moment I was born. I permitted myself to think, to care, to believe.

Q: Who was your favorite President to cover?

THOMAS: Kennedy and Johnson. Kennedy because I think it was the most inspired. I thought he had his eyes on the stars, that he knew where the country should be going. He told young people to give something back to the country. He had ideals. And Johnson moved a mountain the first two years in office. He got through Medicare, civil rights, voting rights for blacks in the South, federal aid to education at all levels from Head Start through college, child and maternal health, public housing, you name it. It was phenomenal.

Q: Even after 9/11, when the press was really tame, there were still charges by some people in the press that there was a liberal media. Do you agree?

THOMAS: I'm dying to find another friend. I am a liberal. I was a liberal the day I was born, and I will be until the day I die. What's a liberal? I care about the poor, the sick, and the maimed. I care whether we go to war for unjust causes. I care whether we shoot people who are innocent. There's no such thing as a liberal media. I think we have a very conservative press. Read the columnists. They are predominantly conservative. I don't relate to them at all. I'm looking for another liberal.

Q: But there was a time when there were more liberal voices.

THOMAS: There were more. But the press has moved with the country to the right. There was a Ronald Reagan revolution. There were many more liberals in the Great Depression, World War II. They had heart and soul and compassion. Reporters see so much more than anyone else, really, if they open their eyes. It's their job to take a very human approach. I don't see how you can see what's all around you and not be liberal. You see the poor. You see the hungry. You see the suffering.

—ELIZABETH DiNOVELLA is the culture editor of *The Progressive* and a volunteer at WORT-FM, the community radio station in Madison, Wisconsin.

# An Interview with Amy Goodman, Founder and Host of Democracy Now!

ELIZABETH DiNOVELLA
FEBRUARY 2008

Q: Talking to people who are the target of U.S. foreign policy is a hallmark of your show. How did that happen?

AMY GOODMAN: We have a special responsibility as American journalists. We live in the most powerful country on Earth. Yet there is probably a level of ignorance about our effect in the rest of the world because the media doesn't bring it to us. It's much more difficult for people at the target end to forget, to be oblivious, because they are right there living it every day. We have a responsibility here to understand what it feels like, because we are the ones who are creating that situation, whether we like it or not.

We're constantly hearing from the small circle of pundits in Washington who know so little about so much, explaining the world to us, and getting it so wrong. Every network is the same. Unfortunately, sometimes public broadcasting sounds the same way.

The United States has the potential to have tremendous power for good. Right now, it just doesn't have that position. But there are many, many people who make up a pro-democracy movement in this country, just like in other countries, people who really do deeply care. If we want to be safer here, we have to extend those voices to the rest of the world. That's going to increase our national security.

Q: The FCC just relaxed media ownership limits. What's your response to that?

GOODMAN: We've got hundreds of channels with fewer and fewer owners and it's a very big problem. There's the illusion of diversity but what matters is who owns these channels. That's why regulations are so important.

The media is the place where we have a discussion with each other. We can't know everyone individually. We do it through the media. When the kitchen table that we all sit around is controlled by a very few, they are deciding who comes to the table, and that can determine the decisions that are made, when we go to war and when we don't.

Q: What do you think was the mainstream media's biggest failing regarding the Iraq War?

GOODMAN: Simply that it beat the drums for war. As Noam Chomsky says, the media manufactures consent, and they did it for war. There were so many people all over the globe who were protesting the war. In February 2003, millions of people marched, yet the Bush Administration went forward, enabled by the Democrats.

The media act as a megaphone for those in power, the Democrats and the Republicans. When the spectrum of debate between them is very small, that's as far as the media will go. In the lead-up to the invasion, the Democrats joined with Republicans in authorizing war. The media overwhelmingly presented that point of view, that pro-war position, even though most people in this country were opposed to the war.

And now the latest news we find is that the Democratic leaders like House Speaker Pelosi, Jay Rockefeller, and former Senator Bob Graham were briefed for years on waterboarding, on torture. Where was the protest?

On *Democracy Now!* we've just spoken to Henri Alleg, the French journalist who was in Algeria, now in his eighties, who describes waterboarding as if it were yesterday. Because when you yourself are tortured, you never forget. He described what it meant to feel like he was suffocating, not "simulated drowning" but actually drowning.

Q: Immigration is such a big issue but there doesn't seem to be any real debate.

GOODMAN: It's the litany of misinformation, of lies, that really makes people afraid and turns fear into full-blown hate. I think that has to be exposed.

The beauty of community media is that we break the sound barriers, we open up the microphones for people to speak for themselves. And then it's harder to call people labels. I think it's an epithet to talk about illegal aliens. They don't sound human. You can set any kind of policy on a population when you don't talk to them as human beings.

Q: More and more people, especially young people, are getting news from "fake news" programs. What do you think of that?

GOODMAN: Well, since the main news programs are filled with falsehoods, at least they are laughing at them and they are making you see. I think it is teaching media literacy. It's challenging the mainlining of lies.

Q: Do you ever get discouraged by your work?

GOODMAN: The more difficult the issue, the more amazing people are in dealing with it. That's where I find the hope. Even in places like East Timor, people had hope that in this terrible slaughter for a quarter of a century, they would see the end of it. They would be independent, a new nation would be born. It's just astounding.

But in the midst of it, it was hard to believe. And yet the people whose families were being killed, they were the ones who were saying there was hope. You find that in some of the most difficult situations, whether it's in another country or right here.

There are a lot of hopeful people who think that things can be better. We need to broadcast those voices. The most hopeless, cynical voices are those we hear or watch on television. And that can be very depressing. It generates apathy.

Q: Your critics say you are too much of an advocate. How do you respond?

GOODMAN: I don't really know what that means. I care deeply about what I cover. And I think we have a tremendous responsibility as journalists to expose what's going on in the world. When you see suffering, you care. We never want to take that out of our work.

Advocating for more voices to be heard? I plead guilty. Opening up the airwaves, joining people around the world in a global discussion about what should happen? I plead guilty.

As for advocacy journalism, I think the corporate journalists are the best model of that. We know their points of view. We know how important they felt it was to invade Iraq. We knew what it felt like to be in a tank or helicopter and to ask the pilot or the soldier to show how the gun was shot or how the helicopter flew. We learned all that from them. We learned who they thought was important to interview, and who was silenced, and that was the majority of people.

Those who are for peace are not a fringe minority. They are not a silent majority, but a silenced majority, silenced by the corporate media.

# PART 10

# Standing Up for Labor

Economic democracy cannot exist without a strong labor movement. To read the magazine in its early years, to see the articles clamoring for the eight-hour day or the end of child labor or the need for a minimum wage or unemployment insurance or occupational safety is to recognize the gains we've made.

Credit for that goes to organized labor, which led the way on each of these campaigns. In these battles, *The Progressive* would lend its pages to the leaders of the American Federation of Labor, just as it would sympathize with the Wobblies and the Congress of Industrial Organizations.

In the 1930s, *The Progressive* began to carry Upton Sinclair, the author of *The Jungle*. He would clamor for labor rights and for worker cooperatives. In his "Letter to Henry Ford" he makes an improbable pitch: to have Ford turn over his company to the workers.

John Kenneth Galbraith could always be counted on for profound insights wrapped in pith. So it is with his essay in this chapter that mocks those who preach the work ethic.

Dolores Huerta, one of the founders of United Farm Workers, understood the work ethic more than most. And she points to an undeniable truth: "We're taught to look up to and respect people who have money, regardless of how they got it. Did they exploit to get it? We need to respect people who work with their hands."

# The Strike of the Shirtwaist Girls

ELIZABETH DUTCHER
APRIL 23, 1910

How did she happen to be on strike in wintertime in a big, careless city?

New York is a great center for the shirtwaist industry, and over forty thousand people, mostly women, are employed in its factories at this work alone. The trade is seasonal. There is little or no work in summer weather, when all the feminine world is wearing the pretty garments, but from New Year's until June the machines whirr almost continuously. Last year, in many of the factories, the girls remained at work four nights in the week until nine in the evening, and then came back for five hours' work on Sunday.

Church, settlement recreation center, and, most alluring of all to these ambitious girls, night school beckoned in vain. The flashing needle was a jealous master. Now, the trade requires deftness and intelligence. And yet, between a grievous system of subcontracting and the firm's cupidity, their wages were small. A low percentage might occasionally get more, but three dollars to nine dollars weekly was the usual amount, and out of this they paid for power and needles and oil—sometimes for thread too. And most vexatious of all were the fines, ranging from ten to seventy-five cents, from dropping their work to stopping for an instant to tuck a troublesome lock of hair into place.

Wages, too, varied amazingly in the same shop. Bertha might get seven dollars "coming to her" in her pay envelope, while Fannie who was an equally good worker, but quieter, meeker, very much afraid of losing her position, and unskilled in repartee, received only four. And if a whisper of "joining the union" went around, the girl agitators were always discovered and locked out.

It was such a lockout of 150 union operators that started everything going. They hadn't demanded anything, but they were just invited to quit. Quit they did, but they immediately started to picket. And the bereaved manufacturers arose to the occasion.

If the little pickets had been left alone to pursue their lawful avocation there would have been no big strike. Instead the masters tried intimidation. They reasoned thus: They were little working girls, many of them foreigners, and without any political influence (since they had no vote). A few good scares—and who would be wiser?

So police protection was summoned, reinforced by well-paid private detectives, and strong-arm men with criminal records and plenty of business sense. The girls were cursed, battered, pummeled, dragged off to police stations, and there brought before magistrates who openly stated that they were on the side of the manufacturers, and had no use for strikes, still less for any peaceful picketing, legal or illegal. Fines were accordingly imposed of from one to ten dollars, and several girls sent to the work-house, there to be shut in with the most degraded of their sex.

Mark you, at this time the girls had committed absolutely no acts of violence. Did you ever hear of a man's strike which did not include scenes of riot? The Ladies Waist-makers, in their most unladylike rages, when they had known privation and want for months, committed no acts more overt than an occasional call of "scab" or a furtive pull at the alluring puffs of the girls who were taking the bread out of their mouths. As Mayor Gaynor himself put it, when it was all over except the shouting, "These girls have been badly treated. There isn't one of them who has deserved more than a twenty-five-cent fine."

Just here, however, was where that new, and as yet unexplained phenomenon—the twentieth-century spirit of solidarity, among women—made itself felt. The Women's Trade Union League heard what was going on and looked into things. They found that not only had the girls a clear legal right to do picket duty, but that sympathizers might help. So they proceeded to help picket. And as speedily were they arrested.

It was a real victory. Three hundred and fifty-two shops settled with the union, granting all the debated points: fifty-two-hour workweek; only three evenings over-time a week; no Sunday work; all disputed points to be settled, not between the indi-vidual girl and her employer, but by one firm in consultation with a committee of the girls themselves. And in all but fourteen instances, the agreement was made on a "closed shop" basis, a basis which, in a seasonal trade, the girls believed to be the only guarantee of a really permanent contract. Two shops have put on the union label, and friends all over the country can, by demanding it on their waist, make sure that they are helping the right girls.

—ELIZABETH DUTCHER was a leader of the Women's Trade Union League.


# Why Wisconsin Gave a Record-Breaking Vote to La Follette

LOUIS D. BRANDEIS
APRIL 13, 1912

The greatest problem now before the American people is the demand for social jus-tice and industrial democracy. Our working men enjoy political liberty, but, in the main, are subject to industrial despotism, and social injustice which, under the trusts, has become particularly oppressive. A large part of our working people are working and living under conditions inconsistent with American standards and ideals—and indeed with humanity itself. The condition of a large body of the steelworkers toiling twelve hours a day, seven days in a week at less than living wages—while the steel trust exacted from the consumer in ten years more than $650 million in excess of a liberal return on the capital originally invested—is one of the results of industrial absolutism. It is obvious that the present conditions cannot continue. Either our people will lose their political independence or they will acquire industrial independence. We cannot exist half free and half slave.

# The Eight-Hour Day Will Come

ROBERT M. LA FOLLETTE
JULY 19, 1913

The wisdom of legislation providing for an eight-hour day, not only for women but for men as well, is no longer a debatable question. All practical experience shows that shorter hours means better health and higher efficiency of employees, the quality of work and the character of the output more than offsetting any loss from cutting down the working hours of the day. In other words, shorter hours means stronger, sounder bodies, greater physical efficiency, a higher degree of mental alertness, keener and more intelligent concentration on the machinery and material handled by the wage earner, fewer accidents, added time for home life, rest, recreation, and reading, all making strongly for moral, mental, and physical improvement.

Congress has given men employed by the government or by contractors employed on government work the eight-hour day. Twelve states limit the working day of miners to eight hours in one day.

The courts have held again and again that rest from labor one day in seven is "essential for health, morals, and general welfare."

The courts will ultimately hold that it is vital to the health and well-being of the toiler and for that reason vital to the general welfare that the state should limit the hours of labor for the day as it limits the days of labor for the week.

Let the wage earner take heart. The eight-hour day will come, and come soon, to all of the workers of every state in the nation.

## Anti-Trust Law and Labor
An Appeal to Congress and the Public

SAMUEL GOMPERS, President, American Federation of Labor
APRIL 11, 1914

The law of the land assures to workers the right to organize. All who have any knowledge of the world of industry concede that without organization the wage-workers are helpless victims of the industrial forces that are seeking their own self-interest. Practical men of business refuse to deal with a weak union, for its agreements would have neither advantage nor force; but as a matter of course they recognize and deal with strong unions, and adjust their business to conform to the new situation. It follows, then, that control of all the workers in a trade increases the success and the efficiency of the organization in securing better terms for a greater number of workers and in turn protects the fair employer from competition with producers who care not how they grind their employees so long as they also grind out profits.

The right to organize is a sham, a trick, a deceit, unless it carries with it the right to organize effectively and the right to use that organized power to further the interests of the workers. This implied right must be assured. In the name of free labor, in the name of free government and free society, let the right to organize never for one instant be menaced or withheld.

—SAMUEL GOMPERS was the founder of the American Federation of Labor.

## The War of Organized Capital Against the People

ROBERT M. LA FOLLETTE
DECEMBER 1920

The labor organizations of the country are to be smashed. The decree has been entered. The orders have been issued. The drive is on.

The railroad corporations, the street car companies, and other public utilities; the big industrial corporations, the coal, copper, and oil combinations, the affiliated commercial and financial groups—the merchants' and manufacturers' associations, the chambers of commerce, boards of trade, bankers' associations, and in fact all large interrelated organizations representing capital are mobilizing for a war of extermination of all labor organizations in the United States.

The object is two-fold. First of all, organized capital would destroy organized labor because of its growing political power. The activity of the sixteen railroad organizations and their alliance with associations of farmers in the late campaigns is a real menace to the political control of Big Business in the near future. Second, organized capital would destroy organized labor in order to deprive the wage earner of the collective bargaining strength which he derives from his organization. This would leave him in a position where, as one of the representatives of a large business concern recently declared, "The employee would have to eat out of the employer's hand."

Already the Kept Press of these masters of business and government are feeding the public the right kind of propaganda to poison its mind against the "Tyranny of the Labor Trust."

This war on labor organizations is to be waged upon the hypocritical pretense that it is for "the individual freedom of the wage earner."

Behold the real leadership of this army as it is marshaled to fight the "Labor Trust!" Here we should have the imposing figure of "General" Gary—United States Steel. He will be an admirable selection for Commander-in-Chief.

He wears the laurels won in the recent steel strike where he succeeded in maintaining the "Open Shop" for the Steel Corporation and its right to work sixty-nine thousand of its men twelve hours a day.

Seventy thousand of the corporation's men receive the lowest wage, or common labor pay.

One-half of all employees of this corporation work twelve hours a day, and one-half of these men are required to work seven days a week.

The annual earnings of more than one-third of all productive iron and steel workers are and for years have been below the level set by government experts as the minimum of subsistence standard for families of five.

There you have the "Open Shop," and all that goes with it in a steel mill which is akin to the bottomless pit.

Do you marvel that the U.S. Steel Corporation resists with bludgeon and bayonet every attempt on the part of the employees to secure the right to bargain collectively for better hours and wages?

Do you not see why this corporation and all of its kind are determined to crush labor organizations, establish the "Open Shop" and arbitrarily deal with helpless employees individually?

There are today more than 5 million wage earners in the ranks of organized labor. This means a population of some 20 million—it may be 25 million—dependent for homes, fuel, food, clothing, medical attendance, to say nothing of the needs of their spiritual lives, dependent upon the wages of these workers within the ranks of organized labor.

And it is against these people, a necessary and vital part of our political and social life, that a ruthless war is to be made.

The mills and shops and factories are closing down, they are to be starved into withdrawing from their organizations and will be reemployed when they are hungry enough to accept wages at and "below the level set by government experts as the minimum subsistence standard for families of five."

That is what the United States Steel, and "Open Shop" industry, pays to more than one-third of all its productive iron and steel workers.

How is this to affect the small trades people and the farmers who sell food and supplies to these millions?

And after organized labor has been broken and crushed, what of the organized farmers? They, too, are a political menace to organized capital.

## Human Wreckage
A Plea for Federal Relief

WILLIAM GREEN, President, American Federation of Labor
FEBRUARY 20, 1932

With city relief breaking down, with private charity totally unable to meet the needs of the unemployment, we are now face to face with an unprecedented unemployment crisis.

With relief provision totally inadequate for even the winter months, we must look ahead now to the needs of the year. Only thus can we prevent a fearful toll of human wreckage.

Already we are hearing from bankrupt cities and towns reports of unprecedented suffering they cannot meet. Some are not even paying their school teachers. Community chests, after a valiant effort to collect funds from private sources, report their funds inadequate; the need is four times that of 1928, their funds only 25 percent more. Isolated industrial sections outside the cities—coal fields, textile-mill villages— have no resources outside their industry to cope with their problem. Even large cities are not meeting their relief needs. Thus the responsibility of caring for those out of work is thrown back on their relatives, friends, and neighbors, who can least afford to give of their own meager incomes. This burden, added to wage cuts and part-time work, reduces our living standards to the point of poverty in millions of homes.

Only one agency can meet the relief problem now that all other resources have been proved inadequate—the federal government. By taxation it can distribute the burden of this year where it can be borne with least injury to our citizenship.

—WILLIAM GREEN was the president of the AFL from 1924 to 1952.

# A Letter to Henry Ford

UPTON SINCLAIR
JANUARY 15, 1938

My Dear Mr. Ford: This letter will reach you just as you are entering a bitter struggle with your employees, who are seeking to attain the status of citizens of industry, hitherto denied them.

As one who has devoted his life to studying the economic forces of the modern world, I am keenly aware of the possibilities, both hopeful and tragic, which lie in this struggle. It represents a culmination of events which I predicted to you nearly nineteen years ago. You promised me smilingly that you would not forget my prophecies, and would give me credit if they came true.

I believe that the desire for human welfare still animates you; on that basis I am speaking to you again. I am going to tell you how you can once more place yourself at the head of our industrial progress, and make yourself a pioneer in the building of industrial peace and security.

The time has come when our system of private ownership and autocratic control of industry is breaking down. You feel that you personally have made the Ford Motor Co., and that you own it, and can do with it what you please. It was so that King George the Third of England felt about his American colonies and holding stubbornly to that idea, he forced a war, and lost his colonies altogether.

Your workers, Mr. Ford, feel they have had something to do with the building of the Ford car. Their lives depend upon these things, and if they are to have no say about them the workers remain forever serfs of industry. I entreat you to take an enlightened view of this problem, and realize that industrial change is on the march, and that it can be guided, but cannot be blocked.

This is what I urge you to do. Invite your workers to select their most competent leaders in a public election. Sit down with these men and women and work out a plan to place the Ford Motor Company upon a cooperative basis. Provide for a gradual process whereby your holdings in the company may be transferred to a corporation in which you and all other workers will each own one share and have one vote. Turn the making of Ford cars into a public service, carried on as nearly as possible at cost. Place yourself at the disposal of your workers; offer them your help, and that of your son and grandsons, in carrying on the business and making it a permanent success. Can you doubt that the workers would hail your offer with acclaim and elect you president of the new corporation, and your son vice president?

In this way, Mr. Ford, you can avoid dreadful suffering and bloodshed; in this way you can banish hatred from your own life, and suspicion and fear from the lives of your workers and their families. Your action will be greeted by the world as the noblest and most enlightened in our time. It will be an advertisement the like of which has never been known to date, and will make the Ford car the only one which forward-looking people will be willing to drive.

What is it you want, Mr. Ford? I know you have money enough; and you have more power than you have been able to use wisely of late years. What is there now in life for you that can equal consciousness of having helped in the building of industrial democracy, and shown mankind the way to industrial peace, plenty, and security?

My earnest prayers go out to you with this letter.

—Upton Sinclair

—UPTON SINCLAIR, journalist, muckraker, author, candidate for governor of California, and founder of End Poverty in California, wrote *The Jungle*, among many other works.

## *The Work Ethic*
### It Works Best for Those Who Work Least

JOHN KENNETH GALBRAITH
JUNE 1981

The last few months have been greatly enriched, in a manner of speaking, by a discussion of the work ethic. The American economy is to be reinvigorated; this requires that Americans everywhere recover their lost appetite for work. Some of the new burst of energy that we are to witness in the months ahead will come from a relaxation of rules on the environment, job safety, and by the Federal Trade Commission. But more is to come from people working harder, relaxing less at the public expense, getting paid in accordance with effort, and retaining more of what they get. Altogether we are to see a revival of the great American work ethic.

This is not a subject on which I am at all disposed to be cynical or even skeptical. I am thought to be a very hard worker—by some, excessively productive. Nothing is more pleasant than a penetrating examination of one's own virtue. But it is no doubt fair to warn those who are now talking about a revival of the work ethic that they are involved with, perhaps, the trickiest concept in all social theory.

There is, first of all, the terrible class aspect of the work ethic. As an ethic, it is especially ethical for the poor and much less ethical for the rich. The very affluent in the United States were for long called the leisure class. A thoughtful, diverse, or aggressively bizarre use of leisure by those who can afford it is still a major mark of distinction and by far the most certain route into the columns of *People* magazine. The big beer companies possibly apart, no one similarly celebrates the leisure-time tendencies of the working class. If, choosing relaxation however intelligent or constructive or therapy however needful, they do not show up on a Monday for work, they are ethically insupportable.

For some twenty-five years I have been coming to Gstaad, a small village in Switzerland, to write and otherwise occupy myself. Gstaad is, very possibly, the geographical nadir of the work ethic; the opulent and idle come here from all over the world to commune on how best to enjoy doing nothing. One day this winter a friend of many years told me that he thought the buggering off (his phrase) by the working classes was the greatest problem of our time. When I reminded him that he had done no work himself, at least since the early Truman Administration, he responded with indignation, "My father worked hard for every cent I've got."

Finally, affecting any discussion of the work ethic is the terrible ambiguity of the word "work" itself. No other word in the language covers such diverse and irreconcilable circumstances. Work is the tedious routine of the assembly line and the far from enchanting toil of those who collect the trash and garbage. It is also the wonderfully self-rewarding occupation of the musician, painter, surgeon, lawyer, engineer, scientist, or business executive. Work is what members of Congress and the President of the United States spend millions of dollars to be allowed to do. It is ridiculous that one word should be used to cover such diverse conditions.

I first learned about work in Ontario while following a team across the fields, removing the winter accumulation of animal nutrients from the barnyard, and helping restore the tile drains in the fields below the house. This was work—and I deeply detested it. In contrast, teaching at Harvard, writing books, or serving as an ambassador are entertainments for which one might reasonably be required to pay, and some would. And here is another problem. Broadly speaking, those who do what is least properly called work get the most for doing it. And those who do what should really be called work get the least. In this springtime of the great conservative revolt, no one would wish to suggest that there are contradictions in the free enterprise system. But there are. There are.

# An Interview with Dolores Huerta, Cofounder, United Farm Workers

SUSAN SAMUELS DRAKE
SEPTEMBER 2000

Q: How did it feel when you won that first labor contract?

DOLORES HUERTA: Great! It showed that our goal was absolutely possible.

Q: Cesar [Chavez] adopted nonviolence as a union strategy. How deep is this commitment these days?

HUERTA: It's very ingrained in the organization. Nonviolence really strengthens the individual. There's a whole transformational process about it. When you use nonviolence to win, you have to involve other people, build relationships with other people, and become more dependent on other people. It makes the organization stronger.

It has a spiritual quality to it, also. In order to work with nonviolence, you have to have a lot of faith. It builds the foundation and strengthens your belief that something can happen. It may not come out the way that you thought it was going to turn out, but you've got to have faith in it as a dynamic that is actually working.

Q: Surely there have been disappointments?

HUERTA: The persistent disappointment is that employers are living with a mindset of the last century. Racism and sexism are just as strong today in the fields. There's also a lack of willingness on the part of the public to dig in and support changes for farm workers the way consumers supported us in the sixties and seventies.

Q: A Watsonville strawberry picker told me that one reason he won't join the UFW is because the union would send him back to Mexico since he's not here legally.

HUERTA: That's what the growers tell them. It's not true. We probably represent more undocumented workers than anybody. We favor an amnesty program not just for farm workers but for all undocumented workers.

Q: Across the nation, a million people tend and harvest our food. Most are Latino. But we don't hear much about them. Any idea why?

HUERTA: If you make people invisible, they don't exist. It's hard to acknowledge the presence of Latino populations and the fact that this land belonged to Mexico. It's kind of a guilt thing. I'm very concerned about what's happening with the Latino population. Something like 80 percent of the children in the LA school system are Spanish-speaking children, Mexican children, and yet we can't teach them in their own language. They're changing the standards for graduation, which means a lot of these kids aren't going to be able to go on to college. It's basically a prison population preparation program. We're setting up this incredible apartheid system. We have thirty-two million Latinos in the U.S., and all these laws are against them.

Q: In our society, we make judgments: for instance, that a lawyer is more valuable than a farm worker.

HUERTA: If you were stranded on a desert island with only one other person, who would you want: a lawyer or a farm worker? What happens in the United States is we have a bigoted society; and we teach bigotry in our educational system. We're taught to look up to and respect people who have money, regardless of how they got it. Did they exploit to get it? We need to respect people who do things with their hands: farm workers, carpenters, mechanics. The people who create the world are the people who work with their hands. Just because you don't have a college degree doesn't make you a lesser person. It takes courage to do what we want to do.

—SUSAN SAMUELS DRAKE is a freelance journalist who wrote *Fields of Courage: Remembering César Chávez & the People Whose Labor Feeds Us.*

# PART II

# Parading Poetry

Since 1995, *The Progressive* has been publishing one original poem a month. We're not a poetry magazine, but we believe in poetry, and we believe in the power of words and the art of arranging them. We appreciate, too, that there are different ways to communicate, and poetry is one of the oldest. The poetry page swings open every month, and a gust of cool air runs in, just as it does now in this chapter.

But it's not decorative poetry. It's poetry that grapples with the world.

Martín Espada and Adrienne Rich nudged us along this path and introduced us to many of the poets we've published. Others have come our way unbidden. We're grateful for all of their visits, and for the presents they have given us.

Each speaks to us in an idiosyncratic voice, and that voice may linger in our ears. Try reading Mahmoud Darwish's "The House Murdered," for instance, and see if you can forget it.

# Solidarity

June Jordan
june 1989

*for Angela*

Even then
in the attenuated Light
of the Church of Le Sacré Coeur
(early evening and folk songs
on the mausoleum steps)
and armed
only with 2 Instamatic cameras
(not a terrorist among us)
even there
in that Parisian downpour
four
Black women (2 of Asian 2
of African descent)
could not catch a taxi
and
I wondered what umbrella
would be big enough to stop
the shivering
of our collective impotence
up
against such negligent assault.

And I wondered
who would build that shelter
who will build and lift it
high and wide
above
such loneliness.

# Sleeping on the Bus

Martín Espada
NOVEMBER 1995

How we drift in the twilight of bus stations,
how we shrink in overcoats as we sit,
how we wait for the loudspeaker
to tell us when the bus is leaving,
how we bang on soda machines
for lost silver, how bewildered we are
at the vision of our own faces
in white-lit bathroom mirrors.

How we forget the bus stations of Alabama,
Birmingham to Montgomery,
how the Freedom Riders were abandoned
to the beckoning mob, how afterwards
their faces were tender and lopsided as spoiled fruit,
fingers searching the mouth for lost teeth,
and how the riders, descendants
of Africa and Europe both, kept riding
even as the mob with pleading hands wept fiercely
for the ancient laws of segregation.

How we forget Biloxi, Mississippi, a decade before,
where no witnesses spoke to cameras,
how a brown man in army uniform
was pulled from the bus by police
when he sneered at the custom of the back seat,
how the magistrate proclaimed a week in jail
and went back to bed with a shot of whiskey,
how the brownskinned soldier could not sleep
as he listened for the prowling of his jailers,
the muttering and cardplaying of the hangmen
they might become.
His name is not in the index;
he did not tell his family for years.
How he told me, and still I forget.

How we doze upright on buses,
how the night overtakes us

in the babble of headphones,
how the singing and clapping
of another generation
fade like distant radio
as we ride, forehead
heavy on the window,
how we sleep, how we sleep.

# To the Poet Whose Lover Has Died of AIDS

KENNY FRIES
MARCH 1996

*. . . then the wasting begins*
*and the disappearance a day at a time.*
—MARK DOTY

The night of your reading I notice he has carved
a place for his wheelchair. But after the first
poem, through the applause, the noise of moving

out of his way. Then, only the space remains
and nobody, not even those standing, eyeing
what was his position, will take his place.

The next day, when you tell me he wet himself
and could not stay, I think how leaving causes so much
commotion, how in school during roll call the teacher

never knew how long to wait for the voice, present,
before moving on to the next name in the order.
The tittering, the shifting in chairs, when it went on

too long. When you first told me he was sick,
I could not ask if you, too, were infected—
I searched your poems for clues. Now he has died

and I have gone back to read your poems, needing
your words to prove love does not disappear
a day at a time. All those years together,

over a decade of loss, and I don't know
what's left to say. If we are given love
only to have it taken away, what solace

can anyone offer but your voice be present
among the shifting chairs, the embarrassed noises
of absence. The wait is always too long.


## Sonnet on the Location of Hell

JACK AGÜEROS
APRIL 1996

You worry about hell: Where it is and what it looks
Like; how far you should go to safely peek at it;
What to do to avoid it; how to get others out of there.

Haven't you seen the sudden dumping of human beings
On all the streets and tunnels of our city? Don't they
Look like Jesus freshly deposed, twisted and limp like
Licorice in the lap and arms of His Holy Mother Mary?
Jesus was dead only momentarily, as these men and
Women are, but there are no holy arms eyes or mothers
To cry and cradle these dead until their resurrection.

We have made this grotesque Hell on Earth and burn the
Helpless with the silent flame of rust. Worriers listen:

Neither God nor rabbit's feet can stamp these fires out
For Hell is our holy arms folded, our holy voice silent.


## Storm

C. K. WILLIAMS
SEPTEMBER 1996

Another burst of the interminable, intermittently torrential dark afternoon
downpour,
and the dozens of tirelessly garrulous courtyard sparrows stop hectoring each
other
and rush to park under a length of cornice endearingly soiled with decades of
wing-grease.

The worst summer in memory, thermal inversion, smog, swelter, intimations of global warming;
   though the plane trees still thrust forth buds as though innocent April were just blooming,
   last week's tentative pre-green leaflings are already woefully charred with heat and pollution.

Thunder far off, benign, then closer, slashes of lightning, a massive, concussive unscrolling,
   an answering tremor in the breast, the exaltation at sharing a planet with this, then sorrow,
   that we really might strip it of all but the bare wounded rock lumbering down its rote rail.

A denser veil of clouds now, another darkening downlash, the wind rises, the sparrows scatter,
   the leaves quake, and Oh, I throw myself this way, the trees say, then that way, I tremble,
   I moan, and still you don't understand the absence I'll be in the void of unredeemable time.

Twelve suns, the prophecies promise, twelve vast suns of purification will mount the horizon,
   to scorch, sear, burn away, then twelve cosmic cycles of rain: no tree left, no birdsong,
   only the vigilant, acid waves, vindictively scouring themselves again and again on no shore.

Imagine then the emergence: Oh, this way, the sky streaked, Oh, that way, with miraculous brightness;
   imagine us, beginning again, timid and tender, with a million years more this time to evolve,
   an epoch more on all fours, stricken with shame and repentance, before we fire our forges.

## *Poem for an Election Year*
The Politics of Bindweed

MAXINE KUMIN
NOVEMBER 1996

I have lived all season among the bindweed.
I have spied upon their silent Anschluss,
the bugles of their flowers, the dark guy wires
they put down into earth from which to fling
slim vines that burgeon into airy traps.

At eye level I have seen them strangle aster,
milkweed, buttercup; I have taken note of
their seemingly random entanglement by tendril
of the whole drowsy meadow. My own ankles
have been tugged at and held fast by these fanatics.

These barbarian cousins of morning glory
mean to smother the clover, drive out the livestock,
send scouts to infiltrate the next hayfield,
exploit the ties of family and class
until they rule from hedgerow to hedgerow

wherefore all season on my hands and knees
I have ripped out roots, stems, ringlets and blossoms.
I have pursued every innocent threadlike structure
to its source, then plucked it. My chosen task is
to reestablish the republic of grasses.

## *Black on a Saturday Night*

RITA DOVE
JUNE 1998

This is no place for lilac
or somebody on a trip
to themselves. Hips
are an asset here, and color
calculated to flash
lemon bronze cerise

in the course of a dip and turn.
Beauty's been caught lying
and the truth's rubbed raw:
Here, you get your remorse
as a constitutional right.

It's always what we don't
fear that happens, always
not now and why are
you people acting this way
(meaning we put in petunias
instead of hydrangeas and reject
ecru as a fashion statement).

But we can't do it—naw, because
the wages of living are sin
and the wages of sin are love
and the wages of love are pain
and the wages of pain are philosophy
and that leads definitely to an attitude
and an attitude will get you
nowhere fast so you might as well
keep dancing dancing till
tomorrow gives up with a shout,
'cause there is only
Saturday night, and we are in it—
black as black can,
black as black does,
not a concept
nor a percentage
but a natural law.

# The Communist Party

PHILIP LEVINE
NOVEMBER 1998

Seven single, formal men slowly circling
the scarred ping-pong table with its sagging net,
with its bottle of pink Michigan wine,
a plate of stale Saltines, the cheese long gone,

one bruised apple, a soda, and nothing more.
Near Eastside, Detroit, October, '48.
My brother and I looking for girls or women
interested in almost anyone, for we
were almost someones. Forty years down the road
the phrase "sexual politics" would surface
only to die into jargon; that night we
could have used it. I'll spare you the argument
with the one decent girl who called Reuther
a little fascist, the turn-table that ground out
"Petrushka" over and over with a will
of its own, the posters for Henry Wallace,
the plywood square for dancing where two girls
in chinos and sweaters frowned under a bare bulb,
the brick and board bookcase with its virgin copies
of *Das Kapital* and Jack London's novels,
the rain-streaked windows opening on a parking lot.
We stayed forty minutes talking to each other
like a husband and wife in a foreign country
and left with nowhere else to go that night.
We called it experience and laughed it off.
I've partly played this for laughs. It wasn't
that funny. The two of us were looking
for what we couldn't articulate, and so
we said "girls." Were we simply idealists?
What I'm certain of is something essential
was missing from our lives, and it wasn't
in that sad little clubhouse for college kids,
it wasn't in the vague talk, the awful words
that spun their own monotonous music:
"proletariat," "bourgeoisie," "Trotskyist."
Whatever it was we didn't find it there
among a dozen strangers of good will,
we didn't find it there or anywhere.
Perhaps that's why I go back again and
again in my imagination to a night
I could have changed my life or ruined it
or found it for a time. What was missing?
This freezing afternoon in early March
on the downtown 6 headed for Bleecker Street
I read a list of plain words—boots, rack, bin,

box, hose, rake, broom, saw, ax—household words
put down by an Australian novelist
in a book of true stories she'd sent me.
A singular woman who'd created herself
out of the need to be only herself.
Her family names, I thought, reborn on my breath
as I spoke them quietly to everyone.
It's never too late, is it, to lose your life.

## La Niña Obediente / The Obedient Girl

MARJORIE AGOSÍN
JUNE 1999

Obediente la niña
con sus zapatos lustrados
el blanco vestido del orden
Obediente la niña
saluda al general
que le rebanó las uñas
al hermano menor
que quemó los pechos
de la hermana mayor.

Obediente la niña
sonríe, hace las reverencias
apropiadas
y toda turbada gime
cuando un soldado la
llama hermosa
y roza su mano de guerra entre
sus piernas adormecidas.

Obediente la niña vive
porque en un país de niños obedientes
los fantasmas jóvenes aparecen
en días de luz salvaje
para secuestrar a las niñas desobedientes,
a las gitanas perdidas entre los bosques
de luz y sombra.

Obediente la niña
se acerca al soldado
y lo besa con temor
es el soldado que incendió
los libros de su casa
que rajó sus vestidos rojizos
y jugó con los candelabros de
plata y sangre.

La niña obediente
no habla
es una muñeca dormida
y se deja hacer
como si su cuerpo fuese un país
de viajeros oscuros.

The obedient girl
with the patent-leather shoes
and starched white dress
The obedient girl
greets the general
who sliced the fingernails
of her younger brother
and burned the breasts
of her older sister.

The obedient girl
smiles, makes the appropriate
curtsies
and moans completely flustered
when the soldier
tells her she is beautiful
and rubs his hand of war between
her lifeless legs.

The obedient girl lives
because in a country of obedient children
young ghosts appear
on days of savage light
to kidnap disobedient girls,
gypsies lost in the forests
of light and shadow.

The obedient girl
approaches the soldier
and kisses him with fear
he is the soldier who burned
the books of her house
who slashed the crimson dresses
and played with the candlesticks of
silver and blood.

The obedient girl
doesn't speak
she is a sleepy doll
that surrenders herself
as if her body were a country
of obscure travelers.

—*Translated by Celeste Kostopulos-Cooperman*

# Veterans Day

ADRIENNE RICH
NOVEMBER 2000

I

No flag heavy or full enough to hide this face
this body swung home from home     sewn into its skin

Let you     entrusted to close the box
for final draping     take care

what might be due
to the citizen wounded

by foreign blast nor shell     (*is this
body a child's?     if?     why?*)

eyes hooded in refusal—
over these to lower the nation's pall, thick flutter

this body shriveled into itself
—a normal process they have said

The face?　　another story, a flag
hung upside-down against glory's orders

2

Trying to think about
something else—what?—when

*the story broke*
the scissor-fingered prestidigitators

snipped the links of concentration
State vs memory

State vs unarmed citizen
wounded by foreign blast nor shell

forced into the sick-field
brains-out coughing downwind

backing into the alley　　hands shielding eyes
under glare-lit choppers coming through　　low

3

In the dream you—is it?—set down
two packages in brown paper

saying, *Without such means*
*there can be no end*

*to the wrenching of mind*
*from body, the degradation*

*no end to everything you hate*
*and have exposed, lie upon lie*

I think: *We've been dying slowly*
*now we'll be blown to bits*

I think you're testing me
*"how vitally we desired disaster"*

You say, *there can be no poetry*
*without the demolition*

*of language, no end to everything you hate*
*lies upon lies*

I think: you're testing me
testing us both

but isn't this what it means to live—
pushing further the conditions in which we breathe?


4

In the college parlor by the fireplace
ankled and waisted with bells

he, inclined by nature toward tragic themes
chants of the eradication of tribal life

in blue-eyed trance
shaking his neckbent silvering hair

Afterward, wine and cake at the Provost's house

and this is surely no dream, how the beneficiary
of atrocities yearns toward innocence

and this is surely a theme, the vengeful rupture
of prized familiar ways

and calculated methods
for those who were there     But for those elsewhere

it's something else, not herds hunted down cliffs
maybe a buffalo burger in the

tribal college cafeteria
and computer skills after lunch     Who wants to be tragic?

The college coheres out of old quonset huts
demolition-scavenged doors, donated labor

used textbooks, no waste, passion


5

Horned blazing fronds of Sierra ice
grow in hidden rivulets, last evening's raindrop pulses

in the echeveria's cup next morning, fogdrip darkens the road
under fire-naked bishop pines

thick sweats form on skins
of pitched-out nectarines, dumpster shrine

of miracles of truths of mold
Rain streaming, stroking

a broken windowpane
When the story broke I thought

I was thinking about water
how it is most of what we are

and became bottled chic
such thoughts are soon interrupted

6

When the story broke we were trying to think
about history     went on stubbornly thinking

though history plunged
with muddy spurs     screamed at us for trying

to plunder its nest     seize its nestlings
capture tame and sell them or something

after the manner of our kind
Well, was it our secret hope?

—a history you could seize
(as in old folios of "natural history"

each type and order pictured in its place?)
—Back to the shambles, comrades,

where the story is always breaking
down     having to be repaired

7

Under the small plane's fast shadow an autumn
afternoon bends sharply

—swathes of golden membrane, occult blood
seeping up through the great groves

where the intestinal the intestate
blood-cords of the stags are strung from tree to tree

I know already where we're landing
what cargo we'll take on

boxed for the final draping
coming home from home      sewn into its skin

eyes hooded in refusal

—what might be due—


# The Avenue of the Americas

ALICIA OSTRIKER
FEBRUARY 2001


Above the tongues of taxicabs, the horns and buyers
the teeth of buildings grin at each other, the institutions
of media medicine publishing fashion

know how to
bite through human flesh
like hinged aluminum traps chopping the necks

of beavers, or like logging rigs, those saws
that go through a hundred year old
redwood in about three minutes

take out a thousand acres
of virgin Oregon forest
annually because loggers need jobs,

intellectuals need the special sections
of the New York Times stacked
on driveways

each rosy dawn, the Japanese need
the splinters these pines and spruces
finally get turned into,

everybody needs what they can get
and more. Yesterday walking
between fifty-third and fifty-second

on the Avenue of the Americas at twilight on my way
to a good restaurant with good friends I passed
three beggars. Wrapped in plastic. Why not say

beggars?
Why invent novelty phrases like "the homeless"
as if our situation were modern and special

instead of ancient and normal,
the problem of greed and selfishness?
The beggars turned toward me

I put money in the woman's cup
though I didn't like her facial sores
her drowned eyes bobbed to the surface

as if they believed for a second
something new was about to happen
but nothing was

so the eyes sank rapidly back
like crabs into sand, and sorrow
pressed into me like a hot iron

after which I hurried through the hurrying crowd
sky overhead primrose and lilac, skyscrapers
uncanny mirrors filled with tender cloud bouquets

to overtake my friends who had strolled ahead
chatting so as not to be embarrassed
by the sight of charity,

the bad wet rag of need.

## Not Spoken

Tim Seibles
MARCH 2002

As if thirst were not a wound.
As if the thirst for company were not a wound.

Consciousness the one shadow
from which light grows.

As if all the ache flowed from the same bruise.

Near dawn. My blood caught in its circle
I think of your body your legs opening.

And the light hairs strung along your wrists.

As if your shoulders.
As if the muscular turn of your hips.
As if I could tilt your mouth
to this dent in my chest.

So, bit by bit, it becomes unmistakable.
This not knowing how to say.

As if I had already broken
into the last room and found the words
still not English.

As if being flesh were not call enough.

Why stay here to be American?
Where what is exactly sexual has no country.

Let's go.
Whole words. Whole worlds slow
between us. Trying to pronounce themselves.
Unlost.

The body, the one sacred book.

My hand. My hands know
so little of your hands.

The names of pleasure held
in chains taken in ships.

## Rue Beaurepaire, I and II

MARILYN HACKER
JULY 2002

I

On a wide side-street that leads to the canal
job-seeking Meridional families,
retired mail-clerks, philoprogenitive Chinese
textile workers, Tunisian grocers
have found an issue everyone agrees

to disagree on—IV drug users'
right to a safe haven among neighbors:
a hostel instead of a hospital
ER, with coffee, washing-machines and showers,
a Moroccan intern who serves as a nurse,
weekly rap groups, small tables to converse
across. From balconies, spanning the street
hang homemade banners, spray paint on white sheets:
send them to another street—not ours.


II

The banners across the rue Beaurepaire
are gone, those "for" and also those "against"
the shop-front drop-in center. Someone's rinsed
away the angry slogans spray-painted
across the elegant discreet façade
stenciled with quotations from Voltaire,
Sartre, Aragon, Camus. The mayor
stayed out of it: nobody was convinced
and rumor once more outweighed evidence.
(The school's one street over—really, next door!
Don't they have AIDS? Dealers will come. They'll steal . . . )
They won't be driven into the canal;
just relocated to the Gare du Nord
a site indicative of transience—

—according to the ACT UP bulletin.
But on a brilliant summer afternoon
below the white, newly anonymous
façade, the door was open nonetheless.
In the doorway, two women and a man
were talking. One woman, I guessed,
might be a client, so I went on past
and sat by the canal, which, in the sun,
looked less like bodily effluvium;
a few discreet minutes later, returned.
The young man, dressed in orange, fresh on brown/
olive skin, was the intern who'd been there last June.
They're backed now by la Ligue des Droits de l'Homme;
keep clinic hours, but quietly. They've learned.

# My Name's Not Rodríguez

LUIS J. RODRÍGUEZ
AUGUST 2002

It is a sigh of climbing feet,
the lather of gold lust,
the slave masters' religion
with crippled hands gripping greed's tail.
My name's not Rodríguez.
It's an Indian mother's noiseless cry,
a warrior's saliva on arrow tip, a jaguar's claw,
a woman's enticing contours on volcanic rock.
My real name's the ash of memory from burned trees.
It's the three-year-old child wandering in the plain
and shot by U.S. Cavalry in the Sand Creek massacre.
I'm Geronimo's yell into the canyons of the old ones.
I'm the Comanche scout; the Raramuri shaman
in a soiled bandanna running in the wretched rain.
I'm called Rodríguez and my tears leave rivers of salt.
I'm Rodríguez and my skin dries on the bones.
I'm Rodríguez and a diseased laughter enters the pores.
I'm Rodríguez and my father's insanity
blocks every passageway,
scorching the walls of every dwelling.
My name's not Rodríguez; it's a fiber in the wind,
it's what oceans have immersed,
it's what's graceful and sublime over the top of peaks,
what grows red in desert sands.
It's the crawling life, the watery breaths between ledges.
It's taut drum and peyote dance.
It's the brew from fermented heartaches.
Don't call me Rodríguez unless you mean peon and sod carrier,
unless you mean slayer of truths and deep-sixer of hopes.
Unless you mean forget and then die.
My name's the black-hooded 98mm-wielding child in all our alleys.
I'm death row monk. The eight-year-old gum seller
in city bars and taco shops.
I'm unlicensed, uninsured, unregulated, and unforgiven.
I'm free and therefore hungry.
Call me Rodríguez and bleed in shame.

Call me Rodríguez and forget your own name.
Call me Rodríguez and see if I whisper in your ear,
    mouth stained with bitter wine.


## *Balance*

MARIO SUSKO
APRIL 2003

maybe some twenty years from now
they'll sit down with their adversaries
and over coffee and assorted drinks
exchange notes and peruse the maps,
entertaining bald historians and strategists
with their now polite explanations
why they had to kill each other.

the atmosphere at a peaceful resort
will be cordial, even some jokes offered
to unburden the collective conscience
while discussing the variables of life
and death that once had to create
the shortest distance between them.

places such as Pig's Head, Turtle Point,
Goats Trail will be revisited, coordinates
re-examined, hands that held the wheel
or hovered above the button will try to be
steady again as the memory searches
for the orgasmic explosion of color particles.

I have now dead future pictures
to show, any unmarked grave that could
be my mother's, any lit window once mine,
as I sit in a dark empty room in a town
pinpointed on some waterproof map
and hold the eviction notice in my hand,
the droning of the landlord's refrigerator
reminding my displaced mind of gravity.

commentators will then talk about the need
to understand the necessary historical balance

in the global scheme of things, and mention
in passing only the unbalanced act of someone
who throws a good refrigerator out of the window
and jumps, trying to beat it to the ground.

# Book Burning

JAY ROGOFF
JANUARY 2004

Fire loves paper
but adores people.
Fire eats our words,
hurling them off
like flaming birds
on bright black wings.
Smoke must cough
but fire sings,
breathing deeper,
sucking down
our oxygen.
Fire is not
our brother's keeper.
It isn't a question
of good and evil;
it guzzles the broth,
consumes the table.
Heine guessed
a modern truth:
they burn books first.

The night of the fire
on Unter den Linden
what rang up the curtain
next door at the Staatsoper?
*Die Zauberflöte*,
its gorgeous noise
lit with love,
a book of seduction,
light, and learning.

We walk through flame,
daring hell and high water,
dancing and burning,
our fancy fired up
till real tears drop;
or *Tristan and Isolde*,
romantic hell
on a Celtic ship,
love mating death
till both look the same.
Fire crests the wave
of the blood-dark ocean,
extinguished breath
blood-wet with kisses:
lovers, poison,
and none left to blame.

On the Opernplatz
the students wave
a sea of dark arms
engaged by armbands
and oozing the spume
of cream-pale hands
awash in the air.
Goebbels commends
their courage to break
the intellectual
reich of the Jew
and homosexual;
and face the blaze,
courage to erect
in this vast empty platz,
banal and funereal,
a tower of books
and feed them to fire
like so many faggots.
The boys pledge death
divinest respect
with courage to burn,
courage to burn
Freud and all joy,

such men as Mann,
heretic Einstein,
and Heine the Jew.

The opera disgorges
its lovers, their eyes
still moist, songs still
in their teeth. They view
the night turned day,
the spring turned hell
this early May night.
The spines crack.
The burning covers
issue a smell
like living leather,
rank with authors.
Kerchiefs mask noses
and hands shield eyes
raised to the skies.

Another decade
and they'll take burning
to the very Beginning,
the primal Word,
spinning the world
back down the commode,
back into its Chaos
of mud and scheiss.
For now, bringing brightness,
words of all people
soar in a tower,
the babble of languages
melting together,
the fire-breathing steeple
drunk on air
and publishing ash,
singing like mad
a single song
in a single tongue.

## Patriotic Poem

RAFAEL CAMPO
DECEMBER 2004

*after Neruda*

The war on words had been declared. A voice
was now considered dangerous,
and could be confiscated by police.
A metaphor lay beaten in the street
while moonlight bathed it in white tears. The war
on words had been declared, in language none
could contradict. A lie ran naked through
the capital, while onlookers looked on.
It seemed that everything stopped making sense:
the punctuation of the traffic lights,
the thudding sound of dictionaries shut,
the heavy heart the poet wore to bed
for love. The war on words had been declared.
A lullaby defied the curfew, night
close in around it like swaddling clothes.
A girl spelled "moratorium" in school;
the next day she was dead, her hands sawn off
as punishment. The war on words had been
declared. Soon, silence stole over the land,
broken only by the piercing protest
of car alarms set off by no one's touch,
a neighbor's wailing weed-whacker, a song
that once remembered one cannot get out
of one's head. WAR ON WORDS DECLARED cried out
the evening paper, soundlessly, too late—
the President was on TV to say
we had won, we had won, we had won.

# sizing up the cost of war

DEVORAH MAJOR
FEBRUARY 2006

what is left but the shoes

shoes scuffed and torn
no longer having
feet to carry them

shoes
empty now

work boots still bearing mud
from the last field
that he had plowed
with his father

empty now

red sneakers with white stripes
brought back from america
by her oldest son given
to her youngest
both of them
immediately running outside
kicking the soccer ball back and forth
the older ruffling the youngster's head
after a well aimed goal

empty now

heavy and white they were
the first pair of shoes she ever walked in
the first she had learned to untie
so that she could wriggle out
and once again feel the sand
sift between her toes

empty now

his work boots were resoled many times
next season he would have bought a new pair
or perhaps the season after that

but these old ones darkened from the oil
had become supple and familiar
they knew his feet
grasped his ankles
and kept them strong

empty now

she had smiled when he offered
the embossed leather pumps
made for her in italy
from the pattern he
had carefully traced
around her narrow feet
long toes tapered
in perfect symmetry

empty now

regulation boots smoothed by the sand salt crystals
seeming to be so much of the desert they had walked
the inside soles showing imprints of thick heavy feet

empty now

and these hand made slippers
that were a vanity only
a grandmother's silk flowered kiss
that never touched the ground
because as her father's favorite
she was still carried everywhere

empty now

the red heels she saved for
the brown loafers passed down
the sandals strapped and tied

all empty now

the flesh gone
the blood gone
the legs gone
all gone

# On the Third Anniversary of the Ongoing War in Iraq

SAM HAMILL
AUGUST 2006

*a letter to Hayden Carruth*

It's been nearly forty years
since you wrote that poem
about writing poems against
all those wars, Harlan County
to Italy and Spain. When your
Selected Poems arrived today,
it was one of the poems that
gave me pause reading it again.

We've been at war ever since.
I too, born in World War,
have lived and written against
that particular stupidity
and pointless, hopeless pain
all my agonizing days.
Has even a single life thereby
been saved? Who can say?
Except that doing so saved mine.

Oh, I could tell you about
saved lives. There was that
beautiful young woman in Sitka
whose husband, jealous
of her poetry, tied
her feet together with a rope
and threw her from his boat.
You have about 12 minutes of life
in those southeast Alaskan waters.

Or the grandmother in Utah
who wrote rhymed, romantic sonnets
and called me late one night
in my motel because her jaw
was broken, and her nose, and because

he was still drinking. Or
I could tell you about Alex,
doing life for murder over drugs,
and how his eyes lit up
when he discovered the classics.

Yes, poetry saves lives.
All wars begin at home
within the warring self.
No, our poems cannot stop
a war, not this nor any war,
but the one that rages from
within. Which is the first
and only step. It is
a sacred trust, a duty,
the poet's avocation.
We write the poetry we must.

# The House Murdered

MAHMOUD DARWISH
NOVEMBER 2006

In one minute, the whole life of a house ends. The house murdered is also mass murder, even if vacant of its residents. It is a mass grave for the basic elements needed to construct a building for meaning, or for an insignificant poem in a time of war. The house, murdered, is the amputation of things from their relations and from the names of emotions, and it is tragedy's need to guide eloquence to contemplate the life of a thing. In each thing there's a being that aches . . . the memory of fingers, of a scent, of an image. And houses get murdered just as their residents get murdered. And as the memory of things get murdered—wood, stone, glass, iron, cement—they all scatter in fragments like beings. And cotton, silk, linen, notepads, books, all are torn like words whose owners were not given time to speak. And the plates, spoons, toys, records, faucets, pipes, door handles, and the fridge, the washer, the vases, jars of olives and pickles, and canned foods, all break as their owners broke. And the two whites, salt and sugar, are pulverized, and also the spices, the matchboxes, the pills and oral contraceptives, elixirs, garlic braids, onions, tomatoes, dried okra, rice and lentils, as happens with the residents. And the lease contract, the marriage and birth certificates, the utility bills, identity cards, passports, love letters, all torn to shreds like the hearts of their owners. And the pictures fly, the toothbrushes, hair combs, make-up accessories, shoes, underwear, sheets, towels, like family secrets hung in public, in ruin. All these things are the memories of people who were emptied of things, and the memories of things that were emptied of people . . . all end in one minute. Our things die like us, but they don't get buried with us!

*—Translated by Fady Joudah*

# No Moon

Spoon Jackson
december 2006

I was afraid this would
happen the way the night
looks with no moon
The way the wind whistles
off the back porch

You want to love me
How can I tell you
I have a life
but I don't have a life

What can I tell you
Shall I tell you about
the bars that don't speak

or the razor wire
that longs to sever
the throat
or the cold winds
that bounce off the emptiness

Shall I tell you
about the trees 200 yards away
across the river of electric wire
How the trees haunt me
like the smell of barbeque
the scent of a mountain meadow
the sight of crimson painted toes.

Across the river, across the fields
across the hills
there is wine that belongs
to no one

What can I tell you
Shall I tell you about
the lovely women
I never had

Shall I tell you
about the moon fading away
like a piece of hard
round candy

I was afraid this would
happen the way the night
feels with no moon
the way the wind whistles off

the back porch pushing
on the screen door
like ten cats, like ten mad
men fighting.

## Prayer for the New Millennium

SANDRA CISNEROS
JULY 2007

In the hour of extremes,
long live the brave
wordsmiths of American letters.

Hallowed be the poets
when the news is diffused
in the name of *susto*.

Viva the citizens of truth.

Hallelujah
the devotees of language,
the languished souls
enamored of the syllable.

In the wake of *políticos*,
blessed be the *relámpagos*,
the border-crossers,
the illegal citizens of American lit.
The syntax-leapers.
The language-benders.
The cross-pollinators.
The decimators of the sacrosanct
ivory tower.

All power to you.
Wary be thy name.
United trespassers,
workers hammering
yammering into something
vital, nourishing, and new.

*Dale gas* until the poem
rings and sizzles and sings.
Word without end,
Amen.

# PART 12

# Waging Peace

"Every nation has its war party," La Follette tells us. *The Progressive* has consistently opposed this war party and advocated peace even—especially—when it was not popular to do so.

Instead of war, *The Progressive* upholds nonviolence. Early on, it paid great attention to Mahatma Gandhi's campaigns, covering him repeatedly before most magazines took him seriously. And it has always put the peace activist in a place of honor.

Leading pacifists, such as Bertrand Russell and Norman Thomas, took to *The Progressive*'s pages to stake their claims. Erwin Knoll, who edited *The Progressive* for twenty-one years, laid out the pacifist argument in the starkest terms in his article "Not a Just War—Just a War."

Nationalism is antithetical to peace, and even dying for one's country is a misnomer, as Howard Zinn points out. Like Bertrand Russell and Norman Thomas, he calls for a world without borders, and begs us to use our ingenuity to find peaceful solutions to the world's problems.

Being a peace activist can be dangerous. Jeff Miller found that out. He was killed by the National Guard at Kent State on May 4, 1970, along with three other students. His mother, Elaine Holstein, wrote about the pain of that loss, many years later. Her article has been reprinted more than almost any other in the history of *The Progressive*, and she still gets letters from people who read it and are moved by it.

# Take the Profit Out of War

ROBERT M. LA FOLLETTE
FEBRUARY 1915

It is repugnant to every moral sense that governments should even indirectly be drawn into making and prosecuting a war through the machinations of those who make money by it. Yet the vast capital privately invested in plants for naval construction, and the manufacture of munitions of war necessary for the equipment of armies, has the strongest possible inducement to employ every means to shape conditions and influence policies which lead on to armed conflict. It means business. It means dividends. It means great accumulations of wealth in private hands to be again turned, though organization, into the building of more plants, more battleships, the manufacture of more powder, more shot and shell. In the end it has but one purpose, and that is to sacrifice human life for private gain.

Back of every big army and any appropriation bill is the organized power of private interest, pressing for larger appropriations, for more battleships, more armor plate, more powder, more rifles, more machine guns, a larger standing army, a bigger navy, because there follows in the wake of such legislation fat army contracts, with attendant opportunity for graft and easy money. Over and over again we have heard the same arguments from the same organs of the great special interests, making their hypocritical appeals on the ground of patriotism; urging that thorough preparation for war is always a sure guarantee of peace.

What state, what city finds security for peace and good order in allowing every man to pack a gun? Why have civilized communities enacted laws and ordinances prohibiting inhabitants from going about armed? States are but aggregations of individuals. Nations are but great groups of human beings. The deadly weapon within ready reach of the hand breeds a murderer. And nations, armed to the teeth, quickly resort to killing as a means of settling their differences.

International agreement for reducing the oppressive expenditures in preparation for war may be remote. But one thing we in America can do and do at once: We can nationalize the manufacture of all munitions of war. We can take away from private interest all the incentive to increase army and navy appropriation bills. We can set a worthy example for the world.

# The Right of the Citizen to Oppose War and the Right of Congress to Shape the War Policy

ROBERT M. LA FOLLETTE
JUNE 1917

In these days, whenever an American citizen presumes to question the justification, either in law or morals, of our participation in the European war, he is at once denounced by the war party and the war press as disloyal to the country.

The war party in the United States seeks to justify our entrance into the bloody conflict on the ground that it is in the interest of democracy. But every man and every woman knows that there is a struggle going on today in every civilized nation between democracy and autocracy.

Every nation has its war party. It is not the party of democracy. It is the party of autocracy. It seeks to dominate absolutely. It is commercial, imperialistic, ruthless. It tolerates no opposition. It is just as arrogant, just as despotic, in London, or in Washington, as in Berlin. The American Jingo is twin to the German Junker.

In times of peace, the war party insists on making preparation for war. As soon as prepared for war, it insists on making war. If there is no sufficient reason for war, the war party will make war on one pretext, then invent another, possibly more effective, pretext after war is on.

Before war is declared, the war party assumes the divine right to denounce and silence all opposition to war as unpatriotic and cowardly.

After Congress has been bullied into a declaration of war, the politicians, the press, and the mercenaries of the war party assume authority to deny the right of American citizens to discuss the necessity for the war, or the ultimate object and purpose of the declaration of war.

Today Secret Service men, United States District Attorneys, United States Marshals, United States Court Commissioners, and other federal officials are rankly abusing their authority on every hand. People are being unlawfully arrested, thrown into jail, denied the right to employ counsel, or to communicate with their friends, or even to inform their families of their whereabouts, subjected to unlawful search, threatened, intimidated, examined, and cross-examined. The most sacred constitutional rights guaranteed to every American citizen are violated in the name of democracy.

It appears to be the purpose of those conducting this procedure to throw the country into a state of terror, to coerce public opinion, stifle criticism, suppress discussion of the issues of the war, and put a quietus on all opposition.

It is time for the American people to assert and maintain their rights.

# Gandhi Opposes Bloodshed

SEPTEMBER 19, 1931

*Special to* The Progressive

Condemnation of bloodshed and violence to attain freedom of other national aims was voiced by Mahatma Gandhi, India's famed Nationalist leader, in a radio speech broadcast throughout the world from London, where the "holy man of India" is visiting to attend the round table conference on Indian independence.

Making the first radio speech in his life, the ninety-two-pound brown little man whose leadership in India is followed by millions of supporters seemed pleased with the opportunity of talking to America and the world through the magic of radio.

"The world is sick of blood spilling," said Gandhi. "I personally would wait for ages rather than attain freedom through bloody means. I flatter myself that India's method—nonviolence—may show the world out of all the violent turmoil.

"I have, therefore, no hesitation in inviting all the great nations of the earth in giving their hearty cooperation to India in her mighty struggle. It must be a sight worth contemplating and treasuring that often millions of people have given themselves to suffering with retaliation, in order that they might vindicate the dignity and honor of the nation. I have called that suffering a process of self-purification.

"May I not on behalf of the semi-starved millions of India appeal to the conscience of the world to come to the rescue of a people dying to regain their liberty?"

# Who Is It That Wants War?

BERTRAND RUSSELL
SEPTEMBER 24, 1932

In every civilized country all persons capable of apprehending plain facts are agreed that the next great war will, in all likelihood, bring the end of civilization. This is in no sense a party question; it has nothing to do with economics or theology or any of the other issues that divide men. It has to do solely with the perfection of war technique, especially of the technique of attack.

Aeroplanes and poison gas have made the attack much stronger than the defense, and have made it easy to make war on civilian populations behind the lines. If there should be a war, say, between England and France it is to be expected that within a few hours of its outbreak practically all the inhabitants of London or Paris would be dead.

Within a few days all the main centers of industry would be destroyed and most of the railways would be paralyzed. The population, maddened with terror, would fight each other for stores of food, and those who were most successful would retire into lonely places, where they could shoot all who approached them. Probably within a week the population of both countries would be halved and the institutions which are the vehicles of their culture would be destroyed forever.

All this is well known, and yet, incredible as it may seem, the governments show a rooted opposition to all serious attempts to prevent war. The disarmament conference, after long deliberation, decided merely to renew certain futile agreements which, as everyone admits, will be broken on the day war breaks out.

The assembled governments decided to flout the intelligence of the civilized world, and to make it clear that they would do nothing whatever to make war less likely or less horrible.

Einstein, who is universally recognized as the greatest man of our age, went to Geneva during the disarmament conference to find out whether there was any hope of anything being done. Since the conference proved futile, Einstein and various other friends of peace, many of them eminent and highly respectable, have been attempting to hold a congress that should consider what intelligent people could do to save Europe from suicide.

The Swiss government refused them permission to meet in Switzerland on the pretext that friends of peace must be Communists. The French government proved equally unfriendly. The British prime minister, personally appealed to, has not even replied. Apparently he is now ashamed of his honorable record in the great war.

The conclusion to be drawn from such facts is that governments of the world, while not positively desiring war, are just as determined as they were in 1914 to obstruct every measure that is likely to prevent it.

It is to be hoped that ordinary citizens will, before it is too late, acquire the common sense required to save themselves and their children from a horrible and futile death.

The first step should be universal compulsory and complete disarmament, the second the creation of an international government. Armies and navies do not make for safety. The only way to be safe in the modern world is not to have the means of fighting.

Men like Einstein proclaim obvious truths about war, but no one listens. So long as Einstein is unintelligible he is thought wise, but as soon as he says anything that people can understand it is thought that his wisdom has departed from him. In this folly governments take a leading part.

It seems that politicians would rather lead their country to destruction than not to be in the administration. A greater depth of wickedness than this it is not easy to imagine.

—LORD BERTRAND RUSSELL, philosopher and campaigner for peace and nuclear disarmament, won the Nobel Prize in 1950.

# We Can Have Peace, If We Want It

NORMAN THOMAS
JULY 9, 1945

This article is begun the day before the San Francisco Charter is to be officially launched as the bearer of the world's sure hope of lasting peace. It is not that. I shall favor its ratification because I am convinced that practically and psychologically we shall be in a better position to work for genuine security and peace.

But basically, the new charter is a device by which the Big 3 can easily and somewhat amiably maintain their collective power over the world, and adjust their own rivalries with a minimum of friction. This is not the basis for peace. That requires a definite and conscious progress towards a federation of free peoples who will seek to use our marvelous machinery for the good of all.

Wars spring from group prejudices and group passions for profit and power. There are in the Charter no adequate provisions to make possible the rule of the sort of a law between nations which by orderly processes can be made to approximate justice. The amoral idea of sovereignty remains, and neither the unreal metaphysical idea of equality of sovereignty of weak nations and strong, nor the grim reality of the imperialism of the strong, is greatly affected by the San Francisco Charter. The business of removing the political and economic causes of war, and organizing the world, regardless of racial and national prejudice, on a basis fit for peace is completely unfinished.

—NORMAN THOMAS, socialist and pacifist, ran six times for president on the Socialist Party ticket.


# Anniversary

ELAINE HOLSTEIN
MAY 1988

At a few minutes past noon on May 4, I will once again observe an anniversary—an anniversary that marks not only the most tragic event of my life but also one of the most disgraceful episodes in American history. This May 4 will be the eighteenth anniversary of the shootings on the campus of Kent State University and the death of my son, Jeff Miller, by Ohio National Guard rifle fire.

Eighteen years! That's almost as long a time as Jeff's entire life. He had turned twenty just a month before he decided to attend the protest rally that ended in his death and the deaths of Allison Krause, Sandy Scheuer, and Bill Schroeder, and the wounding of nine of their fellow students. One of them, Dean Kahler, will spend the rest of his life in a wheelchair, paralyzed from the waist down.

That Jeff chose to attend that demonstration came as no surprise to me. Anyone who knew him in those days would have been shocked if had decided to sit that one out. There were markers along the way that led him inexorably to that campus protest.

At the age of eight, Jeff wrote an article expressing his concern for the plight of black Americans. I learned of this only when I received a call from *Ebony* magazine, which assumed he was black and assured me he was bound to be "a future leader of the black community."

Shortly before his sixteenth birthday, Jeff composed a poem he called "Where Does It End?" in which he expressed the horror he felt about "the War Without a Purpose."

Was Jeff a radical? He told me, grinning, that though he might be taken for a "hippie radical" in the Middle West, back home on Long Island he'd probably be seen as a reactionary.

So when Jeff called me that morning and told me he planned to attend a rally to protest the "incursion" of U.S. military forces into Cambodia, I merely expressed my doubts as to the effectiveness of still another demonstration.

"Don't worry, Mom," he said. "I may get arrested, but I won't get my head busted." I laughed and assured him I wasn't worried.

The bullet that ended Jeff's life also destroyed the person I had been—a naive, politically unaware woman.

Until that spring of 1970, I would have stated with absolute assurance that Americans have the right to dissent, publicly, from the policies pursued by their government. The Constitution says so. Isn't that what makes this country—this democracy—different from those totalitarian states whose methods we deplore?

And even if the dissent got noisy and disruptive, was it conceivable that an arm of the government would shoot at random into a crowd of unarmed students? With live ammunition? No way! Arrests? Perhaps. Tear gas? Probably. Antiwar protests had become a way of life, and on my television set I had seen them dealt with routinely in various nonlethal ways.

The myth of a benign America where dissent was broadly tolerated was one casualty of the shootings at Kent State. Another was my assumption that everyone shared my belief that we were engaged in a no-win situation in Vietnam and had to get out. As the body counts mounted and the footage of napalmed babies became a nightly television staple, I was certain that no one could want the war to go on. The hate mail that began arriving at my home after Jeff died showed me how wrong I was.

We were enmeshed in legal battles for nine years. The families of the slain students, along with the wounded boys and their parents, believed that once the facts were heard in a court of law, it would become clear that the governor of Ohio and the troops he called in had used inappropriate and excessive force to quell what had begun as a peaceful protest. We couldn't undo what had been done, but we wanted to make sure it would never be done again.

Our 1975 trial ended in defeat after fifteen weeks in federal court. We won a retrial on appeal, and returned to Cleveland with high hopes of prevailing, but before the trial got under way we were urged by both the judge and our lawyers to accept an out-of-court settlement. The proposal angered us; the case wasn't about money. We wanted to clear our children's names and to win a judicial ruling that the governor and the National Guard were responsible for the deaths and injuries. The defendants offered to issue an apology. The wording was debated for days, and the final result was an innocuous document stating that "in retrospect, the tragedy . . . should not have occurred" and that "better ways must be found to deal with such confrontations."

Reluctantly, we accepted the settlement when we were told this might be the only way that Dean would get at least some of the funds to meet his lifelong medical expenses. He was awarded $350,000, the parents of each of the dead students received $15,000, and the remainder, in varying amounts, was divided among the wounded. Lawyers' fees amounted to $50,000, and $25,000 was allotted to expenses, for a total of $675,000.

Since then we have lived through Watergate and Richard Nixon's resignation, crises in the Middle East and in Central America, and the Iran-contra affair. To most people, Kent State is just one of those traumatic events that occurred during a tumultuous time.

To me, it's the one experience I will never recover from.

—ELAINE HOLSTEIN is the mother of Jeff Miller, who was killed by the Ohio National Guard at Kent State.

## Not a Just War, Just a War

ERWIN KNOLL
JUNE 1991

Last fall, when the U.S. government was assembling more than a half million U.S. troops in Saudi Arabia for what was sure to be a bloody war against Iraq, I participated in a panel discussion of the Persian Gulf crisis at a small church-affiliated liberal arts college. The speaker who preceded me was the school's chaplain, who delivered a learned and, it seemed to me, interminable disquisition on the theory of just and unjust wars. He quoted Thomas Aquinas and other sages, and concluded, after much rumination, that American military intervention in the Persian Gulf would not meet the traditional criteria of a just war.

I was impatient because I could have been marching that very night, back home, in a militant street demonstration against the coming war. I wasn't at all sure that I had done the right thing by leaving town to add my comments to an abstract, academic discourse. The situation called for protest, not chatter.

What's more, I was simply bored with the whole "just-war" argument, having re-hashed it so many times, over the years, in my own mind. So when it came my turn to speak, I heard myself saying in a tone verging on incivility, "There's no such thing as a just war," and adding for good measure, "Never has been. Never will be."

To my surprise, nobody in the college audience—not even the chaplain—chal-lenged my summary dismissal of centuries of "just-war" doctrine. But when a front-page editorial in the March issue of *The Progressive* repeated the assertion that "there is no such thing as a just war," there was swift and angry reaction from many readers.

One irate correspondent characterized the statement as "mush" and asked, "What about the Vietnamese, the Sandinistas, the nations victimized by the Nazis? Weren't their wars just?" Another asserted, "I do not remember seeing before in your maga-zine such a statement of a principled pacifist position. For example, you have not adopted this position in regard to wars waged by progressive forces against the United States and its allies in El Salvador, Southern Africa, and Vietnam. . . . Your new-found pacifism has the ring of inconsistency."

One letter-writer demanded to know how I could tell a Salvadoran teenager that he had no right to take up arms against his government's oppressive army. Still another found the renunciation of the just-war concept "self-righteous, condescending, and imperious," and urged me to "tell it to the countless number of thoughtful people who, through the ages, have agonized over the question of just war. Or . . . to the fallen black soldiers of the 54th Massachusetts, or the guys dead on the beaches of Normandy, or the young people throwing stones at Brezhnev's tanks in the streets of Czechoslovakia."

Having done my own agonizing—for several decades—over the question of just war, I can sympathize with such outraged reactions. The idea that it is sometimes nec-essary and, indeed, proper to slaughter our fellow human beings to stamp out a great evil or advance a noble cause has, after all, been drummed into all of us by Church and State, School and Family. To reject that notion is to dismiss the ultimate sacrifice made by ancestors, friends, relatives, and compatriots who laid down their lives in wars they—or, at least, their governments—deemed worthy. Perhaps it is self-righteous, condescending, even imperious to suggest that their last measure of devotion—as Lincoln described it at Gettysburg—was neither just nor justifiable.

I make no apology.

The reader who suggested that we supported "wars waged by progressive forces against the United States and its allies in El Salvador, Southern Africa, and Vietnam" is simply mistaken. We supported the goals of those progressive forces; we supported their cause; we did not support the use of violence to attain those goals or to promote that cause. We have, for example, called for justice for the Palestinians since the state of Israel was established in 1948, but we have never condoned violence by the PLO (or by the Israelis).

It's a difficult argument to make, of course. How can I say to a long-suffering vic-tim of South Africa's apartheid regime that he or she should not take up arms against such brutal oppression? How can I tell the Salvadoran teenager cited by one of my correspondents that he or she must resort only to nonviolent resistance against the savagely greedy oligarchs who exploit the people of that land?

I respond that the casualties of war are hardly ever the patriarchs and oligarchs and despots who are supposedly its targets. Just wars claim the just—not the unjust—as their victims.

About the only thing we know with certainty about the casualties U.S. troops inflicted in Iraq—not a just war by any standard—is that of the 100,000 or 200,000 or 300,000 dead, not a single one was Saddam Hussein. The desperate resident of Soweto who picks up a rifle or a bomb will not kill one of the gold-mine proprietors who batten on the sweaty labor of indentured Bantu workers; he'll kill a soldier or a cop who can't find anything better to do with his life than don a uniform. And that teenaged Salvadoran revolutionary is most likely to shoot another Salvadoran teenager just like himself who was unlucky enough to be impressed into his government's army.

What can I say to urge nonviolence on a frustrated and furious Palestinian whose people have been abandoned by the whole world? I can say, Friend, I support your cause though I can't begin to share the depths of your pain. But from my safe distance I can tell you this: If you should succeed against all odds in obtaining justice by force of arms, the victory will turn to ashes, as all such victories have. The guns that were used to free your people will be used to re-enslave them. Every revolution, every national-liberation movement that achieves its ends by dealing in death continues dealing in death once its ends have been achieved.

And I can say, Friend, violence is a terrible taskmaster: It compels its victims to emulate their oppressors. And what's the point of doing that?

All this I've understood for most of my life. Why, then, did I spend so many years agonizing over the question of just and unjust wars? Because the first question you are asked when you say there's no such thing as a just war is the question that was put to me by so many of *The Progressive*'s readers: What about Nazi Germany? For a long time, I wasn't able to answer that question.

I was born in Austria, and at the age of six I watched jackbooted Nazi troops march into Vienna. (Millions of Austrians cheered.) I was fortunate enough to escape with my life, but many members of my family weren't that lucky; they died in the camps. The Holocaust is, I suppose, the formative experience of my life.

As a teenager, even as a young adult, I loved to go to old World War II films so that I could watch Germans die. It gave me special pleasure to see the violent end inevitably allotted to officers of the Waffen SS who invariably wore monocles, permanent sneers, and black uniforms adorned with swastikas and death's-head insignia. I assumed, somehow, that all the German soldiers who froze to death in the siege of Stalingrad and all the German civilians cremated in the firestorm bombing of Dresden were officers of the Waffen SS who wore monocles, black uniforms, and permanent sneers. It took me an embarrassingly long time to figure out that wasn't the case. Apparently, some people still haven't figured it out.

But wasn't it necessary, after all, to stop Hitler? Sure it was; it was necessary, in fact, not to let him get started. But of all the ways to stop Hitler or to keep him from getting started, war was the worst—the way that inflicted the most pain, the most suffering, the most damage on everyone—especially on Hitler's victims. A few months ago, when I read and reviewed Howard Zinn's latest book, *Declarations of Independence*, I was deeply moved by the account of his moral and intellectual journey from World War II bombardier to pacifist. Zinn offers persuasive evidence that the war magnified rather than diminished Nazi atrocities. And he writes, "History is full of instances of successful resistance (although we are not informed very much about this) without violence and against tyranny, by people using strikes, boycotts, propaganda, and a dozen ingenious forms of struggle."

I believe in ingenious, nonviolent struggle for justice and against oppression. So I won't support our troops—not in the Persian Gulf or anywhere else. And I won't support anyone else's troops when they go about their murderous business. And I'll say, regretfully, to the fallen black soldiers of the 54th Massachusetts, and the guys dead on the beaches of Normandy, and the young people who threw stones at Brezhnev's tanks in the streets of Czechoslovakia, that they died in vain perpetuating a cycle of human violence that must be stopped, because there's no such thing as a just war. Never was. Never will be.

—Erwin Knoll edited *The Progressive* from 1973 to 1994 and was a voice in the wilderness on the *MacNeil/Lehrer NewsHour*.

## Dying for the Government

HOWARD ZINN
JUNE 2003

Our government has declared a military victory in Iraq. As a patriot, I will not celebrate. I will mourn the dead—the American GIs, and also the Iraqi dead, of whom there have been many, many more.

I will mourn the Iraqi children, not just those who are dead, but those who have been blinded, crippled, disfigured, or traumatized. We have not been given in the American media (we would need to read the foreign press) a full picture of the human suffering caused by our bombing.

We got precise figures for the American dead, but not for the Iraqis. Recall Colin Powell after the first Gulf War, when he reported the "small" number of U.S. dead, and when asked about the Iraqi dead, replied: "That is really not a matter I am terribly interested in."

As a patriot, contemplating the dead GIs, I could comfort myself (as, understandably, their families do) with the thought: "They died for their country." But I would be lying to myself.

Those who died in this war did not die for their country. They died for their government. They died for Bush and Cheney and Rumsfeld. And yes, they died for the greed of the oil cartels, for the expansion of the American empire, for the political ambitions of the President. They died to cover up the theft of the nation's wealth to pay for the machines of death.

The distinction between dying for your country and dying for your government is crucial in understanding what I believe to be the definition of patriotism in a democracy. According to the Declaration of Independence—the fundamental document of democracy—governments are artificial creations, established by the people, "deriving their just powers from the consent of the governed," and charged by the people to ensure the equal right of all to "life, liberty, and the pursuit of happiness." Furthermore, as the Declaration says, "whenever any form of government becomes destructive of these ends, it is the right of the people to alter or abolish it."

It is the country that is primary—the people, the ideals of the sanctity of human life and the promotion of liberty. When a government recklessly expends the lives of its young for crass motives of profit and power, always claiming that its motives are pure and moral ("Operation Just Cause" was the invasion of Panama and "Operation Iraqi Freedom" in the present instance), it is violating its promise to the country. War is almost always a breaking of that promise. It does not enable the pursuit of happiness but brings despair and grief.

Mark Twain, having been called a "traitor" for criticizing the U.S. invasion of the Philippines, derided what he called "monarchical patriotism." He said: "The gospel of the monarchical patriotism is: 'The King can do no wrong.' We have adopted it with all its servility, with an unimportant change in the wording: 'Our country, right or wrong!' We have thrown away the most valuable asset we had—the individual's right to oppose both flag and country when he believed them to be in the wrong. We have thrown it away, and with it, all that was really respectable about that grotesque and laughable word, Patriotism."

If patriotism in the best sense (not in the monarchical sense) is loyalty to the principles of democracy, then who was the true patriot, Theodore Roosevelt, who applauded a massacre by American soldiers of 600 Filipino men, women, and children on a remote Philippine island, or Mark Twain, who denounced it?

With the war in Iraq won, shall we revel in American military power and—against the history of modern empires—insist that the American empire will be beneficent?

Our own history shows something different. It begins with what was called, in our high school history classes, "westward expansion"—a euphemism for the annihilation or expulsion of the Indian tribes inhabiting the continent, all in the name of "progress" and "civilization." It continues with the expansion of American power into the

Caribbean at the turn of the century, then into the Philippines, and then repeated Marine invasions of Central America and long military occupations of Haiti and the Dominican Republic.

After World War II, Henry Luce, owner of *Time, Life,* and *Fortune,* spoke of "the American Century," in which this country would organize the world "as we see fit." Indeed, the expansion of American power continued, too often supporting military dictatorships in Asia, Africa, Latin America, the Middle East, because they were friendly to American corporations and the American government.

The record does not justify confidence in Bush's boast that the United States will bring democracy to Iraq. Should Americans welcome the expansion of the nation's power, with the anger this has generated among so many people in the world? Should we welcome the huge growth of the military budget at the expense of health, education, the needs of children, one-fifth of whom grow up in poverty?

I suggest that a patriotic American who cares for his or her country might act on behalf of a different vision. Instead of being feared for our military prowess, we should want to be respected for our dedication to human rights.

Should we not begin to redefine patriotism? We need to expand it beyond that narrow nationalism that has caused so much death and suffering. If national boundaries should not be obstacles to trade—some call it "globalization"—should they also not be obstacles to compassion and generosity?

Should we not begin to consider all children, everywhere, as our own? In that case, war, which in our time is always an assault on children, would be unacceptable as a solution to the problems of the world. Human ingenuity would have to search for other ways.

## An Interview with Cindy Sheehan, "The Peace Mom"

DAVID BARSAMIAN
MARCH 2006

Q: You've said, "We get up every morning, and every morning we see this enormous mountain in front of us. We can't go through it, we can't go under it, so we have to go over it."

CINDY SHEEHAN: Just waking up and getting out of bed after you've buried a child is almost too much to ask one person to do. I realize that bringing the troops home and having somebody held accountable for Casey's needless death is an immense undertaking, but we can't go back. As much as we'd like to go back to before Casey was killed, we can't. So we have to go forward and we have to go up. Every day is an uphill battle. Sometimes you make progress, sometimes you slide back. But it's the only way to go.

Q: Talk about the support you've received from other military families.

SHEEHAN: It's so important. I know in my own organization, Gold Star Families for Peace, not only do we advocate for an immediate withdrawal of the troops, we're also a support group. We all have lost a loved one in war. I say *lost*, but I don't like that euphemism because Casey wasn't *lost*; he was killed by George Bush's murderous policies in the Middle East.

Q: Why do you think Bush went to war in Iraq?

SHEEHAN: I really think you would have to look at where these billions of dollars are going. They're going to the Halliburtons, the Bechtels, the Blackwaters. If you read something like *War Is a Racket* by General Smedley Butler, then you know why our country goes to war. A hundred percent of the time it's to feed the war machine, it's to make the war profiteers richer.

Q: What do you think about the uses of faith and the invocation of God to justify war?

SHEEHAN: George Bush has made the Christian faith an obscenity. To rationalize what he's doing in Iraq because God told him to do it or to make Jesus some kind of warmonger is another immorality. And for people in America to buy that? I was a Catholic youth minister for eight years. I am a follower of the teachings of Jesus Christ. And I know that the Jesus that I studied about in the Gospels would not approve of what George Bush is doing. I believe that religious extremism, whether it's Jewish, Muslim, or Christian, has caused a lot of problems in the world for centuries. Leaders misuse religion to have the masses follow them. You can't invoke your religion to do things that you know the founder or the prophet of that religion would be against.

—DAVID BARSAMIAN, the director of *Alternative Radio*, is the author of many books, including *Imperial Ambitions: Conversations with Noam Chomsky on the Post-9/11 World*, *Original Zinn*, and *Louder than Bombs: Interviews from* The Progressive *Magazine*.

# PART 13

# Opposing Nuclear Weapons

E
ver since the United States dropped nuclear weapons on Hiroshima and Nagasaki, *The Progressive* has been in the forefront of the disarmament movement. The article by Ernest L. Meyer in the August 20, 1945, edition, set the tone, noting how ghastly it is to "gloat and sing paeans on the edge of that enormous crater where tens of thousands of mangled bodies fester in the stench of death."

Sidney Lens, who wrote for *The Progressive* for four decades, took pains to show how Washington's nuclear planners were engaged in a "lunatic process" that was designed to end in catastrophe. He also noted that the American public had dozed off to the craziness.

Waking the public up was the genesis of the story that brought *The Progressive* its greatest notoriety. In the spring of 1979, freelance writer Howard Morland was on assignment for the magazine to crack the secret to the hydrogen bomb and by so doing to underline the fact that nuclear secrecy provides no safety—only disarmament does. The U.S. government, in an unprecedented display of censorship, slapped a prior restraint order on *The Progressive*, which prevented the magazine from publishing the article for six months. Erwin Knoll, who was editor at the time, conveys the drama of that moment.

# Plunderers in Paradise

ERNEST L. MEYER
AUGUST 20, 1945

It's always bound to happen like that. You are relaxing in a chair on the lawn, weary after a session of chopping down underbrush with a weed-cutter none too sharp. You reflect, gratefully, that never before have the flower and vegetable beds behind the little house looked so lush. The long rows of zinnias, portulacas, bee-balm, petunias, and nasturtiums pattern a gay flag at the foot of the terrace, and in the back garden the vines hang heavy with tomatoes, and the bold yellow of squash already ripe speckles the shadows under the great dark leaves.

Above all, besides all, and permeating everything is that indefinable feeling of peace that you soak in through your pores as you absorb the sunlight. It is accented by the little noises that, compounded, make up the so-called silence of the country: the chirk of a colony of katydids sliced by the more strident sawing of a distant cicada, the staccato scolding of a red squirrel infuriated by a gray cousin, and the wash of the wind through the roadside maples.

The sounds blur as you doze a bit. And in that moment of utter contentment you are aware of a twinge of selfishness that you should, even for a little space, inhabit this corner of Shangri-La from which so many, so fearfully many, have been banished by the flaming sword.

And then it happens. The back door of the house bangs, and your son, who has been listening to the radio in his room, comes dashing across the lawn, hair flying, eyes wide with excitement. He blurts the news that the miracle has happened. The atom has been split, its terrific power controlled and shaped into a thunderbolt of a vengeful Jahveh.

President Truman has announced that a single atomic bomb has been dumped on a Japanese city of 340,000, probably wiping it and most of its inhabitants off the blasted acres of the Earth. The President has added with gratification that the atomic bomb means "harnessing the basic power of the universe." The very stuff of God, then, molded into the hands of Satan but used—oh, to be sure—in a righteous, a glorious cause, and all people of peace, goodwill, and kindliness should gloat and sing paeans on the edge of that enormous crater where tens of thousands of mangled bodies fester in the stench of death. Gloria in excelsis.

You enter the house to hear the radio, with details red and raw as dripping flesh, elaborate on the theme that humanity has been advanced by the holocaust. And when you return to the outdoors, spent and shaken, you become aware suddenly that even here in this slice of Shangri-La the feeling of peace is but a fraud and delusion.

# The Doomsday Strategy

SIDNEY LENS
FEBRUARY 1976

The nuclear menace is not apparent to the naked eye: America's policymakers cloak its self-propelling nature—and their intent—in defensive rhetoric. The United States, they argue, has no choice: It is under intensive and long-term siege by a gruesome enemy, and it needs a massive nuclear stockpile to "deter" that enemy. The deception begins with the word "deter." In the early 1960s, some of Kennedy's advisers were saying privately that the United States could "deter" the Russians with 100 nuclear missiles. That would be enough or more than enough, they argued, to knock out the nine Soviet cities with a million or more population; the USSR could no longer function as a viable society. Why, then, do we need 30,000 nuclear bombs, 8 billion tons of dynamite-equivalent, more than 1,000 times the firepower used in World War II?

While denying that it contemplates the possibility of a surprise attack, the Pentagon has been developing weapons systems whose only purpose is to make a first strike feasible. Meanwhile, the Ford Administration is focusing on an area it feels holds greater promise—*limited* nuclear war.

Those who have made policy for the United States since 1945 are driven by a "win syndrome" that refuses to accept stalemate, that seeks victory with religious fervor—no matter how long it takes, how many of our resources it diverts to the moloch of militarism, or how totally it transforms America into a secret, repressive, security state. The search for a "win" formula has coalesced with a technology that is capable of inflicting total annihilation on the human race.

Because of its catastrophic scope, the nuclear menace is neither believable nor believed by the general public. It has been absorbed, grain by grain, over a period of thirty years, so that its impact has been lost. Americans have become immunized to the permanent emergency, the permanent war economy, the permanent national security state. Crises arise in endless procession, but somehow they are resolved without triggering the big boom. We all know the firecracker is there—the nuclear arsenal—but the match to light it does not seem to be in sight. And we refuse, quite properly, to believe that the potential match-lighters are lunatics.

Yet, we are confronted by a lunatic process, in which every participant is sane but all collectively are trapped in psychosis. The process propels itself, like a machine gone mad. The atom bomb of 1945 encourages a win syndrome in which the bomb is to create a Pax Americana; the nuclear win syndrome gathers a massive constituency, in finance, business, the Pentagon, science, government, even labor; that constituency is compelled to overwhelm its opponents by concocting a synthetic anti-communism; anti-communism offers the pretext for more armaments and for the "mad momentum" in technology; technology spreads the illusion of power, and the illusion reinforces the win syndrome, so that the cycle continues on its own, human beings in high places serving merely as puppets. Technology, abetted by the win syndrome, now encompasses the possibility—the likelihood—of total annihilation.

The most important change needed today is—as Einstein noted—a change in thinking, a recognition that in a milieu of nation-states the splitting of the atom is, itself, the enemy. There can be no security for any people anywhere until that enemy is mastered. The superpowers should be able to arrive at an agreement for destroying their nuclear weapons stockpiles. The alternative is to wait for mutual destruction, and that is no alternative at all.

—SIDNEY LENS was a journalist, peace activist, and labor organizer. His memoir was entitled *Unrepentant Radical.*

# Radiation
## Unsafe at Any Level

DR. HELEN CALDICOTT
DECEMBER 1978

Radiation, the particles and waves emitted by unstable elements, has saved the lives of thousands of people when used to diagnose and treat disease. But little more than thirty years after its discovery in the late 1890s, scientists began to find that radiation had a schizophrenic nature: It could kill as well as cure. Studies conducted over the past forty years have shown that many people irradiated in infancy and childhood for such minor maladies as acne, enlarged thymus, bronchitis, ringworm, tonsillitis, and adenoids have developed cancer of the thyroid, salivary glands, brain, pharynx, and larynx as much as thirty years later. Studies of uranium miners and people engaged in commercial activities, as well as of Japanese survivors of atomic explosions, have yielded enough evidence to demonstrate beyond doubt that cancer of the blood, lung, thyroid, breast, stomach, lymph glands, and bone occur in human beings as a result of exposure to radiation.

It is difficult to predict how many mutated children will be born in the world as a result of nuclear power and weapons production, or what the nature of their defects may be. But it is indisputable that the mutation rate will rise—perhaps far higher than we would care to contemplate. The massive quantities of radiation that would be released in a war fought with nuclear weapons might, over time, cause such great changes in the human gene pool that the following generations might not be recognizable as human beings.

It is important that we keep in mind the fact that the nuclear industries are relatively young. Nuclear power has been in commercial production in the United States for only twenty-five years; arms production for thirty-five. Since the latency period of cancer is twelve to forty years, and genetic mutations do not often manifest themselves for generations, we have barely begun to experience the effects radiation can have upon us.

Nuclear power plants and military facilities will continue to release radioactive materials into the environment until public pressure becomes great enough to bring such releases to a halt. Because the effects of these materials on us, our children, and our planet will be irreversible, we must take action now. We are entering a danger zone—an unchartered territory—from which we may never return.

—HELEN CALDICOTT, the founder of Women for Nuclear Disarmament, helped galvanize the nuclear freeze movement in the 1980s.

## *Born Secret*

The Story Behind the H-Bomb Article
We're Not Allowed to Print

ERWIN KNOLL
MAY 1979

On Monday, March 26, 1979, a federal judge did what no federal judge had ever done before in the 203-year history of the American republic: He issued a preliminary injunction, at the request of the government of the United States, barring a publication from printing and distributing an article.

Behind Judge Robert W. Warren, an American flag was mounted on the ornate, oak-paneled wall of his Milwaukee courtroom. Before him sat the plaintiffs, officials of the government and their attorneys, and the defendants, the editors of this magazine and a thirty-six-year-old freelance writer, named Howard Morland, and their attorneys.

The article was "The H-Bomb Secret: How We Got It, Why We're Telling It."

All copies of that article that were in our possession, as well as the proofs from which it would have been printed, and the headlines, sketches, and covers that would have accompanied it are, at this writing, locked away.

Under the terms of Judge Warren's preliminary injunction, we, Howard Morland, and our "agents, servants, employees and attorneys, and all other persons in active concert or participation with them" are barred from "publishing or otherwise communicating, transmitting or disclosing in any manner any information designated by the Secretary of Energy as Restricted Data contained in the Morland article."

The judge said he had "agonized" over his decision and did not welcome the "notoriety" it would bring him. He acknowledged that the injunction would "curtail defendants' First Amendment rights in a drastic and substantial fashion," and would "infringe upon our right to know and to be informed as well."

Still, he assumed "the awesome responsibility of issuing a preliminary injunction against *The Progressive*'s use of the Morland article in its current form" because, he said, "a mistake in ruling against the United States could pave the way for nuclear annihilation for us all."

How did all this happen? How did the full force of the federal government come to be arrayed against a small, perpetually struggling magazine published in Madison, Wisconsin? How did *The Progressive*, which has fought against militarism throughout its seventy-year history and crusaded against the nuclear arms race more persistently than any other publication in America, suddenly find itself accused of threatening to "pave the way for nuclear annihilation"?

Samuel H. Day Jr., the managing editor of *The Progressive*, joined our staff about a year ago. He is the former editor of the *Bulletin of the Atomic Scientists*, and one of his first projects for us was a tour of some of the key facilities involved in the production of nuclear weapons—a tour arranged for him by the Department of Energy.

As he embarked on his tour of nuclear facilities in June of last year, Sam Day met Howard Morland, a freelance writer engaged in a similar project. Morland was a former Air Force pilot, an antinuclear activist, who held a passionate conviction that Americans needed to be aroused to the dangers inherent in nuclear power and nuclear weaponry. Though Morland had taken only a few college undergraduate science courses, he had begun to educate himself on the nuclear arms race and its links to the nuclear energy industry.

Day encouraged Morland to pursue his research with a view toward writing a series of articles for *The Progressive*. He urged Morland, in particular, to explore the secrecy that surrounds the nuclear weapons program.

It was our feeling, last summer, that the government had invoked secrecy for thirty years to keep Americans from questioning the nuclear arms race: How much justification was there for the secrecy, we wondered, and what kind of information was being withheld that might help people formulate informed judgments on such vital questions as environmental risks, occupational health and safety threats, nuclear proliferation and the continuing arms race, and the astronomical costs of the nuclear weapons program?

*The Progressive* advanced him $500. Morland read extensively in the open literature available to anyone who has a library card: physics texts, encyclopedia articles, magazine pieces, unclassified government publications. By arrangement with the Department of Energy, he began visiting nuclear production facilities.

A rough draft of Morland's major article on secrecy in the weapons program came to us in January. It ran to about eighteen manuscript pages and was accompanied by seven sketches hand-drawn by the author. The sketches were captioned "How a Hydrogen Bomb Works." In consultation with the author, we subjected the draft to routine editing. As is our practice when dealing with a subject in which we have no particular expertise, we sent copies of the manuscript to half a dozen qualified experts for review of its accuracy.

Without our consent—without our knowledge, in fact—one of those reviewers passed a copy of the manuscript to George Rathjens, a professor at the Massachusetts Institute of Technology who also serves as a government consultant. On February 15, Rathjens called Sam Day and expressed concern that Morland's article contained "secrets" which should not be published. Ironically, Rathjens was one of the authorities Morland had consulted in preparing his article.

Rathjens's secretary called Day the next morning. Professor Rathjens was "in conference," she said, but he had asked her to advise us that he was sending a copy of the Morland manuscript to the Department of Energy.

By this time, we were worried. Gordon Sinykin has been *The Progressive*'s friend, legal counsel, business adviser, and chairman of the board for close to four decades. We gave him a copy of the Morland article.

That evening he sat down after dinner to read the Atomic Energy Act of 1954. My home telephone rang at about 9:30 p.m. "Do you know what's in this law?" Sinykin asked. I said I didn't, and he proceeded to tell me.

The Atomic Energy Act declares: "The term 'Restricted Data' means all data concerning (1) design, manufacture, or utilization of atomic weapons; (2) the production of special nuclear material; or (3) the use of special nuclear material in the production of energy, but shall not include data declassified or removed from the Restricted Data category."

That language means, Gordon Sinykin explained to me, and later explained to the court in *The Progressive*'s brief, that "every bit of information, then, every scrap of knowledge—whether theoretical or practical—is classified, restricted, protected unless, of course, it is declassified by the government." It need not be government information; it can be information private citizens create, or conjure up out of their feverish imaginations. If it pertains to nuclear weapons or, for that matter, to nuclear energy, it is automatically classified: It is, as the government was to tell Judge Warren, "data restricted at birth." That such language, which is, in our judgment and that of our attorneys, unconstitutionally broad and in clear violation of the First Amendment, should have stood unchallenged for decades is, in itself, evidence of the oppressive secrecy that has surrounded the nuclear program.

Sinykin, explaining the act to me in that late-evening telephone call, was clearly alarmed. He had one bit of reassuring news: The act no longer carried a death penalty; that had been repealed several years ago. But he warned that publication of the article could result in government seizure of an entire issue of *The Progressive*. It could also result in criminal prosecution, and convictions could mean sentences of up to twenty years' imprisonment.

By February 26, *The Progressive* was approaching the production deadline for its April issue. We had received no reaction of any kind from the DOE. The response came early in the afternoon of Thursday, March 1, in a telephone call from Lynn R. Coleman, General Counsel for the Department of Energy. He read us the relevant portions of the Atomic Energy Act and asserted that Morland's article fell within the area of "Restricted Data" as defined in the law, though he declined to specify which portions of the article were objectionable. Coleman said he had discussed the matter with Secretary of Energy James Schlesinger and with officials of the Departments of State, Defense, Justice, and the Arms Control and Disarmament Agency. Unless we agreed to refrain from publishing the article, Coleman said, the government would subject us to legal action. We asked for time to consult with our counsel.

We called Coleman's office at the DOE late that afternoon to report our readiness to be in Washington the next morning. That would not be necessary, we were told; a group of federal officials would be in Madison the next day to talk to us.

On the afternoon of Friday, March 2, we met in the conference room of the law firm LaFollette, Sinykin, Anderson, and Munson with a federal delegation consisting of four representatives from the Department of Energy and two from the Department of Justice. The chief spokesman was Duane C. Sewell, Assistant Secretary of Energy for Defense Programs, who again read to us from the Atomic Energy Act—a piece of legislation we have almost learned to recite by rote.

Sewell said all of Morland's sketches and captions, and about 20 percent of the text of his article, were "Restricted Data." He offered to have the Department of Energy "rewrite" our article in a form that would make it acceptable to the government.

Once again we withdrew to talk with our attorneys. My reaction to the government's offer to "rewrite" our article was expressed in a few blunt expletives. (Gordon Sinykin, with characteristic understatement, would later advise the officials that we found their offer "more than objectionable.") But our formal response was that we would take a few days to consider our position, and that we would, in the meantime, refrain from publication of the Morland article.

Gordon Sinykin notified the government that we saw no reason to withhold the Morland article, that we would not permit it to be "rewritten" by the Department of Energy, that we intended to publish it, and that if the government planned to move in court to restrain us, it should do so with dispatch.

After hearing brief arguments from the government and *The Progressive* on Friday afternoon, March 9, Judge Warren granted the government's request for a ten-day restraining order. He acknowledged that he had not read Howard Morland's article—but he delivered himself of a line that would haunt us for weeks, providing fodder to hostile editorial writers and racist cartoonists: "I want to think a long, hard time before I'd give a hydrogen bomb to Idi Amin. It appears to me that is just what we're doing here."

That comment illustrated, in itself, the heavy price we have paid in public ignorance for thirty years of official secrecy. As Howard Morland's suppressed article makes abundantly clear, there is no way that Idi Amin could build a hydrogen bomb even if *The Progressive* provided the instructions—which we would not and could not do. There is no way terrorists or hoodlums or anyone but a large, highly industrialized nation could build a hydrogen bomb.

By the time he issued his preliminary injunction on March 26, even Judge Warren had apparently come to understand that the Morland article would not "give a hydrogen bomb to Idi Amin." In his opinion he wrote: "Does the article provide a 'do-it-yourself' guide to the hydrogen bomb? Probably not. A number of affidavits make it quite clear that a sine qua non to thermonuclear capability is a large, sophisticated industrial capability coupled with a coterie of imaginative, resourceful scientists and technicians. One does not build a hydrogen bomb in the basement."

When we walked out of Judge Warren's courtroom on the afternoon of March 9, we were "under restraint." We had decided that we would comply strictly with the court's order while we pursued our fight for our First Amendment rights, but it was only gradually that we began to understand the full implications of being muzzled. We are, and have been since that day, the only journalists in America who are compelled to keep "secrets" under penalty of the law, "secrets" available to anyone who goes looking for them. It is an unenviable state, and one we hope no other American journalist will ever have to share.

## The H-Bomb Secret

To Know How Is to Ask Why

HOWARD MORLAND
NOVEMBER 1979

What you are about to learn is a secret—a secret that the United States and four other nations, the makers of hydrogen weapons, have gone to extraordinary lengths to protect.

The secret is in the coupling mechanism that enables an ordinary fission bomb—the kind that destroyed Hiroshima—to trigger the far deadlier energy of hydrogen fusion.

The physical pressure and heat generated by x and gamma radiation, moving outward from the trigger at the speed of light, bounces against the weapon's inner wall and is reflected with enormous force into the sides of a carrot-shaped "pencil" which contains the fusion fuel.

That, within the limits of a single sentence, is the essence of a concept that initially eluded the physicists of the United States, the Soviet Union, Britain, France, and China; that they discovered independently and kept tenaciously to themselves, and that may not yet have occurred to the weapon makers of a dozen other nations bent on building the hydrogen bomb.

I discovered it simply by reading and asking questions, without the benefit of security clearance or access to classified materials.

Why am I telling you?

It's not because I want to help you build an H-bomb. Have no fear; that would be far beyond your capability unless you have the resources of at least a medium-sized government.

I am telling the secret to make a basic point as forcefully as I can: Secrecy itself, especially the power of a few designated "experts" to declare some topics off limits, contributes to a political climate in which the nuclear establishment can conduct business as usual, protecting and perpetuating the production of these horror weapons.

Of all the world's nuclear weapons secrets, none has eluded publication more successfully than the secret of the H-bomb. In the twenty-five years since its first successful field test in the South Pacific, no description of how it works has ever been made public.

The energy of an exploding fission bomb is transferred by means of radiation pressure to the hydrogen part of the weapon. Radiation pressure—a term never mentioned in the open literature—is the essence of what remains of the H-bomb secret.

The weapons are harder to believe than to understand.

There are three stages to the detonation of a hydrogen weapon: fission, fusion, and more fission. Although one event must follow the other for the weapon to work, they happen so rapidly that a human observer would experience only a single event—an explosion of unearthly magnitude. Within the bomb, however, fission—the splitting of uranium and plutonium nuclei—comes first.

The mechanism for the first fission stage is a miniaturized version of the Nagasaki bomb. It has roughly the same explosive power as the World War II weapon, but it measures less than twelve inches in diameter. This fission "trigger" vaguely resembles a soccer ball, with the same pattern of twenty hexagons and twelve pentagons forming a sphere. Detonator wires are attached to each pentagonal or hexagonal face. When its full explosive energy is realized, this oversized cantaloupe becomes the source of the radiation pressure which ignites the fusion stage.

Weapon designers call this miniature A-bomb the "primary system." The rest of the nuclear part of the weapon is called the "secondary system." In published accounts, the primary system is often referred to as the "trigger." By itself, it could level a small city, but in a hydrogen weapon it merely provides the energy necessary to ignite the second stage, which releases energy by fusing hydrogen to form helium. A fission bomb is the only force on Earth powerful enough to provide the compression and heat needed to detonate a fusion bomb.

The secondary system is the mechanism which captures the fission energy of the primary system and puts it to work in the fusion process. The design of the secondary system is the H-bomb secret.

The challenge in designing a hydrogen weapon is to make the secondary system finish its task of fusion before the expanding fireball of the primary systems engulfs and destroys it. About a millionth of a second is all the time available for doing the job.

Pure radiant energy, in this case the energy of x and gamma radiation, is the only thing fast enough and manageable enough to be harnessed for that purpose.

X and gamma radiation travel at the speed of light, more than a hundred times faster than the expanding debris from an exploding A-bomb. If the primary system and the fusion fuel are located some distance apart, say twelve inches, the radiant energy of the primary system will have time to race ahead of the expanding nuclear debris and reach the fusion fuel first.

The third and final stage in the explosion of the weapon is virtually an afterthought. In fact, it is optional, although in most hydrogen weapons it is a highly desired option— it provides roughly half the total energy release of the weapon and most of the fallout. In this third stage, the uranium-238 casing, which was used to capture and focus the radiation, undergoes fusion as a result of bombardment by the high energy neutrons released by the second-stage fusion process.

The result can be an explosion a thousand times more powerful than the blast that destroyed Hiroshima.

Do we need to possess this technical information? Yes. Without it, there is little hope of understanding the vast industrial complex that turns out three new nuclear weapons a day.

In the business of nuclear weaponry, as in science and technology itself, no secret, once discovered, can long endure, as Einstein observed. The practical effect of secrecy is to discourage and inhibit public participation in the formulation of public policy— in this case not only nuclear weapons policy but also a broad spectrum of related policies (national security, energy, environmental protection, natural and human resource allocation) with which it is inextricably intertwined.

Since World War II, the process of secrecy—the readiness to invoke "national security"—has been a pillar of the nuclear establishment. That establishment, acting on the false assumption that "secrets" can be hidden from the curious and knowledgeable, has successfully insisted that there are answers which cannot be given and even questions which cannot be asked.

The net effect is to stifle debate about the fundamentals of nuclear policy. Concerned citizens dare not ask certain questions, and many begin to feel that these are matters which only a few initiated experts are entitled to discuss. This self-imposed restraint only entrenches further those who are committed to the nuclear arms race.

The secret of how a hydrogen bomb is made protects a more fundamental "secret": the mechanism by which the resources of the most powerful nation on Earth have been marshaled for global catastrophe. Knowing how may be the key to asking why.

—HOWARD MORLAND is a freelance writer and anti-nuclear activist.

# Why We Seized the Hammer

PHILIP BERRIGAN
MAY 1981

*They will hammer their swords into plowshares.*
—ISAIAH 2:4

One question nagged at us: How does one survive sanely, nonviolently, faithfully in a society mobilized against such survival? To put it another way, given corporate capitalism's appetite for war, given the Bomb as diplomatic bargaining chip, what is the meaning and price of discipleship?

Our answer—it is by no means the only one—was to form the nonviolent community of resistance. The Community for Creative Nonviolence began in Washington in 1972 and Jonah House in Baltimore in 1973. With little notice and less media coverage, we took up resistance to the war again—tons of rubble dumped on Pentagon approaches, civil disobedience at the White House over violations of the Paris Peace Accords, two raids on the Vietnamese Overseas Procurement Office, several sit-ins against President Ford's "amnesty" program, arrests at the National Security Agency, a whole summer (1974) of tiger cages outside the Rotunda of the Capitol. Small actions, but something during a disillusioned and jaded time.

Resistance communities sprouted and slowly grew—out of vision, pain, and necessity. Friends formed the Pacific Life Community (an anti-Trident coalition) in Washington, and it spread to California and Oregon. Others collected East Coast resisters into the Atlantic Life Community, concentrating on the Pentagon, Electric Boat in Groton, Connecticut (producer of the new Trident), United Technologies in Hartford, GE in the Philadelphia area, Rockwell in Pittsburgh, and assorted war-making think tanks. At the Pentagon, we sustained a five-year campaign—thousands of arrests (a thousand in 1980, alone).

A student wrote recently, "Your protest was futile! It hasn't changed public opinion; it hasn't reduced nuclear arms." He attends a Catholic high school and studies justice and peace in one of his classes. In answering him I wrote, "Why do you say 'futile'? Our action is making you think, isn't it?"

Perhaps that's a key, however imperfect. The struggle to prevent nuclear war is, in an altogether unprecedented way, a struggle for spirit, heart, and mind. The intention to use the Bomb—most Americans would use it, in one circumstance or another—evidences a moral paralysis, a militarization of soul, a submission to violence as necessity, a bankruptcy of ethical option that amounts to slavishness.

Official propaganda peddles the Bomb as guarantor of our freedoms. That is a stupefying lie: It is, to the contrary, a symbol of moral and physical slavery, of mass suicide, and, perhaps, of omnicide.

Civil disobedience offers the hope of liberation, the hope of survival. In his classic essay, Thoreau called civil disobedience a "duty"—personal and political. Personal duty because enslavement of blacks and exploitation of Mexicans enslaved and exploited every American. Political duty because government, then as now, was unrepresentative, was the slaveholders, the exploiters, the devious and ruthless enemy of the people.

Thoreau's grasp of the law was incisive: "It is not desirable to cultivate a respect for the law, so much as for the right. . . . Law never made men a whit more just; and by means of their respect for it, even the well disposed are daily made the agents of injustice."

Two convictions support our civilly disobedient attitude toward the law: First, the State has perverted law to the point of legalizing its nuclear psychosis. Second, the State is invincible unless such legalizing is rendered null and void by nonviolent civil disobedience. We cannot leave the State invincible in its determination to initiate (or provoke) nuclear war.

Who expects politicians, generals, and bomb makers to disarm? People must disarm the bombs. That's the only way it will happen.

> —PHILIP BERRIGAN, pacifist and practitioner of civil disobedience, was a leading peace activist against the Vietnam War and against nuclear weapons with his brother, Daniel, and his wife, Elizabeth McAlister, of Jonah House.

## An Interview with Sam Day, Peace Activist

MATTHEW ROTHSCHILD
MARCH 2001

Q: You just got out of prison. What were you in for?

SAM DAY: I was in for six months for crossing the line at Offutt Air Force Base in Nebraska, the headquarters of the U.S. Strategic Command, which controls the launching and targeting of every long-range missile in the nuclear arsenal.

Q: Why did you decide to trespass there?

DAY: To try to lift the veil of secrecy and numbness which covers that and other nuclear installations in our country, and to help the people of Omaha and the people of America understand that this is a very, very dangerous facility having control of some 8,000 nuclear warheads, all of them still aimed at targets all over the world and ready to go just as surely now as they were at the height of the Cold War.

Q: A lot of people assume that the threat of nuclear war has passed. Why is that not the case?

DAY: Because, while it's true that there's no longer a confrontation between two nuclear superpowers, one of those superpowers—namely, the United States—continues using nuclear weapons and the threat of the use of nuclear weapons as the basis for projecting power. And by doing that, we set an example for other countries to say that nuclear weapons are the way for them to protect their interests, too.

Q: How has the United States used this threat to protect its interests?

DAY: Ever since the beginning of the nuclear era, we have been using our nuclear weapons as a way of reinforcing our economic and diplomatic positions. First of all, in a dispute over Iran way back in 1946, we directly threatened the Soviet Union with a possible nuclear strike. And as late as the Persian Gulf War, President Bush directly threatened Saddam with a nuclear strike. Now, the United States is saying that only it and the small group of nuclear powers can legitimately have these weapons of mass destruction. That's a way of keeping our dominance in perpetuity. And it's maintaining the double standard of a few privileged countries having nuclear weapons, while the rest of the world either doesn't have them or pretends not to have them.

Q: So how should we work toward zero?

DAY: We should start by stopping the production of nuclear weapons, just ceasing altogether and dismantling our 15,000 to 16,000 remaining nuclear warheads, and doing it regardless of what any other nation does. Simply because it's in our own interest to get out of the nuclear weapons business.

Q: But that's not self-evident, at least to many people.

DAY: It's in our interest because sooner or later they're going to be used. We may think it's a long time—fifty years—to have gone without the use of nuclear weapons. But fifty years is the blink of an eyelid in human history. It's axiomatic that eventually these weapons are going to be used, just as every other weapon that's been developed by humankind eventually has been used. And we still have no conception— we as a society—of the incredible, uniquely devastating, destructive force of nuclear weapons. Not just the blast, which is thousands of times greater than any other weapon that has ever been developed, but the radiation effect, which is of incalculable damage to the environment and to the human genetic system.

It's the most urgent cause that exists: Sooner or later, we've got to come to terms by getting out of this venture into nuclear weapons. Either we will do it through the democratic process, or we will do it in the aftermath of some god-awful tragedy, which has wiped out maybe half a dozen cities of a million or more people overnight.

If that happens, we will get out of the nuclear business, but it will be over the dead bodies of untold millions.

# PART 14

# Weaving a Safety Net

In 1909, Jane Addams talked about the need for "humane legislation," and *The Progressive* has consistently campaigned for a tightly woven safety net for all Americans.

Senator Robert Wagner in 1930 put it well when he wrote that the worker must be given "some protection against the haunting fear of enforced idleness," and Wagner made the compelling case for a federal jobs program more than two years before FDR introduced one.

To pay for crucial social programs, *The Progressive* has understood the need for a progressive income tax and an estate tax and has never been shy about defending them. "Isn't $10 million to $100 million enough for any one man?" asked Huey Long. "What's he going to do with any more?"

Providing universal health care in America is a long-deferred dream. *The Progressive* wrote about it back in 1917. Truman proposed it when he was president. So did Clinton. We're not there yet. Michael Feldman, the radio showman, lampoons the failure of the Clinton proposal. (We've counted on him and Molly Ivins and Will Durst and Kate Clinton for much-needed comic relief over the last couple of decades.) Meanwhile, Barbara Ehrenreich shows how devastatingly cruel it is to not have health insurance in America.

The novelist Edwidge Danticat, in discussing the disaster of Hurricane Katrina, gives us a "passport to an America where citizens do not always have bus fare, much less an automobile, where health insurance is as distant a dream as a college education, where poverty is a birthright." She calls this "the America of the needy and never have enoughs."

Enacting "humane legislation" remains an imperative.

# The Reaction of Moral Instruction upon Social Reform

JANE ADDAMS
MAY 1, 1909

We are failing to meet the requirements of our industrial life with courage and success simply because we do not realize that unless we establish some of that humane legislation, which has its roots in a consideration for human life, our industrialism itself will fall behind. It is suffering from inbreeding, growing ever more unrestrained and more ruthless. It would seem obvious that, in order to secure relief in a community dominated by commercial ideals, an appeal must be made to the old moral sanctions for human conduct, that we must reach motives more substantial and enduring than the mere fleeting experiences of one phase of modern industry which vainly imagines that its growth would be curtailed if the health of its employees were guarded by the state.

And yet when we attempt to appeal to these old sanctions, the conclusion is often forced upon us that they have not been ingrained in the present generation, that they have never been worked over into character, that they cannot be relied upon when they are brought into contact with the arguments of commercialism, that the colors of the flag flying over the fort of our spiritual resources wash out and disappear when the storm actually breaks.

Educators, moralists, clergyman, publicists, all of us forget how very early we are in the experiments of founding a first civilization in the trying climate of America, and that we all are making the experiment in the most materialistic period of all history, having as our last court of appeal against that materialism, only the wonderful and inexplicable instinct for justice which resides in the heart of man. This instinct may be cultivated or neglected as we choose to give it opportunity for expression, and it is never so irresistible as when the heart is young.

It is as if we ignored a wistful creature who walked through our city streets calling out, "I am the spirit of youth, with me all things are possible." We fail to understand what he wants or even to see that he is caught into all sorts of movements for social amelioration, some of them abortive and foolish simply because they appeal to him as an effort to moralize our social relations. We may either feed the divine fire of youth with the historic ideals and dogmas which are after all the most precious possessions of the race, or we may smother it by platitudes and heavy discourses. We may listen to the young voice rising clear above the roar of industrialism and the prudent counsels of commercialism, or we may become hypnotized by the sudden new emphasis placed upon wealth and power and forget the supremacy of spiritual forces in men's affairs.

# How Shall We Pay for Industrial Accidents?

ROBERT M. LA FOLLETTE
JULY 17, 1909

What is the human eye worth? Or an arm? Or a leg? These questions are not to be lightly answered. If one were asked to place a money valuation on any part of his body, or on life itself, he would be likely to answer that they are all priceless possessions and that their loss is not to be measured in dollars and cents.

It is a fact, however, that such valuations are made constantly. In our great industries, particularly in the most hazardous ones, scarcely a day passes that does not take its heavy toll of maimed or killed workingmen. Sometimes the accident is the result of the man's own carelessness; sometimes it is due to the negligence of the employer, who thinks it too costly to provide adequate safeguards; sometimes it is unavoidable—and then we say it is inherent in the business. But in every case it has been found necessary to set a price upon the workingman's body.

The amount fixed varies astonishingly in individual cases. The Pittsburgh Survey recently made an investigation of the actual amounts paid as compensation by employers to twenty-seven workingmen permanently injured in Allegheny County, Pennsylvania. Following is the result:

> For loss of an eye. . . . . Nothing to $200
> For loss of an arm. . . . . Nothing to $300
> For loss of two fingers . . . Nothing to $100
> For loss of leg. . . . . . . . Nothing to $225

How do those figures impress you? Do you think the amounts given cover the loss? Notice that the largest sum paid in any one case was $300 for the loss of an arm. Observe more particularly that the minimum compensation was nothing! Those injured workmen who were fortunate enough to get any compensation at all received barely enough to pay the doctor's bill, and, in the case of the most lucky ones, perhaps, to help keep the family from starvation while the wound was healing. But how about the men who received nothing? How were they to keep the wolf from the door until they got well again—at least well enough to find work that a crippled man could do? Perhaps his wife found employment cleaning railroad cars at $1.21 a day; perhaps the oldest boy was big enough to get a job in a factory at $2.50 a week. If so, that family was kept from the limit of human misery. If not—who is there to measure the terrible price that was paid for the accident?

Nothing could more vividly illustrate the injustice of the present system of compensating injured workingmen than the figures given. They represent the kind of appraisals that are actually placed upon eyes and arms and fingers and legs.

The necessity of making such valuations has given rise to an important problem. It is the problem of industrial insurance. You who read this are interested in this problem because at present you help bear the cost of these industrial accidents. The workingman is interested because it is a question of comfort or misery for him and his family, the employer is interested because it means dollars and cents to him; but you also are interested because you are a member of society, and society must care for those who are rendered dependent through injury.

# Why We Need an Income Tax

SENATOR WILLIAM E. BORAH
JULY 17, 1909

The income tax is the fairest and most equitable of the taxes. It is the one tax which approaches us in the hour of prosperity and departs in the hour of adversity.

The farmer, though he may have lost his entire crop, must meet the taxes levied upon his property.

The merchant, though on the verge of bankruptcy, must respond to the taxes imposed.

The laborer, who goes to the store to buy his food, though it be his last, must buy with whatever extra cost there may be imposed by reason of custom duties.

But the income tax is to be met only after you have realized your income. After you have met your expenses, provided for your family, paid for the education of your children for that year, then provided you have an income left, you turn to meet the obligations you owe to the government. For instance, according to amendments recently pending relative to the income tax, a man with an income of $10,000 would pay the modest sum of $100. "Man as a human being owes services to his fellows and one of the first of these is to support the government which makes civilization possible."

I think those who advocate the income tax merely as a revenue-producing proposition rob the proposition of its moral foundation. We should contend for an income tax not simply for the purpose of raising revenue but for the purpose of framing a revenue system which will distribute the burdens of government between consumption and accumulated wealth, which will enable us to call upon property and wealth not in an unfair and burdensome way but in a just and equitable way to meet their proportionate expenses of the government, for certainly it will be conceded by all that the great expense of government is in the protection of property and of wealth.

A tax placed upon consumption is based upon what men want and must have. A tax placed upon wealth falls upon those who have enough and to spare and therefore have more which it is necessary for the government to protect.

The general government has its armies and its navies and its great burden of expense for the purpose among other things of protecting property, protecting gathered
and accumulated wealth, and enabling men to make fortunes and to preserve their
fortunes, and there is no possible argument founded in law or in morals why these
protected interests should not bear their proportionate burden of government.

We simply call upon those who have the good fortune to have accumulated wealth
to respond to the expenses of the great government under which they live and thrive.

## The Need for Health Insurance

IRVING FISHER
JANUARY 1917

At present the United States has the unenviable distinction of being the only great
industrial nation without universal health insurance. For a generation, the enlightened nations of Europe have one after another discussed the idea and followed discussion by adoption. It has constituted an important part of the policy and career of
some of Europe's greatest statesmen, including Bismarck and Lloyd George.

The need of health insurance, like that of most other forms of insurance, is twofold.
There is the need of indemnification against loss and the need of diminishing the loss
itself. It is more economical to pay a little premium for the fire insurance each year
than to suffer a big loss when the fire comes.

It is the poor whose need of health insurance is greatest. Millions of American work-
men cannot at present avail themselves of necessary medical, surgical, and nursing aid.

Health insurance is like elementary education. In order that it shall function properly its needs must be universal and in order to be universal, it must be obligatory. In
health insurance, as in education, we are dealing not with obligatory burdens, but with
obligatory benefits.

Certain interests which would be, or think they would be, adversely affected by
health insurance have made the specious plea that it is an un-American interference
with liberty. They forgot that compulsory education, though at first opposed on these
very grounds, is highly American and highly liberative.

According to the logic of those now shedding crocodile tears over health insurance,
we ought, in order to remain truly American and truly free, to retain the precious liberties of our people to be illiterate, to suffer accidents without indemnification, as well
as to be sick without indemnification.

It is by the compelling hand of the law that society secures liberation from the evils
of crime, vice, ignorance, accidents, unemployment, invalidity, and disease.

—IRVING FISHER was the president of the American Association for Labor Legislation.

# Wagner Urges Unemployment Relief Action

Senator Robert Wagner
June 14, 1930

During the winter of every depression I have heard the fair-weather prophets make the smug prediction that the spring would bring relief. Unfortunately when the spring arrived the winter was never far behind, and again the unemployed were treated to the cold comfort of the exasperating pronouncement from Washington that "spring would bring relief." I wish the public could in some way express its unmitigated weariness of this sort of soothsaying. Too long already has sham propaganda served to excuse the failure to take hold of the problem of unemployment rationally and effectively. It is time we become impatient with inaction.

Will not our grandchildren regard it as quite incomprehensible that in 1930 millions of Americans went hungry because we had produced too much food; that millions of men, women, and children were cold because we had produced too much clothing?

I am not speaking in parables. It is the literal truth that today we are suffering want in the midst of unprecedented plenty; our workers go without wages because they had learned to work too well.

It is this condition which justifies our impatience with statesmanship which regards unemployment as inevitable and poverty as incurable. I do not believe that unemployment is inevitable. We have never tried to do anything about it. We have never assembled the necessary information. We have never applied to the problem the organized intelligence of our people.

The worker must be given a greater measure of security, some protection against the haunting fear of enforced idleness, before he can lead the broad and full life which the rich endowment of natural resources of this country intended he should enjoy.

To me it seems plain that the responsibility of the federal government must not be shirked, for the prevention of unemployment is a distinctly national obligation.

Unemployment today is not produced by local causes. The forces which make for the shutdown of factories, the curtailment of activity in the mines and on the railroads, are forces which operate on a national and worldwide scale. The individual workman, the individual business, the state, are helpless when an economic storm breaks upon the country. Only the coordinated strength of the entire nation is competent to deal with such powerful economic forces.

The federal government is always engaged in constructing highways, developing rivers and harbors, erecting flood-control structures and public buildings. It should plan these projects in advance and time them so as to make available opportunities for employment when private business slackens.

And the government should join with the states in the establishment of a nation-wide system of public employment offices so as to assist workers to find jobs and to assist employers to find workers with the least amount of delay and the least amount of friction.

This is but a bare outline of what the federal government can do toward the prevention of unemployment.

If there were political advantages to be secured by championing the cause of the unemployed, this problem would have been tackled long ago. The unemployed never make campaign contributions. They do not control any portion of the press through which to bring their plight home to the American people. They maintain no lobby in Washington to tell their depressing story to their representatives in Congress. Their only spokesmen are those who have responded to the common call of humanity; the only advocates of their cause are those who pursue the welfare of our country irrespective of party advantage.

Will Congress choose the way out of unemployment, the way of intelligent organization, the way of responsible action, the way of sensible prevention? Or I hesitate to suggest the alternative: Will America continue to walk the rutted road of want in this age of plenty?

> —Robert Wagner was a U.S. senator from New York from 1927 to 1949 and author of the labor legislation that bears his name.

## The Long Plan for Recovery

Senator Huey P. Long
APRIL 1, 1933

With the one law which I propose to submit, I think most of our difficulties will be brought to an almost immediate end. To carry out President Roosevelt's plan as announced in his inaugural address for redistribution and to prevent unjust accumulation of wealth, I am now drawing a law, but without consort with the president, for the following:

A capital levy tax, principally on fortunes above $10 million graduated so that when a fortune of $100 million is reached, the capital tax levy will take all the balance above that sum. This will not prevent aggregated capital, that is, several persons combining their wealth in one big enterprise, but will prevent only one man owning from $10 million to $100 million without paying the government a substantial part and will further prevent any man from owning anything at all above the value of $100 million.

An inheritance tax, heavier in the higher brackets than at present, graduated so that no one person can inherit more than $5 million, the balance to go to the government.

An income tax about the same as now exists except that it shall be heavier in the higher brackets and finally providing that no one will be permitted to keep more than $1 million from earnings of one year.

Because of the fact that in some cases it would be difficult for large property to be sold at a fair value to pay the inheritance and capital levy taxes, the proposed law will provide that such taxes may be paid in a course of several years and that in case a fair price for the property cannot be obtained in that length of time by the tax debtor, that the government will take its percent of the property and market it along such lines as may be best for general welfare.

This proposed legislation will operate to down the big fortunes so that they cannot be so powerful to crush out the little men and little businesses. It will mean the solution of the problem of financing all such things as the guaranteeing of bank deposits and the public construction works, including roads, navigation, flood control, reforestation, unemployment, farm relief, canals, irrigation, etc. And with this law passed, no one can ever again say that our government has not a satisfactory basis for an adequate and sufficient currency. All such can be amply financed by the government without any burden on the common citizen at all and in a manner that accomplishes the still better object of the decentralization of wealth. Such public works of the government will provide employment for everyone in the country not otherwise gainfully employed, and it will so stimulate all private endeavors and business that little additional legislation will be necessary.

Isn't $10 million to $100 million enough for any one man? What's he going to do with anymore?

Isn't $5 million enough for one child to inherit, who never hit a lick of work for it?

Isn't $1 million enough for any one man to make in one year?

Decentralize wealth, is the command of the Lord. See Leviticus, chapters 24 to 27; St. James, chapter 5.

Let your president, your two U.S. senators, and your congressman know how you feel about this plan. Why starve while our food rots for lack of a place to sell it?

—Huey P. Long was governor of Louisiana from 1928 to 1932 and U.S. senator from 1932 to 1935.

## The Taxing Power Is Only Effective Way to Redistribute Wealth and Break Down Vast Fortunes

William T. Evjue
June 29, 1935

No one who has lived through the last five and a half years of the depression and observed the economic consequences of the hectic so-called boom years prior to 1929 can deny the future welfare of this nation is inextricably dovetailed with the problem of wealth distribution.

It should now be apparent to everyone that the continued concentration of wealth is responsible for the destruction of purchasing power and the inevitable consequence of depression. Business and industry, both big and little, need a market to prosper. That market must rest on the ultimate consumer—the masses of the people. When they have no power to buy, the whole structure topples.

What has happened to the purchasing ability of the consumer has been well illustrated by Senator Robert M. La Follette Jr. in the following example:

"Let us assume that $100 represents the entire vast wealth of this nation and its people. Let us assume that 100 people represent our entire population. If we divide this $100, representing our total wealth, among these 100 people, representing our total population, as wealth is actually distributed in this country today, we get the following results: One person would have $59 out of the hundred; one would have $9; 22 people would have $1.22 each, and 76, all the rest, would have less than 7 cents apiece out of the $100, representing our total wealth."

While the nation was going through what was supposed to have been one of the greatest periods of prosperity—1923 to 1929—what really was happening was an accelerated concentration of income and wealth in even fewer hands.

One study of the "beautiful boom" reveals the following results:

From 1923 to 1929 the top 400,000 persons in America who reported incomes of over $10,000 each had increased their incomes by more than 76 percent; the top 40,000 of these favored few increased their profits by 129 percent and the top 4,000 plutocrats of this class multiplied their gains by 207 percent. But the cream of the top, the 400 real rulers of America, increased their income 234 percent. The bigger the ownership, the bigger the profits was the rule during these six years of rugged individualism. In sad contrast to this unequal division of profits, the laborer at the end of the table, increased his earning by less than 5 percent. During the fictitious prosperity of Hoover the national income was being grossly redistributed but always upwards in favor to the concentration of wealth.

The economic trend toward concentration of wealth and income in the hands of a select group of favorably situated persons did not end with the Wall Street crash of 1929 and the swift coming of depression.

Despite all the agencies of the Roosevelt new deal calculated to benefit the wage earner, the farmer, and other "forgotten men" of the present social order, centralization of wealth has continued. In 1933 taxpayers with incomes of less than $10,000 annually saw their incomes decrease 5 percent under 1932, while those receiving $50,000 or more a year increased their takings by 10 percent; those with $200,000 increased their incomes by 16 percent, and the number of persons with annual incomes of $1,000,000 or over increased their profits 20 to 46 percent.

During 1934 the real weekly wage of industrial workers (wages figured on the basis of buying power) decreased 2 percent. At the same time, corporations' dividends rose 17 percent. Industrial profits soared 76 percent over the previous year.

If this country is to continue the institutions and philosophy of equality and free-dom upon which it was established, it is clear that vast fortunes that continue to multiply at the expense and to the impoverishment of the American people must be checked.

This great wealth must be redistributed on a basis that will allow our economic system to breathe. The only effective means is taxation.

> —WILLIAM T. EVJUE was the founder of the *Capital Times* in Madison, Wisconsin, and the editor of *The Progressive* from 1929 to 1940.

# Look at America

GOVERNOR PHILIP LA FOLLETTE
APRIL 30, 1938

Look at America: We occupy 6 percent of the world's area. We have about 7 percent of the world's population. Under normal conditions we have consumed about one-half of the world's coffee, half of its tin, half of its rubber, a fifth of its sugar, two-thirds of its silk, a third of its coal, nearly half of its pig iron, half of its copper and over two-thirds of its crude oil.

We operate over half of the world's telephone and telegraph; we own over three quarters of the automobiles and a third of the world's railroads; we produce nearly three-fourths of the oil, over half of the wheat and cotton, and the lead and coal of the world.

We dug a hole in Kentucky in which to hide over $12 billion in gold, over half of the world's monetary metal. We have two-thirds of the world's banking resources, and it has been estimated that our people have a purchasing power greater than that of the 500 million people of Europe and considerably larger than that of the billion people who live in Asia.

Yet, here we are at the end of ten years still in a depression, nearly one out of every four living off some kind of relief. Half our people are back where they were in 1931, and the country is headed for conditions as bad or worse than 1933.

A program of constructive action is not difficult to think of or agree upon. Our great difficulty is getting a government that sees the problem and has the courage to act.

I emphasized a government that will act because if anything is clear this is clear: The question of prosperity or hard times—of liberty or dictatorship—will be made by government.

Here above all else is a problem we as individuals cannot solve. A farmer may be industrious, thrifty, and intelligent. But that farmer is helpless against an economic storm sweeping across the nation. An employer may follow the best methods, may be thrifty, prudent, and far-sighted, and yet he has no alternative but to close his plant when there are no longer orders to fill. Millions of industrious and willing workers lose their jobs through no fault of their own. We cannot answer these questions as lone individuals. They can be solved only by acting together as an organized people.

—Philip La Follette was governor of Wisconsin for six years in the 1930s.

## A New Economic Bill of Rights

Harry Magdoff
November 1990

Most of us have been sold a bill of goods on what ails the United States. We've been told that reforms for the sake of human needs are impractical, if not impossible. The deficits in the federal budget and foreign trade are supposed to be twin evils that have crippled the economy.

In light of these perceptions, accepted wisdom touts such remedies as greater competitiveness in industry, higher labor productivity, reduced consumption, cuts in welfare spending, and a tax system that favors the rich. In reality, however, the conventional diagnosis has the cart before the horse. The deficits and related problems are symptoms, not causes, of our troubled economy.

The disease is a long-lasting stagnation, one that we have been suffering from for more than two decades. Simply put, the economy has run out of steam and has sunk into a morass of stagnation.

Lacking sufficient profit opportunities in productive activities, money capital shifted to financial sectors, producing a spiral of debt, speculation, and inflation of capital assets.

Tinkering with the money supply, interest rates, and other devices favored by economic orthodoxy will not get us out of the mess we are in. Nor will attempts to reduce the budget and trade deficits, even if successful, overcome stagnation and help the economy escape the perils lurking in the financial superstructure. In fact, the remedies proposed by the conventional wisdom would make things worse for the vast majority.

The main question is whether government policy is to be aimed at social justice, in defense of the poor and oppressed, or at protection of the business system in its present form.

In Franklin D. Roosevelt's 1944 State of the Union message to Congress, he called for an Economic Bill of Rights. This Bill of Rights was to include "the right to a useful and remunerative job in the industries or shops or farms or mines of the Nation; the right to earn enough to provide adequate food and clothing and recreation; the right of every farmer to raise and sell his products at a return which will give him and his family a decent living; the right of every family to a decent home; the right to adequate medical care and the opportunity to achieve and enjoy good health; the right to a good education."

Not a bad start for a people's progressive program.

—HARRY MAGDOFF was the longtime coeditor of the *Monthly Review* with Paul Sweezy.

# Cutting the Lifeline
## The Real Welfare Fraud

RUTH CONNIFF
FEBRUARY 1992

All across the country, the poor are getting one message: America has no tolerance for the needy; if the poor are going to survive, they had better clean up their act and get to work.

This past year, under the federal government's Family Support Act, people who rely on Aid to Families with Dependent Children (AFDC)—the government safety net for families so impoverished that their children are officially labeled "deprived"—must take job-training programs and meet a variety of other requirements. If they don't, they lose their welfare checks.

Many of these welfare reform or "workfare" requirements are intrusive and punitive. The programs don't begin to address the root problems of poverty. Often, they don't help participants find jobs, and they exact a terrible toll on the children of the poor.

But as states scramble to reduce their welfare rolls, programs that treat poverty as an attitude problem are catching on.

In Wisconsin, Governor Tommy Thompson has pioneered the welfare reform movement with his Learnfare program, which cut government aid to hundreds of families when their teenagers missed too many days of school.

In Michigan, Governor John Engler cut off support last October to 90,000 "able-bodied" unemployed people—many of whom were mentally and physically disabled—telling them to go out and find jobs because, he said, the state could no longer afford to support them.

In California, Governor Pete Wilson proposed in December a referendum called the Taxpayers Protection Act, which would cut AFDC benefits by as much as 25 percent and deny any increase in grant money to women who have more than one child.

Republicans and Democrats alike are discovering a scapegoat for America's social and economic ills in an "underclass" which conservative political scientist Lawrence

Mead describes as "street hustlers, welfare families, drug addicts, and former mental patients."

The idea of a vast, free-loading "underclass" in America is pure myth. Two-thirds of the families that rely on welfare do so only for brief periods during times of intense economic distress. And AFDC payments are so low in most states that they no longer cover families' basic needs for food and shelter—hardly a free ride. Finally, despite the racial stereotype of large black families on welfare that "underclass" theorists evoke, the great majority of the poor in America are white.

But none of that matters. As the economic crisis worsens in the United States, contempt for the poor, particularly poor black women with children, is proving to have enormous political appeal. Welfare reform programs build on that contempt, while driving the neediest segment of our population deeper into despair.

## To Your Health

MICHAEL FELDMAN
NOVEMBER 1994

Well, maybe it wasn't a health care crisis after all; maybe we were just a bit under the weather. The way things were going, I wasn't even surprised when the watered down version of the health plan—stay warm and drink plenty of fluids—was blocked by the Republican leadership. Now I understand they want "in sickness and in health" out of the marriage vows.

The last report from Mrs. Clinton's task force—"three quarters of a cup of brown sugar and not a cup as stated earlier"—illustrated the degree to which the issue had gotten away from the Administration. The flak from all sides took its toll; I don't think I was alone in beginning to feel I would be the single payer in a single-payer system, or that managed care could manage without me.

The political maneuvering was occasionally brilliant; you've got to hand it to Bob Dole and Newt Gingrich for coming up with the notion that everything is a preexisting condition.

While the sheer scale of the original proposal may have led to its annihilation, after all, it wouldn't have been a comprehensive plan if it didn't have something to alarm everybody. Doctors complained long and hard about having been left out of the decision-making. Perhaps so, but in an age when only Dr. Kevorkian makes house calls and magnetic resonance imagers have filled the void left by x-ray shoe machines, it's nice to see them take an interest in health care again. Small business owners weren't excited about becoming health care providers, and you've got to admit it's a leap of faith to imagine the same guy who hasn't changed the Krackels in the break room vending machine since the late 1980s taking responsibility for your health and well-being.

Initially, the insurance industry was in a panic. Who could blame it, with all those dependents in state legislatures and Congress to look after? That's a lot of mouths to feed, not to mention guaranteed insurance jobs when they get out (even though some of these guys have a demonstrated inability to sell policies).

Meanwhile, the pharmaceuticals, fearing their halcyon days were over and they'd have to compete on the street with everybody else (and with the phone in front of the liquor store out of service), recovered from their initial misstep of threatening to withhold vaccines from schoolchildren, and put their money and samples on the true torchbearers of the democratic process, the Business Roundtable. In short, everybody did his part, or, as Senator Dole put it, "That's the way it is supposed to work."

Now it's clear that the Greatest Nation on Earth is going to have to improvise if it wants medical coverage for all its citizens. The near-term solution seems obvious: marry a Canadian. If we all married Canadians we'd be covered by one of the most comprehensive health care plans in the world, all for the daily cost of a twelve pack of Moosehead. Call it a marriage of medical convenience, if you will, but in the long run it's what goes on under the coverage, not the covers, that counts. Love comes and goes, but major medical goes on and on.

—MICHAEL FELDMAN is creator and host of Public Radio International's *Whad'Ya Know?*

# Another Country

EDWIDGE DANTICAT
NOVEMBER 2005

*The folks in the quarters and the people in the big houses further around the shore heard the big lake and wondered. The people felt uncomfortable but safe because there were the seawalls to chain the senseless monster in his bed. The folks let the people do the thinking. If the castles thought themselves secure, the cabins needn't worry.*

*—*ZORA NEALE HURSTON, *Their Eyes Were Watching God*

In Zora Neale Hurston's visionary 1937 novel, Janie Crawford and her boyfriend Tea Cake, an African American day laborer, refuse to evacuate their small unsteady house before a deadly hurricane batters the Florida Everglades.

"Everybody was talking about it that night. But nobody was worried," wrote Hurston. "You couldn't have a hurricane when you're making seven and eight dollars a day."

Turns out you could have a hurricane even if you're making considerably less than that. And if you manage to survive, you might end up with nothing at all. No home.

No food or water. No medical care for your sick and wounded. Not even body bags for your dead.

Americans have experienced this scenario before. Not just in prophetic literature or apocalyptic blockbusters, but through the very real natural disasters that have plagued other countries. Catastrophes that are eventually reduced to single, shorthand images that, if necessary, can later be evoked.

Take for example, visions of skyscraper-size waves washing away entire crowds in Thailand and other Asian countries devastated by last year's tsunami.

Or remember Sophia Pedro? The Mozambican woman who in March 2000 was plucked from a tree by a South African military helicopter four days after giving birth?

And, for a personal example, let's not forget Haiti's September 2004 encounter with hurricane Jeanne, which left 3,000 people dead and a quarter of a million homeless. In that disaster too, patients drowned in hospital beds. Children watched as parents were washed away. Survivors sought shelter in trees and on rooftops while corpses floated in the muddy, contaminated waters around them.

As I watched all this unfold again on my television set, this time in the streets of New Orleans where I also have friends and loved ones, I couldn't help but think of the Bush Administration's initial response to the Haitian hurricane victims the year before: a mere $60,000 in aid and the repatriation of Haitian refugees from the United States back to the devastated region.

New Orleans's horrific tragedy had been foreshadowed in America's so-called backyard, and the initial response had been pretty much the same: Let's pretend it didn't happen and hope it goes away.

In the weeks since Hurricane Katrina struck, I have heard many Americans, pundits and citizens alike, make the case that the types of horrors we have seen and heard about—the desperation of ordinary citizens, some of whom resorted to raiding stores to feed themselves and their families, the forgotten public hospitals where nurses pumped oxygen into dying patients by hand, the makeshift triage wards on bridges and airports, the roaming armed gangs—are more in line with our expectations of the "Third World" than the first. Turning to Kenyan CNN Correspondent Jeff Koinange on "American Morning" a week after hurricane Katrina struck New Orleans, anchorwoman Soledad O'Brien opined, "If you turned the sound down on your television, if you didn't know where you were, you might think it was Haiti or maybe one of those African countries, many of which you cover."

"Watching helpless New Orleans suffering day by day left people everywhere stunned and angry and in ever greater pain," echoed *Time* magazine's Nancy Gibbs. "These things happened in Haiti, they said, but not here."

Not to be outdone, even the Canadians jumped in the act. Chiding her fellow citizens for their self-righteous attitude toward American poverty, Kate Heartfield of the *Ottawa Citizen* nevertheless added, "Ottawa is not New Orleans. And it is definitely not Freetown or Port-au-Prince."

It's hard for those of us who are from places like Freetown or Port-au-Prince not to wonder why the so-called developed world needs so desperately to distance itself from us, especially at a time when an unimaginable tragedy shows exactly how much alike we are. The rest of the world's poor do not expect much from their government, and they're often not disappointed. The poor in the richest country in the world, however, should not be poor at all. They should not even exist. Maybe that's why both their leaders and a large number of their fellow citizens don't even realize that they do.

This is not the America we know, chimed many field reporters who, haunted by the faces and voices of the dying, the stench of corpses on city streets during the day and screams for help rising from attics at night, recorded the early absence of first responders with both sorrow and rage. Their fury could only magnify ours, for if they could make it to New Orleans, Mississippi, and Alabama and give us minute-by-minute accounts of the storm and its aftermath, why couldn't the government agencies find their way there? Indeed, what these early, charged news reports offered, before the spin and public relations machines kicked into full gear, was a passport to an America where citizens do not always have bus fare, much less an automobile, where health insurance is as distant a dream as a college education, where poverty is a birthright, not an accident of fortune.

This is the America that continues to startle, the America of the cabins and not castles, the America of the needy and never have enoughs, the America of the undocumented, the unemployed, the elderly, and the infirm. An America that remains invisible until a rebellion breaks out, gunshots ring out, or a flood rages through. Perhaps this America does have more in common with the developing world than the one it inhabits. For the poor everywhere dwell within their own country, where more often than not they must fend for themselves. That's why one can so easily become a refugee within one's own borders because one's perceived usefulness and precarious citizenship is always in question in that other America, the one where people have flood insurance.

As some residents return to their houses and businesses in New Orleans in the following weeks and others, renters not owners, remain forever barred from places they once called home, this catastrophe too will gradually be reduced to images that we may or may not want to evoke for a while. However, never again can we justifiably deny the existence of this country within a country that is always on the brink of massive humanitarian and ecological failure. No, it is not Haiti or Mozambique or Bangladesh, but it might as well be.

—EDWIDGE DANTICAT is a novelist, short story writer, and nonfiction writer. Her books include *The Farming of Bones* and *Brother, I'm Dying.*

# President Bush, Meet Lorraine

BARBARA EHRENREICH
APRIL 2006

Here's the news that rocked my little world this month: We got a message that a family friend, let's call her Lorraine, was in an ICU, barely able to breathe on her own. In the last few weeks, there'd been some mumblings about "not feeling a hundred percent," but no hint of anything seriously wrong. The diagnosis came back in a couple of days: fourth-stage breast cancer, which has spread to a number of other organs, including her lungs. If you know anything at all about breast cancer "staging," you know there is no fifth stage.

Lorraine has no health insurance. We didn't know that. In fact, we'd been content to believe that her consulting business was going as well as she said it was. In her late forties now, she's a former accountant who never could find another decent job—also a news junkie, an avid reader, and an energetic volunteer in a number of worthy causes. But it turns out she's been struggling with the cell phone bill and the rent. A few weeks ago, unbeknownst to us, she'd moved out of her apartment and into a free room offered by one of the nonprofits she volunteers for. The cost of a mammogram—well over $100—must have been out of reach.

President Bush, in his State of the Union address, said we should each have a "catastrophic" health insurance policy for the big ticket items like breast cancer, plus a tax-deductible savings account for the little things, like mammograms. If we have to take "personal responsibility" for our doctor visits and routine care we'll be thrifty about it—or so the thinking goes—and the nation's medical expenditures will stop spiking like an Ebola fever.

It's an old idea, going back at least to the Clintons, that the problem with the American health system is that we, the consumers, just consume too much. Make us mindful of the costs by raising co-payments and other out-of-pocket costs, and we'll stop indulging in blood workups, MRIs, prostate exams, and all those other fun things.

President Bush, meet Lorraine. Her problem wasn't that she feasted on unnecessary care, but that like so many of the 45 million uninsured Americans, she wasn't getting any care at all. Maybe, when she first noticed the lump, she should have staged a sit-in at the nearest clinic until it sprang for a free mammogram. But her idea of "personal responsibility" was not to be a bother to anyone.

And how much does the "personal responsibility" theory even apply to the insured population? I have insurance—at enormous cost, because I'm not part of a group plan and I'm an ex-breast cancer patient myself—but that doesn't mean I choose what care I get. It's not my idea to have an annual mammogram and pap smear. The doctor had to threaten tears before I'd submit to a bone scan, and they'll have to drag me in for a colonoscopy. No one aside from the rare victim of Munchausen's syndrome goes looking for recreational medical care.

The fact is there's a big difference between the economics of health care and that of, say, costume jewelry. We the consumers control the demand for costume jewelry; we can splurge on it or leave it alone. But we have precious little control over our demand for health care. Sure, we can exercise and refrain from smoking and sky-diving and swimming with sharks. We can eat right, too (whatever that may mean, with the dietary advice fluctuating from month to month). But it's the medical profession that determines how often we need our blood drawn, our breasts squished, our cervixes scraped, or any of the other nasty interventions they have to offer.

If the medical care we consume was under our own control, I'd say, sure, save up for it and use it wisely. But it's no more in our control than the wind and floods we insure our homes against.

You think it's too expensive to have universal health insurance? Let's be hard-headed about Lorraine's case. If she'd been diagnosed earlier, she might have gotten by with a mastectomy and a bout of chemotherapy instead of burning up Medicaid dollars in an ICU. She might be out volunteering for the needy right now, instead of lying in terror in a hospital bed.

# PART 15

# Upholding Human Rights

In 1910, Teddy Roosevelt asserted that "human rights have the upper hand" over property rights. That belief remains central to progressivism.

But there were other human rights challenges over the last 100 years, including the fight against fascism. Heywood Broun stood up for the Abraham Lincoln Brigade in the Spanish Civil War. And William T. Evjue, who edited *The Progressive* for a decade, defied La Follette's sons, who were isolationists, by publishing an article about the need to take on Hitler and the Nazis. Evjue was eventually fired for continuing to do so.

One vexing human rights problem over the last sixty years has been the plight of the Palestinians. I. F. Stone, Edward Said, and Hanan Ashrawi provide their own perspectives on that crisis.

This chapter also contains interviews with four Nobel Peace Prize winners: Aung San Suu Kyi, Desmond Tutu, Shirin Ebadi, and the Dalai Lama. Says Ebadi: "You do not throw down human rights like bombs."

# Human Rights Higher Than Property Rights

PRESIDENT THEODORE ROOSEVELT
MAY 7, 1910

*From his address at the Sorbonne, France, April 23, 1910*

While not merely acknowledging, but insisting upon, the fact that there must be a basis of material well-being for the individual as for the nation, let us with equal emphasis insist that this material well-being represents nothing but the foundation, and that the foundation, though indispensable, is worthless unless upon it is raised the superstructure of a higher life.

That is why I decline to recognize the mere multimillionaire, the man of mere wealth, as an asset of value to any country, and especially as not an asset to my own country. If he has earned or uses his wealth in a way that makes him of real benefit, of real use—and such is often the case—why, then he does become an asset of worth. But it is the way in which it has been earned or used, and not the mere fact of wealth, that entitles him to the credit.

It is a bad thing for a nation to raise and admire a false standard of success; and there can be no falser standard than that set by the deification of material well-being in and for itself.

My position as regards the moneyed interests can be put in a few words. In every civilized society property rights must be carefully safeguarded. Ordinarily and in the great majority of cases human rights and property rights are fundamentally and in the long run identical. But when it clearly appears that there is a real conflict between them, human rights must have the upper hand, for property belongs to man and not man to property.

—THEODORE ROOSEVELT was the twenty-sixth president of the United States.

# Still Those Who Prize Freedom

HEYWOOD BROUN
JANUARY 8, 1938

Everybody, save his supporters in this country, seems to admit readily enough that Franco is a Fascist. In several authorized interviews, the general himself has made no bones about it. The earlier pretense of fighting for "liberty" has been dropped, and the opposition to any form of democratic government is now candidly and even proudly proclaimed.

The early sham about warring to restore the rights of the Spanish people was always a little thing. It was pretty hard to put that over in the face of the fact that a very large proportion of the "liberator's" forces were made up of Moorish mercenaries, together with the troops of Hitler and Mussolini.

"Our new state is to be a totalitarian instrument at the service of national integrity," he said. And he explained, "We have abolished implacably the old parliamentary system of multiple political parties."

It is true that when he was asked whether he intended to establish a dictatorship, he replied, "Absolutely not."

But whatever distinction lies in Franco's mind can be explained by the seventh son of the seventh son of a hair splitter. And the differentiation becomes even more difficult since the general also stated that the regime he has in mind "will be similar to the regimes of Italy and Spain."

"Spain," he declared, "has not foolish dreams." But in spite of the little Caesar's cynicism the cables still indicate that there are Spaniards who dream of democracy and liberty and resent the effort which is being made to transform their land into a Fascist province of the Duce and the Führer. And that dream has animated the oppressed of the earth from the beginning of time.

By what right, then, does any American refer to the valiants who fight for freedom as Reds and anarchists? If it is anarchical to struggle against alien mercenaries, then George Washington was quite a prominent Red when he fought the Hessians.

Of course, it is not the business of the United States to intervene, but we dishonor ourselves and our own tradition as well as the cause of liberty if, as individuals, we refuse to realize the spiritual bond between ourselves and the people of Spain who stand against the tyrant and echo the grand old cry of "Give me liberty or give me death!" And if this be anarchy, make the most of it!

—HEYWOOD BROUN, journalist and columnist, founded the Newspaper Guild.

## Against Isolationism

WILLIAM T. EVJUE
SEPTEMBER 30, 1939

This column is written by one who experienced the intolerance, the hatred, and the persecution of the World War. This writer was burned in effigy on the university campus. I have always fought the ugly institution of war, and we have loathed war as a means of settling disputes between nations and people.

But much as I loathe war and all its horrors, I seem to feel differently about this war than I did concerning the World War of 1917. It was not difficult to justify one's opposition to the World War. It was evident that the struggle, started in 1914, was simply an imperialistic war in which the various nations engaged were seeking more power, colonies, and resources. The slogan of the last war that this was a battle "to save the world for democracy" was a fake and a delusion. But now I feel that there are real issues at stake in this war—that liberty and human freedom, heritages that are precious to Americans, that even civilization itself are at stake in the outcome of this conflict, and that the world may be returned to barbarism and slavery if the mad forces now loose in the world are not stopped and exterminated.

And then I begin to ask myself: How can a person who has been raised on concepts of liberty, freedom, and human dignity be indifferent and neutral when the rights of free peoples are being challenged by forces that are seeking to smash democracy and all it stands for?"

I start from the premise that Adolph Hitler is the greatest menace to free institutions and human freedom in the world today. He has expressed his contempt for democracy time and time again, and he is now engaged in a worldwide attempt to smash democracy and substitute the totalitarian concept of government under which human liberty and freedom are suppressed. Hitler is drunk with power and he continues from one aggression to another. All of Europe lives in dread of this monster Machiavelli, and small nations live in consternation because of the fear that they will be next as he proceeds to the dismemberment of one nation after another. The world is in a continual state of crisis because of the aggressions of Hitler and the gang of Nazi warlords surrounding him, and it is evident to everyone that there can be no peace in the world until Hitler and all he stands for are smashed. It must be admitted that the person to whom the principles of democracy are precious and dear cannot be indifferent to the continued and progressive enslavement of peoples brought on by these totalitarian warlords.

# Let Me In on the Kill

MILTON MAYER
OCTOBER 14, 1946

I see by the papers that you are going to hang the Nazi war criminals unless, after communing with the God of Love, you decide that hanging is too good for them.

I have a stake in this matter. I have been personally offended by these Enemies of Humanity (as the Czar Alexander called the French in 1812). These Nazi Beasts offended me in several respects. Because of them, most of my fellow Jews, who had never been bothered by anybody before, were tortured. Because of them, some of my dearest friends lost their lives. Because of them, no end of my attractive acquaintances lost their wives while no end of my obnoxious acquaintances got rich. Because of them I was, myself, slurred as a defeatist and appeaser and almost, but not quite, sent to jail. Because of them my taxes are high, my income is low, and my babies are meatless.

I respectfully request an opportunity to participate personally in the punishment of the Devil. It was all right for Job to forgive his fallen foe—and to ask God's consideration on that single count—but as for me, I am only human, and my patience is exhausted. I want to drink blood. Mulled, with cloves.

Let me in, at least to slaver and drool. And consider my application for a pound of Nazi hamburger.

You know, dear Allied Control Council, how I hated the Nazis. I hated them even before they were Nazis; even before, if you will pardon my impudence, you did. I hated them when they sent Gene Debs to jail—and that is going back some. And when they crucified Isaiah and Socrates and Jesus—and that is *really* going back some. My vengeance is overdue.

In the new triumph of international justice—hailed by all humanitarians everywhere—you generals are the court of last appeal. The fact that you are at one and the same time generals and the court of last appeal is itself proof of the new triumph of international justice. I know that in your high hands, dear Allied Control Council, there will be no miscarriage of justice.

I know, for instance, that while you are hanging Goering for deportation and slavery, you will not reach down and hang Mayer, who feasted, only last spring, at a Southwestern ranch maintained by enslaved and deported German prisoners of war. I know you will not reach up, either, and hang the governments of the United States, England, France, and Russia for deporting 11 million Germans into postwar slavery. I know that you know better—in a word—than to carry international justice too far.

I know that I may count on your discretion. May I count on your cooperation? May I count on getting in on the kill?

Here are the Enemies of Humanity, all bundled up and brought to book at last. I have been waiting for this—for a chance at the Antichrist—for going on two thousand years. Can I persuade you to let me in on the fun?

My wants are simple enough. As a friend of mankind—I *think* I'm a friend of mankind—I have been personally affronted by the suffering visited upon my fellow men in Warsaw; Rotterdam; Coventry; Hamburg; Hiroshima; Dresden; Passaic, New Jersey; and Decatur, Alabama. Here you have, all in one caboodle, the Enemies of Humanity whom I have been fighting all my life. Let me at them.

Let me have the gizzard of Field Marshal Keitel, with whom you, dear Allied Control Council, were hobnobbing when I was opposing ROTC in the American public schools.

Let me have the heart of Foreign Minister von Ribbentrop, whose giggle-water you were drinking in London when I was blubbering over the shelling of the Karl Marx houses in Vienna.

Let me have the liver—on toast—of Julius Streicher, who didn't bother you a bit when I was howling against the Nazi-Soviet pact, Churchill's policy in India, the talk of General Moseley, and the racism of West Point.

Let me have a morsel—just a tidbit, a soupçon, a second joint—of the Enemies of Humanity, now that they are going to be carved up.

Let me in, dear Allied Control Council, on the punishment of the Enemies of Humanity and the birth of international justice and the death of the Devil.

Let me out, dear Allied Control Council, of my failure to do anything at all for my neighbor across the street and my brother across the tracks.

Let me drink the blood of the Beast, and I shall be new and pure.


# On Justice for the Palestinians

I. F. STONE
JANUARY 1975

I have not spoken in a synagogue for a long time. I was welcome in synagogues when I spoke about Jewish refugees, but the plight of Arab refugees is not a popular subject in synagogues.

From the beginning of Zionism we have hated to admit that the Arabs were there. We knew they were there, but we pretended that they weren't. Or we talked about helping them. We didn't talk about dislodging them—very few of us thought the day would come when we would dislodge a kindred people. Nothing seems to me more dreadful than that, in the effort to resettle our own people, we have been drawn into the terrible moral fate of treating another people with injustice.

We cannot ignore the problems of the Arab refugees, and of Palestinian national aspirations, nor blind ourselves to their realities. We cannot say that Jews have a right to yearn for Palestine after 1,900 years and deny the Arabs the right to yearn for their homes after nineteen years. These were their homes; they are not all Bedouins. But anyone who wants to regard them as Bedouins must remember that Abraham, Isaac, and Jacob were Bedouins. Any Jew with historical imagination who sees the tents of the Bedouins can't help but see the tents of our forefathers.

In any case, we are not dealing with Bedouins. The Arab world is in many stages of development. We are dealing with a contemporary people—many radical young people, many good older people.

Imagine that you are an Arab. Imagine that you were a dentist or a doctor in Jerusalem or Haifa, or that you had a villa along the little Arab Riviera in Jaffa—there were some lovely Arab villas there. Or imagine that you were a farmer, or that you had a business, or that you went to school. Then, suddenly, everything was swept away.

You lost your home, your business, your school, your country. You would feel bitter—there is nothing mysterious about that—and you would feel desperate.

Terrorism is a reflection of that desperation. I do not favor terrorism, and I do not excuse it, but let's be honest: If the situation were reversed, Jewish boys would be doing what Arab boys are doing. Jewish terrorists did it in 1946 and 1948. They killed women and children in Jerusalem, they blew up the King David Hotel, they destroyed Arab villages.

The way to end the terror, the way to heal the breach, is first of all to recognize (as Chaim Weizmann, the first president of Israel, recognized from the beginning of Zionism) that this is a struggle of right against right, that there is an Arab side and a Jewish side, that we must find a way to live together. We must begin to see the problem through their eyes, and thus have the right to ask them to see it through ours.

I want to see Israel live.

If we do not pursue the path of reconciliation, the Jewish people will be transformed in the span of a generation; we cannot harden our hearts against our Arab brothers and remain the kind of people we have been proud of being for 2,000 years. We will begin to turn our backs on everything we have been proud of, everything that the Bible and the Prophets stand for. It would not be the first time. Every time God has given the Holy Land back to us, we have gone after strange gods. Now we are in danger of bowing down to the idols of militarism and force and realpolitik.

Isaiah says, "Israel shall be redeemed by justice," and for me, this time around, that means justice for the Arabs as well as for the Jews.

—I. F. STONE, independent journalist and critic of U.S. foreign policy, published *I. F. Stone's Weekly.*

## A Palestinian Versailles

EDWARD W. SAID
DECEMBER 1993

Now that some of the euphoria has lifted, it is possible to look at the agreement between Israel and the Palestine Liberation Organization with the common sense it requires. What emerges from such scrutiny is a deal that is more flawed and more weighted against most of the Palestinian people than many had first supposed. The fashion show vulgarities of the White House ceremony, the degrading spectacle of Yasir Arafat thanking everyone for the suspension of most of his people's rights, and the fatuous solemnity of Bill Clinton's performance, like a twentieth century Roman emperor shepherding two vassal kings through rituals of reconciliation and obeisance: All these only temporarily obscure the truly astonishing proportions of the Palestinian capitulation.

So first let us call the agreement by its real name: an instrument of Palestinian surrender, a Palestinian Versailles.

To go forward in the march toward Palestinian self-determination—which has meaning only if freedom, sovereignty, and equality, and not perpetual subservience to Israel, are its goals—we need an honest acknowledgement of where we are.

The primary consideration in the document is Israel's security, with none to protect the Palestinians from Israel's incursions. In a mid-September press conference, Prime Minister Yitzhak Rabin was straightforward about Israel's continuing control over sovereignty; in addition, he said, Israel would hold the River Jordan, the boundaries with Egypt and Jordan, the sea, the land between Gaza and Jericho, Jerusalem, the settlements, and the roads. There is little in the document to suggest that Israel will give up its violence against Palestinians or compensate the victims of its policies for forty-five years.

Neither Arafat nor any of his Palestinian partners with the Israelis in Oslo has ever seen an Israeli settlement. There are now more than 200 of them, principally on the hills, promontories, and strategic points throughout the West Bank and Gaza. An independent system of roads connects them to Israel and creates a disabling discontinuity between the main centers of the Palestinian population.

Was there a single Palestinian watching the White House ceremony who did not also feel that a century of sacrifice, dispossession, and heroic struggle had finally come to naught?

So far from being the victims of Zionism, the Palestinians saw themselves characterized before the world as its now repentant assailants, as if the thousands killed by Israel's bombing of refugee camps, hospitals, schools in Lebanon, its expulsion of 800,000 people in 1948 (whose descendants now number about 3 million, many of them stateless refugees), its conquest of their land and property, its destruction of more than 400 Palestinian villages, the invasion of Lebanon, to say nothing of the ravages of twenty-six years of brutal military occupation, were to be dropped from reference entirely. Palestinian resistance was renounced and reduced to simple "terrorism and violence." Israel has always described Palestinian resistance in such terms, so even in the matter of diction it received a moral and historical gift.

By accepting that land and sovereignty are being postponed until "final status negotiations," the Palestinians in effect have discounted their internationally acknowledged claim to the West Bank and Gaza: These have now become "disputed territories." Thus, with Palestinian assistance Israel has been awarded at least an equal claim to them.

For at least twenty years, Yasir Arafat has been portrayed as the most unattractive and morally repellent man on earth. Whenever he appeared in the media or was discussed by them, their audience could not imagine him without the thought that he supposedly entertained at all times: Kill Jews, especially innocent women and children.

Within a matter of days, though, the "independent media" totally rehabilitated Arafat. He became an accepted, even lovable figure, whose courage and realism bestowed on Israel its rightful due. He had repented, he had become a "friend," and he and his people were now on "our" side. Thus, even if it is patently obvious that Palestinian freedom in any real sense has not been—and is clearly designed never to be—achieved beyond the meager limits imposed by Israel and the United States, the famous handshake broadcast all over the world is meant to symbolize a great moment of success as well as to blot out past and present realities.

The march toward self-determination can only be undertaken by a people with democratic aspirations and goals, or it is not worth the effort. After all the hoopla celebrating "the first step toward a Palestinian state," we should remind ourselves that having a state is much less important than the kind of state it is. The modern history of the post-colonial world is disfigured with one-party tyrannies, rapacious oligarchies, economic ruin, the distortion of society caused by Western "investments," and large-scale pauperization through famine, civil war, and outright robbery. Mere nationalism is not and can never be "the answer" to the problems of new secular societies, any more than religious fundamentalism can. Potential statehood in Palestine is no exception.

—EDWARD W. SAID, Columbia University professor and leading defender of the Palestinian cause in the United States, wrote *Orientalism* and *The Politics of Dispossession*, among many other works.

## An Interview with Aung San Suu Kyi, Nobel Peace Prize Winner

LESLIE KEAN and DENNIS BERNSTEIN
MARCH 1997

Q: There is a movement in the United States and Europe to pressure corporations to stop doing business in Burma. How do these investments—such as those from Unocal and its partner, Total Oil of France—affect the prospects for democracy for Burma?

AUNG SAN SUU KYI: These companies do create jobs for some people but what they're mainly going to do is make an already wealthy elite wealthier, and increase its greed and strong desire to hang on to power. So immediately and in the long run, these companies harm the democratic process a great deal.

Q: The SLORC [State Law and Order Restoration Council] claims that its economic programs for modernization, such as building roads and infrastructure, are helping the people and bringing them benefits.

SUU KYI: A lot of the roads, bridges, railways, and such are built through the use of forced labor, and that is causing the people great suffering. What we put into this in the form of human suffering is not worth what comes out of it.

I think corporations should give more attention to this suffering and should wait to invest until there is a responsible government in Burma. I do not think it is a good idea to separate economics from politics; in fact, I do not think economics can be separated from politics. It's quite understandable that many business concerns think only about their own profits. It's up to the public to put as much pressure as it can on these companies, through shareholder resolutions and public actions. It's good to know that the people of different countries are really concerned and involved in the movement to help Burma. I think in some ways it's better to have the people of the world on your side than the governments of the world.

Q: What do you tell people when they get discouraged?

SUU KYI: We are confident that our cause will prevail, because that is what the great majority of the people in Burma want. We all want justice and human rights. Since what we want will benefit all the people in Burma, our cause is bound to win.

And for those who get discouraged, I would say they should search their own hearts. I have a strong belief that those working for the truth will never lose. Sacrificing for the truth means victory. The National League for Democracy has promised the people that we will continue working for their benefit, knowing that we will have to sacrifice and there will be many difficulties. Our promise to them will never be broken. And we will not use any methods that require the people to take risks. If there is something to sacrifice for, we will take the risks. That is why our League has been formed. We will sacrifice ourselves at the forefront, but we will also need the goodwill, trust, and strong determination of the people.

—LESLIE KEAN is a journalist in San Francisco. DENNIS BERNSTEIN is an investigative reporter, human rights activist, poet, and radio host for KPFA in Berkeley, California.

# An Interview with Desmond Tutu, Nobel Peace Prize Winner

ZIA JAFFREY
FEBRUARY 1998

Q: Can you speak a little about the concept of *ubuntu*, which is the goal of the Truth and Reconciliation Commission.

TUTU: The Act says that the thing you're striving after should be *ubuntu* rather than revenge. It comes from the root [of a Zulu-Xhosa word], which means a "person." So it is the essence of being a person. And in our experience, in our understanding, a person is a person through other persons. You can't be a solitary human being. It's all linked. We have this communal sense, and because of this deep sense of community, the harmony of the group is a prime attribute.

And so you realize, in this worldview, that anything that undermines the harmony is to be avoided as much as possible. And anger and jealousy and revenge are particularly corrosive, so you try and do everything to try and enhance the humanity of the other, because in that process, you enhance your own, since you are bound up with each other.

Q: What has been the most surprising thing you've observed during the Truth and Reconciliation hearings, and what has been the most shocking?

TUTU: The most surprising is to discover the central role that women played in our struggle. In a very real sense, without women, we would not have had our liberation. You'll say I'm saying the obvious, but I think women are quite extraordinary— their resilience. You saw Mrs. Seipei. Her son was killed. And to hear the gruesome way in which they killed him. And there she can walk across and go kiss Winnie, who is alleged to have given orders for the killing of her son, and who has been convicted of abducting her son. That is one of the most extraordinary things that I think has come out of this.

Then you say, "What are the worst things?" It's in imagining that we thought we knew how awful things were, and then we discover they were worse. I found it very difficult to hear how, say, the police abducted someone and drugged his coffee, shot him behind the ear, and then had a barbecue. I mean, they burned him up, and whilst they were doing that, which was bad enough, they were having a barbecue. I don't know why I found that particularly gruesome because some of the things that have happened are awful. I mean, the necklacing is not beautiful, you know, and it was done largely by young people, and you wonder how that could have been thought to advance the struggle, the cause. Or when they used to force people who didn't observe a consumer boycott to drink cooking oil out of the bottle. I mean, awful, awful things. I think our commission has done very well in unearthing all of that.

Q: You were saying that there's something extraordinary in the way Mrs. Seipei behaved. But do you think Winnie Mandela actually deserved that embrace from Mrs. Seipei?

TUTU: Well, you could just as well expect a fish not to swim as expect Mrs. Seipei not to operate in the way that she's operated. You know, people sometimes are wonderful. You don't "deserve" grace. Otherwise, it would not be grace. It's there. It's given.

—ZIA JAFFREY is a journalist and nonfiction writer. Her works include *The Invisibles* and *The New Apartheid*.

# *Where We Went Wrong*
## A Palestinian's Soul Search

HANAN ASHRAWI
FEBRUARY 2002

Why and when did the drive for revenge overtake our pursuit of human rights and the struggle for human dignity and liberty, thereby making us fall in the trap of the reactive mode as deliberately set up by the occupation?

How did we allow Sharon to formulate our agenda and dictate our timing by responding to his calculated provocations specifically designed to draw us within his cycle of retribution? Pain, grief, and the impulse for revenge are negative motivations that give rise to mutually destructive acts of desperation. No relief and no remedy can be found in that course.

Why and when did we allow a few from our midst to interpret Israeli military attacks on innocent Palestinian lives as license to do the same to their civilians? Where are those voices and forces that should have stood up for the sanctity of innocent lives (ours and theirs), instead of allowing the horror of our own suffering to silence us?

How did some from amongst us take up the tools and weapons (however ineffectual) that are chosen by others and on their own terms instead of fending off and exposing Israeli military violence with our own empowerment as advocates of freedom, justice, and peace? Turning our reality into a battlefield plays directly into the Israeli government's hand, not only by allowing it to use its superior military strength, but also by eradicating the fact of the occupation from public discourse and by creating false impressions depicting the Palestinians as aggressors and the Israelis as engaging in self-defense.

When and why did we allow the concept of resistance (and the right to resist) to become the exclusive domain of armed struggle rather than the expression of our human will and spirit in defiance of subjugation, intimidation, and coercion?

How did we allow ourselves those modes of behavior that we abhor or condemn in others? When and why did our nation-building process become subject to the narrow agenda of the few who consider themselves above the law and beyond accountability, and who have persisted in their politics of proprietorship despite their dismal record and inability to deliver?

How did our principles of democracy and the rule of law become subsumed by practices of intimidation, exclusion, and lawlessness? When and why did our elected legislative council become a political instrument for the few or a self-negating, powerless body for the many?

How did the right to hold free and fair elections become a one-time indulgence in some instances and a suspended exercise in others?

When and why did our Basic Law and other unsigned bills disappear, our judiciary become impotent, and our law enforcement agencies sever their ties with the law?

How did we leave a whole people vulnerable, at the mercy of rhetorical bombast on the one hand and relentless military assaults on the other, with no political strategy and no reprieve or protection?

When and why did international public opinion become desensitized to the plight of Palestinians under occupation, with the silence of the Arabs and the duplicity of the rest?

How did the public presentation of the people and the cause become hostage to the excesses of the few, and fall victim to the distortions and fabrications of official Israeli malice?

Whether targeted by an immoral and brutal occupation or suffering silently from internal inequities, the people of Palestine do not deserve their perpetual victimization.

Whether deafened and terrorized by exploding shells and missiles or stunned by the silence of their officials and allies, the Palestinian people deserve better.

Whether grieving for their murdered children and their destroyed homes and crops or smarting at the indignity and deliberate humiliation of the siege and checkpoints, the Palestinian people will not be dehumanized.

Who has the courage now to restore hope to a people whose spirit has ever been broken and whose will remains undefeated despite intolerable adversity?

Who has the courage once again to intervene in the course of history and to change its direction from death and destruction to the promise and release of a just peace?

—HANAN ASHRAWI is a scholar, a spokesperson for the Palestinian cause, and a member of the Palestine Legislative Council.


# An Interview with Shirin Ebadi, Nobel Peace Prize Winner

AMITABH PAL
SEPTEMBER 2004

Q: You're the first Muslim woman to receive the Nobel Peace Prize. Do you feel it to be a burden to be representing Muslim women?

SHIRIN EBADI: I have to begin by saying that the prize does not belong to me alone. This prize truly belongs to all of those who have worked for the cause of human rights in Iran. The awarding of this prize to me is a recognition by the international community of the cause of Islamic feminism. Therefore, Muslim women around the world and all of those who have worked for the cause of human rights in Iran are partners in this award.

Q: Could you tell us your assessment of the state of women in Iran and in the Muslim world?

EBADI: Let me start with Iran. Sixty-three percent of our university students are female. But you still see violations of women's rights in Iran. A Muslim man can have up to four wives. He can divorce his wife without offering any reason, while it is quite difficult for a woman to get a divorce. The testimony of two women is equal to that of one man. Any woman who wishes to travel needs the written permission of her husband. And the number of unemployed women is four times that of men.

Whenever women protest and ask for their rights, they are silenced with the argument that the laws are justified under Islam. It is an unfounded argument. It is not Islam at fault, but rather the patriarchal culture that uses its own interpretations to justify whatever it wants. Needless to say, the dominant culture is going to insist on an interpretation of religion that happens to favor men.

Before the revolution, there were the first 100 female judges in Iran. I was one of them. After the 1979 revolution, they argued that women cannot be judges, and they made us all into peons in the ministry of justice. But women resisted. We wrote essays, held protests, and organized conferences to insist that women being judges was not incompatible with Islam. After twenty years, they finally accepted the argument and said, OK, women can be judges. So, as you can see, one day they interpret Islam in such a way that women cannot be judges and the next day they manage to reverse themselves.

The condition of women in Islamic societies as a whole is also far from desirable. However, we should acknowledge that there are differences. In certain countries, the conditions are much better and in others much worse. For example, the conditions women face even in Egypt differ a whole lot from what their Iranian counterparts deal with. The condition of women in Pakistan is far different from that in Saudi Arabia. This shows that you can have different interpretations of Islam. There is no "true Islam," just different interpretations.

Q: Who have been your role models and inspirations?

EBADI: I have never been convinced throughout my life that one needs to be imitating others. I even tell my daughters not to look at me as a model. Everyone's condition is different, and the way that each person lives his or her life is different. What is important is that one utilizes one's intellect and not to be 100 percent sure about one's convictions. One should always leave room for doubt.

Q: Two criticisms of your approach have been that you are hesitant to fundamentally challenge the Islam-based sociopolitical system in Iran and that you favor Islamic democracy rather than a truly secular government. How do you respond?

EBADI: I am Muslim, to begin with. It's perfectly OK that there are certain people who do not accept Islam at all. Therefore, to announce that I am a Muslim can rub some people the wrong way. But my aim is to show that those governments that violate the rights of people by invoking the name of Islam have been misusing Islam. I'm promoting democracy. And I'm saying that Islam is not an excuse for thwarting democracy. Don't forget, I'm not here to promote Islam. Islam has its own preachers. But some, as you said, criticize me, thinking I'm too tolerant of the clerical regime in Iran. In response, I have to say, I have served time in prison, I have lost my position [as a judge]. Do I need to prove that I am brave? Do I need to be killed?

Q: What's your response to the argument that the concept of human rights is just a Western invention and is not applicable to the Middle East?

EBADI: The idea of cultural relativism is nothing but an excuse to violate human rights. Human rights is the fruit of various civilizations. I know of no civilization that tolerates or justifies violence, terrorism, or injustice. There is no civilization that justifies the killing of innocent people. Those who are invoking cultural relativism are really using that as an excuse for violating human rights, and they're putting a cultural mask on the face of what they're doing. They argue that cultural relativism prevents us from implementing human rights. This is nothing but an excuse. Human rights is a universal standard. It is a component of every religion and every civilization. Democracy doesn't recognize east or west; democracy is simply people's will. Therefore, I do not acknowledge that there are various models of democracy; there is just democracy itself.

Q: I wanted to move on to President Bush's war on terrorism.

EBADI: Certainly, the fight against terrorism is a legitimate fight. And certainly whoever commits terrorism should be brought to justice. Unfortunately, the United States and a few other governments have used the war on terrorism as a way of violating human rights.

Q: President Bush has said the Iraq War would further the cause of freedom and democracy in the region. What's your view?

EBADI: Americans do not understand that you do not throw down human rights like bombs. People's ignorance of the region and Western imperial interests over oil are the main reasons why we are where we are now in the region. I wish there was no oil in the Middle East, and more water. People would have been much happier than they are right now.

# An Interview with the Dalai Lama, Nobel Peace Prize Winner

AMITABH PAL
JANUARY 2006

Q: What are the sources of terrorism, and what is its solution?

THE DALAI LAMA: Such acts are not possible unless you have very strong hatred and very strong willpower and determination. That tremendous hatred comes from many reasons. The causes of this hatred may be going back centuries. Some people say that the West has a cruel history. These people also may see the achievements of Western countries—in terms of the economy, education, health, and social achievements—as a result of exploitation of poorer countries, including Arab countries. Western nations get rich by using resources such as Arab oil. Meanwhile, the countries supplying them raw materials remain poor. Due to such injustices, jealousies are created. Then, there's perhaps a religious factor. In some places, there's the concept of one religion, one truth. In the Muslim world, there's the notion of Allah. The Western, multireligious modern society is some kind of a challenge to this. These, I feel, are the main causes, and, when combined with lots of anger and frustration, cause a huge amount of hate.

The countermeasures for such things are not easy. We need two levels. One level—the immediate—various governments are taking, including some violent methods, right or wrong. But we have to have a long-term strategy, too. In the Muslim world, certain mischievous individuals will always be there, just like among Christians, Hindus, and Buddhists. We can't blame the entire Muslim society because of the mischievous acts of a few individuals. Therefore, at the general public level we must cultivate the notion of not just one religion, one truth, but pluralism and many truths. We can change the atmosphere, and we can modify certain ways of thinking.

Then, second, there should be a spirit of dialogue. Whenever we see any disagreements, we must think how to solve them on the basis of recognition of oneness of the entire humanity. This is the modern reality. When a certain community is destroyed, in reality it destroys a part of all of us. So there should be a clear recognition that all of humanity is just one family. Any conflict within humanity should be considered as a family conflict. We must find a solution within this atmosphere. It's not easy. If we tackle these problems the wrong way, then while today there is one bin Laden, after a few years there will be ten bin Ladens. And it is possible that after a few more years, there will be 100 bin Ladens.

Q: Apart from Buddhism, what are your sources of inspiration?

THE DALAI LAMA: Human values. When I look at birds and animals, their survival is without rules, without conditions, without organization. But mothers take good care of their offspring. That's nature. In human beings also, parents—particularly mothers—and children have a special bond. Mother's milk is a sign of this affection. We are created that way. The child's survival is entirely dependent on someone else's affection. So, basically, each individual's survival or future depends on society. We need these human values. I call these secular ethics, secular beliefs. There's no relationship with any particular religion. Even without religion, even as nonbelievers, we have the capacity to promote these things.

Q: What do you hope for as a just settlement with China, and what sort of system and society do you foresee in Tibet once that happens?

THE DALAI LAMA: Meaningful autonomy. Autonomy is provided for in the Chinese constitution for minorities and special rights are guaranteed for Tibet. In communist states, sometimes the constitutions they write are not sincerely practiced. It's a special sort of case with Tibet. It becomes possible to have one country, two systems. Why not? Let's consider Tibet historically: Different language, different culture, different geographical location. So in order to get maximum satisfaction for the Tibetan people, I think a higher degree of autonomy should be given. Then Tibetan loyalty to the people of China will naturally come. Tibetans will enjoy true autonomy. That is the guarantee for preservation of our identity, our culture, our spirituality, our environment.

# PART 16

# Democratizing Democracy

Private money corrupts public life. To end this corruption was "the great issue" of La Follette's life. It remains one of the great issues of our democracy. That is why progressives demanded, and still demand, public financing of elections.

Letting the people decide—and not corporate interests or party bigwigs—is elemental. So La Follette campaigned for a system of primaries to elect presidential candidates, and within states, for the process of initiatives, referendums, and recalls. So, back in 1922, Senator George Norris called for the abolition of the Electoral College.

Also elemental is curbing the power of the Executive Branch. Neil Sheehan, writing in 1972 (though it easily could have been in 2004), warns: "If we do not find a way to make the Executive Branch of government our servant again, then the executive branch will make servants of us."

# Restrict Use of Money in Campaigns

SENATOR A. W. SANBORN
MARCH 20, 1909

The qualifications of two men being equal, the power of one with a large amount of money to spend should be no greater, in securing votes, than the one without money. The amount of money the one has to spend does not add one iota to his qualifications to hold that office.

Wherein lies the power of the man with money? He can bribe. He can influence votes with money. He can buy newspapers. He can indirectly buy the editorial columns of newspapers for the campaign. He can hire a large number of people to work for him, which implies that they will vote for him for the same consideration. He can prevent others from being candidates for the same office. He can hire others to become candidates in aid of his candidacy. He can make himself feared and dreaded by the force of power his money gives him. He can practically purchase the office.

—A. W. SANBORN was a Wisconsin state senator.

# Initiative, Referendum, and Recall

ROBERT M. LA FOLLETTE
DECEMBER 10, 1910

The initiative and referendum will place in the hands of the people the power to protect themselves against the mistakes or indifference of their representatives in the legislature. Then it will always be possible for the people to demand a direct vote and to repeal a bad law which the legislature has enacted, or to enact by direct vote a good measure which the legislature has refused to consider.

The recall will enable the people to dismiss from the public service a representative whenever he shall cease to serve the public interest. Then no jackpot politician can hold his office in defiance of the will of a constituency whose commission he has dishonored.

Wherever representative government fails, it fails because the representative proves incompetent or false to his trust. Entrenched in office for his full term, his constituency is powerless and must submit to misrepresentation. There is no way to correct his blunders, or to protect against his betrayal. At the expiration of his service he may be replaced by another who will prove equally unworthy. The citizen is entitled to some check, some appeal, some relief, some method of halting and correcting the evils of misrepresentation and betrayal.

The initiative, referendum, and recall will insure real representative government and will prove so effective as a check that it will rarely be found necessary to invoke the powers conferred against unworthy representatives in any enlightened and progressive commonwealth. When finally invested through constitutional amendment with this supreme power, the electorate can always enact such laws as the ever-changing industrial and political conditions require for the common good.

## Election of National Delegates and the Nomination of President by Direct Vote

ROBERT M. LA FOLLETTE
JANUARY 7, 1911

To Wisconsin belongs the honor of enacting the first primary law for the election of delegates to a national convention by direct vote of the people. The Wisconsin delegates to the Republican National Convention of 1908 were elected under the law. They stood in that convention, a little band of fearless men fighting to the last ditch for platform pledges vital to the public interest. Their contest in the Chicago convention fixed the attention of the country and forced the candidate nominated for the President to broaden the platform by declarations in his speech of acceptance in favor of several of the important Wisconsin propositions which the convention had impatiently rejected.

The lesson is obvious. Every state in the Union should adopt a primary law for providing for the election of delegates to the National Conventions of 1912 by direct vote of the people. With such a law in each state, the delegates will be chosen by the voters instead of by the machine managers, and the national platforms of both political parties will represent the interests of the people rather than the interests of the system.

Wall Street has already selected the Presidential candidates of both political parties. There is just time to defeat the Wall Street plan.

## The Great Issue

ROBERT M. LA FOLLETTE
FEBRUARY 17, 1912

The great issue before the American people today is the control of their own government. In the midst of political struggle, it is not easy to see the historical relation of the present progressive movement. But it represents a conflict as old as the history of man—the fight to maintain human liberty, the rights of all of the people against the encroachment of a powerful few.

A tremendous power has grown up in the country in recent years. Again and again it has proven strong enough to nominate the candidates of both political parties. It rules in the organization of legislative bodies, state and national, and of the committees which frame legislation. Its influence is felt in cabinets and in the policies of administrations. Its influence is seen in the appointment of prosecuting officers and the selection of judges upon the bench.

In business it has crippled or destroyed the competition. It has stifled individual initiative. It has fixed limitations in the field of production. It makes prices and imposes its burdens upon the consuming public at will.

In finance its power is unlimited. In large affairs it gives or withholds credit, and from time to time contracts or inflates the volume of the money required for the transaction of the business of the country, regardless of everything excepting its own profits.

It has acquired large control of the public domain, monopolized the natural resources: timber, iron, coal, and oil.

And this mighty power has grown up in a country where, under the Constitution and the law, the citizen is sovereign!

The official in every department of government, executive, legislative, and judicial, is the servant of the people. And, yet, within the lifetime of this generation this power has come between the people and these servants.

At any time within the last ten or fifteen years whenever a voice has been raised in protest, it has been silenced or discredited as an attack upon business and prosperity. Honest, unselfish, patriotic effort to awaken the public to an appreciation of the dangers threatened by this great power has been denounced as the work of the demagogue and self-seeker. Whoever has been conspicuous in any movement, municipal, state, or national, that man has been marked and proclaimed dangerous, and wherever such a leader has been thorough-going and effective in his work—through a controlled press, and upon the highest business authority, every such man has been especially characterized and the public particularly warned against him. But finally, the time seems to have arrived when even the most conservative citizen admits the gravity of the problem confronting the American public!

It is a simple matter to define the present day progressive movement. It can be expressed in a single sentence. It comprehends the aspiration of the human race in its struggle from the beginning down to the present time.

*The will of the people shall be the law of the land.* Constitution, statutes, courts, and all the complex details of government are but instruments to carry out the will of the people, and when they fail—when constitutions and statutes and all of the agencies employed to execute constitutions and statutes, fail—they must be changed so as to carry out and express the well formulated judgment and the will of the people.

For over all and above all and greater than all and expressing the supreme sovereignty of all, are the people. Government shall be brought to and committed to the hands of the people; that they are supreme over legislatures, over government, over Presidents, over constitutions, over courts.

The people have never failed in any great crisis in our history. The composite judgment is always safer and wiser and stronger and more unselfish than the judgment of any one individual mind. The people have been betrayed by their representatives again and again.

The real danger to democracy lies not in the ignorance or want of patriotism of the people, but in the corrupting influence of powerful business organizations upon the representatives of the people.

The real cure for the ills of democracy is more democracy.


# Elect President by Direct Vote

SENATOR GEORGE W. NORRIS
JANUARY 1922

In order to be elected President of the United States it is necessary to be nominated by some political party. There is no other practical way of electing a President so long as our antiquated Electoral College system remains a part of the Constitution. The practical result is that any man or set of men who are able, through any means whatever, to control presidential conventions, do in fact, through such means, select the President and Vice President of our country. The only voice that the voter has in the entire transaction is to register a choice between the nominees of the different political conventions.

It is common knowledge that the people have very little, if anything, to say in regard to the nomination of presidential candidates by political parties. Nominations for President are in fact made, as everybody knows, by a few so-called leaders, who through various and devious ways known only to the politician control and handle the misled and worn-out party convention delegate in accordance with the wishes and the decrees of political bosses. On election day the people find that the voter has nothing left to decide except to choose between two evils, and there is no way by which he can properly protest against such arbitrary control of nominations. He is as helpless on election day as though he were entirely disfranchised.

The abolishment of the Electoral College would make it not only possible but practical for the people to disregard party entirely and elect independent candidates to the offices of President and Vice President. In addition to this, such change would have the beneficial effect of restraining political leaders and machines from imposing upon the party and the people unworthy candidates for the office. If the Electoral College were abolished, an independent candidate for President would be not only a possibility but a probability whenever the conventions of the great political parties were manipulated and controlled by unfair and dishonorable means.

—GEORGE W. NORRIS represented the state of Nebraska in the U.S. Senate from 1913 to 1943.

# The Power and Duty of the Senate

Expenditure of Huge Sums for Seats in Congress Cannot Be Justified; "Pay As You Enter" Policy Denounced

SENATOR GEORGE W. NORRIS
JANUARY 1927

The moral conscience of the nation was deeply shocked when it learned from undisputed and admitted evidence that there had been spent in the Illinois and Pennsylvania primaries several millions of dollars in an effort to obtain nominations for candidates for the United States Senate. In Pennsylvania more than $3 million was expended by the various candidates. Of this amount, $800,000 was spent for the nomination of Mr. Vare. In Illinois, $458,000 was spent to secure the nomination for Mr. Smith.

The expenditure of such huge sums for seats in the United States Senate cannot be justified unless we desire to turn over that great legislative body to the multimillionaires of the country who are willing to buy legislation the same as though it were merchandise sold for cash to those who are willing and able to pay the price. If this practice is to be condoned then we have placed seats in the highest legislative assembly of the world, upon the auction block, and we have, by indirection, defeated every fundamental principle that underlies our government.

If we take this step we have nullified every effort made by our forefathers when they laid the foundation of the Republic, and have established a government not based upon the consent of the governed, but dependent on the power of those who have the money to buy and the will of those ready to sell.

We have made it impossible for any citizen of the United States to become a member of the Senate unless he himself is many times a millionaire, or unless he sells out in advance to those who are billionaires and are willing to put up the money in order to secure the legislation which they want.

If Mr. Smith and Mr. Vare must be seated and the precedent thus established is carried to its logical end, the country will soon discover that the Senate is not a club of millionaires, but a club of multimillionaires, or what is still worse, a club of the tools and slaves of multimillionaires.

# What Democracy Means

UPTON SINCLAIR
MARCH 25, 1939

Our fathers understood democracy as something applying to government; they never dreamed that it might someday have application to industry. But in the century and a half which has passed since our American revolution, new inventions have revolutionized industry; the village blacksmithy has been replaced by the steel trust, the village candlemaker by the power trust, and the family stocking by the Wall Street credit monopoly.

The system of autocracy which prevails in American industry today is in all essentials the same as that which drove our forefathers to revolt. In the automobile industry, Mr. Henry Ford is "the state" just as much as King Louis ever was in France—and just as fully convinced of his divine right.

So long as human beings have to have food, clothing, and shelter in order to live, just so long will freedom and democracy be incompatible with the private ownership and autocratic control of the instruments and means of production.

A nation which has democracy in its political affairs and autocracy in its industrial and financial affairs is a house divided against itself, a house built upon sand, a pyramid resting upon its apex. The two systems by their very nature are driven to war upon the other; and there will never again be peace in America, or anywhere else in the world, until the right to fix the wages of labor and the prices of products has been taken over by the people, and is administered under a system of industrial government by popular consent.


# The Erosion of Liberty

NEIL SHEEHAN
JULY 1972

The constitutional system of checks and balances in government envisioned by the Founding Fathers of our country no longer exists in fact. This is one of two central lessons to be drawn from the Pentagon Papers, which provide us with a vast body of facts through which we can see how our government really functions, in contrast to how we imagine it to function. What we have learned from this archive of American involvement in Indochina over the last three decades is that the American Presidency—and the state machinery that has grown up under it in the Executive branch since World War II—now far outweighs in power and influence the other two, supposedly counterbalancing, branches of government. The Executive branch of our government has become a centralized state in the European sense of the word. The Executive branch has become the state in America, to all intents and purposes.

The second lesson to be drawn from the Pentagon Papers is that the requirements of the Executive branch to maintain and enlarge our overseas empire have become incompatible with the preservation of our domestic liberties. And I do not use the word empire here in a pejorative sense, but rather in its simplest meaning—to describe the system of overseas dependencies and interests we have acquired in the course of the Cold War.

What is emerging from the current structure of our government and its constant struggle to maintain this empire is the working concept that the citizen exists to serve the needs of the state. This concept is directly contradictory to the idea that was central to the thinking of the Founding Fathers—that government exists to preserve the liberties of the citizen.

Unless we can find some way to bring the American Presidency and the state machinery of the Executive branch under control, unless we can find some means to restore a system of checks and balances to our government, unless we can somehow dismantle our overseas empire, we are, I believe, going to see this centralized state turn into an authoritarian state. Unless we can reverse the historical trend that has us in its grip, we are in danger of losing the domestic liberties that have made this country, in the words of Abraham Lincoln, "the last, best hope on earth."

Through these decisions taken in secret the Executive branch has made war in Indochina, either indirectly through French or indigenous forces or directly with American troops, for most of the past twenty-three years. The conflict has cost the lives of 95,000 members of the French expeditionary forces, some 55,000 American servicemen so far, and no one knows how many Indochinese—the estimates run from a million to two million men, women, and children. A hundred billion to a hundred and fifty billion dollars of the treasure of the American people have been lavished on this war.

I submit that the power to make war on this scale is power indeed. It is a measure of how much authority the Executive branch has arrogated to itself. It is a dramatic warning of how gravely the constitutional processes of our system of government have been distorted and thrown out of balance. If we do not find a way to make the Executive branch of government our servant again, then the Executive branch will make servants of us.

—NEIL SHEEHAN, journalist, received the Pulitzer Prize for publishing the Pentagon Papers.

# Wall Street's Mascots

MOLLY IVINS
SEPTEMBER 2002

Remember the old saying about how to get the mule's attention? First you hit it upside the head with a heavy plank, then you gently say, "Hey, mule." The American people have just been hit upside the head with a plank: $7 trillion of what people thought they were worth disappeared in a giant "earnings restatement." And now it is time to gently suggest what can be done to fix this.

Or maybe not so gently, since failure to fix it is likely to cost so much that $7 trillion will look like chump change. Our political system is so broke it took seven years to react to the savings and loan crisis, which was caused by the political system in the first place. That cost us only $500 billion. If they take seven years to stop this hemorrhage, we'll be totally sunk.

Step Numero Uno: public campaign financing. This mess is not just about corporate greed; it is just as much about political corruption.

Perhaps the least edifying sight so far is that of politicians pointing their fingers at the CEOnistas and clucking over their greed. First and funniest was President Junior, whose entire business career was this very same corporate scandal writ small. The man is the mascot of crony capitalism. Listening to his lecture to Wall Street about their need for moral rearmament and better business ethics was first-rate entertainment.

There are basically only two ways to control capitalism: One is by government regulation, and the other is through the courts. Wave after wave of "tort reform" made corporations increasingly sue-proof. The much maligned trial lawyers and their so-called frivolous lawsuits actually functioned like the sharks they are so often compared to. If a corporation stuck a hand outside the law, a shark would swim by and bite it off, as it were, by suing for lots of money, a lovely incentive for decorous corporate behavior. But the politicians have been killing off the sharks.

All of this is not the fault of corporate greedheads; it is the fault of a corrupted political system. It is a consequence of legalized bribery. It is about campaign finance. *That* is the "without which" nothing will come out of this mess.

# PART 17

# Providing a Platform for Writers, Musicians, and Performers

Here's the fun part. When *The Progressive* started doing monthly interviews, we wanted to enliven our pages. There are only so many weighty essays and grim investigative reports that any one person can take. So we offered a section of the magazine every month to a progressive writer, musician, or performer—people who are doing politics in their own arena, people who speak their minds in their own way.

Take Frank Zappa. "You celebrate mediocrity, you get mediocrity," he says. "Few people who do anything excellent are ever heard of. You know why? Because excellence, pure excellence, terrifies the fuck out of Americans."

Or take Susan Sarandon, who says, "I don't pick issues. They pick me."

Or Allen Ginsberg: "Safe sex is just as good as unsafe sex."

Or Harold Pinter: "We are mostly told lies."

George Carlin agrees. He says we're falling for "the official bullshit story."

Or Chuck D: "Now, rappers have become the status quo themselves. You can't rebel against the Queen and then become the Queen yourself."

Note to reader: Included in this chapter you'll find a silly little riff by Will Durst. Just because it's funny.

# An Interview with Pete Seeger, Folksinger

MIKE ERVIN
APRIL 1986

Q: How do you define folk music?

PETE SEEGER: The term was invented about 130 years ago in Europe, and it meant "the music of peasant classes, ancient and anonymous." By that standard, of course, America has no folk music. But around the turn of the century, people in this country began collecting cowboy songs and Negro spirituals, and they said, "This is folk music, too."

Then along came people like Woody Guthrie. Until he met some folklorists, he had never heard the term folk music. They said, "Woody, you're a true folk musician," and he said, "Am I?" He wrote a little magazine piece called "Ear Music," where he wrote: "By this I don't mean that you strum the guitar with your ear. I mean you learn it just by hearing it and other people learn it just by hearing you." It was a beautiful description of folk music.

Q: You suggested once that *Sing Out!* magazine ought to change its name from "the magazine of folk music" to "the magazine of homemade music." Why?

SEEGER: It would be more accurate and more important, too. It would signify being more concerned with the kind of music people make, not the kind people listen to. I don't want to ignore those who just sit and listen, but I'm really hipped on the subject that this world won't survive unless people realize that it's a lot of fun to do things yourself.

Q: Why not?

SEEGER: Well, we live a much more comfortable life than our ancestors, who had to endure cold and heat and hunger and often an early death. But I don't think we're happier. Anthropologists tell us about tribes in far-off places where life is less rushed and often full of laughter. We've forgotten what fun it is to lead a well-rounded life in which you do a little of this and a little of that. Our age of specialization makes for efficient production, but not for happiness.

Q: Tell me about Clearwater [the group he helped found that tries to clean up the Hudson River]. Does your heavy involvement mean you believe environmental protection is the big issue?

SEEGER: No. The key issues are those that are close to you, geographically as well as spiritually. If someone says, "I want to change the world. Where do I go?" I answer, "Stay right where you are. Don't run away. Dig in."

Q: But then who will work on such global issues as the arms race?

SEEGER: My guess is that a lot of people will work on those, but they can still work on local issues at the same time. The world needs a certain number of traveling salesmen and diplomats, but maybe they should just be traveling salesmen and diplomats for part of their lives. After you've done your job nationally or internationally, go back home.

# An Interview with Frank Zappa, Musician

BATYA FRIEDMAN and STEVE LYONS
NOVEMBER 1986

Q: You have said that "art is dying in this country." What do you mean?

FRANK ZAPPA: Much of the creative work I find interesting and amusing has no basis in economic reality. Most decisions about what gets produced and distributed are made strictly on a bottom-line basis. Nobody makes a move without talking to an accountant first. There will always be people who will take a chance, but their numbers are dwindling. The spirit of adventurousness at any level of American society has been pretty much legislated away.

Q: Do you think anything can be done to reverse the trend?

ZAPPA: Perhaps. It is no accident that the public schools in the United States are pure shit. It is no accident that masses of drugs are available and openly used at all levels of society. In a way, the real business of government is the business of controlling the labor force. Social pressure is placed on people to become a certain type of individual, and then rewards are heaped on people who conform to that stereotype.

Take the pop-music business, for example. Look at the stereotypes held up by the media as examples of great accomplishment. You see guys who are making millions of dollars and selling millions of units. And because they are making and selling millions they are stamped with the seal of approval, and it is the millions which make their work quality. Yet anyone can look at what is being done and say, "Jesus, I can do that!"

You celebrate mediocrity, you get mediocrity. People who could have achieved more won't because they know that all they have to do is be "that," and they too can sell millions and make millions and have people love them because they're merely mediocre.

Few people who do anything excellent are ever heard of. You know why? Because excellence, pure excellence, terrifies the fuck out of Americans, who've been bred to appreciate the success of the mediocre. People don't wish to be reminded that lurking somewhere there are people who can do some shit you can't do. They can think a way you can't think; they can run a way you can't run; they can dance a way you can't dance. They are excellent. You aren't excellent. Most Americans aren't excellent, they're only okay. And so to keep them happy as a labor force, you say,

"Let's take this mediocre chump and we say, 'He is terrific!'" All the other mediocre chumps say, "Yeah, that's right and that gives me hope, because one day as mediocre and chumpish as I am, I can." It's smart labor relations. An MBA decision. That is the orientation of most entertainment, politics, and religion. So considering how firmly entrenched all that is right now, you think it's going to turn around? Not without a genetic mutation, it's not!

—BATYA FRIEDMAN is currently a stone carver, designer, innovator, and professor in the Information School at the University of Washington. Putting his University of California, Berkeley degree in electrical engineering to good use, STEVE LYONS writes stage plays and is a house husband for his wife and son.

# An Interview with Yevgeny Yevtushenko, Poet

KATRINA VANDEN HEUVEL
APRIL 1987

Q: What role did you and your fellow artists play in bringing about the changes that are under way in the Soviet Union?

YEVGENY YEVTUSHENKO: Who are these people who lead our country? They are people who were listeners of our poetry readings in the late 1950s and early 1960s. That's true. That's reality. Some people absorbed my message that bureaucracy is stifling them. We created a new generation with our poetry. We created people who now are recreating our country. For instance, there is a new openness in the Soviet Union. This is an echo of our poetry.

Q: Are you saying that writers and poets prepared the way for Gorbachev?

YEVTUSHENKO: Of course. Absolutely. I'm sure. They absorbed our spirits. They were students—some of them were students—squeezing without tickets on the balcony of our poetry readings.

I think my generation of poets did a lot of things to break the Iron Curtain. We wounded our hands breaking this Iron Curtain with our naked hands. We didn't work with gloves on. Sometimes there were victories, sometimes there were defeats. Some retreats were preparatory, and sometimes we sat under the ground after a hail of insults. But our literature, our art, didn't come as a gift from the so-called upstairs.

We worked for it. We didn't get this as a gift. We forged this gift for ourselves and for future generations. Of course, we didn't think that we would produce new kinds of people. But it's happened. We've produced a new kind of person, a new-minded person. Poetry plays a great role in the Soviet Union, and so I am very happy that we worked for it not in vain.

Q: What are some of the areas where you would like to see the policy of openness extended?

YEVTUSHENKO: We don't have enough openness when we speak about our past. Without having more open conversations about the problems of our past, we can't decide the problems of our present. To put sugar on the open wounds is even more dangerous. Ever since ancient times, professional seamen have cured their wounds with salty water. It was the only way for them. Salt, honest salt, could be more helpful than dishonest sugar. Yes, we must not only put salt on open wounds, we must dig into them as deep as possible, because there is still some infection which doesn't give us the possibility to be absolutely healthy.

Great literature is always a great warning. If we see some danger, we must prophylactically write about it. Even if it's very painful. This literature must be like acupuncture. We mustn't be afraid to put needles into the most painful points of the conscience. It's painful, it's unpleasant, but you might be saved.

Q: Your critics ask why the Soviet state, which will not tolerate others, tolerates you.

YEVTUSHENKO: Some of the American press accuse some Russian writers of being conformist, not rebellious enough, et cetera, et cetera, et cetera. I am a victim of this accusation, because I am not in prison, I am not in a mental hospital, nothing like that. Such a writer's life is sometimes interpreted in your country as a kind of dishonesty.

But I am a poetician, not a politician. As a poet, I don't like any kind of borders, prisons, any kind of police, army, missiles, anything which is connected with repression. I don't like it. And I never glorified it. And I did everything that was possible. I am not God. Nobody is God—not even God himself.

I am absolutely convinced that all poets, all real poets, are rebels. In all centuries simple honesty looks like courage. Rebels are not only very famous people who make public statements. If someone doesn't give to others the possibility of engaging him in their hypocrisy, he is a rebel. Not famous, but a rebel. There are so many unknown rebels in the world, just simple, honest people. Any kind of honesty is rebellion.

—KATRINA VANDEN HEUVEL is the editor of *The Nation* magazine.


# An Interview with Alice Walker, Novelist

CLAUDIA DREIFUS
AUGUST 1989

Q: Do you think some of the attacks on you are really jealousy of your worldly attainments? You've got the prizes, the money, the fame—many of these gentlemen critics would like that stuff, too.

ALICE WALKER: I suppose. There is nothing I can say about it except I've worked very hard all my life. I have not had an easy life. I did not start out writing to attain worldly goods. I started out writing to save my life. I had a childhood where I was very much alone and I wrote to comfort myself. I've been very suicidal at times in my life, for various reasons that I don't want to go into here. But I've had some really hard times. And whenever that has happened, I have written myself out of it. And it may look to other people like "silver platter time," but to me, it's just been a very long struggle; so it was always just astonishing to me that anyone would be envious.

Q: When you say you've written yourself out of depressions, is that because you created characters to keep you company?

WALKER: No. It's because of the act of creation itself. It's like in Native American cultures, when you feel sick at heart, sick in soul, you do sand paintings. Or you make a basket. The thing is that you are focused on creating something. And while you're doing that, there's a kind of spiritual alchemy that happens and you turn that bad feeling into something that becomes a golden light. It's all because you are intensely creating something that is beautiful. And in Native American cultures by the time you've finished the sand painting, you're well. The point is to heal yourself.

Q: More than many writers, you are known as a political activist. What do you get from activism?

WALKER: Well, it pays the rent on being alive and being here on the planet. There are things that you really owe, I feel. If I weren't active politically, I would feel as if I were sitting back eating at the banquet without washing the dishes or preparing the food. It wouldn't feel right to me.

Q: In your work, you've tried to go to other myths and histories than the ones that are standard.

WALKER: It's amazing to me that the white male establishment in literature and other areas really seems to believe that because they buy the myth that they have always been wonderful, that they've always done everything, and that the only thing worth knowing is what they produced—it's amazing to me that they think we should think it. We don't. If ever the emperor had no clothes, this is it. Whatever their worldview is, it is certainly not shared by me.

I am not they. My life has not been theirs. My life has been one of everyone in the culture acknowledging that I, as a black woman, am the least respected person in the society. I'm the one expected to do most of the work and not complain, and a long list of other things, over hundreds of years. They, on the other hand, have been brought up to think that they are to rule, that their word is law. But just because they have the power to do that does not mean it is right or that I think they are great. I don't. I think any twelve black women anywhere in the world could do a much better job of running the world than they are doing. And I say twelve because if I had to create a structure for governing, it would never have one person at the head of it. To me that is really totally obsolete.

—CLAUDIA DREIFUS works for the *New York Times.*

# An Interview with Susan Sarandon, Actress

CLAUDIA DREIFUS
OCTOBER 1989

Q: You are probably the most politically active of all the working movie stars these days.

SUSAN SARANDON: Well, I don't think you have a choice, really. If you believe in something, it's just hard to keep your mouth shut. But why shouldn't I have the right to be outspoken about what I consider my own survival? I'm not an expert on anything, and I don't pretend to be. But I do have a point of view. I talk about specific things that touch me personally.

Q: Name one area where you feel personally touched.

SARANDON: AIDS. I've lost good friends to AIDS. In the beginning, in the early 1980s, you couldn't talk to people about AIDS. Most people thought, "It doesn't affect me. It only affects gays and IV users and people who deserve it." And there really was a long period when nothing was done. I work with a group called ACT UP.

Q: Isn't that the group that does civil disobedience as part of its AIDS consciousness-raising?

SARANDON: It does lots of things. It publishes all the facts people need to know about possibly beneficial anti-AIDS drugs, which drugs are available and which are not. When necessary, the group does civil disobedience—such as, recently, taking over the offices of the Food and Drug Administration to make it clear to the FDA that if it can't run things smoothly, someone else will. The issue of contention was that the FDA was not making important drugs available to people who need them.

Q: You said a friend's death pushed you to act on AIDS.

SARANDON: Yes. An actor died a terrible death, all alone and isolated, in the early 1980s. He didn't want people to know about this strange rare disease that he'd contracted. After he died, I went to one of the first anti-AIDS marches from Sheridan Square to New York's City Hall. And I was the only woman there. This was very early, when most people didn't know about AIDS yet and when it was still called "the gay cancer." I remember everyone was quite shocked to see me there. And to me, it seemed like a normal thing. I didn't question it for a second. I was just going to walk in memory of my friend.

When we got down to City Hall, they asked me to speak. And I remember I didn't have the faintest idea what to say. I think I said something like, "I hope people start to understand what's happening—and start supporting each other—because to have to deal with AIDS in isolation and secrecy at a time when you are needing just the opposite is even more of a tragedy than dying."

Q: About five years ago, you made a well-publicized trip to Nicaragua.

SARANDON: I went to Nicaragua in 1984 with a group I'm active in called MADRE. I didn't go so much to get a message across, but more to humanize the issue of

Nicaragua and to inform myself as to what was going on. When I first decided to make the trip, I decided to go and do something specific. I ended up bringing baby food and milk to mothers.

At the particular moment I went there, the U.S. government was most active in destabilizing the Nicaraguan government. I wanted to know, "What does that mean?" With my own eyes, I got to see that it meant women and children were being killed. It meant that we were strangling this tiny place the size of Iowa. I saw that everyone was armed. I saw some people bitching about the government, the way they do here. I saw people that never had been able to read or write learn through a national literacy campaign. I saw people there from all over the world building churches. I saw bombed-out day-care centers that we had bombed. I saw the oil depots that we had dropped bombs on, without even disguising our planes. I was embarrassed. I was confused. This was all being done with my tax money.

I also wasn't prepared for the differences between what I saw and what was reported. For instance, while I was there, Corinto Harbor was mined [by CIA operatives]. I happened to be at a party where I ran into the *New York Times* person in Managua, and I said to him, "Why haven't you covered this?" And the answer was, "Well, we're supposed to be up at the border and we don't know if there really was an explosion. It could have been an implosion, and blah, blah, blah."

Q: Do you ever worry that your outspokenness will leave you without work?

SARANDON: It's a little like worrying whether your slip is showing while you flee a burning building. I don't know. I can't dwell on it. Maybe it has. Maybe being outspoken can cost you work. It's a very subjective business. It's not like being an athlete and you're the fastest. If you're an actor, it's real subjective what makes you hot or cool. But no, I can't think about things like that.

Q: You don't pick safe issues, though.

SARANDON: Well, I don't pick issues. They pick me. I mean, it's not an intellectual choice. And it's not a hobby. I don't say, "This year, I'm going to be interested in this." These are things that you can't not be involved in, that's all.

# An Interview with Allen Ginsberg, Poet

MATTHEW ROTHSCHILD
AUGUST 1994

Q: In *Cosmopolitan Greetings*, you have a phrase, "radioactive anticommunism." What do you mean by that?

ALLEN GINSBERG: Well, the bomb was built up beyond the Japanese war as a bulwark against communism. The military extremism was not much help in overthrowing communism, except maybe in bankrupting both sides, but that only left the communist countries helpless when they switched over to the free market.

But beyond that I think as much was done to subvert Marxist authoritarian rule by Edgar Allan Poe, blue jeans, rock 'n' roll, Bob Dylan, the Beatles, modern American poetry, and Kerouac's *On the Road*—that was more effective in subverting the dictatorship and the brainwash there than all the military hoopla that cost us the nation, actually.

Q: Why did these works undermine communism?

GINSBERG: The authoritarian mind—Maoist, Hitler, Stalinist, monotheist, Ayatollahist, fundamentalist—shares a fear and hatred of sexual libertarianism, fear of free-association spontaneity, rigid control over thought forms and propaganda, fear of avant-garde and experimental art. The Stalinist word for this kind of avant-garde is "elitist individualism" or "subjectivism"; the Nazi word was "degenerate art"; the Maoist word was "spiritual corruption"; the fundamentalist word is "spiritual corruption and degenerate art"; the Jesse Helms argument is why should the average American taxpayer have to pay for this "elitist individualistic filth"? It's exactly what Stalin used to say: "Why should the Russian people have to pay for the avant-garde to display their egocentric individualism and immorality and not follow the Communist Party line?"

The whole authoritarian set of mind depends on suppression of individual thought, suppression of eccentric thought, suppression of inerrancy in the interpretation of the Bible, or of Marx, or *Mein Kampf*, or Mao's *Little Red Book* in favor of mass thought, mass buzz words, party lines. They all want to eliminate or get rid of the alien, or the stranger, or the Jews, or the gays, or the Gypsies, or the artists, or whoever are their infidels. And they're all willing to commit murder for it, whether Hitler or Stalin or Mao or the Ayatollah, and I have no doubt that if Rush Limbaugh or Pat Robertson or Ollie North ever got real power, there would be concentration camps and mass death.

Q: The specter of AIDS is in many of the poems in your latest work. How has the AIDS plague affected you?

GINSBERG: There's this decimation of genius, particularly in theater and film and music and poetry. One of the greatest modern poems is called "Ward 7," written by Tim Dlugos, who was dying of AIDS. It's one of the most humane, heartfelt, sincere poems I've ever read. It's one of the great poems of this part of the century. So there's been a lot of loss.

My taste tends to be for young men and straight young men, so in a way in the early days of AIDS that sort of kept me a little bit safe. Now I'm very careful. It hasn't affected me all that much in terms of my love life, though lately I must say I'm getting older, I'm less successful in bedding young men and young straight men. And I like to be screwed, or screw, but I can't get it up anymore anyway (because of diabetes and other things that I mention in this book) unless there's a great deal of stimulation and rapport and real interest, so I'm not inclined to screw anybody because it's hard and I'd be a little scared to be screwed—though with people that I know real well and I know their situation and their history and have been tested, I wouldn't mind. But I don't know anyone that I like that well or that likes me enough to get it up.

Q: Even in these days of AIDS, you're like the last apostle of desire. You still celebrate sex.

GINSBERG: Safe sex is just as good as unsafe sex. And with safe sex you get something which I always liked anyway—you have these long pillow talks about what you're going to do with each other, how you're going to make love to each other, what you should do, and what you want to do, and who's going to be on top, and who's going to be on the bottom. You have a chance to talk it over if you're verbal at all, and that's fun because it's like opening up your secret recesses of desire to each other.

I always remember Kerouac saying, "Woe to those who deny the unbelievable joy of sexual love." The joy, the exquisite joy. I've found sexual communication to be one of the most thrilling and exquisite experiences in my life. With people I love, all shame is gone, everybody is naked, as Hart Crane said, with "confessions between coverlet and pillow." And I think the best teaching is done in bed also, by the way, as did Socrates. It is an old tradition: transmission in bed, transmission of information, of virtue. Whitman pointed out that "adhesiveness" between the citizens was the necessary glue that kept democracy from degenerating into rivalry, competition, backbiting, dog-eat-dog. I think that's true. One of the problems of the Reagan-Bush era was the lack of cohesiveness, the competition, the rivalry, the Darwinian dog-eat-dog, which fed egocentricity, exploitation, and cruelty and indifference and left three million people out on the streets homeless.

Q: You have a couple of criticisms of 1960s activists, New Leftists—"peace protesters angrier than war's cannonball noises," and you talk about "the scandal of the '60s"—people carrying pictures of Mao and Che and Castro.

GINSBERG: It seems to me that the extreme one-dimensional politics of the New Left—which had no spiritual or adhesive element or direction but relied on "rising up angry" rage, which was considered by some to be the necessary gasoline or fuel for political action—was a great psychological mistake. Any gesture made in anger is going to create more anger. Any gesture coming from rage and resentment creates more rage and resentment. Any gesture taken in equanimity will create more equanimity. The 1968 Chicago police riot was, after all, to some extent provoked by the attitude, behavior, and propaganda of some of the members of the New Left, who had promised a Festival of Light but delivered an angry protest. The original Yippie idea, as announced, was to have a festival that would be cheerful, affirmative, ecologically sound, and generous emotionally so that it would outshadow the "Death Convention" of Johnson's war.

Before the Chicago thing, Jerry Rubin came over to my house, and I wanted reassurance that he didn't have any intention of starting a riot. I didn't want any blood. He swore, "not at this time." I should have suspected it then and there, but actually

I do think unconsciously or consciously some wanted to precipitate an "exemplary" riot.

Q: Do you ever get tired of being Allen Ginsberg?

GINSBERG: No, there's no Allen Ginsberg. It's just a collection of empty atoms.

Q: But in several of your latest poems, you seem to be wrestling with immortality.

GINSBERG: No, I'm not wrestling. I'm saying, "Immortality comes later," by definition. It's a joke.

Q: I can understand the need to feel that your life's work was worthwhile, but to feel the need that people will be reading you when you're gone I don't understand. You're not going to be around to enjoy it, anyhow. What's the big deal about immortality?

GINSBERG: There's no total immortality. "The sun's not eternal, that's why there's the blues," as I wrote in a previous book. However, it is important if you have the impulse of transmitting dharma or whatever wisdom you've got, writing "so that in black ink my love might still shine bright"—Shakespeare. There is a Buddhist reason for fame and for immortality, which is that it gives you the opportunity to turn the wheel of dharma while you're alive to a larger mass of sentient beings, and after you're dead that your poetry radio continues broadcasting dharmic understanding so that people pick up on it and the benefits of it after you're dead. To the extent that your ambition is to relieve the mass of human sufferings, that can be accomplished with art.

## An Interview with Patti Smith, Musician

JOHN NICHOLS
DECEMBER 1997

Q: As an artist, did you feel you had to pick up a guitar and form a band to get your message across?

PATTI SMITH: I've always loved the format of rock 'n' roll. I remember, as a child, watching rock 'n' roll develop. I grew up with it. I was certainly comforted by it, inspired by it, excited by it.

Then in the early 1970s, when I really felt that rock 'n' roll was losing some of its strength when it just seemed like a format people were visiting for some kind of glamorous lifestyle, or to take a lot of drugs, twist people's minds, make a lot of money, and then exit—I reacted. I had never had any aspirations toward being a musician. I'm not a musician. I'm not really much of a singer. I wasn't brought up in a time where females even thought of things like that. In terms of female performers, we had memories of Edith Piaf, Billie Holiday, jazz singers, then you had Janis Joplin coming up, and Tina Turner. But in terms of a singer-songwriter leading a rock band, there really wasn't anyone I could think of. So I just didn't think about it.

To me, rock 'n' roll is a totally people-oriented, grassroots music. It came up from the people, from the blues. The roots are deep. It came from the earth. It's our thing. Rock 'n' roll is great because it's the people's art. It's not an intellectual art. It's totally accessible. The chords are totally accessible. The format is totally accessible. But it's not ours anymore. Right now, rock 'n' roll belongs to business. We don't even own it.

The people have got to wake up and reclaim what belongs to them. The music business should be working for us; artists should not be working for the music business.

It's the same with America. The country belongs to us. The government works for us. But we don't think of it that way. We've gotten all twisted around to a point where we think that we work for the government.

Q: Almost twenty years ago, you wrote a song called "Citizenship." Can you describe your sense of the role of the artist as citizen?

SMITH: When I was younger, the last thing I wanted to be was a citizen. I wanted to be an artist and a bum—what Genet would call one of "the sacred bums of art." That's pretty much all I wanted to be. I was concerned about certain things—about censorship, about nuclear power, about the Tibetan situation, and the famine in Ethiopia. I did have concerns, but still, as an artist and a human being and an American, I was basically self-centered. I didn't really have an understanding of what it was like to be a citizen.

In 1979, when I moved to Detroit to live with Fred, my life changed drastically. I came to understand George Washington's quote after he left the Presidency, when he said, "I have resumed my life as a citizen." I took comfort from that, because I actually became "as a citizen." I gained a lot of respect for people. It's not my bent. I'm just not a middle-class person. I don't have middle-class sensibilities, desires. But I would never again be so snooty about the middle class and middle-class struggles.

Q: Has that changed your sense of art? Do you feel different responsibilities?

SMITH: I think the artist's first responsibility is to his work, to the quality of his work. An artist must concern himself with what's motivating him, whether it's a spiritual motivation, or a vision thing, an abstract principle, or something totally intellectual.

An artist must concern himself with the quality of his work. What it does out in the world is not always of the artist's choosing. I don't think it's the artist's duty to be political. It's the artist's duty to do good work. If that work inspires people— if he's a politically articulate artist—that's great. But the main thing is to inspire people or to comfort them or to touch them in some way.

—JOHN NICHOLS is the associate editor of the *Capital Times* of Madison, Wisconsin, and the Washington correspondent for *The Nation*. He also cofounded the media reform group Free Press and has written several books, including *The Genius of Impeachment* and, with Robert W. McChesney, *It's the Media, Stupid.*

# An Interview with Harold Pinter, Playwright

ANNE-MARIE CUSAC
MARCH 2001

Q: Early on, you didn't talk about some of your plays, like *The Birthday Party*, *The Dumb Waiter*, or *The Hothouse*, as political. But more recently you've started to talk about them that way. Why?

HAROLD PINTER: Well, they were political. I was aware that they were political, too. But at that time, at whatever age I was—in my twenties—I was not a joiner. I had been a conscientious objector, you know, when I was eighteen. But I was a pretty independent young man, and I didn't want to get up on a soapbox. I wanted to let the plays speak for themselves, and if people didn't get it, to hell with it.

Q: What was your experience like as a conscientious objector?

PINTER: I was quite resolute. This was 1948, I remind you. And I was simply not, absolutely not, going to join the army. Because I had seen the Cold War beginning before the hot war was over. I knew the atom bomb had been a warning to the Soviet Union. I had two tribunals and two trials. I was prepared to go to prison. I was eighteen. It was a civil offense, you know, not a criminal offense. I had the same magistrate at both trials, and he fined me twice. My father had to find the money, which was a lot of money at the time, but he did. But I took my toothbrush with me to court both times. I was prepared to go to prison.

And I haven't changed a bit, I have to say.

Q: What changed your way of approaching your plays?

PINTER: I became less and less reticent about saying what I felt, and therefore I was able to talk about the plays in a slightly different way, too.

I really did have a great jolt in 1973, when the Pinochet coup overthrew Allende. It really knocked me, as they say, for six. I was appalled and disgusted by it. And I knew how the CIA and the U.S. were behind the whole damn thing. So that really jolted me into another kind of political life.

Q: This appears on your website. "In 1958, I wrote the following: 'There are no hard distinctions between what is real and what is unreal, nor between what is true and what is false. A thing is not necessarily either true or false; it can be both true and false.'" But then you make the note, "I believe that these assertions still make sense and do still apply to the exploration of reality through art. So as a writer I stand by them, but as a citizen I cannot. As a citizen, I must ask: What is true? What is false?" Do these two ways of seeing and experiencing ever come into conflict for you?

PINTER: When you are writing a work of fiction, you're inhabiting a very different kind of world from the world we actually live in every day of the week. It's simply different, the world of imagination. You can't make those determinations—about truth and lies—in what we loosely call a work of art. You've got to be open and explore. You've got to let the world find itself, speak for itself. Whereas, in the actual, practical, concrete world in which we live, it's very easy, from my point of view, to see a distinction between what is true and what is false. Most of what we're told is false. And the truth is, on the whole, hidden and has to be excavated and presented and confronted, all along the line.

We are mostly told lies. Or, where we are not told lies, we are told a lot of bull- shit. The actual propaganda of our democracies is palpably hypocritical. Who are they kidding? The trouble is, they do manage to kid an awful lot of people. That's a terrible thing.

And the complicity is a fact—the complicity between government, business, and media, which few people care to contemplate. The structures of power essentially treat people with contempt because that's the way they survive. But they say the opposite. They say, "We love you." It's the Orwellian thing: "We're taking the great- est care of you."

Even while they're torturing them, they're saying, "We love you. Please trust us and rely upon us." And what appalls me is, "We're looking after your best interests by torturing you."

You know T. S. Eliot said something about, "Don't expect serenity from old men." Well, you certainly won't get it from me, because I have become more and more disgusted by that kind of lie.

Q: What kind of torture are you talking about?

PINTER: All kinds of torture, including the torture in American prisons. I'm not really saying that the United States would assert that they are looking after the best inter- ests of the two million people in prison. But they would say they are looking after the best interests of society. And they're not. They're not by a very long way. They're doing something quite different. They are suppressing a great body of people, you know, thousands upon thousands for obviously very minor offenses—very small drug offenses and so on. The proportion of black prisoners is extraordinary.

Q: How did you get involved in this issue?

PINTER: I do have friends in America, one or two, who do, believe me, keep me up- to-date and well informed. They're pretty beleaguered, I have to say. It's not just a U.S. domestic affair with nothing to do with anybody else. Not at all.

Since the U.S. makes so many pronouncements about the world it sees before it, I think I am entitled to make pronouncements about what actually is taking place in the United States. I'm always looking for those schisms between language and action, what you say and what you do. This is where I find constant sources of curiosity and disgust.

# An Interview with George Carlin, Comedian

MARC COOPER
JULY 2001

Q: How cynical or pessimistic are you about politics in general?

GEORGE CARLIN: I'm certainly a skeptic. But to me the cynics are the ones in the boardrooms with the reports from the focus groups. And the belief that there's a man in the sky watching us, watching everything we do, is so ingrained: First thing they do is tell you there's an invisible man in the sky who's going to march you down to a burning place if he doesn't like you. If they can get you to believe that, it's all over. Before you're six years old, they've got you thinking that, they've got you forever on anything else they want. There's no real education. It's an indoctrination training little producers of goods who will also be consumers of goods. Some will be on the producer side, and more will be on the consumer side. But you're all being trained to be a part of this big circle of goods being pumped out and everyone buying them and everyone going to work to help make more of them for other people to buy.

I've given up on the whole human species. I think a big, good-sized comet is exactly what this species needs. You know, the poor dinosaurs were walking around eating leaves, and they were completely wiped out. Let the insects have a go. You know, I don't think they'll come up with sneakers with lights in them, or Dust Busters, or Salad Shooters, or snot candy.

But, you know, life is dual. If you'll scratch a cynic, you'll find a disappointed idealist. And the fire never goes out completely. And that part of me that made my mother say, "You have a lovely nature" is very true.

Q: Is there anything out there happening that would check your despair with the human species? Or are we on the big slide down, here?

CARLIN: It's called CTD—Circling The Drain. But I do cherish, and love, and am thrilled by individuals. People, one by one as I meet them, I find are wondrous. When you have time to listen and watch them, when you look in the eyes, you see all the potential of the whole thing, this whole species that had such a wonderful gift that was given by nature. The mind, the ability to objectify and to think abstractly. And we've wasted it by everyone wanting a fanny pack and to go to the mall and to be paying 18 percent interest on things that we don't need, don't want, don't work, and can't give back.

Q: There are very few places, even in the comic world, where people are so openly blasphemous as you are. Why the absolute, unremitting scorn for religion?

CARLIN: I take pride in it. Sometimes people will say, "That's bigotry, can't you see? You wouldn't attack blacks, you wouldn't attack Jews." I say, "Wait a minute, religion is a self-conferred intellectual decision; it's not something you get at birth and is unchangeable. You're collusive with the religion when you accept it; you have a choice." So I think intellectually if you accept it, intellectually I have every right to question that choice you made. Whereas your blackness, ethnicity, homosexuality is something that might be genetic, I can't touch that, and I have no right.

I saw religion as the first big betrayal of me. You know, they promised everything. I remember at first communion I was seven years old, and they said, "You're going to feel different, you're going to get the blessed sacrament in your mouth, and you will be in a state of grace, you will feel God's presence." I thought, "None of that happened."

I think religion is a terrible distortion and exploitation of a very natural urge every human has—to be rejoined with the one somehow, to become a part of the universe. Once the high priests and the traders took over, we were lost as a species.

Q: You talk about businessmen with such scorn. That's the lifeblood of America, isn't it?

CARLIN: It absolutely is, and that's probably why there is so much scorn. Everybody in America is a part of this big herd of cattle being led to the marketplace, not to be sold, which is usual with cattle, but to do the buying. And everyone is branded. You see the brands—Nike, Puma, Coke—all over their bodies. Pretty soon you'll go to a family and say, "$100,000 if we can tattoo Pepsi on your child's forehead, and we'll have it removed when he's twenty-one. A hundred grand." I'm sure the George Washington Bridge will someday be the Ford Motor Company George Washington Bridge. It's gone beyond what you can merely mock, so it has to be a frontal attack. Folks, this is bullshit. This is jerk-off time. Don't you see what's happening? What you're doing? What you're participating in? You know, that justice is blind, everyone's equal, the press is fair and impartial. It's what I call the "American Okey-Dokey." It's the official bullshit story.

—MARC COOPER, journalist, writes for *The Nation* and *The Huffington Post*. The author of *Pinochet and Me*, he also teaches at the University of Southern California Annenberg School of Journalism.

# An Interview with Janeane Garofalo, Actress

ELIZABETH DiNOVELLA
MAY 2003

Q: Why are you speaking out against this war in Iraq?

JANEANE GAROFALO: I'm so public about this because I've been asked to do so and because I painfully felt that the antiwar movement was being ignored. If I thought the antiwar movement was getting proper coverage in the mainstream media, I would have said no. You don't need actors to make this a mockery.

But as it became abundantly clear that no one was getting on TV talking about this, and when I was specifically approached by the founders of Win Without War and some people at MoveOn.org, I said yes. And I wasn't reluctant about it. I can't stand watching history roll right over us. It's like they're asking you to bend over, put your head in the sand, and put a flag in your ass.

Q: You've been on CNN, MSNBC, and Fox speaking out against the war. How has that gone?

GAROFALO: On the one hand, it's so bad that it's enjoyable. Some of the anchors or journalists or whatever you want to call them, personalities, have been kind and it's been fine. But for the most part, you just have to defend yourself. You don't get a chance to have a real debate. You don't get a chance to discuss anything. You defend your position, defend your career choice, defend your patriotism, defend your intelligence level, and then no information has been disseminated to people watching the show.

Q: Have you gotten a lot of hate mail?

GAROFALO: Oh shit, yeah. I had to change my home phone number. A lot of the hate mail I get is clearly misogynist. I am a proud liberal, feminist woman, and the hate mail I get for those three things is not about me. It's about those signifiers, and about what the right in this country has managed to do to perpetuate anger over what they mean.

Then there is a lot of the hate mail that says actors are too wealthy to understand what's going on. The actors live in Hollywood, all this kind of nonsense. Do they realize how wealthy the Bush family is, or the Cheney family? If you are going to talk about somebody not understanding the common man, then look no further than the Beltway.

Q: What's your opinion on the current state of the mainstream media?

GAROFALO: The mainstream media has, in my opinion, been so grossly negligent, so disturbingly devoid of authentic debate, and actual dissemination of information. They are, in theory, the custodians of fact, the watchdogs of government. That's the theory. At a time as important as this, they have absolutely rolled over to the conservative hawkish agenda.

The parents of the troops who die and the parents of Iraqi civilians who die should have the right to slap a lot of these media outlets with a suit of criminal negligence. Military parents would have a legitimate case, especially against Fox and the *New York Post* for cheerleading this thing the whole way, for waving the flag, and using knee-jerk, sycophantic, pseudo-patriotism as a tool to galvanize public opinion.

Q: How do you react when people say you are brave to speak out?

GAROFALO: What's brave about it? There's nothing brave in saying, "Hey, I don't think this is right." There's nothing brave about saying, "I feel we are not functioning under a true democracy, I feel like we are being manipulated." That's not brave, that's common sense. I guess it's brave to go on television. It's certainly brave and sadomasochistic to go on Fox. But my choice is either I can yell at Fox on my couch or I can get in there and voice my opinion.

Q: Are you expecting a blacklist to come out in Hollywood?

GAROFALO: No. Plus the fact that I'm on the Hollywood "rarely works" list, so to blacklist me would be extraordinary. It would be an actual compliment to be black-listed because I barely work. Not that I wouldn't love to get good parts, but I bowed out of that because it's not worth the rat race. I don't go to the gym. I'm thirty-eight years old. I don't care to invest the time and energy to perfecting my physical appearance so that I'm at least acceptable to play the waitress. It is of no concern to me.

Q: Have you lost work for your antiwar position?

GAROFALO: I have. And that's irrelevant to me. I actually lost a potentially lucrative job as the voice for a software company. That's OK. It's no big loss in the big picture. Nobody gives a shit whether I'm the voice of it or not. The more I became involved with the antiwar movement, the more it was clear that they were not going to use me. That's fine. That's their choice.

But the point is I'm not sorry for speaking out for my First Amendment rights. I'm not sorry that I have demanded that my news do its job. I'm not sorry about that. There's been such an assault on democracy here, and the mainstream media is complicit in it. We are living in neo-McCarthy, post-democratic times. Democracy is being criminalized. Democracy is being ignored.

I never imagined this would be my life. I never imagined that I would never care about dumb things anymore. I never imagined I'd be a person who could transcend that kind of nonsense. But beyond that, I never imagined I would be penalized for speaking out in favor of social justice. I never thought that anyone who spoke out for peace, and diplomacy, and social justice would be pilloried.

I'm frequently depressed—just have a general malaise. And I don't mean a malaise of indifference; I mean a malaise of sadness and fear. I've always been alarmed by some of the things that the mainstream media does and by what the government does, no matter who's in office, but the broken heart is new.

# *An Interview with Kurt Vonnegut, Novelist*

DAVID BARSAMIAN
JUNE 2003

Q: What's your take on George Bush?

KURT VONNEGUT: We have a President who knows absolutely no history, and he is surrounded by men who pay no attention to history. They imagine that they are great politicians inventing something new. In fact, it's really quite old stuff: tyranny.

Q: Today, war is being produced as a made-for-TV event; war is turned into a video game for the army of couch potatoes.

VONNEGUT: It's incumbent on the President to entertain. Clinton did a better job of it—and was forgiven for the scandals, incidentally. Bush is entertaining us with what I call the Republican Super Bowl, which is played by the lower classes using live ammunition.

Q: You live just a few blocks from the United Nations. On February 15, there was a mass demonstration in New York. You took part in it?

VONNEGUT: I was simply there, but I didn't speak.

Q: What do you think of the efficacy of people turning out at protests and marching?

VONNEGUT: I'm an old guy, and I was protesting during the Vietnam War. We killed fifty Asians for every loyal American. Every artist worth a damn in this country was terribly opposed to that war, finally, when it became evident what a fiasco and meaningless butchery it was. We formed sort of a laser beam of protest. Every painter, every writer, every stand-up comedian, every composer, every novelist, every poet aimed in the same direction. Afterwards, the power of this incredible new weapon dissipated. Now it's like a banana cream pie three feet in diameter dropped from a stepladder four feet high. The right of the people to peacefully assemble and petition their government for a redress of grievances is now worth a pitcher of warm spit. That's because TV will not come and treat it respectfully.

The government satirizes itself. All we can wish is that there will be a large number of Americans who will realize how dumb this all is, and how greedy and how vicious. Such an audience is dwindling all the time because of TV. One good thing about TV is, if you die violently, God forbid, on camera, you will not have died in vain because you will be great entertainment.

Q: When Bush began to play the Iraq card, it was exactly at a moment when there was an enormous amount of attention paid to the scandals on Wall Street. It distracted the public from what was going on in the corporate sector.

VONNEGUT: One thing I learned, with permission of the school committee of Indianapolis, was that when a tyrant or a government gets in trouble it wonders what to do. Declare war! Then nothing else matters. It's like chess; when in doubt, castle.

The polls demonstrate that 50 percent of Americans who get their news from TV think Saddam Hussein was behind the Twin Towers attack. TV is a calamity in a democracy.

Q: What about the importance of reading books?

VONNEGUT: It's hard to read and write. To expect somebody to read a book is like having someone arrive at a concert hall and be immediately handed a violin and told to go up onstage. It's an astonishing skill that people can read, and read well. Very few people can read well. For instance, I have to be very careful with irony, saying something while meaning the exact opposite. *Slaughterhouse-Five* is read in high schools, and sometimes the teachers tell the students to write the author.

Some of them write that the events are not sequential! It's hard enough to read a book with Wednesday followed by Monday.

Q: You take pride in being from Indiana, in being a Hoosier.

VONNEGUT: For being from the state that gave us Eugene Debs. Eugene Debs said (and this is merely a paraphrase of the Sermon on the Mount, which is what so much socialist writing is), "As long as there's a lower class, I'm in it; as long as there's a criminal element, I'm of it; as long as there is a soul in prison," which would include Timothy McVeigh, "I am not free." What is wrong with that? Of course, Jesus got crucified for saying the same thing.

Q: With two million souls in prison today in the United States, Debs would be very busy.

VONNEGUT: Debs would've committed suicide, feeling there was nothing he could do about it.

Incidentally, I am honorary president of the American Humanist Association. John Updike, who is religious, says I talk more about God than any seminarian. Socialism is, in fact, a form of Christianity, people wishing to imitate Christ.

Q: Christianity pervades your spirit.

VONNEGUT: Well, of course. It's good writing. I don't care whether it's God or not, but the Sermon on the Mount is a masterpiece, and so is the Lord's Prayer: "Forgive us our trespasses as we forgive those who trespass against us." The two most radical ideas, inserted in the midst of conventional human thought, are $E=MC^2$— matter and energy are the same kind of stuff—and, "Forgive us our trespasses as we forgive those who trespass against us."

# Crack Kills, Pot Giggles

WILL DURST
AUGUST 2003

Straight off, I got to tell you, I don't smoke pot. Used to. Used to deal it. Bad Midwestern weed. Indiana gold. $95 a pound. We'd roll skinny little toothpick joints and smoke all day long. Right around 8:00 at night, we'd start to wonder, "Hey, am I actually getting high?" The answer, of course, was no, we had just spent the entire day hyperventilating. I quit smoking around 1978 when the heathen devil weed got too good. But you know what? I miss it. Not for the high. For all the wrong reasons. I miss rolling a joint one-handed while driving. I miss being illegal. I miss being a rebel. But it seems the U.S. government is determined to maintain that rebel status for its estimated 80 million pot smokers.

You wouldn't be accused of being one toke over the line if, after U.S. District Judge Charles Breyer refused to sentence Ed Rosenthal on federal charges of growing more than 100 plants, you assumed it was a victory for the pro-pot movement.

But if you think this action will cause the Bush Administration to slow down its feverish crackdown on medical marijuana, you might want to hold off on investing all your money in rolling paper manufacturers. Richard Meyer, spokesman for the San Francisco division of the DEA, said, "The so-called medical marijuana initiative was a smokescreen: The real agenda of these people was to legalize not only marijuana but all drugs."

Can you believe these guys? A third-grader can tell you that crack is to pot as an Uzi is to a banana. Crack kills, pot giggles. Say you do run into a crazed pothead, what's the worst thing that's going to happen? You might get fleas, that's about it. OK, there's Twinkie creme on your shirt, wipe it off.

—WILL DURST, stand-up comedian and political satirist, is the author of *The All-American Sport of Bipartisan Bashing.*


# An Interview with Tom Morello, Musician

ELIZABETH DiNOVELLA
JANUARY 2004

Q: When did you first learn guitar?

TOM MORELLO: I started kind of late, when I was seventeen. I got the Sex Pistols record, and had the punk rock epiphany of "I can do this, too." Prior to that, I was a big fan of heavy metal music, which involved extravagance. You had to have huge walls of Marshall amplifiers and expensive shiny Gibson, Les Paul guitars. You had to know how to play "Stairway to Heaven" and have a castle on a Scottish loch, limos, groupies, and things like that. All I had was a basement in Illinois. None of that was going to come together for me.

When I heard the Sex Pistols and the Clash and Devo, it was immediately attainable. I thought, this music is as good as anything I have ever heard, but I can play it this afternoon. I got the Sex Pistols record, and within twenty-four hours I was in a band.

Q: Rage Against the Machine is overtly political. Audioslave does not have politically charged lyrics. How did that happen?

MORELLO: There are many overtly political bands that do not sell 14 million records like Rage Against the Machine because the first thing they have to take care of is the musical chemistry. You can have all of your politics lined up and all of your analyses together, but it's got to be a great rock 'n' roll band.

And the way great rock 'n' roll bands happen is organically. The convergence of those four musicians made a band called Rage Against the Machine that had a political content. Had we started out saying it must be a, b, c, d, trying to shoehorn ideas and music into a little box, it wouldn't have worked. When bands do that, it's either derivative or it's not compelling.

With Audioslave, the four of us got in a room and we said, what's this going to be? We're not going to try to be Rage Against the Machine; we're not going to try to be Soundgarden; we're going to see what develops. It developed musically, very successfully for us, in a way that felt just great in the room.

For me, Audioslave didn't have political content. And that's when I formed Axis of Justice. It's important to me to have both great rock 'n' roll and to be able to fight the power on a daily basis. That's where that divergence happened, to do my politics via Axis of Justice and my music via Audioslave.

Q: What is Axis of Justice?

MORELLO: Axis of Justice is a nonprofit political organization formed by me and Serj Tankian, singer of System of a Down. We formed the organization a little over two years ago to build a bridge between progressive-minded musicians, fans of rock and rap music, and local grassroots organizations.

For ten years in Rage Against the Machine, kids were asking me, "I love your band. I feel motivated. How do I get involved?" We formed this organization to answer that question for the kids who were basically like I was. I grew up in a small, conservative Midwestern town. I had these ideas in my head but there was nothing to connect to. I wouldn't have known if there was an anti-nukes rally happening in the next town over.

So we send an Axis of Justice tent on anybody's tour that asks, free of charge. We organize the booths at the shows. We invite local grassroots groups and speakers. We play videos. And kids come.

Q: I've read that an ambition of yours is to unionize rockers and rappers.

MORELLO: That's correct. There's a cabal of record companies, management companies, entertainment firms, booking agencies, and concert promoters. They are the slumlords of the music industry. We artists rent a room. Sometimes you get the fleabag room, sometimes you get the penthouse suite. But all those people have been having dinner together and have been scratching each others' backs long before you put your band together, and they'll still be there long after they drop your band. The structure is set, and it's not artist-friendly.

Q: Are you feeling any backlash for speaking out against the war in Iraq?

MORELLO: No more than usual. I guess some artists like the Dixie Chicks had a tremendous media backlash. But having controversial left opinions is nothing new to me in my work. Especially with the war in Iraq, I thought it was very important to help galvanize young people who are in my audience.

There's only been a few times in my history as a musician and an activist where I've ever felt "the Man" push back. One of them was the immediate aftermath of 9/11. Clear Channel banned all Rage Against the Machine songs from all their radio stations. They faxed this memorandum to all the stations that listed specific songs that could not be played, including John Lennon's "Imagine" and the Gap Band's "You Dropped a Bomb on Me." The only artist whose entire catalog was singled out was Rage Against the Machine.

Q: How do you reconcile being anti-corporate and being on a major label?

MORELLO: Rage Against the Machine sold 14 million records of totally subversive revolutionary propaganda. The reason why is that the albums were released on Sony and got that sort of distribution.

You have two choices. I admire bands like Fugazi that take the other route. They are completely self-contained and independent. But if you do that, then you have to be a businessman. Then I have to sit there and worry about the orders to Belgium and make sure they get there. That is not what I'm going to do.

We've had, in Rage Against the Machine and Audioslave, complete artistic control, 100 percent over everything. Every second of every video, every second of every album, every bit of advertisement comes directly from us. I don't even look at it as a tradeoff. You live in a friggin' capitalist world. If you want to sell 45s out of the back of your microbus, God bless you. And maybe that works better, I don't know. I'll see you at the finish line.

## An Interview with Chuck D, Hip-Hop Artist

ANTONINO D'AMBROSIO
AUGUST 2005

Q: Do you think that hip-hop can escape the corporate grip?

CHUCK D: I always remain optimistic. There are three levels of music production: the majors, indies, and what I call "inties," music distributed via the Internet. The Internet is one area that I have used pretty effectively to break free of corporate control. Alternative spaces, independent media, satellite, these all provide some tools by which we can work more independently and deal more directly with communities we hope to reach. Distribution is key, and finding alternative ways to do that with new media is critical.

Q: Why did you get involved with the Internet?

CHUCK D: I became tired of submitting my art to a panel of corporate strategists who decide if it meets their standard of what gets into stores or not. It was quite simple for me: They act like judge and jury of my art, and that is unacceptable. I wanted to give it right to the public.

Q: How would you describe Public Enemy?

CHUCK D: Public Enemy started out as a benchmark in rap music in the mid-1980s. We felt there was a need to actually progress the music and say something because we were slightly older than the demographic of rap artists at the time. It was a time of heightened right-wing politics, so the climate dictated the direction of the group. The Berlin Wall was up. Nelson Mandela was in prison. Margaret Thatcher was running the U.K. Reagan was out of control in the White House. And Bush Senior was Vice President soon to be President. You can say we were up against it.

Q: What kind of political and cultural resistance did Public Enemy encounter?

CHUCK D: We were coming out of the black community with this thing called rap music, which was basically black men yelling at the top of their lungs about what we liked and what we didn't like. It was disturbing to the status quo. It really shook things up. And those in power didn't know what to make of us, but they knew that we had to be silenced, stopped in any way from expressing our outrage.

Q: Hip-hop is thirty years old and now a dominant global musical force. What has been the biggest change in hip-hop over this period?

CHUCK D: The biggest thing that has happened to hip-hop in the last ten to twelve years is the clinging on to the corporation as the all-mighty hub of the music. When culture is created in boardrooms with a panel of six or seven strategists for the masses to follow, to me that is no different than an aristocracy. It's not created from the people in the middle of the streets, so to speak. It is created from a petri dish for the sake of making money, and it is undermining the longevity of the culture.

Rap comes from the humble beginnings of rebelling against the status quo. Now, rappers have become the status quo themselves. You can't rebel against the Queen and then become the Queen yourself. I attribute much of the blame to testosterone—male dominance and patriarchy.

Q: Then music for you is about building a community.

CHUCK D: I don't think that the music should be above the people. Class doesn't cost a dime, and you spread it around. Knowledge, wisdom, and understanding don't come out of the microwave. You got to keep moving forward because the evil doesn't sleep.

—ANTONINO D'AMBROSIO, a writer and filmmaker in New York, is the author of *Let Fury Have the Hour: The Punk Politics of Joe Strummer.*

# PART 18

# Envisioning a Better World

Progressivism points the way forward to a more just society. "It holds up a vision of a society redeemed by true democracy," as La Follette put it.

To get there, we need to respect the contributions that all Americans can make, a fact June Jordan drives home with a flourish.

And to get there, we need to take action, even when the odds seem insurmountable. Howard Zinn points out how fragile the powerful can be once people unite against them. Remember, he says, "a flash of the possible."

Paul Wellstone, the great senator from Minnesota who died tragically in a plane crash, warns against "cynics and people who sit on the sidelines." Instead, he urges us to "step up to the plate."

Bill Moyers reminds us that we are "heirs of one of the country's great traditions," and that the noble fight we are engaged in is "between democracy and oligarchy." With historical sweep, he tells our story better than anyone else can. So enjoy it. As he says, it's yours.

# The Basis of the Struggle

ROBERT M. LA FOLLETTE
JULY 31, 1909

Here is the basis of the struggle in America: There are those, high in power and strong in intellect, many of them, who do not believe that the evils we suffer come from social maladjustments.

They think the poor man, or the criminal, or the ignorant, or the weak, the architect of his own fortune.

They can thread the slum or inspect the tenement with a sincere belief that these people are so situated by reason of inevitable evils, or of their own fault or failure, and not because of misdirected social forces which are capable of correction by an aroused democracy.

They regard the industrial situation in America as, on the whole, about what it should be.

They look upon the huge accumulations of capital and huger accumulations of power which we call the trusts as agencies of men who rule because on the whole they are best fitted for the rulership.

They may not be religious men, but they fervently believe that the obscure and indigent should follow the text of the ritual which bids us to be content in that sphere to which Providence has called us, and they regard as a Divine recognition of an immutable condition the passage which said of Judea of old, "The poor ye have always with you."

Such men and such statesmen do not exactly believe that whatever is, is right, but they believe fully in the game as it is played, in the huge percentage that it gives to the "house," the system of chances that divides the wealth of the nation into two piles, one of which is the spoil of the very few who get it in immense lots, and the other the pittances of the very many who get it in pitifully small portions. They believe that the game should be played "on the square" but that any other game than this prince-making, pauper-creating game of monopoly and exploitation is possible they do not for a moment believe.

There is another plane of thought into which some have entered.

It holds up a vision of a society redeemed by true democracy.

It believes in a time when monopoly shall be no more, and labor and capital, no longer at war, shall cooperate to the wiping out of involuntary and undeserved poverty in an era of industrial equality and social peace.

Believers in this may not be very religious either, but they thrill to the divine democracy of the Golden Rule and the Sermon on the Mount. They believe in the changing of the rules of the game.

They seek to eliminate the percentage that goes to the nonproductive "house" and to make production a sure thing for all, open to all hands on equal terms, wherein wealth shall go to the producers in proportions fixed by their individual contribution to production.

In short, these have the vision of a society redeemed by the institutional application of the principles of Jesus, of Jefferson, of Lincoln.


# Toward a Manifest New Destiny

JUNE JORDAN
FEBRUARY 1992


I have worked here, inside this country, and I have kept my eyes open, everlastingly. What I see today does not support a media-concocted controversy where my life or the lives of African Americans, Native Americans, Chicano Americans, Latin Americans, and Asian Americans amount to arguable fringe or freak components of some theoretical netherland. We have become the many peoples of this nation—nothing less than that. I do not accept that we, American peoples of color, signify anything optional or dubious or marginal or exotic or anything in any way less valuable, less necessary, less sacred, than white America.

I do not perceive current issues of public education as issues of politically correct or incorrect curriculum. In a straight line back to James Baldwin who, twenty-eight years ago, begged us, black folks, to rescue ourselves by wrestling white people out of the madness of their megalomania and delusion, I see every root argument about public education turning upon definitions of sanity and insanity. Shall we submit to ceaseless lies, fantastic misinformation, and fantastic omissions? Shall we agree to the erasure of our beleaguered, heterogeneous truth? Shall we embrace traditions of insanity and lose ourselves and the whole real world?

Or shall we defend and engage the multifoliate, overwhelming, and ultimately inescapable actual life that our myriad and disparate histories imply?

In America, in a democracy, who shall the people know if not our many selves? What shall we aim to learn about the universe if not the entire, complicated truth of it, to the best of our always-limited abilities? What does public education in a democratic state require if not the rational enlightenment of as many of the people as possible? But how can you claim to enlighten a child and then tell him that the language of his mother is illegal?

Most Americans are not even distant relatives of the nice guys who run the country. And so there's not a lot of emotional blur to our perceptions. We've had to see them as clearly as the hunted need to watch the ones who hunt them down.

Some of us sit in front of a young man, a member of the Creek nation, and we hear his voice break, and we feel his hands trembling, and we avoid staring at the tears that pour from his eyes as he tells us about the annihilation of his ancestors, about the bashing of babies' heads against trees, about the alternate, nearly extinct worldview that his forefathers and foremothers embraced. Between convulsions of grief, he speaks about the loss of earlier, spirit relations between his hungering people and the foods of the Earth.

Some of us must devise and improvise a million and one ways to convince young African American and Chicana women that white skin and yellow hair and blue eyes and thin thighs are not imperative attributes of beauty and loveliness.

Some of us must reassure a student born and raised in Hong Kong that we do not ask her to speak aloud in order to ridicule her "English" but in order to benefit from the wisdom of her intelligence.

Some of us search for avenues or for the invention of avenues for African American boys to become men among men beyond and without surrendering to that racist offering of a kill-or-be-killed destiny.

And we move among the peoples of this nation on an eyeball basis. We do not deny the heterogeneity that surrounds our bodies and our minds. We do not suppress the variegated sounds of multiple languages spoken by so many truly different Americans all in one place, hoping for love.

I am just one among an expanding hard-core number of American educators who believe that an American culture requirement, for instance, is not a laughable or subversive or anti-intellectual proposal. On the contrary! We are teachers running as fast as we can to catch up with the new Americans we are paid to educate.

The current distribution and identity of power will have to change or we will have to laugh the word "democracy" out of our consciousness forever.

And that is the political crisis that each of us personifies, one way or the other.

Since the demographics of our nation state do not even forecast English as the usual first language of most of our future children, what is the meaning of "English Only" legislation?

What does that reveal besides the politics of culture?

And who shall decide what these many peoples of America shall know or not know?

And what does that question underscore besides the political nature of knowledge?

And what shall be the international identity and what shall be the national identity of these United States when a white majority no longer exists inside our boundaries even as a white majority has never existed beyond these blood-and-gore-begotten boundaries of our nation state?

This moment of ours is just an obvious, excellent moment to declare for Americans, and for ourselves, a Manifest New Destiny: a destiny that will extricate all of us from the sickness of egomania and ignorance, a destiny that will cherish and delight in the differences among us, a destiny that will depend upon empowerment of the many and merciful protection of the young and the weak, a destiny that will carry us beyond an eyeball basis of knowledge into an educated, collective vision of a really democratic, a really humane, a really, really good time together.

# A Flash of the Possible

HOWARD ZINN
JANUARY 2000

In the year 1919, when the city of Seattle was brought to a halt by a general strike—beginning with 35,000 shipyard workers demanding a wage increase—the mayor reflected on its significance:

"True there were no flashing guns, no bombs, no killings. Revolution . . . doesn't need violence. The general strike, as practiced in Seattle, is of itself the weapon of revolution, all the more dangerous because quiet. To succeed, it must suspend everything, stop the entire life stream of a community. . . . That is to say, it puts the government out of operation. And that is all there is to revolt—no matter how achieved."

What happened in Seattle recently was not as large an event as the general strike of 1919. But it showed how apparently powerless people—if they unite in large numbers—can stop the machinery of government and commerce. In an era when the power of government, and of multinational corporations, is overwhelming, it is instructive to get even a hint of how fragile that power is when confronted by organized, determined citizens.

When the civil rights activists of the South in the early sixties put into practice the principle they called "Nonviolent Direct Action," they were able to make heretofore invincible power yield. What happened recently in Seattle was another working out of that principle.

Let's face it: Many of us—even old veterans of social movements—had begun to feel helpless as we observed the frightening consolidation of control by the interests of capital, the giant corporations merging, the American military machine grown to monstrous proportions. But we were forgetting certain fundamental facts about power: that the most formidable military machine depends ultimately on the obedience of its soldiers, that the most powerful corporation becomes helpless when its workers stop working, when its customers refuse to buy its products.

The strike, the boycott, the refusal to serve, the ability to paralyze the functioning of a complex social structure—these remain potent weapons against the most fearsome state or corporate power.

Note how General Motors and Ford had to surrender to the strikers of the thirties, how black children marching in Birmingham in 1963 pushed Congress into passing a Civil Rights Act, how the U.S. government, carrying on a war in Vietnam, had to reconsider in the face of draft resistance and desertions en masse, how a garbage workers' strike in New York immobilized a great city, how the threat of a boycott against Texaco for racist policies brought immediate concessions.

The Seattle protests, even if only a gleam of possibility in the disheartening dark of our time, should cause us to recall basic principles of power and powerlessness, so easily forgotten as the flood of media nonsense washes over the history of social movements.

It has been discouraging to watch the control of information in this country get tighter and tighter as megacorporations have taken over television and radio stations, newspapers, even book publishing. And yet, we saw in Seattle that when tens of thousands of men and women fill the streets and halt the normal flow of business and march with colorful banners and giant puppets and an infectious enthusiasm, they can break through the barriers of the corporate media and excite the attention of people all over the country and around the world.

Of course, the television cameras rushed to cover the fires (many actually produced by the police with their exploding tear-gas bombs) and the broken windows. The term "anarchist" was used to describe the perpetrators, by journalists ignorant—as were the window-smashers themselves—of the philosophy of anarchism. But it was not lost on viewers that the vast majority of people marching through the streets were angry, even obstructive, but peaceful—yes, nonviolent direct action.

In Seattle, the demonstrators were grappling with impossibly complex economic issues—globalization, protectionism, export trade, intellectual properties—issues the most sophisticated experts have had a hard time explaining. But through all of that complexity, a certain diamond-hard idea shone through: that the schemes of well-dressed men of finance and government gathering in ornate halls were dangerous to the health and lives of working people all over the world. Thousands in the streets, representing millions, showed their determination to resist these schemes.

In one crucial way, it was a turning point in the history of the movements of recent decades—a departure from the single-issue focus of the Seabrook occupation of 1977, the nuclear freeze rally in Central Park in 1982, and the gatherings in Washington for the Equal Rights Amendment in 1978, for lesbian and gay rights in 1993, for the Million Man March in 1995, and Stand for Children in 1996. This time, the union movement was at the center. The issue of class—rich and poor, here and all over the globe—bound everyone together.

It was, at the least, a flash of the possible. It recalled the prophecy of A. Philip Randolph in November of 1963, speaking to an AFL-CIO convention shortly after the civil rights march brought 200,000 people, black and white, to the nation's capital. Randolph told the delegates: "The Negro's protest today is but the first rumbling of the underclass. As the Negro has taken to the streets, so will the unemployed of all races take to the streets."

There will be more rumblings to come.

# History Is a Dance of Life

S ENATOR  P AUL  W ELLSTONE
D ECEMBER  2002

*Adapted from a speech given in 1999 at the ninetieth-anniversary celebration of*
The Progressive.

Whenever I'm speaking in schools, I always say to the students, "The future will not belong to those who are content with the present. The future will not belong to cynics and people who sit on the sidelines. The future will belong to people who have passion and are willing to work hard to make this country better."

Most of the people in cafés don't care about left, right, or center. They care whether the politics you represent speaks to the concerns and circumstances of their lives. That is the center. That is what most people believe in. We shouldn't give any ground on that.

If every two years our politics are based on what some pollster tells us are the key hot-button issues to get the swing vote, then we don't really represent all that much. And what we need to challenge is this downsized politics, which just invites cynicism. This is not a good politics. It is no wonder that we have a huge hole in the electorate.

People are so focused on how to earn a decent living. People are so focused on how to do well by their kids. People are so focused on health care and on affordable child care. And they want reform. They want to see a government they can believe in. And there's a lot of goodness in people. They believe in human rights. They believe in the environment.

So we should step up to the plate, the progressive community, and I will just highlight a few ways we can do that.

First, we ought to put clean money, clean election reform, at the top of the agenda. Get the big money out, and let the people back in. We ought to seize the clean money, clean election initiative that passed in Massachusetts and Arizona and take it all around the country and push as long and as hard as we can to restore democracy in America. Make reform a huge issue!

And second of all, we need to put on the table a plebiscite about children in America. We are still being told that we should accept the fact that one out of every four children under the age of three is growing up poor, and one out of every two children of color is growing up poor. Children are the most poverty-stricken group in our country. This is a betrayal of our heritage. It is a national disgrace.

And third of all—and I could do a tenth of all—now we have 44 million who don't have health insurance, and we have another 44 million who are underinsured, and everywhere I go people are talking about health care. It's staring them in the face. The insurance industry took universal health care coverage off the table. As progressives, we're going to put it back on the table, and fight for universal health care coverage in this country. It's a political majority issue. It's the right thing to do. It's what we stand for.

History is a dance of life. We have celebrated the past, we've talked of the challenges of the present, and now what we have to do is build the future.

—PAUL WELLSTONE represented Minnesota in the United States Senate from 1991 to 2002.

# Our Story

BILL MOYERS
MAY 2004

Fifty-three years ago, on my sixteenth birthday, I went to work for the daily newspaper in the small East Texas town where I grew up. I soon had a stroke of luck. Some of the old-timers were on vacation or out sick and I got assigned to cover what came to be known as the Housewives' Rebellion. Fifteen women in my hometown decided not to pay the Social Security withholding tax for their domestic workers. They argued that Social Security was unconstitutional, that imposing it was taxation without representation, and that—here's my favorite part—"requiring us to collect the tax is no different from requiring us to collect the garbage."

In one way or another, I've been covering the class war ever since. Those women in Marshall, Texas, were its advance guard. They were not bad people. They were regulars at church, their children were my friends, many of them were active in community affairs, their husbands were pillars of the business and professional class in town. They were respectable and upstanding citizens all. So it took me a while to figure what had brought on that spasm of reactionary rebellion. It came to me one day, much later. They simply couldn't see beyond their own prerogatives. Fiercely loyal to their families, to their clubs, charities, and congregations—fiercely loyal, in other words, to their own kind—they narrowly defined membership in democracy to include only people like them. The women who washed and ironed their laundry, wiped their children's bottoms, made their husband's beds, and cooked their family meals—these women, too, would grow old and frail, sick and decrepit, lose their husbands and face the ravages of time alone, with nothing to show from their years of labor but the crease in their brow and the knots on their knuckles. Security was personal, not social, and what injustice existed this side of heaven would no doubt be redeemed beyond the Pearly Gates.

This is the oldest story in America: the struggle to determine whether "we, the people" is a spiritual idea embedded in a political reality—one nation, indivisible—or merely a charade masquerading as piety and manipulated by the powerful and privileged to sustain their own way of life at the expense of others.

It's the difference between a society whose arrangements roughly serve all its citizens and one whose institutions have been converted into a stupendous fraud. It's the difference between democracy and oligarchy.

You are the heirs of one of the country's great traditions—the Progressive Movement that started late in the nineteenth century and remade the American experience piece by piece until it peaked in the last third of the twentieth century. Its aim was to keep blood pumping through the veins of democracy when others were ready to call in the mortician.

Step back with me to the curtain raiser, the founding convention of the People's Party—better known as the Populists—in 1892. Mainly cotton and wheat farmers from the recently reconstructed South and the newly settled Great Plains, they had come on hard, hard times, driven to the wall by falling prices for their crops on one hand and racking interest rates, freight charges, and supply costs on the other. All this in the midst of a booming industrial America. They were angry, and their platform—issued deliberately on the Fourth of July—pulled no punches. "We meet," it said, "in the midst of a nation brought to the verge of moral, political, and material ruin. . . . Corruption dominates the ballot box, the state legislatures, and the Congress and touches even the bench. . . . The newspapers are largely subsidized or muzzled, public opinion silenced. . . . The fruits of the toil of millions are boldly stolen to build up colossal fortunes for a few."

Furious words from rural men and women who were traditionally conservative and whose memories of taming the frontier were fresh and personal. But in their fury they invoked an American tradition as powerful as frontier individualism—the war on inequality and especially on the role that government played in promoting and preserving inequality by favoring the rich. The Populists knew it was the government that granted millions of acres of public land to the railroad builders. It was the government that gave the manufacturers of farm machinery a monopoly of the domestic market by a protective tariff that was no longer necessary to shelter "infant industries." It was the government that contracted the national currency and sparked a deflationary cycle that crushed debtors and fattened the wallets of creditors. And those who made the great fortunes used them to buy the legislative and judicial favors that kept them on top. So the Populists recognized one great principle: The job of preserving equality of opportunity and democracy demanded the end of any unholy alliance between government and wealth. It was, to quote that platform again, "from the same womb of governmental injustice" that tramps and millionaires were bred.

But how were Americans to restore government to its job of promoting the general welfare? Here, the Populists made a breakthrough to another principle. In a modern, large-scale, industrial, and nationalized economy it wasn't enough to curb the government's reach. That would simply leave power in the hands of the great corporations whose existence was inseparable from growth and progress. The answer was to turn government at least into the arbiter of fair play, and when necessary the friend, the helper, and the agent of the people at large in the contest against entrenched power.

So the Populist platform called for government loans to farmers about to lose their mortgaged homesteads, for government granaries to grade and store their crops fairly, for governmental inflation of the currency, which was a classical plea of debtors, and for some decidedly nonclassical actions like government ownership of the railroad, telephone, and telegraph systems and a graduated, progressive tax on incomes, as well as a flat ban on subsidies to "any private corporation." And to make sure the government stayed on the side of the people, the "Pops" called for the initiative and referendum and the direct election of Senators.

Predictably, the Populists were denounced, feared, and mocked as fanatical hayseeds ignorantly playing with socialist fire. They got twenty-two electoral votes for their candidate in '92, plus some Congressional seats and statehouses, but by 1904 Populism was a spent rocket. But if political organizations perish, their key ideas don't—keep that in mind because it gives perspective to your cause today. Much of the Populist agenda would become law within a few years of the party's extinction because their goals were generally shared by a rising generation of young Republicans and Democrats who, justly or not, were seen as less outrageously outdated than the embattled farmers. These were the Progressives, your intellectual forebears and mine.

They were a diverse lot, held together by a common admiration of progress—hence the name—and a shared dismay at the paradox of poverty stubbornly persisting in the midst of progress like an unwanted guest at a wedding. Of course they welcomed, just as we do, the new marvels in the gift bag of technology: the telephones, the autos, the electrically powered urban transport and lighting systems, the indoor heating and plumbing, the processed foods and home appliances and machine-made clothing that reduced the sweat and drudgery of home-making and were affordable to an ever-swelling number of people. But they saw the underside, too, the slums lurking in the shadows of the glittering cities, the exploited and unprotected workers whose low-paid labor filled the horn of plenty for others, the misery of those whom age, sickness, accident, or hard times condemned to servitude and poverty with no hope of comfort or security.

In a few short years, the progressive spirit made possible the election not only of reform mayors and governors but of national figures like Senator George Norris of Nebraska, Senator Robert M. La Follette of Wisconsin, and even that hard-to-classify political genius Theodore Roosevelt. All three of them Republicans. Here is the simplest laundry list of what was accomplished at state and federal levels: publicly regulated or owned transportation, sanitation, and utilities systems; the partial restoration of competition in the marketplace through improved antitrust laws; increased fairness in taxation; expansion of the public education and juvenile justice systems; safer workplaces and guarantees of compensation to workers injured on the job; oversight of the purity of water, medicines, and foods; conservation of the national wilderness heritage against overdevelopment, and honest bidding on any public mining, lumbering, and ranching.

We take these for granted today—or we did until recently. All were provided not by the automatic workings of free enterprise but by implementing the idea in the Declaration of Independence that the people had a right to governments that best promoted their "safety and happiness."

The mighty progressive wave peaked in 1912. But the ideas leashed by it forged the politics of the twentieth century. Like his cousin Theodore, Franklin Roosevelt argued that the real enemies of enlightened capitalism were "the malefactors of great wealth"— the "economic royalists"—from whom capitalism would have to be saved by reform and regulation. Progressive government became an embedded tradition of Democrats—the heart of FDR's New Deal and Harry Truman's Fair Deal. Even Dwight D. Eisenhower honored the tradition. He didn't want to tear down the house progressive ideas had built—only to put it under different managers. The progressive impulse had its final fling in the landslide of 1964 when LBJ—a son of the West Texas hill country, where the Populist rebellion had been nurtured in the 1890s—won the public endorsement for what he meant to be the capstone in the arch of the New Deal.

I had a modest role in that era. I shared in its exhilarations and its failures. We went too far too fast, overreached at home and in Vietnam, failed to examine some assumptions, and misjudged the rising discontents and backlash engendered by war, race, civil disturbance, violence, and crime. The failure of Democratic politicians and public thinkers to respond to popular discontents allowed a resurgent conservatism to convert public concern and hostility into a reactionary crusade.

You have to respect the conservatives for their successful strategy in gaining control of the national agenda. Their stated and open aim is to strip from government all its functions except those that reward their rich and privileged benefactors. They are quite candid about it, even acknowledging their mean spirit in accomplishing it. Their leading strategist in Washington, Grover Norquist, has famously said he wants to shrink the government down to the size that it could be drowned in a bathtub. The White House pursues the same homicidal dream without saying so. Instead of shrinking down the government, they're filling the bathtub with so much debt that it floods the house, waterlogs the economy, and washes away services that for decades have lifted millions of Americans out of destitution and into the middle class. And what happens once the public's property has been flooded? Privatize it. Sell it at a discounted rate to the corporations. It is the most radical assault on the notion of one nation, indivisible, that has occurred in our lifetime.

While the social inequalities that galvanized progressives in the nineteenth century are resurgent, so is the vision of justice, fairness, and equality. That's a powerful cause, if only there are people around to fight for it.

What will it take to get back in the fight? The first order of business is to understand the real interests and deep opinions of the American people.

And what are those?

That a Social Security card is not a private portfolio statement but a membership ticket in a society where we all contribute to a common treasury so that none need face the indignities of poverty in old age.

That tax evasion is not a form of conserving investment capital but a brazen abandonment of responsibility to the country.

That concentration in the production of goods may sometimes be useful and efficient, but monopoly over the dissemination of ideas is tyranny.

That prosperity requires good wages and benefits for workers.

That the rich have the right to buy more cars than anyone else, more homes, vacations, gadgets and gizmos, but they do not have the right to buy more democracy than anyone else.

And that our nation can no more survive as half democracy and half oligarchy than it could survive "half slave and half free," and that keeping it from becoming all oligarchy is steady work—our work.

What's right and good doesn't come naturally. You have to stand up and fight for it, as if the cause depends on you, because it does. Allow yourself that conceit, to believe that the flame of democracy will never go out as long as there's one candle in your hand.

So go for it. Never mind the odds.

"Democracy is not a lie"—I first learned that from Henry Demarest Lloyd, the progressive journalist whose book *Wealth Against Commonwealth* laid open the Standard Oil trust a century ago. Lloyd came to the conclusion that to "regenerate the individual is a half truth. The reorganization of the society which he makes and which makes him is the other part. The love of liberty became liberty in America by clothing itself in the complicated group of strengths known as the government of the United States." And it was then he said: "Democracy is not a lie. There live(s) in the body of the commonality unexhausted virtue and the ever-refreshed strength which can rise equal to any problems of progress. In the hope of tapping some reserve of their power of self-help," he said, "this story is told to the people."

This is your story, the progressive story of America.

Pass it on.

—BILL MOYERS, journalist, worked in JFK's Peace Corps and for Lyndon Johnson, whom he served as press secretary. Moyers went on to be the editor of *Newsday* and to host programs on PBS.